"A searing indictment of the power and exploitation at the heart of big-money college athletics. . . . A clarion call for anyone who believes that hardworking people deserve fairness, respect, and a level playing field."

—**SENATOR CORY BOOKER**

"Shocking and stunning. Two of the nation's finest newspaper writers have delivered an absolute masterpiece."

—**PAUL FINEBAUM**, ESPN

"Painstakingly reported and deftly written, *Indentured* shines the brightest light yet on the hypocrisy and injustice perpetrated by the NCAA."

—**GEORGE DOHRMANN**, author of *Play Their Hearts Out*

"When I was in college, I felt like an indentured servant, exploited and controlled by all the people who were getting rich off my labors and my talent. This book is not only a must read for college athletes and fans but a call to action."

—**ARIAN FOSTER**, Houston Texans running back

PORTFOLIO / PENGUIN

# INDENTURED

JOE NOCERA is an op-ed columnist for *Bloomberg View*. His previous books include *All the Devils Are Here* (with Bethany McLean), *Good Guys and Bad Guys*, and *A Piece of the Action*. He has won three Gerald Loeb awards for excellence in business journalism and was a finalist for a Pulitzer Prize in 2006. He lives in New York City.

Ben Strauss has covered sports and politics for the *New York Times* and *POLITICO Magazine*. He lives in Washington, D.C.

# INDENTURED

## THE BATTLE TO END THE EXPLOITATION OF COLLEGE ATHLETES

## Joe Nocera
## and Ben Strauss

Portfolio / Penguin

Portfolio/Penguin
An imprint of Penguin Random House LLC
375 Hudson Street
New York, New York 10014

First published in the United States of American by Portfolio/Penguin 2016
This paperback with a new afterword published 2018

Most Portfolio books are available at a discount when purchased in quantity for sales promotions or corporate use. Special editions, which include personalized covers, excerpts, and corporate imprints, can be created when purchased in large quantities. For more information, please call (212) 572-2232 or e-mail specialmarkets@penguinrandomhouse.com. Your local bookstore can also assist with discounted bulk purchases using the Penguin Random House corporate Business-to-Business program. For assistance in locating a participating retailer, e-mail B2B@penguinrandomhouse.com.

"Excuses, Not Reasons" by Andy Schwarz. Reprinted by permission of the author.

"National Letter of Indenture" by Andy Schwarz and Jason Belzer. Reprinted by permission of the authors.

ISBN 9780143130550

The Library of Congress has catalogued the hardcover edition as follows:
Names: Nocera, Joseph, author. | Strauss, Ben.
Title: Indentured : the inside story of the rebellion against the NCAA /
    Joe Nocera and Ben Strauss.
Description: New York : Portfolio, [2016] | Includes index.
Identifiers: LCCN 2015044500 (print) | LCCN 2015048037 (ebook) |
    ISBN 9781591846321 (hardcover) | ISBN 9781101619919 (ebook)
Subjects: LCSH: National Collegiate Athletic Association. | College sports—
    Economic aspects—United States. | College athletes—United States—
    Economic conditions. | College sports—United States—Management.
    | College sports—Moral and ethical aspects—United States.
Classification: LCC GV351 .N64 2016 (print) | LCC GV351 (ebook)
    | DDC 796.04/30973—dc23
LC record available at http://lccn.loc.gov/2015044500

Printed in the United States of America
10  9  8  7  6  5  4  3  2  1

Set in Diverda Serif Com
Designed by Daniel Lagin

*For Macklin*

—Joe Nocera

*For my parents, Leslie and Jonathan*

—Ben Strauss

# CONTENTS

# INDENTURED

# PROLOGUE

# "WHY DO THEY HATE ME SO MUCH?"

Ryan Boatright was in trouble with the National Collegiate Athletic Association even before he played his first game as a freshman point guard for the University of Connecticut Huskies.

Boatright had arrived at UConn in the fall of 2011 from Aurora, Illinois, a town of two hundred thousand an hour west of Chicago, with a per capita income that ranks it 261st among Illinois cities. His mother, Tanesha Boatright, was a single mom struggling to raise four children; her job as a customer service representative for a health care company earned her a paycheck that was not much better than minimum wage. Her father had been a well-known local track coach, and she'd run track herself in high school, before she got pregnant with Ryan when she was seventeen. It was obvious early on that her son was also athletically gifted; despite his lack of size—he never grew taller than five foot ten—basketball was his game, and both he and his mother came to see the sport as his ticket to a better life, not just for himself but for his family. When he was thirteen, he attended a basketball camp run by Tim Floyd, then the basketball coach at the University of Southern California. Floyd became so enamored with Boatright that he offered him a scholarship on the spot. (Floyd resigned a few years later, after being tarred by a recruiting scandal.) At East Aurora High School, Boatright started as a freshman; three years later, as the team's senior point guard, he averaged over 30 points a game and was named Illinois's co–Mr. Basketball.

Like many top high school athletes, Boatright also played for a local Amateur Athletic Union (AAU) team. His coach, Reggie Rose, the brother of Chicago Bulls star Derrick Rose, was a long-standing friend of his mother's, and over time he became a father figure to Boatright. During a particularly stressful period in the Boatright household, Rose got Ryan out of Aurora, taking him to California, where he spent several days working out with other good players—another thing the best high school players commonly do. When Tanesha bought a used car, a 2008 Chevrolet Impala she needed to get to her job, Rose helped her with some of the payments. And when Boatright went on his recruiting visits—he made four trips in all, including one to the UConn campus in Storrs, Connecticut—Rose covered the cost of an additional plane ticket so that Tanesha could go too. Most people would views these as acts of generosity, a friend helping out a friend with fewer resources. But the NCAA, which had been tipped off about the money Rose gave Tanesha, saw them as potential—nay, likely—violations of its "amateurism" rules. That's why Boatright was in trouble.

Since the early 1950s, the NCAA has served as the powerful overlord of college sports, with one central tenet: that college athletes, whether gymnasts or quarterbacks, must be unpaid amateurs, for whom sports is little more than a sideline to their academic pursuits. As the NCAA puts it in its bylaws, "Student participation in intercollegiate athletics is an avocation, and student-athletes should be protected from exploitation by professional and commercial enterprises."

The NCAA's long-standing insistence that amateurism is the "core value" of college sports has always been more than a little hypocritical— as has the idea that the NCAA was somehow preventing (as opposed to enabling) their exploitation. Has there ever really been a time when the athletes in the so-called revenue sports that are the focus of this book— football and men's basketball—weren't expected to put their sport first and their studies a distant second, while helping to bring glory and money to their school? Has there ever been a time when college athletes weren't at some level exploited? Long before coaches made millions and the NCAA turned its annual basketball championship into the financial windfall known as March Madness, critics have complained about the pervasive commercialism of college athletics.

But with the NCAA now generating over $900 million in annual revenue; with athletic conferences owning their own lucrative all-sports cable networks; with coaches making $5 million (Jim Harbaugh, Michigan football) or $7 million (Nick Saban, Alabama football) or even $10 million (Mike Krzyzewski, Duke basketball); and with ESPN paying $7.3 billion over twelve years for the rights to the new college football playoff, the idea that the players who make all this possible should not get much more than a scholarship isn't just hypocritical. It's offensive. An economist named Dan Rascher, who is a character in this book, estimates that college sports in its totality generates some $13 billion, which, incredibly, is more than the most lucrative professional sports league in America, the National Football League.

Before we go any further, a few facts: More than 460,000 NCAA athletes participate in twenty-four sports across its three divisions. Supporters of the status quo like to point out that the system as currently constructed maximizes opportunities for the largest number of athletes—think of all the scholarships for tennis players and swimmers. Our book is focused on the 15,000 athletes playing top-level football and nearly 5,500 in Division I men's basketball, because they produce the revenue that pays for everything from those expensive football coaches' salaries to track and field scholarships. Indeed, most schools' athletic department budgets remain separate from central administration. But while the college sports establishment squeezes every last dollar out of their marquee athletes—weekday night games, schools jumping from conference to conference, and a rash of corporate sponsors—they must remain amateurs, while a little more than 5 percent of them go on to careers in the NBA or NFL.

The NCAA has consistently refused to acknowledge this hypocrisy; instead, it has held tightly to the centrality of amateurism, even as it has encouraged the commercialization of college sports in every other way imaginable. And over the years, it has enforced its amateurism rules with a Javert-like zealotry. Until very recently, athletes could receive nothing for playing their sports beyond their athletic scholarship, plus a Pell Grant if they were poor enough to qualify. (As this book details, the NCAA has recently allowed schools to add a stipend to cover the "full cost of attendance" beyond the scholarship itself.) Anything else these athletes receive that the NCAA deems to be the result of their skill or fame, no matter how inconsequential, is considered a violation of its rules and is therefore punishable.

And it's not only while they're in college: if a high school athlete, or his parents, gets money or gifts as a result of his status as an athlete, that too is punishable once the player gets to college and comes under the scrutiny of the NCAA. Eight months before Boatright's problems, for instance, a freshman basketball player named Perry Jones III, the star center for the Baylor University Bears, was suspended for six games because his mother, who had been out of work due to a heart condition, had accepted—and quickly repaid—several short-term loans from Jones's AAU coach to cover her rent. Jones had been in the tenth grade when this happened and had never known about the loans. Although the NCAA had earlier allowed Auburn's star quarterback, Cam Newton, to play in a lucrative bowl game after it was alleged that his father had tried to auction him off to the highest bidder—on the grounds that Newton hadn't known what his father was doing—it took the opposite stance with Jones. His suspension was announced, cruelly, just before Baylor's opening-round conference tournament game, creating a swirl of publicity that humiliated the teenager while dooming the Baylor team to defeat with Jones out of action. When I asked an NCAA spokeswoman why it had let Newton play while punishing Jones, all she would say is, "Every situation is different." Really?

It was Boatright's new coach, Jim Calhoun, who first informed Tanesha in November 2011 that her son had been declared ineligible by the school because the NCAA had some questions "about his recruitment," as he put it to her. (That's the way the system works: the NCAA itself doesn't declare a player ineligible; it forces the school to do so, because if the school doesn't and the NCAA rules against the player, the team will forfeit any game he has played when he should have been ineligible. Plus that allows the NCAA to claim piously that it isn't the responsible party when a player becomes ineligible—the university is.)

Within a day or two, members of the NCAA's enforcement staff began calling her at work on her cell phone. They didn't even attempt to make an appointment; they simply started asking questions. She would try to answer a few, but then she would have to tell the investigators that she had to be back to work. The fact that her son was being held out because of an NCAA investigation was all over ESPN. "It was embarrassing," she says. "I had to tell my supervisor that this was the reason I was on my cell phone all the time. It got to the point where it was a real problem at work." Because she couldn't drop everything and answer their questions, the investigators reported back to their supervisor that Tanesha was not being responsive. This went on for several weeks. She would go home and cry herself to sleep. "You're so paranoid," she says. "Your son's future is at stake, and you don't know what you can say that will satisfy them."

Finally, someone at UConn told her to set up a meeting with the investigators. She did; it was to be held in a nearby hotel. But instead of meeting her there, the investigators first showed up at her office, dressed in ties and jackets, looking as though they belonged to the FBI. More humiliation. They took her to the hotel around 5:30 p.m., where Tanesha was grilled until 1 a.m. She still had no idea what wrongdoing she was being accused of—or who had made the allegations against her. And the NCAA investigators refused to tell her. Instead, they asked the same set of questions again and again: "How did you pay for your visit to UConn? Who got you your tickets? Who gave you the $3,000?"

Tanesha says they kept referring to secret deliveries of money she was supposed to have gotten. She had no idea what they were talking about. They refused to let her use the phone to call her parents, who were taking care of her other three children. They told her they thought she was lying. She was a single black woman alone in a room with four white men she had never met. She had no one to help her or represent her. She wasn't just embarrassed anymore. She was terrified.

The NCAA likes to say that because it lacks subpoena power, it has to find other means to get people to cooperate with its investigations. But it has far more power than a mere subpoena. It controls the fate of eighteen-year-old athletes, many of whom have dreams of playing professionally someday, but whose careers the NCAA can destroy on a whim, simply by declaring them permanently ineligible. What mother can stand up to that kind of raw power?

By the NCAA's own rules, the money that Rose spent on the Boatright family really shouldn't have been a problem. The rules state that a player or his family can't take money from someone trying to steer him to a particular school, or from anyone fronting for a professional agent. Rose was neither of those things. An athlete or his family can accept money from someone who is genuinely a close family friend—which Rose was. But the NCAA harbors a deep suspicion of father figures of talented athletes, especially when those athletes are African Americans who come from disadvantaged families. It also intensely dislikes AAU basketball, viewing it as a cesspool of corruption full of hangers-on, a netherworld where money exchanges hands and basketball players are steered to schools by coaches who are on the take. And it was particularly suspicious of Reggie Rose, who was a peripheral figure during the NCAA's investigation of his younger brother Derrick after the 2007–08 season when he was playing for the University of Memphis. Without the slightest proof he had done anything wrong, the NCAA would later describe Rose as a person "linked to non-scholastic basketball and professional sports"—as if that were somehow damning.

As her ordeal continued, Tanesha couldn't eat. She started losing weight. Unable to concentrate on work, she lost her job. She tried to explain to the NCAA that Rose was a family friend; there was no agent or booster involved; nothing untoward had taken place. It didn't matter. When the NCAA made its ruling in December, it took the position that Rose's financial assistance was an "impermissible benefit." It ruled that Boatright would have to sit out six games and pay $100 a month until he had repaid $4,100, which the NCAA calculated was the cost of the impermissible benefit. NCAA investigators even told Tanesha that she should "stay away" from Reggie Rose, as if controlling her relationships was somehow within its purview. Finally, in late November, Boatright was cleared to play in his first game for UConn.

By then, Tanesha had figured out who had tipped off the NCAA. It was her ex-boyfriend. In addition to telling the NCAA about Rose, he was also the one who alleged that she was getting secret payments. The man, who had seen Boatright as his meal ticket, was exacting revenge on his mother. Did it give the NCAA pause that its star witness was an angry ex-convict with questionable motives? Clearly not.

Tanesha had also finally hired a lawyer, whom she found with UConn's help. His name was Scott Tompsett, and he had spent most of his career defending clients who had gotten crosswise with the NCAA. He harbored a deep cynicism about the NCAA's brand of justice, and was appalled by what Tanesha had been put through. What he quickly realized, though, was that her ordeal wasn't close to being over.

In mid-January 2012, for reasons that have never been clear, the enforcement staff decided to reopen its investigation—which meant that once again Boatright had to be declared ineligible by UConn. The investigators could not have chosen a more humiliating moment for the young freshman. He had flown with the team to South Bend, Indiana, where UConn was scheduled to play Notre Dame that evening. South Bend is only a few hours from Aurora, and some three hundred people from his hometown had bought tickets to the game. It was snowing, and they drove slowly, with Tanesha's car in the lead, as they approached South Bend for the game. At 5 p.m., Calhoun got the call from UConn's compliance official telling him that he would have to sit Boatright again. Calhoun was enraged. "Here he was about to play in front of his hometown fans," he says. "I'm supposed to be his mentor and there's nothing I can do. I felt a real sense of guilt."

When Calhoun conveyed the news to Boatright, the player collapsed, weeping, in Calhoun's arms. Then he called his mother, whose car had just turned onto the street where their hotel was located. "I started screaming and crying," she says. "I couldn't drive. I'm thinking, *what do you want from me?*"

Tanesha pulled over to the side of the road and let someone else drive the rest of the way. She walked into the lobby of the hotel "still screaming and crying," she says. She ran into her son; they hugged and he told her they would get through it, but she was inconsolable. "I kept saying, 'Why do they hate me? Why do they want to embarrass me and destroy me?' I'm a single mother. Reggie was like a father. How is this wrong? I don't understand."

It's hard to know even now what the NCAA was trying to pin on her, but the pressure its investigators put on Tanesha was unrelenting. It demanded that she account for every deposit from February 2009 to October 2011. It then extended the demand to January 2012. For some of that time, Tanesha hadn't used a bank, so the NCAA demanded to see all her money orders and other nonbank transactions. Where did this $200 cash deposit come from? How about that $1,000? At one point, she explained, family and friends had given her money so that she could buy her children Christmas presents. The NCAA investigators then went to her friends' workplaces and demanded that they confirm her account. It demanded to see the paperwork for the Impala she had bought, even going to the dealer to obtain it. Of course, there was no $3,000 deposit, nor any secret transactions, as the ex-boyfriend had claimed. It didn't matter. Until Tanesha could account for every deposit, the NCAA would not allow Ryan to play basketball for UConn.

It was right around this time, the latter part of January 2012, that I became aware of Boatright's situation. Three weeks earlier, I had written an essay in the *New York Times Magazine* making the case that college football and men's basketball players should be compensated, given all the money they were generating for everyone else in college sports. In the course of reporting that article, I had come to certain conclusions about the NCAA—conclusions that aligned me squarely with a small group of people who were trying to reform it, most of whom I met while working on the story. One was that the NCAA was a classic cartel, the OPEC of sports, which existed in no small part to artificially suppress the wages of its labor force—namely the players.

The second was that the ubiquitous term "student-athlete," which the NCAA had first trotted out in the mid-1950s, was a farce. College football and men's basketball players worked fifty hours or more a week on their sport, and they knew full well that their university expected them to make athletics their top priority. They couldn't take any classes that interfered with practice or other team events. Their travel caused them to miss numerous classes and exams. Many of them majored in "eligibility"—that is, they took courses that made no particular sense other than to ensure that their grades were good enough to stay on the basketball court or the football field. Many of them were poor, meaning that on campuses filled with upper-middle-class kids who had plenty of spending money, they had next to nothing—and anybody who helped them was potentially violating NCAA rules. They also were likely to have come from a substandard high school, so the academic work they faced in college was a struggle. "Many athletes feel the same sense of fear in the classroom that you or I would feel if we stepped out onto a football field," one agent said. Their scholarships had to be renewed annually, so if they got hurt or didn't play up to expectations—or if a new coach came in with a different approach—they could be cut and lose their chance at a college degree.

My third conclusion was that the hundreds of bylaws in the NCAA rulebook—ostensibly aimed at furthering the amateur ideal and ensuring competitive balance on the field—were more appropriately seen as a means of keeping the players in their place. There were rules about how many times a player could eat in someone's home; rules that forced a player to lose a year of eligibility if he transferred to a different school (unless the NCAA gave him a waiver); rules that limited how many miles a coach could drive a player in his car. "I spent part of my life investigating coaches making too many phone calls," says one former NCAA investigator. "That's a pathetic commentary on lots of things, including my life at that time. When you think about it, it's insanity."

The fourth thing I had come to understand was that for all the seeming glory that surrounds them, college athletes in the revenue sports were exploited. It was as simple as that. "When you are profiting off someone else, while restricting them from earning a profit, that's exploitation," one of the most prominent reformers, Jay Bilas of ESPN, told the *Wall Street Journal*. Another important reformer, the historian Taylor Branch, wrote a seminal article in the *Atlantic* in which he compared the NCAA to "the plantation." Yet a third reformer, Andy Schwarz, a Bay Area economist and litigation consultant, who is also a character in this book, coauthored a persuasive paper comparing college athletes to indentured servants. (It is reprinted in appendix 2.)

These were all issues that spoke mainly to the economic underpinnings of college sports and the NCAA, which was the thrust of my article. What I was seeing with Ryan Boatright was something else: raw injustice. Did the NCAA really have the power to punish an athlete because his mother was friends with someone the NCAA disapproved of? It did. Could it make accusations against an athlete or a coach without allowing the accused to know who made the charges and give them a chance to cross-examine their accuser? It could. Did it hold the power to destroy careers using evidence that was little better than hearsay? It did.

As my coauthor, Ben Strauss, and I explain in chapter 2, the NCAA had won an important Supreme Court case in 1988 that meant that it was not required to give due process to those it accused of wrongdoing. And so it didn't. When it brought a case against a school or a player, it acted as investigator, prosecutor, and judge. "The moment the NCAA sends you a notice of allegations," one prominent coach told me, "they are sending you an indictment." There were lawyers who specialized in counseling universities in trouble with the NCAA whose basic advice was that they should get down on their knees and beg for mercy, no matter how wronged they felt. That way the punishment would be lighter than if they contested the charges—which they were bound to lose anyway. There were veterans of college sports, jaded by the system, who shrugged their shoulders at its fundamental unfairness. But when you are seeing how the NCAA dispenses "justice" for the first time, as I was in the Boatright case, it's really quite shocking.

I wrote several columns about Boatright, in which I expressed that shock. "One question keeps reverberating in my head," I wrote in one of them. "How can this be happening in America? . . . How can [the NCAA] act so ruthlessly to enforce rules that are so petty?" As I would later realize, this is often people's reaction when they first see the NCAA up close. Trying to answer that question was part of the reason I kept writing about it over the next few years.

During the time that I've been covering the NCAA, public perception has undergone significant change. Fans of teams that have been punished by the NCAA have always had their grievances—that's nothing new—but what is new is that there are many more people, sportswriters in particular, who are questioning whether amateurism should be the basis upon which college sports is built, as the NCAA has long insisted.

Part of the reason for this change is a series of missteps by the NCAA over the past few years, which Ben and I have documented. Another reason is all the money that has poured into college sports, making it increasingly difficult to swallow the idea that athletes should get none of it. And a third reason is the efforts of a small handful of dedicated reformers who are at the heart of this book. Their collective efforts have exposed the foibles and hypocrisy of the NCAA to the larger public. And as you'll see in the last few chapters, they've even taken the NCAA to court.

As for Ryan Boatright, he did get back on the court not long after I wrote my second column about his and his mother's troubles. Even then, though, the NCAA couldn't resist heaping a final dose of humiliation on the Boatrights. The NCAA's public relations staff issued a lengthy—and malicious—press release, laying out its skewed version of events in a fashion designed to put Boatright, Tanesha, and Reggie Rose in the worst possible light. It made it sound as if Boatright had been given a car, that Tanesha had refused to cooperate, and that Rose had an ulterior motive for befriending the player. It also included material that the NCAA had told Tompsett would remain confidential.

Furious, Tompsett sent out a press release of his own, accusing the NCAA of violating his client's confidentiality and invading the Boatrights' privacy. The Boatrights, he said, would consider their legal options. But of course Tanesha was hardly in a position to sue; she just wanted to get her son back on the court. And the NCAA knew it.

Even so, the NCAA had to take one last shot. "Had Ms. Boatright cooperated fully from the beginning," its next press release stated piously, "this matter could have been solved months ago."

—Joe Nocera

# CHAPTER 1
# THE TURNCOAT

It's easy enough to mark the moment when the NCAA began its rise to power: it was 1951, when an ambitious twenty-nine-year-old former sportswriter named Walter Byers became its first executive director. Though founded in 1906, the NCAA had long been a toothless association comprised of fewer than four hundred universities with athletic programs. Within a few years after Byers's arrival, however, the NCAA was striking fear into the hearts of college athletic officials, coaches, university presidents, and athletes alike. The essential rules governing amateurism were written on his watch. He built and nurtured the enforcement staff that investigated schools accused of breaking the rules. He invented the term "student-athlete," which he coined to evade efforts by several states to classify athletes as employees, and thus allow them to collect workers' compensation if they were injured. He negotiated television contracts, cut licensing deals, and helped elevate the NCAA's college basketball tournament into the commercial spectacle we now know as March Madness, where fans are not allowed to bring a drink to their seats that is not from a tournament sponsor, and where even the ladders that the players climb to cut down the nets at the Final Four are made by an official NCAA sponsor. He crushed the AAU, which had held power over amateur athletics before he took over the NCAA, brushed aside congressional calls for reform, and fought anyone who stood in his way. Though universities often resented the NCAA and Byers, they felt they had no choice but to join: by the time he retired, the NCAA had over a thousand member schools. Largely forgotten today, Byers was a force of nature in his prime: secretive, despotic, stubborn, and ruthless. Although he left the NCAA nearly three decades ago—he died in May 2015, at the age of ninety-three—his imprint was so strong that the NCAA's culture today is not very different from the one he imposed on it all those many years ago.

But while the NCAA didn't change in the intervening years, Byers did. He eventually turned against his creation, becoming one of its fiercest critics. Having fought all manner of opponents while he ran the NCAA, he joined them after he left, calling for the kinds of radical reforms that would not gain traction for another two decades.

The original purpose of the NCAA was to devise rules that would make football less risky. At the turn of the last century, football was a new game, and an exceedingly dangerous one; during the 1905 season, 18 athletes died, while nearly 160 others were seriously injured. Alarmed, President Theodore Roosevelt called upon the presidents of Harvard, Yale, and Princeton—football powers in those early days—to fix the problem. The newly formed NCAA wound up eliminating some of the most hazardous plays—out went the flying wedge—while legalizing the forward pass. "I must say that football has been greatly improved this year," said Harvard president Charles William Eliot as the 1906 season came to an end. "It has less injuries and is much more openly played."

By the 1940s, football was by far the most popular college sport, a position it has never yielded—and a fact that drives the decision making at most university athletic departments to this day. In addition to the Ivy League schools, Notre Dame was nationally known for its football team, as were the Big Ten schools like Michigan and Ohio State. Then, as now, the athletes were supposed to be matriculating students who played solely for the glory of their school. And then, as now, there was plenty of cheating, with under-the-table payments, loosened academic standards, no-show jobs, and the like.

Byers, who grew up in Kansas City, had been a good high school football player, but when he went out for the team as a freshman at Rice University, the coach told him that, at five foot eight, he was too small to play in college. He transferred to the University of Iowa, where he worked on the student paper, only to drop out a few courses short of graduation to join the army after Pearl Harbor. Discharged because he was cross-eyed, he went to work in New York for the news agency that was then called United Press. In 1947, wanting to return to the Midwest, he took a job in Chicago with the Big Ten, as an assistant to its commissioner, Kenneth "Tug" Wilson.

In addition to his day job, Wilson was the secretary of the NCAA, which operated out of a room at the Big Ten's Chicago headquarters. Unhappy about the rampant cheating, Wilson proposed that the NCAA establish uniform national rules that all universities would have to abide by. "We must set up a policy whereby a boy will choose a school for its educational value rather than the school choosing a boy for his athletic ability," he said. In 1948, at the NCAA's annual convention, he helped push through something called the Purity Code (the name was later changed to the Sanity Code), which banned off campus recruiting, prohibited "subsidies and inducement" to athletes, and insisted that athletes meet a school's "normal academic requirements" to be admitted. It even barred athletic scholarships, which became a source of contention with other NCAA schools, especially in the South, which felt they had to award scholarships to catch up with the high-profile teams in the East and Midwest. Though it still had no full-time employees, the NCAA was supposed to enforce the new code.

The Sanity Code didn't last long. By 1950, seven schools had admitted to violating the rules—mainly by giving athletic scholarships—and essentially dared the NCAA to toss them out, which was its only recourse. (The NCAA finally approved athletic scholarships in 1956.) At its convention that year, the schools that made up the NCAA failed to gain the two-thirds vote necessary to expel the "Seven Sinners." It was in the aftermath of that failure that Wilson turned to Byers and put him in charge of the NCAA, with an initial salary of $11,000.

Byers immediately moved the NCAA headquarters to Kansas City, which not only got him closer to home, but also created some necessary distance between the NCAA and the Big Ten, and hired a secretary. In the summer of 1952, he added an assistant, Wayne Duke, who would eventually become Big Ten commissioner himself. "It was a pretty humble beginning," Duke told the journalist Keith Dunnavant, the author of *The*

*Fifty-Year Seduction*, a book about the symbiotic relationship between college football and television. "But there was a feeling that we were getting in on the ground floor of something big."

Byers burned with ambition for his new organization. "He wanted to build something meaningful," says Chuck Neinas, an early hire who worked for the NCAA for a decade. "Walter was an entrepreneur," says Wally Renfro, who spent forty years at the NCAA, beginning in 1972. "He built the NCAA largely through the force of his personal will, his charisma, and his genius." Jack McCallum, the longtime *Sports Illustrated* writer, once wrote that Byers "made a kingdom out of what once was a dot on the American sports scene."

Like Byers, the NCAA was secretive, despotic, stubborn, and ruthless. It also quickly became bureaucratic and rules-driven, lacking both flexibility and empathy—two qualities Byers also did not possess—in applying its myriad rules. Byers mistrusted the press, and so did the NCAA. He was a classic control freak who played power politics with the best of them, usually maneuvering behind the scenes. (He rarely spoke at NCAA conventions, for instance.) NCAA rules were "bylaws" that were first proposed as "legislation," making them sound like actual laws, which of course they weren't. His managerial style was often likened to that of J. Edgar Hoover; like Hoover, Byers didn't allow coffee breaks and he insisted that the desks of NCAA staff members be spotless. (He was also obsessed with how the Mafia worked; one of his ex-wives once said that he read a copy of *The Godfather* so many times that he had to get a second one.) He had NCAA staffers who sat next to windows report to him about who came to work late. ("Discipline is necessary," he later said. "That is why I ran a tight ship.") He used to tape phone calls with conference commissioners and others. He had no real friends to speak of—just "acquaintances and colleagues," says Neinas, who often had drinks with him after work.

Byers was also completely sincere about the importance of amateurism as the sine qua non of college athletics. "I passionately believed NCAA rules could preserve the amateur collegiate spirit I so much loved as a youth and admired as a young sports reporter," he wrote in his memoir. He abhorred what he used to call "the power coaches"—the ones, like Bobby Knight, the basketball coach at the University of Indiana, or Joe Paterno, Penn State's legendary football coach—who dominated their campuses and could run roughshod over the university president. He viewed himself as single-handedly restraining the forces of commercialism, and claimed that as much as he loved college sports, if he were forced to choose between athletics and academics, he would choose the latter. He believed that his enforcement staff, which was so distrusted by most member schools, was on the side of the angels, rooting out college sports' bad apples. Yet at the same time, his push to make the NCAA powerful—and college sports right along with it—had the practical effect of enabling the power coaches, of shoveling ever more money into athletics and turning it, year by year, into less of an avocation and more of a business. The contradictions that are now so glaring in college sports could also be seen in Walter Byers's life and career.

The NCAA's power, as Byers first constructed it and then fortified it, stood on two pillars. The first was enforcement. The second was television.

Having watched the collapse of the Sanity Code, Byers realized that he had to show that he could punish schools short of kicking them out of the NCAA. Less than a month after he took the job as NCAA executive director, he got his first opportunity when the New York District Attorney's Office picked up two recently graduated Kentucky basketball players, Alex Groza and Ralph Beard, on suspicion of point shaving during their college days. After New York's investigation came to a close six months later—there was no jail time for the players, though they were banned from professional basketball—Byers and Bernie H. Moore, the commissioner of Kentucky's conference, the Southeastern Conference, agreed that all the other SEC basketball teams should cancel their games with Kentucky for the 1952–53 season. Byers then went a step further. He insisted that *every* school in the NCAA boycott Kentucky for that season. When Kentucky decided not to fight the boycott, Byers had what he needed: proof that he could impose a punishment that would stick.

Within a decade, the NCAA was handing out all gradations of punishments. A school accused of recruiting violations might be forbidden from playing in a televised game for a year or two, or prevented from playing in the postseason. Schools were regularly put on "probation." Athletes who took money from boosters could lose their eligibility—and their prospective careers. In severe cases, coaches could lose their jobs because their programs had violated the rules. Enforcement gave the NCAA immense power over universities, athletic departments, coaches, and athletes—and it wasn't shy about using that power.

With its enforcement powers, the NCAA under Byers ruled primarily by fear. Maybe things might have been different if the enforcement staff— and the NCAA's Committee on Infractions, which made the final rulings based on the enforcement staff's findings—had respected rights, shown compassion when circumstances warranted, and created an ethos that all the participants felt was fair. But the enforcement process simply wasn't set up that way. Lacking subpoena power, NCAA investigators gathered information any way they could, no matter how dubious or conflicted the source, or underhanded the method. There was no pretense that there were "rules of evidence" as that phrase is commonly understood. And it was merciless in enforcing rules even when they caused an unjust outcome.

Investigators would often act on tips—yet the tipster was never revealed, so that a school had no way to defend itself or question the informant's motive. Members of the NCAA enforcement staff didn't tape-record their interviews, and often didn't take notes until hours or even days later. Athletes or coaches who were charged with violations were allowed to have a lawyer at some, but not all, interviews. Nor could they mount any kind of defense that involved cross-examining witnesses, since that was not part of the process. The moment a player came under suspicion, he was assumed to be guilty, and the school had to render him immediately ineligible or risk forfeiting games it had played using an "ineligible" player. Indeed, because the player was not even a member of the NCAA—only universities were—he essentially had no standing to defend himself against any charges that were brought against him. With his career on the line, the player would be questioned without knowing why, and would be told that he couldn't discuss the interrogation without further jeopardizing his eligibility.

After the enforcement staff finished its work, the case went before the NCAA's Committee on Infractions, which met a handful of times each year and was made up of law professors and other academics at NCAA member schools. Then, and only then, would the school or the player be given a chance to defend themselves—not that it was ever a fair fight. The enforcement staff and the Committee on Infractions were invariably on friendly terms—dinner and drinks were not unusual when the committee was in town—and the enforcement staff had ex parte communications with the committee that were never afforded school officials. Because of the way the NCAA put together investigations—with hearsay evidence, interview notes that were often inaccurate, and unnamed sources—universities were invariably forced into a he-said, she-said conflict with the enforcement staff. The Committee on Infractions almost never voted against the enforcement staff.

As the NCAA rulebook grew ever larger, eventually ballooning to over four hundred pages, many people in college sports came to believe that the NCAA could make a case against any school, at any time, if it so chose: it was simply impossible to always stay on the right side of so many rules. This was especially true in the two big-money sports, football and men's basketball, where the players often came from disadvantaged backgrounds and lacked the kind of pocket money that other students on campus took for granted. Allowing an athlete a free phone call from the coach's office was impermissible. Giving him money for a ticket back home to attend his grandmother's funeral was impermissible. Allowing an athlete free food in between mealtimes was an impermissible benefit. (This rule was finally changed in 2014, after Shabazz Napier, the University of Connecticut guard who was the star of that year's March Madness tournament, complained on national television that he often went to bed hungry.) In 1978, during a series of congressional hearings about the NCAA, one of its former investigators, Brent Clark, said, "Give me six weeks and I can put any school in the country on probation."

In 1978, Representative John Moss, a California Democrat, led a year-long series of hearings into the NCAA's enforcement practices. "I have been writing administrative law in this House for more than a quarter of a century and I have never seen anything even touching upon this kind of inequity in procedure," Moss said at one point. "It appears that they are far more interested in punishment than in justice."

The committee heard from witnesses who described examples of the NCAA's investigative methods and its version of justice. Investigators interviewed athletes not on campus but in their homes or neighborhoods, where they bought them food, provided them transportation, and hung out with them—doing things, in other words, that violated the NCAA's own rules. "The ostensible purpose for conducting interviews under those conditions was to catch the young man off guard, and wield a good deal of authority over him," said Clark, who had quit the NCAA's enforcement staff to join the subcommittee, and was also its star witness. (He was also a highly controversial witness. Three months after his testimony, a Republican subcommittee member, Norman Lent of New York, issued a forty-two-page report describing him as a "deceptive and misleading witness." A closer look shows that he had a penchant for inflammatory language like "bribery" and "flesh peddling" that gave his allegations an exaggerated quality. He resigned from the subcommittee staff several months after he delivered his testimony.)

Officials at Mississippi State University told the committee how they had been advised not to take the NCAA to court over a case where they felt they had been punished unfairly. "I was told by my co-counsel and clients that if we fought the NCAA by going to court, we would have our heads bloodied." Indeed, the NCAA was so furious when Mississippi State did ultimately take it to court that Warren Brown, the head of enforcement, told an underling that it should look for new infractions even though the investigation was closed.

Committee members learned that Byers would sometimes secretly tape telephone calls, and that he would also sit in on hearings by the Committee on Infractions, which suggested to the committee that he had an interest in the outcome. They heard how an investigator had set up one player with a pro tryout to get him to give information, and offered another "legal representation" in the pros. One member of Congress quoted Al McGuire, the former Marquette coach turned sportscaster, as saying that the NCAA's investigative tactics were "Gestapo-like."

At those same hearings, Burton Brody, a law professor at the University of Denver who was also the school's faculty representative to the NCAA, said of the NCAA's enforcement process, "It was at best a burlesque of fairness. No evidence was presented, only the conclusions of staff members. No witnesses were called. The only 'testimony' was by the enforcement staff members, without oath, stating the rankest sort of mixture of hearsay and opinion as part of his prosecutorial arguments."

The perception that the deck was stacked against them was only one reason why schools, coaches, and players all feared NCAA investigations.

In addition, the NCAA could seem vindictive if an institution dared to fight back. "Most member institutions bow down without a whimper," Mississippi State attorney Erwin Ward said during the hearings. "Those that stand up against the NCAA do so with trembling and continuing fears of retaliatory retribution that can be dispensed without warning by a powerful arm of arbitrary force."

Adding to the sense of unfairness, certain schools were viewed as untouchable, no matter how egregious their violation of NCAA rules. The most notorious example was the UCLA basketball team during the John Wooden era. Between 1964 and 1975, when Wooden retired, UCLA won a remarkable ten NCAA championships, becoming the dominant program in the history of men's college basketball. Wooden himself was portrayed as a teacher of men, whose Pyramid of Success—fifteen tenets that built the foundation for personal and athletic success—was as famous as his full-court zone press defense. And his UCLA teams were always portrayed as beyond reproach.

They were anything but. During almost the entirety of Wooden's championship reign, a prominent booster, a construction magnate with reputed mob connections named Sam Gilbert, served as a fixer for the players. Gilbert arranged for food, clothes, and housing for players; he provided them cars, stereos, airline tickets, money, and other perks. Players went to see him in his office, a penthouse on Ventura Boulevard with a view of the San Fernando Valley, or hang out with him on weekends at his home. No matter what they needed, Gilbert delivered. He facilitated cars for players by helping them sell season tickets to home games for as much as $1,000 and then sending them to a friendly salesman. He paid for players' attorneys if they needed them and even for abortions for their girlfriends.

When a radical sports activist named Jack Scott wrote a book in the mid-1970s about Bill Walton, the great UCLA All-American center, he called up Gilbert to ask about a letter from a UCLA player—presumably Walton—that promised to reimburse Gilbert $4,500 for all he had given him in college. Gilbert, known to be gruff and profane, instantly changed his tune. "Are you going to use that letter?" he asked Scott. "UCLA would have to return four championships. What I did is a total violation of NCAA rules."

"It's hard for me to have a proper perspective on financial matters since I've always had whatever I wanted since I enrolled at UCLA," Walton said after he graduated.

Gilbert's role was an open secret in college basketball circles. NCAA investigators interviewed him on more than one occasion. Brent Clark, the former NCAA investigator, testified during the 1978 congressional hearings that he had first been alerted to Gilbert after learning that he may have represented several players in negotiations with NBA teams while the players were still juniors. That was (of course) a violation of NCAA rules. According to Clark's testimony, he interviewed Gilbert and others and presented his findings, but was told by a superior, "We're just not going after the institution right now."

Why not? One possibility is that UCLA's athletic director, J. D. Morgan, was a close friend of Walter Byers. There was always speculation that that relationship kept investigators at bay. (As for why UCLA never cracked down on Gilbert, Charles Young, UCLA's chancellor from 1968 to 1997, says, "John must have known, but concluded there was nothing he could do. J.D. once told me he didn't want to end up encased in concrete at the bottom of the ocean. He was physically afraid of Sam.")

Another reason the NCAA left UCLA alone was because the basketball team was so important financially. For years, the National Invitation Tournament (NIT) had been more prestigious than the NCAA championship. (Byers took care of that problem by having the NCAA pass a rule in 1981 that any team chosen for the NCAA tournament could not opt for the NIT instead.) Indeed, until the 1970s the men's championship was not even shown live—it was on tape delay. UCLA's championship run gave the tournament a storyline that excited fans and gave reporters something to write about. Clark told the subcommittee that it was his belief that the NCAA chose "not to pursue the individual"—Gilbert—"since it would involve one of the NCAA's leading moneymakers, a major basketball power." He added, "In this instance politics and balance sheets seemed to dictate that the NCAA take no action."

Then there was the second pillar, television, which translated into money. In modern times, the March Madness tournament has served as the NCAA's primary profit center: its deals with "corporate partners," ticket sales, and television contracts with TBS and CBS for the rights to the men's basketball championship bring in around $900 million a year. But for most of Byers's tenure, it was televised football that the NCAA relied on to generate revenue, both for itself and for its member schools. Indeed, one of Byers's early moves was to wrest control of televised football from the universities themselves. "Wrest," however, is probably the wrong word; most universities were begging him to do it. In the early 1950s, most big football schools feared the effect television would have on their ticket receipts, which were their primary revenue source. With the NCAA as a sole negotiator for all member schools, it could ration the supply of games on television—and protect the all-important gate. Or so the thinking went.

Not every school agreed with this approach. In particular, the University of Pennsylvania, as well as Notre Dame, resisted turning over their television rights to the NCAA. Both schools argued that the TV rights to their football games were their intellectual property, and that taking them away amounted to an antitrust violation. The two schools also argued, presciently, that it was shortsighted to view television as the enemy; television could one day be college football's best friend.

Byers made no attempt to negotiate or reason with the two recalcitrant schools; that was hardly his style. With Penn determined to go ahead with its own television contract, Byers had the NCAA declare that it was "not a member in good standing," which meant that every other NCAA member school would have to boycott it. Reluctantly, Penn backed down. Notre Dame, seeing what had happened to Penn, abandoned a television deal it had negotiated with the old DuMont network. But it did so with considerable bitterness. "The NCAA started as an advisory body, then became a regulatory body, and now has become a confiscatory one," groused Notre Dame athletic director Moose Krause.

The rationing that Byers developed with his television plan was severe: each school was allowed a total of five appearances over a two-year span, divided between national and regional games. In 1954, ABC paid the NCAA $2 million for the rights to those games. By 1974, the contract was worth $16 million, with schools receiving $487,856 for a national appearance and $355,000 for a regional one. Byers insisted that smaller schools appear in some of the regional games, and that the Division II and Division III championships be televised. Although the networks complained, they went along. Byers didn't treat them any better than he treated member schools.

By the 1970s, however, the big football schools had come to see the error of their ways. They realized, first of all, that television was a potential gold mine. Football fans were clamoring to see the best teams—and those schools wanted to oblige, but couldn't, thanks to the NCAA's television plan. A classic example, as Dunnavant points out in his book, was the famous 1966 game between Notre Dame and Michigan State, both undefeated and ranked number 1 and number 2 in the country. (The game stirred up enormous controversy when, late in the fourth quarter with the score 10–10, Notre Dame coach Ara Parseghian chose to run out the clock instead of going for the win.)

By the time the game took place, late in the season, Notre Dame had already played in one nationally televised game. Michigan State had played in one regional game. The NCAA's television rules said that a team could only play in one national game or two regional games a year. Thus the NCAA opted to make this highly anticipated matchup a regional game, meaning that half the country was not able to see it live. Instead, they were shown a meaningless "national" game between Kentucky and Tennessee. College football fans were irate.

The football powers had other frustrations with the NCAA. Because they were outnumbered by the smaller schools in the association, they were regularly outvoted on items they cared about, such as scholarship limits and other cost-cutting measures. Indeed, when the NCAA member schools voted to limit football scholarships to ninety-five per school—an attempt both to save money and to prevent the football powers from stockpiling players—the football powers were outraged. Thus it was that in early 1977 some sixty-three universities formed a new group, called the College Football Association, or CFA. It included all the big football powers except the schools in the Big Ten and the Pac-10, which decided to remain allied with the NCAA. Chuck Neinas, Byers's former employee, who had become the commissioner of the Big Eight Conference, was named executive director of the CFA in 1980.

Although the CFA had been formed to deal with a variety of grievances, it soon narrowed its focus to the television rights issue. The only football games the conferences themselves controlled were the season-ending bowl games. By the late 1970s, conferences were receiving $1 million–plus paydays for their contractual deals with the big bowl games, like the Rose Bowl or the Sugar Bowl. Just think of what they could earn if they controlled *all* their games! What's more, the NCAA had never had any interest in controlling the televising of men's basketball; that was left to the individual conferences. How could the NCAA argue that it needed to control football but not basketball?

In August 1981, after several years of trying to have their concerns taken seriously by Byers and the NCAA, the CFA took a drastic and provocative step. Neinas announced that the CFA had signed a four-year, $180 million deal with NBC. And the money from the contract would flow only to the CFA schools, not to the larger NCAA membership.

A different kind of leader—a leader who was willing to listen to his most important constituents and craft compromises—could have easily found a way to keep the CFA schools on the reservation. The schools that comprised the CFA did not want to leave the NCAA—its running of various championship tournaments was (and remains) a very useful function, and most schools wanted to have some level of enforcement, if only to keep their competition in line. Besides, if they split off, and the Big Ten and Pac-10 schools remained part of the NCAA, the subsequent fracturing of college sports would be a nightmare.

But Byers was not that kind of leader. Without so much as a phone call to any members of the CFA, he threw down his usual gauntlet: any school that went through with the NBC deal would be expelled from the NCAA. It was an astonishing act of brinksmanship.

The CFA had two responses. First, it abandoned the NBC contract, as Byers had insisted. Second, it took the NCAA to court. Officially titled *NCAA v. Board of Regents of the University of Oklahoma*, the suit became known as the *Regents* case. It alleged that the NCAA, in controlling the television rights for the schools, was violating the Sherman Antitrust Act. "The plaintiffs argued that the NCAA artificially limited the number of games on the air which, coupled with the governing body's coercive tactics, represented a restraint of trade," explained Dunnavant. "They also asserted that price-fixing resulted from these practices."

Was Byers willing to compromise *now*? Not a chance. At the district court level, the NCAA lost badly, with many court observers believing that Byers's own testimony—grudging, argumentative, and evasive—helped lose the case for his side. The district court judge, Juan Burciaga of New Mexico, ruled that the NCAA was a "classic cartel" that enjoys "almost absolute control over the supply of college football which is made available to the networks." The cartel, he added, was able to seek "a price for their product which is, in most instances, artificially high."

After the ruling, Byers convened a conference call of the NCAA executive committee. "How does the decision read?" asked one committee member. "Like a goddamn CFA press release," Byers replied.

After its victory, the CFA approached the NCAA about a possible settlement. Stubborn to the end, Byers wasn't interested. When the case got to the Supreme Court in 1984, the outcome was no different: the justices ruled 7–2 against the NCAA, which meant that its television contracts—by then with ABC, CBS, and the cable network WTBS—were voided. One of the dissenting judges was Byron "Whizzer" White, the only Supreme Court justice who had ever been an All-American football player, at the University of Colorado. Whereas the opinion by Justice John Paul Stevens had used much the same language as the district court—"restraint upon the operation of a free market," "anticompetitive effects," "a price structure that is . . . unrelated to the prices that would prevail in a competitive market"— White bemoaned the ruling's emphasis on the commercial nature of college football. When the case was argued in front of the Supreme Court, White told one of the lawyers for Oklahoma and Georgia that he might win the case, but he would one day regret it. What he feared more than anything was that this ruling would push college sports—especially big-time football—to become even more money-oriented now that the NCAA was no longer in control of the television rights. In this he was entirely right.

One of the reasons Byers gave for restricting the number of games a college football team could appear on television was to keep the commercialism under some semblance of control. In 1981, around the same time the CFA was suing the NCAA, a man named Jim Host approached Byers during that year's Final Four in Philadelphia. A former Kentucky baseball player, Host had been a radio announcer before spending several years in Procter & Gamble's legendary marketing department and then returning to broadcasting. Among other things, he had created a radio network for the NCAA and had the contract for the NCAA tournament programs.

Now Host wanted to market the NCAA itself—and turn it into a real brand. After all, he reasoned, advertisers were looking to differentiate themselves in the marketplace, and the NCAA tournament was growing in popularity. The potential was enormous, he thought. But when he broached the idea to Byers, on the Sunday before the championship game, Byers responded angrily. "Over my fucking dead body," he told Host.

A year later, however, Byers called Host and asked him to come to Kansas City. By then, the NCAA had trademarked the phrase "Final Four," and Byers had decided he was indeed open to the idea of capitalizing financially on the tournament's growing popularity. Byers wanted to know how much a sponsor might pay to use the NCAA's logo. Maybe $250,000, Host replied. Now Byers was really interested: he soon signed a deal with Host in which they would split the revenue fifty-fifty. The NCAA maintained strict approval rights for the companies Host signed and how they would use the logo. It also insisted on no beer sponsors. But Pandora's box had been opened.

The first company Host signed was Gillette, and in 1984 the company ran its first campaign, which featured newspaper inserts around the country: buy Gillette razor blades and get a chance to win two tickets to the Final Four. The company asked Host how much he was looking for. Host said $500,000 a year for a guaranteed three years. Gillette immediately agreed; "I knew I had priced it too low," he says now. (By 2002, when Host signed Coca-Cola to a sponsorship deal, it was worth $135 million over eleven years.) It took Byers a whole year to approve the contract, but eventually he did.

Valvoline was next, and before long the number had jumped to four, then eight, then twelve and sixteen sponsors. An NCAA executive named Tom Jernstedt suggested the word "sponsor" sounded too commercial, so the companies were renamed "corporate partners." Host later created tiers—"champions" for the richest deals and "partners" for the others.

The marketability of the NCAA was evident to Host when he ran a deal with Pizza Hut to sell mini-basketballs promoting the Final Four ahead of the 1987 tournament. Pizza Hut executives were reluctant, but agreed to have Rawlings—another sponsor—make two million. They sold out in less than two weeks, and the pizza chain ran the promotion for a number of years.

Byers was also changing his tune in another important way. In 1984, he gave a short interview to Jack McCallum, a star writer at *Sports Illustrated*, in which he essentially denounced the principle of amateurism that he had clung to for so long.

"We're in a situation where we, the colleges, say it's improper for athletes to get, for example, a new car," he told McCallum. "Well, is that morally wrong? Or is it wrong because we say it is wrong? . . . It's only the colleges with the rules that say it's wrong. . . . The public doesn't think it's so wrong."

A short while later, at a closed-door meeting of the NCAA Council—a forty-member body that served as the NCAA's chief legislative arm—Byers was asked what he had meant by his *Sports Illustrated* comments. "I believe it's time to change what we're doing," he said. A year after that, during another meeting with the NCAA Council, he expanded on his earlier statements. "I suggested allowing student-athletes to endorse products, with the income going first into a trust fund, then to players when they graduate or complete eligibility," he later wrote. "I argued that since the colleges were exploiting their talent, the athletes deserved the same access to the free market as the coaches enjoyed."

These views were heresy, of course; not even the schools that made up the CFA—which had sued precisely to be able to enjoy the fruits of the free market—were interested in extending the market's beneficence to their football and basketball players. In Byers's recounting, his new, radical ideas were met with a stony silence—and "a hardening of the NCAA position on 'amateurism.'" Within three years, he had stepped down as executive director and retired to a ranch in Kansas.

What had caused this profound change of heart? Byers wouldn't be interviewed for this book, but in his memoirs, published in 1995, he obliquely attributed his awakening to sitting in the courtroom during the *Regents* case, listening to university presidents describe their athletic programs, under oath, as "commercial enterprises." He said that the coaches and athletic directors and university presidents had undermined his desire "to keep college athletics more a student activity than a profession."

He noted that John Wooden had made only $32,500 in 1975—and a decade later, Jim Valvano of North Carolina State was grossing $850,000 a year. "It finally became clear," he wrote, "that the new generation of coaches and staff didn't know and didn't care to learn about old ideals."

Yet he also had to acknowledge that he "had joined college leaders in fighting to prevent college sports from paying the taxes levied against entertainment businesses." He had negotiated television contracts that had enriched conferences and schools. He had allowed the NCAA to market its own logo. Though he placed most of the blame on the schools and their athletic departments, he couldn't completely ignore his own role in turning big-time college sports into a lucrative and commercial entertainment business. As Wally Renfro would later put it, "Walter went about, in a controlled way, to monetize the interest in intercollegiate athletics with the happy blessing of higher education."

But there may be another, simpler answer for his sudden turnabout. He had fought the *Regents* case to the bitter end—and lost. His powerful grip over college sports was loosened for the first time. Byers couldn't abide no longer being in control. Having lost the battle, he turned against his creation.

Byers's memoir, entitled *Unsportsmanlike Conduct: Exploiting College Athletes* and published by the University of Michigan Press, is poorly written and hard to follow. The bulk of it focuses on bringing enforcement cases and negotiating television contracts. His recounting of the CFA battle is told with considerable bitterness. When it was first published, the book sank like a stone.

Yet it remains one of the most stinging indictments of college sports ever written. Byers wrote at length about the greed of university athletic departments and the various ways college athletes are cheated, especially academically. He described the NCAA as a cartel, and called amateurism a "modern day misnomer for economic tyranny." He mocked the NCAA's purported mission of protecting athletes "from exploitation by professional and commercial enterprises," as the association described it.

"The NCAA constitutional restriction prevents direct dealings between the commercial, for-profit world and the athlete," he wrote. "This is not about amateurism. This has to do with who controls the negotiations and gets the money." He condemned the myriad rules that college athletes had to abide by to retain their amateur status. He even compared college sports to "the plantation" nearly two decades before Taylor Branch made the same analogy.

Byers's reform agenda included paying the players and having Congress pass an athlete's bill of rights that would mean that players didn't "sign away freedoms available to other students solely because they engage in college athletics." He argued that players should be able to transfer to other schools if they wanted, without having to sit out a year. He said that most of the petty rules should be abolished, and that players should be able to make money from their names—from endorsements, for instance.

It would take years for other reformers to pick up on Byers's complaints, though very few of them realized that was what they were doing. But it was true: virtually everything the reformers would call for had been laid out long before by the very man who made the NCAA a cartel.

# The First Activist

**GARY SHAW WAS AN ALL-STATE FOOTBALL PLAYER AT DENTON HIGH** School in North Texas in the early 1960s. A bulky lineman, he received scholarship offers from across the state, settling finally on the burnt orange of the University of Texas, the state's flagship school. With the Longhorns, Shaw played for one of the most successful coaches in college football history, Darrell Royal, the man who built Texas into a college football power and won three national championships. Today, the Longhorns' football stadium is named after Royal.

Arriving at Austin in the fall of 1963, Shaw struggled to crack the lineup, and shortly before the end of his final season he quit the team. A few years later, he published a heartwrenching book called *Meat on the Hoof,* one of the first critical looks at the underbelly of big-time college football. Nearly half a century later, the book reads like a blueprint for many of the scandals—and lawsuits—college sports have faced in the ensuing decades: the forty-hour workweek players endured; athletes funneled into classes that would keep them eligible; athletic department officials asking professors to change grades; physically abusive coaches; hazing (Shaw used to have to strip naked and carry a record between his butt cheeks); and denying players proper medical care.

Shaw interviewed a handful of former teammates who not only corroborated his experience as a college football player but had many stomach-churning anecdotes of their own. One involved teammate Wesley Barnes, a five-foot-ten dynamo and former All-State high school performer. Barnes had torn cartilage in his knee and was told to stay out of spring practice. But when an assistant coach spotted him on the sidelines one day—in sweats and with his knee wrapped—he ordered Barnes to dress for practice.

"Coach, I can't even run on it," he replied. The coach said, "Barnes, as of right now, you are officially cured—get your gear on." Barnes spent the next week as the running back in linebacker tackling drills.

Another teammate, Charlie "Chachie" Owens, sustained a serious calf injury but wasn't allowed to see the doctor. "It's just a bruise," he was told. A week passed and Owens, in searing pain, finally went to see a doctor on his own. He had blood clots in his calf. Without medical attention, he could have died.

Shaw shed light on another unsavory practice of the time, writing in great detail of Royal's practice of running off players he had soured on. In that era, scholarships were given for four years—players couldn't be cut for not living up to their coaches' expectations, the way they could be later—and though the NCAA had no policies on scholarship limits, the Southwest Conference limited teams to around a hundred at a time. That made each scholarship valuable to coaches.

Royal signed huge numbers of players; there were forty-four in Shaw's recruiting class, for instance. When he decided he wanted to get rid of a player, Royal put him through brutal exercises. Shaw and his teammates called them "shit drills," convinced they had no other purpose than to convince players to quit. In one drill, players ran at each other and collided at full speed. In another, a player was given the ball and then tackled by more than a dozen teammates. "They would pit us in a way to most quickly eliminate people," Owens told Shaw. "Our punishment was injuries." By Shaw's fourth year at Texas, only eleven of the original forty-four members of his recruiting class remained on the Longhorn squad.

*Meat on the Hoof* was released in 1972 and sold more than 350,000 copies. For a time, Shaw was a mini-celebrity, interviewed by Howard Cosell and written about in *Newsweek* and *Cosmopolitan*. Sadly, though, he spent much of the 1980s homeless, and was later diagnosed with paranoid schizophrenia. He died of an apparent heart attack in 1999 at the age of fifty-three.

# CHAPTER 2

# "HOW DO I GET ONE OF THOSE DEALS?"

"**I** always believed the kids got the shaft," said Sonny Vaccaro.

It was a sunny afternoon in 2013, and Vaccaro was sitting at a small dining room table in his modest home in Pebble Beach, California. The room was cluttered with boxes filled with letters, newspaper clippings, magazine articles, documents, and photographs: the detritus of his very long career, first as a marketer of basketball shoes, and since 2007 as perhaps the most prominent critic of the NCAA in the country. At seventy-four, Vaccaro is an excitable man; from time to time he would pick up something from one of the boxes and begin to tell the story behind it, his arms waving, his words tumbling out in almost stream-of-consciousness fashion, his voice rising so high it practically squeaked. He had been giving interviews to the press for some forty years, but he had never mastered the art of the sound bite. Clearly, he never would.

Sitting next to him was his wife, Pam, an oasis of cheery calm, who seemed to know her husband's stories almost as well as he did. As well she should. Eighteen years his junior, Pam Vaccaro started dating her future husband when she was twenty. They have worked hand in glove for the last sixteen years of their thirty-year marriage. Pam had originally been an actress in television commercials—she appeared in several of Michael Jackson's Pepsi spots—but in the early 1990s she gradually gave up acting as she assumed a larger role in her husband's work in sports marketing.

When Vaccaro decided to take on the NCAA, she was fully in favor. By Vaccaro's estimation, he had only taken two airplane flights since 1992 without her. She had long since become not just his traveling companion, but also his aide-de-camp, senior adviser, and sounding board.

Vaccaro had once been the most notorious figure in college basketball, the so-called sneaker pimp, who peddled basketball shoes first for Nike, then for Adidas, and finally for Reebok. At Nike, he had come up with one of the great marketing ploys ever: getting college players to wear Nike sneakers by paying their coaches. He persuaded Nike to sign Michael Jordan, straight out of college, and make him the company's signature athlete, with his own line of sneakers. At Adidas, he signed Kobe Bryant to a $1 million shoe contract straight out of high school. And all the while, he ran a basketball camp and an all-star game for the most prominent high school players in the land, both of which regularly aroused the suspicion of the NCAA. Many of those players, even in high school, somehow wound up wearing Vaccaro's sneakers.

The corporatization of college sports—with logos on uniforms, bowl games sponsored by Chick-fil-A, and naming rights for college stadiums—would surely have happened even without Vaccaro. But it's not too much to say that it began with him, and for many years he was its personification. "We created the commercialism," he happily concedes. "We were the first corporate entity to be involved with a coach or a university."

When he turned his back on his former career—something he did without a great deal of money in the bank—many college sports observers said he was trying to atone for his sins. No, disagreed Vaccaro, that wasn't the case. Was it because of his own run-ins over the years with the NCAA? Not really, he said. What motivated him, he said, was getting to know so many high school players over the years and being appalled at the way they were treated by the NCAA. His objections to the NCAA were visceral and personal—the result of what he had seen in the course of his life. It was his view, for instance, that the NCAA was systematically biased against impoverished black athletes. How often did a white, middle-class athlete become the subject of an NCAA investigation? he asked. It almost never happened, because their parents had money. It was only those who didn't have money—and who were supposed to stay that way so long as they were playing "amateur" college sports—who found themselves in trouble with the NCAA.

"I have always had these feelings," Vaccaro said. "The NCAA would never allow the kids to have anything."

"There was never any epiphany," agreed Pam.

"I approached the NCAA once about having the sneaker companies put up $500,000 so that they could fly the parents of the athletes in for the Final Four," Vaccaro continued. "They laughed at me. They had no incentive to do the human thing." Another time, he said, he persuaded Nike to fund an antigambling movie with Billy Packer and Al McGuire, who were then the country's preeminent college basketball announcers. "We delivered it to the NCAA to give to the schools. They did nothing with it."

"They never wanted anything to do with Sonny," nodded Pam. Not that they had any choice anymore. Vaccaro had seen to that.

Vaccaro's lifelong involvement with college basketball came about in a roundabout way. Growing up in Trafford, Pennsylvania, a tiny town (population four hundred) outside of Pittsburgh, he played baseball and football. He wanted to play football at the University of Kentucky, but his grades were lacking, so he wound up at Reedley College, in Reedley, California. While there, however, he suffered an injury that was serious enough to cause Division I programs to lose interest in him. So instead he accepted an athletic scholarship from Youngstown State University, where he promptly got injured again and never played a down. Thanks to the rules in that era, he was able to keep his scholarship and graduate.

One of the assistant football coaches at Youngstown State doubled as the basketball coach. He asked Vaccaro to help him recruit basketball players from the Pittsburgh area. As Vaccaro befriended these high school athletes, he began driving them to different local tournaments. That experience gave him his first big idea: to create an all-star game consisting of the best high school seniors around the country. He based it in Pittsburgh, named it the Dapper Dan Roundball Classic, and sold—he still has the number at his fingertips—10,344 tickets. The year was 1965; Vaccaro was twenty-four years old.

Vaccaro spent the rest of his twenties and early thirties on the periphery of both college and professional basketball. He started his summer camp, which drew not only the best high school athletes but also many of the most prominent college coaches, who came to scout the players. Vaccaro had a knack not just for befriending young African American basketball players, many of whom came from disadvantaged backgrounds, but for earning their trust (Vaccaro likes to say he was the only white guy in Pittsburgh with an afro back then). When George Gervin, a sensational shooter who had been one of his Roundball all-stars, got kicked out of Eastern Michigan University after getting in a fight during a game, it was Vaccaro to whom he turned to help him get a contract with the Virginia Squires in the upstart American Basketball Association, which was trying to compete with the NBA. (Gervin, of course, went on to become one of the most prolific scorers in the history of professional basketball.) For the next few years, Vaccaro served as a basketball headhunter for the ABA, which paid him $3,500 for every college player he convinced to join the ABA instead of the NBA.

In 1977, Vaccaro approached Nike with his next big idea. At the time, the dominant basketball sneaker—indeed, for most college and professional basketball players, the *only* sneaker—was the thin-soled canvas shoe made by Converse. Nike was then a small company that focused on track shoes; CEO Phil Knight had been a middle-distance runner at the University of Oregon under the legendary coach Bill Bowerman, and the two men had started the company—originally called Blue Ribbon Sports—with the dream of designing better running shoes. (Famously, Bowerman poured rubber into a waffle iron to make the sole for Nike's first lightweight running shoes.) By the time Vaccaro showed up, Nike was thirteen years old, but had only been manufacturing its own sneakers for a half dozen years.

Vaccaro was interested in having Nike do for other kinds of sports shoes what it had done for running shoes—make them better. He went so far as to have a shoemaker friend of his design some prototypes of various sneakers, which he took to Oregon to meet Knight and Rob Strasser, Nike's head of marketing. One of the things he discovered at the meeting was that Nike was already making basketball shoes, though it hadn't begun selling them. The meeting ended with Vaccaro inviting Strasser to that year's Roundball Classic.

That year, says Vaccaro, seventeen thousand fans showed up for his all-star game, including dozens of college coaches. Impressed by the obvious pull Vaccaro had in the basketball world, Strasser invited him back to

Oregon for further discussions. They first talked about getting high school athletes to wear Nike basketball shoes. Then, suddenly, Vaccaro blurted out: "If you guys really want to get into basketball," he said, "you should aim at college teams. You could pay the coaches and give them free shoes for the team to wear." Strasser loved the idea.

"I knew all these guys," Vaccaro said years later, referring to the coaches, "and none of them had any money." It was the same principle as an endorsement: if people saw their favorite team wearing Nike sneakers, they would be inclined to buy them. Was this the kind of "commercial exploitation" of athletes that the NCAA had sworn to prevent? You could certainly make that case; indeed, Walter Byers used to rail about Vaccaro inside the NCAA's Kansas City headquarters. But there wasn't much he could do about it. College athletes had to have shoes, and schools had to provide them, just as they had to provide uniforms. Besides, unlike the athletes, coaches weren't bound by the rules of amateurism. They could make any financial side deals they wanted to.

It only made sense that Vaccaro would be the one to approach the coaches with this idea—after all, he was the one who knew them. So he became first a Nike marketing consultant, and then a full-time employee. That first year, he recalls, he rounded up a dozen or so coaches. The first was Jerry Tarkanian at the University of Nevada, Las Vegas. Tarkanian and Vaccaro were close friends; he and Pam had lived for a time in Las Vegas, where Vaccaro had moonlighted as a radio announcer for UNLV games. Vaccaro wrote Tarkanian a check for $5,000, and promised him $5,000 more, plus 120 pairs of shoes to get UNLV through its season. The team also got shirts and sweatshirts. Another early signee was an up-and-comer named Jim Valvano, then the coach at Iona College. Vaccaro recalls Valvano being taken aback at first—"You're going to give me *money*?" he asked. "And I don't have to do anything? Is that legal?" Vaccaro assured him that it was. It wasn't long before Mark Asher, a reporter for the *Washington Post*, heard about what Vaccaro was doing and wrote a story about it. Vaccaro and Nike expected a fierce blowback. Instead, he says, "The next day, I got a call from Lute Olson." Olson was then the basketball coach at the University of Iowa. "How can I get one of those deals?" Olson asked. The following year, Nike had some eighty college basketball coaches under contract.

Over the next dozen years—years in which Vaccaro became a quasi-celebrity in the basketball world because of his willingness to throw around Nike's money, while Nike became the country's dominant maker of basketball shoes, thanks to Vaccaro's efforts—Vaccaro and Nike achieved at least three other milestones.

In 1983, Valvano, by then the coach at North Carolina State, won the national championship in a stirring upset, defeating a mighty University of Houston team that included Hakeem Olajuwon and Clyde Drexler, two future NBA All-Stars. That was the first time a Nike-clad team had won it all, though it would hardly be the last.

The following year, Michael Jordan, a junior at the University of North Carolina, decided to skip his senior year and join the professional ranks. It was going to be one of the greatest drafts ever, including not only Jordan but Olajuwon, Charles Barkley, and several others who would go on to enjoy long and prominent careers in the NBA. At the time, shoe companies were just beginning to pay professional basketball players to wear their shoes. Nike had set aside $250,000 and assumed that that would be enough to sign half a dozen members of the incoming class. Instead, Vaccaro, sensing the kind of impact Jordan was likely to have in the NBA, pushed Nike to spend the entire sum on him. And once the company did that, he encouraged Nike to create a signature shoe for its new marquee basketball star. That shoe, first introduced in 1985, was the Air Jordan, which would go on to become the best-selling basketball shoe ever.

And in 1988, Vaccaro was approached, through an intermediary, by the University of Miami, which wanted Nike to deal directly with the school's athletic department rather than with its basketball coach. This led to the first "all sports" deal with Nike, which allowed the Miami athletic department to control the Nike money and decide how much to hand out to individual coaches.

"The 1980s," Vaccaro said, "was when they figured out how to commercialize college sports."

"I think our problems with the NCAA really started with the Jerry Tarkanian case," said Pam.

*Jerry Tarkanian.* To most fans, he was Tark the Shark, the colorful, towel-chomping coach who put together some of the most dynamic teams in college basketball history. They included the 1990 UNLV squad with Greg Anthony and Larry Johnson that won the national championship, beating Duke by 30 points, the largest margin of victory ever in an NCAA tournament championship game.

But to college basketball insiders, Tarkanian was known for something else: he was the coach who sued the NCAA rather than accept its punishment for alleged violations of NCAA rules. Like the *Regents* case, the *Tarkanian* lawsuit went all the way to the Supreme Court; also like the *Regents* case, the *Tarkanian* decision reverberates to this day. Although the NCAA consistently portrayed Tarkanian as a rogue coach, there were plenty of others, including Vaccaro, who believed that the NCAA's investigation into Tarkanian and UNLV was a prime example of the essential unfairness that characterized so many NCAA investigations. Like Vaccaro, Tarkanian had a gift for befriending exactly the kind of player the NCAA viewed with deep suspicion—an inner-city African American, with suspect grades, a flamboyant game, and sometimes a troubled past. He also recruited heavily from junior colleges, which was where good players wound up when, for one reason or another, they couldn't get into a Division I school straight from high school.

In the interview notes that Walter Byers's ghostwriter compiled as he prepared to write Byers's memoirs, he quoted Byers as saying of Tarkanian, "Tark thinks he is doing a public service for these kids, but his humanitarianism is limited to high leapers." With Tarkanian's shoe deal, added Byers, "He's a guy who epitomizes on cashing in on amateur sports. He's the worst of the breed." That's how the NCAA viewed Jerry Tarkanian.

Indeed, the very genesis of the *Tarkanian* case showed that the NCAA often had an agenda when it targeted a coach or a player. In the early 1970s, while coaching at Long Beach State, Tarkanian wrote two columns in a local paper accusing the NCAA of playing favorites. "The NCAA investigates and then places on probation the New Mexico States, Western Kentuckys, Centenarys and Florida States, while the big money-makers go free," he wrote in the second of those columns. "It is a crime." (Years later, he would rephrase that sentiment in one of his most memorable lines: "The NCAA is so mad at Kentucky, it's going to give Cleveland State two more years' probation.")

Shortly after the columns ran, Warren Brown, the NCAA's enforcement chief, wrote a note to the commissioner of Long Beach State's conference. Its implicit threat was unmistakable.

"It always amazes me when successful coaches become instant authorities," wrote Brown. "As in the case of this article, such instant authorities reflect an obvious unfamiliarity with the facts. Tarkanian is no exception in this regard.

"I wonder whether he considers California State University at Long Beach in the 'big money maker' category.

"Keep smiling," Brown concluded ominously. The NCAA quickly ratcheted up an investigation into Long Beach State's football and basketball teams.

Then, in March 1973, within days of Tarkanian agreeing to take the UNLV job—and well before he could have possibly broken any rules—the NCAA reopened a long-dormant investigation into violations at his new school. Vaccaro was one of the first people the NCAA investigators interviewed. "They wanted me to turn on Jerry, who was one of my best friends," he says. Vaccaro liked to gamble, and "they insinuated that they knew I was doing things in Vegas that could cause me problems, and they would make trouble for me if I didn't tell them what they wanted to hear. 'If you don't tell us how he cheats, you are going to have a miserable life,'" Vaccaro recalls being told. "They threatened me," he adds. "I'll never forget that." (A few years later, Vaccaro had problems with the IRS for not listing such Las Vegas amenities as comped rooms on his tax return. Though they have no proof, he and Pam are convinced that the NCAA was behind his troubles with the government.)

Did Tarkanian violate NCAA rules in the course of his long coaching career? Almost certainly. But despite spending years investigating Tarkanian and UNLV, the NCAA never found anything resembling the kind of systematic cheating that went on at UCLA during the Wooden years. And what it did claim to find—violations ranging from academic fraud to interfering with the investigation—were largely discredited.

That's because even as the NCAA was investigating UNLV, the university, which strongly backed its coach, with the help of the Nevada attorney general's office, was conducting an inquiry into the NCAA's methods. It found witnesses who insisted they had been misquoted by the lead NCAA investigator, Dave Berst. Others who were quoted in the enforcement staff's report claimed they had never even been interviewed—and those who had often recounted chilling statements by the investigators:

"Why do you want to stay loyal to Tarkanian; all he ever did was screw you."

"Tarkanian is like a pimp to you ballplayers."

"They said they were going to get Jerry Tarkanian no matter how long it took."

"We're out to hang him."

"David Berst stated that they wanted me to help them in their investigation of Tarkanian and the basketball program. . . . I explained that I knew of no wrongdoing by Tarkanian. . . . One of [the investigators] stated that Tarkanian exploited black athletes and must be stopped. I told him the whole world exploited blacks. David Berst said, 'We don't have him yet but we really want to get him.'"

Later, under oath, Berst was forced to admit that, on at least one occasion, he had called Tarkanian, whose mother had escaped the Armenian genocide, a "rug merchant," though he claimed he meant it as a term of affection.

(Berst, who retired from the NCAA in 2014 after a forty-three-year career, declined to be interviewed for this book. He did, however, send a lengthy e-mail defending his tenure as an enforcement staffer and later as head of enforcement. "I never have discussed details of cases even at cocktail hour and I'm still not inclined to do so," he began. "I recognize that there are plenty of comments and stories written by others that you may well treat as fact to make your own theories work."

He continued: "I operated with full autonomy when running the enforcement and eligibility programs from 75–98, without any political considerations. . . . I ensured that we did our/my own mea culpas when human mistakes occurred and I learned from everyone and did not avoid exculpatory information that might aid those under inquiry. We at all times attempted to meet the high standards of integrity expected in a self policing environment with rules that are not laws of the land and which involve people who are dedicated to collegiate athletics. It was a constant point of emphasis for me that the issues in athletics are not good and evil issues and whether you like or dislike a person makes no difference whatsoever to the matter at hand.

"I regret as much as anyone that some of our own errors and missteps bring into question how a fair and efficient program can continue. . . . I offer these comments mostly for peace of mind and to ensure that you know that the easy task of flogging an acronym will be built on tales and opinion that I suspect will not meet my standards of inquiry.")

UNLV, meanwhile, compiled mounds of evidence disproving the most serious charges, like academic fraud, with sworn affidavits from everyone involved, professors included. When the *Tarkanian* case came before the Committee on Infractions in 1977, the university countered with all the evidence it had gathered that cast doubt on the enforcement staff's work— and on the accusations themselves. Members of the committee expressed outrage—not at the enforcement staff's shoddy work, but at the university for daring to question the investigators' methods. Byers, who sat in on the hearing, loudly defended the enforcement staff. When the committee handed down its ruling, it ordered that Tarkanian be suspended from his coaching duties for two years, an unusually harsh penalty. On the day before the suspension was to take effect, Tarkanian sued UNLV in Nevada state court, arguing that the school had violated his right to due process.

Due process—the idea that people have legal rights that the state must respect, including the right to defend themselves when accused of wrongdoing—was something the NCAA grappled with in the 1970s. Under the Fourteenth Amendment to the Constitution, only government entities are required to afford due process protections, such as the ability to question witnesses and produce evidence. Nonetheless, players who were found guilty of an NCAA infraction—and who felt they had gotten a raw deal but had no means within the NCAA's structure to try to clear their name—began suing, claiming their due process rights had been violated. As Ellen Staurowsky, a Drexel University professor and NCAA critic, discovered during a search in the NCAA archives, back in 1973 Byers had asked the NCAA's outside counsel, George H. Gangwere, to offer a "position statement" on whether the NCAA should begin offering due process protections to those it accused of violating its rules. His answer was yes.

"Even though there may be no constitutional right to participate in intercollegiate athletics," Gangwere wrote, "there may be sufficient interest in such participation that requires the observance of due process." Noting that several courts had talked of the need for "fundamental fairness," Gangwere concluded that "it is our recommendation, therefore, that member institutions be urged to give notice and an opportunity for a hearing to student athletes in any infractions actions where it is proposed to suspend eligibility or aid."

Byers and the NCAA not only ignored Gangwere's advice of outside counsel, but actively took steps to insulate themselves from having to provide due process protections. For instance, they passed something they called the Restitution Rule, which provided that any university that allowed a player to continue playing after he sued the NCAA—even if he got a court injunction—would be punished retroactively if the NCAA ultimately won the case. Thus not only did the NCAA deprive players of due process during the NCAA process, but now it was even trying to keep players from using the courts to obtain a measure of fairness.

Second, the NCAA passed a rule at its 1975 convention that put the burden of declaring a player ineligible on the school rather than on the NCAA. This was called the Penalty Structure Rule, and when it was submitted for a vote at the convention, the man introducing it admitted forthrightly that it was aimed at "keep[ing] us from getting into legal difficulties." It passed by a voice vote. As a lawyer and NCAA critic named Richard Johnson would write years later in a law review article, "With the stroke of a pen, the NCAA enacted the charade that, since it does not directly punish college athletes, it does not have to afford them any due process whatsoever." Indeed, when Long Beach State president Steve Horn rose to offer a motion that would "allow the student-athlete, just as any other human being in our Anglo-Saxon judicial oriented society . . . to receive notice and have an opportunity for a hearing with respect to his ineligibility," he was voted down.

Tarkanian knew full well that the NCAA did not believe it was required to provide due process to the people it accused. But his argument had a different twist. As an employee of a state-run university, he had an inviolable right to due process protections from his employer, UNLV. The only reason UNLV hadn't provided them was because the NCAA wouldn't allow it. Tarkanian argued that because the NCAA was acting in concert with a government entity, it was a "state actor," and thus was also required to afford him due process. ("State actor" is the legal term for when private institutions act on behalf of government entities—and assume government responsibilities.)

By 1979, the NCAA had been added to the case, which of course was Tarkanian's goal all along. But that was just the beginning of Tarkanian's legal odyssey. The case took a decade to wind its way through the Nevada courts—a decade during which Tarkanian continued to coach basketball at UNLV. Ultimately both the Nevada trial court and the state supreme court decided in Tarkanian's favor. The trial court judge described the NCAA's prosecution of Tarkanian as a "star chamber proceeding," and said that Berst had "an obsession bordering on paranoia" toward Tarkanian. The state supreme court ruled that the NCAA was indeed a state actor.

But in late 1988, the U.S. Supreme Court overturned the Nevada Supreme Court by a 5–4 vote, ruling that the NCAA was *not* a state actor after all. (As with the *Regents* decision, Justice Byron White was in the minority.)

It would be hard to overstate the importance of the *Tarkanian* decision—or the harm it would inflict on future generations of athletes and coaches who found themselves in the NCAA's crosshairs. Thanks to *Tarkanian*, the NCAA would continue to base many of its findings on shaky or nonexistent evidence; continue to allow the enforcement staff to maintain a too-close relationship with the Committee on Infractions; continue to deny those accused an ability to cross-examine their accusers—or even to know who they were. And it would continue to rule by fear.

"The despicable thing is that every time you see some egregious thing happen at a university, the guy who suffers the most is the kid," Vaccaro says. "The coach moves on. The president is still there. But the kid is the one on the hook. And once the NCAA nails him, he's done. The public looks at him like he's committed a crime."

Over the years, the NCAA took tepid steps that created the illusion of reform without doing anything truly meaningful. After those 1978 congressional hearings, for instance, which were prompted by the NCAA's investigation into Tarkanian, the NCAA promised to seriously consider a series of reforms suggested by the committee. But because the committee was unwilling to write its reforms into law, the NCAA was able to ignore its suggestions—which it did. In the early 1990s, again at the urging of Congress, the NCAA established a commission, chaired by Rex Lee, a former solicitor general, to make recommendations to make the enforcement process fairer. The NCAA accepted a number of its recommendations, including allowing the accused to have lawyers, tape-recording its interviews, and allowing the accused access to the evidence—though not its sources. These were all useful reforms. But the commission's two most important recommendations were that NCAA enforcement hearings should be held in public instead of behind closed doors, and that retired federal judges, completely independent of the NCAA, should replace the Committee on Infractions. These, however, the NCAA declined to implement. To this day, Committee on Infractions hearings are held in secret, and the committee members are too close to the enforcement staff.

As for Tarkanian, after losing in the Supreme Court, he sued the NCAA a second time, in 1992, this time alleging harassment. In April 1998, the NCAA agreed to pay him $2.5 million to settle the litigation. Though most of the money went to pay his lawyers, Tarkanian was nonetheless exultant, proclaiming that the settlement, which included a conciliatory statement by the NCAA, was vindication. "The biggest mistake I ever made was taking them on," he told the Associated Press. "The average coach has no chance. It's been a terrible ordeal."

Many in the college sports establishment thought Tarkanian got a raw deal, but few were willing to say so out loud. Bill Walton, however, was an exception. "I can't be quiet when I see what the NCAA is doing to Jerry Tarkanian," he is quoted as saying in Jack Scott's book. "The NCAA is working day and night to get Jerry, but no one from the NCAA ever questioned me during my four years at UCLA." ("Tarkanian's violations are nickel-and-dime stuff compared to what goes on at UCLA and USC," Sam Gilbert once said.)

Tarkanian stepped down as the coach of UNLV in 1992, after a local newspaper published a photograph of several of his players in a hot tub with a known gambler. He never shed his reputation as a cheater; sports fans simply weren't ready to accept the idea that the NCAA was anything but the good cop on the beat. Not until 2013, when, as a sickly man who could barely speak, he was inducted into the Basketball Hall of Fame, did he finally get his due. He died in February 2015 at the age of eighty-four.

———————

Sonny Vaccaro was fired by Nike in 1991. He was never told why, he says, and he was embittered for years afterward. Vaccaro's theory is that he had become too close to Jordan; they used to take jaunts together to Europe and elsewhere. Vaccaro believes that Nike didn't want him serving as a liaison between the company and its most important athlete-endorser. It's just as likely, though, that as Nike became a larger and more professionalized corporation, it no longer had a place for a scrappy hustler like Vaccaro.

For several years Vaccaro worked for a small marketing company, while continuing to run his summer camp and all-star game. But when two of his old Nike bosses, including Strasser, asked him to join them at Adidas America, a subsidiary of Adidas that had fallen on hard times and that they had been hired to revive, Vaccaro jumped at the chance. For him, it was an opportunity to hit back at the company that had cut him loose. "How many people get to climb the same mountain twice?" he recalls Strasser telling him. (Strasser died of a heart attack shortly afterward, at the age of forty-six.)

With Vaccaro leading the charge, Adidas and Nike engaged in what became known as the Sneaker Wars. It was a dirty business. Suddenly stories began appearing about Vaccaro's supposedly unsavory ways, stories he is convinced originated from Nike. The two companies even began signing high school coaches to sneaker contracts. Lamar Odom, widely considered the best player in New York City in the mid-1990s, actually switched high schools because Vaccaro, who had become his mentor, wanted him to be at an Adidas school.

Vaccaro also began signing promising high school basketball players who were skipping college and going straight to the pros. He served as an adviser to Kevin Garnett, who entered the NBA draft in 1995 right out of high school. After Kobe Bryant played in his summer camp and Vaccaro realized that he too was headed straight to the pro ranks, he convinced Strasser to offer Bryant a sneaker endorsement contract. Adidas agreed to pay Bryant, barely eighteen years old, $1 million a year, the most any basketball player had ever received for endorsing a brand of sneakers. By 1996, Adidas had created a signature shoe under Bryant's name, just as Nike had done with Jordan.

Even as he got older, Vaccaro never lost his ability to connect with young African American men. Promising high school basketball players trusted him in a way they trusted few other adults. Many of the athletes came from broken homes and were surrounded by people looking to take advantage of them. Vaccaro did them favors, listened to them, and gave them advice. And while his own self-interest was obviously at work, the athletes never felt he was playing them. "I was nobody coming out of high school," Shaquille O'Neal once said. "But he always treated me nice. The better-known players got everything—jackets and bags. But I was in a mismatched pair of raggedy shoes, and he made a phone call to get me a pair of size 17s."

"There's no prejudging on Sonny's part," Odom told *ESPN The Magazine* years later. "If you're a C student, he doesn't assume you're dumb. If you need help, he's willing to give it. He treated me like family, and Pam is like a mother to everyone." Although Odom signed a Nike deal once he turned pro, Vaccaro bore no grudge.

Vaccaro's closeness to so many high school athletes drove the NCAA crazy—as did his eagerness to help top high school players bypass college for the NBA. One year, he was supposed to do radio commentary during the Final Four for a big Los Angeles station; when he arrived in Tampa, the scene of that year's tournament, he was told that the NCAA would not give him credentials and he wouldn't be able to call the game. It regularly sent him letters after his summer camp was finished, alleging this or that offense, which he would have to try to refute. In the early 1990s he took in a young Senegalese basketball player named Makhtar N'Diaye, and soon became his legal guardian in the United States. The NCAA immediately began a no-holds-barred investigation, which ended only when Vaccaro showed the investigators a letter from N'Diaye's mother, written in French, confirming that he and Pam were N'Diaye's guardians. N'Diaye spent the last two years of his college career at the University of North Carolina. But Vaccaro had become such a prominent target that as N'Diaye's senior night approached, an event in which each senior is accompanied onto the floor by his parents, his coach, Bill Guthridge, asked him not to bring Vaccaro and Pam, for fear of how the NCAA would react. (N'Diaye told Guthridge that if his guardians couldn't come, he wouldn't be there either. UNC relented.)

Sometimes, though, athletes befriended by Vaccaro wound up being punished by the NCAA. When he saw that a player had no money, he would often buy him clothes, or give him sneakers, or even hand him cash—gestures that were not, on their face, violations of the NCAA rulebook, since Vaccaro was neither an agent nor a booster of a particular school. "There is no hard-line rule against it and it would be asinine to put one in because you couldn't monitor it," he told the *Boston Globe*. Nonetheless, because Vaccaro was a person it viewed suspiciously, the NCAA ruled that his gifts were "impermissible benefits." He bought a plane ticket for Felipe López and Zendon Hamilton, two St. John's players, so they could work out with an assistant with the Seattle SuperSonics; the tickets were ruled an impermissible benefit, and the players had to repay the sum to charity. In the late 1980s, he was accused of steering Alonzo Mourning to Georgetown because of his friendship with its basketball coach, John Thompson. (This allegation, which both Vaccaro and Thompson denied, did not lead to any NCAA sanctions.) In the case of Odom, the NCAA discovered that Vaccaro had bought him clothes, and forced Odom to repay the money to a charity.

"I was their piñata," Vaccaro says of the NCAA now. But turning the other cheek was not his style. He took to calling the NCAA "The Machine." "There is incredible hypocrisy," he told *New York* magazine in 1997. "The networks, the colleges, the sneaker companies, the coaches, the NCAA—they all make tons of money. The only ones who don't make money are the kids." At the height of his notoriety, and very much feeling his oats, Vaccaro was beginning to speak out about the things that bothered him about the world he lived in and had, in truth, helped create.

Two other events took place right around that time that had a powerful effect on Vaccaro's thinking. In March 1997, he was part of an ESPN "Town Meeting" about sports and race that was moderated by the ABC journalist Ted Koppel. Another member of the panel was Chris Webber of the Sacramento Kings, who had been part of Michigan's "Fab Five" in the early 1990s. The Fab Five—the others were Jalen Rose, Jimmy King, Ray Jackson, and Juwan Howard—had all been starters for Michigan as freshmen. They were an absolute sensation, taking the basketball world by storm, players with their own style—they were the first to wear the baggy shorts that all players wear to this day—who packed arenas everywhere Michigan played. They played hip-hop basketball, you might call it—flamboyant, cocky, immensely fun to watch, with strong undercurrents of black pride. The real stars of college basketball were usually the coaches like North Carolina's Dean Smith or Georgetown's John Thompson. But at Michigan, the coach, Steve Fisher, was a nonentity; the stars were the Fab Five. Michigan made millions selling their jerseys.

Vaccaro had been close to all five athletes in high school. Although Michigan was a Nike school, and Vaccaro left Nike just as they were entering college, he watched their success from afar and the way they had become marketable commodities. Nike quickly started selling baggy shorts, as did its competitors.

That night on ESPN, he heard Webber allude to his feelings of being exploited in college, about how he and his teammates at Michigan had revolutionized what basketball players wore—new styles that had made millions for clothing companies—but he couldn't even give a jersey to his own parents without violating NCAA rules. "That hit me hard," says Vaccaro.

The second event, which also took place in 1997, was the purchase of a small cable channel, called Classic Sports Network, by ESPN, whose own success had been very much tied to the popularity of college sports. Classic Sports Network showed old game footage for which it had bought the rights from various professional leagues, college conferences, and the NCAA. Though it had only been on the air for two years, ESPN paid $175 million for it.

As Vaccaro watched old college games on the new ESPN Classic channel, that $175 million purchase price stuck in his craw. "I watched all these kids I had known intimately," he said. Not all of those players had made it big in the pros; most of them, in fact, had not. Pearl Washington, for instance, the legendary Syracuse University point guard in the mid-1980s, had had a short-lived pro career and had bounced around ever since. ESPN often showed games in which he starred. "Why can't Pearl Washington get some of that money?" Vaccaro wondered. It didn't seem right to him that these players, long out of college and certainly no longer "amateurs," still received nothing for the rights to their images in these games. That feeling that something was wrong—it never left him.

In 2001, while still with Adidas, Vaccaro was invited to testify before the Knight Commission on Intercollegiate Athletics, a group funded by the Knight Foundation, which sought, mostly in vain, to keep the creeping commercialism of college athletics from infecting the academy. The meeting was held behind closed doors at the Willard Hotel in Washington, D.C.

The commission rarely heard from someone who was actually a part of that commercialization. And they were not prepared for Vaccaro's bluntness. Instead of defending the commercialization of college sports, Vaccaro accused the universities of being complicit. "We want to put our materials on the bodies of your athletes, and the best way to do that is to buy your school," he said. "Or buy your coach."

"Why should a university be an advertising medium for your industry?" Bryce Jordan, the president emeritus of Penn State University, asked indignantly.

"They shouldn't, sir," Vaccaro replied, according to the historian Taylor Branch. "You sold your souls and you're going to continue selling them. You can be very moral and righteous in asking me that question, sir, but there's not one of you in this room that's going to turn down any of our money. You're going to take it. I can only offer it."

Slowly, Vaccaro's own mind-set was changing; although the NCAA had always been a burr in his side, it was becoming bigger than that. And although he remained in the sneaker business for another six years—the last three with Reebok—his heart was elsewhere. He was angry about the way the players were treated by the NCAA, especially black players. He was angry at the way he himself had been treated over the years. And as college sports became an ever-bigger business, he was angry that the players did not share in the spoils.

Finally, in 2007, with two years remaining on his contract with Reebok, and after long discussions with Pam, he quit. His contract called for him to make $500,000 a year—the most money he'd ever made in his life. He didn't care. He got rid of his summer camp and his all-star game. He and Pam sold their house and began living off their savings. "As long as I'm working," he said, "people won't take me seriously."

"I woke up and said, 'I need to do this other thing.'" This "other thing" was spending every waking moment fighting the NCAA.

# The $12 Suspension

**IN THE FALL OF 1974, LARRY GILLARD, A FRESHMAN FOOTBALL PLAYER**
at Mississippi State, passed through the small town of Okolona, Mississippi,
where he stopped at Howard's Clothing Store. There, Gillard picked out a pair of
pants and a shirt, for which he paid $25, about a 20 percent discount from the
sticker price. He made the same trip again later that semester and bought another
shirt and pants for another $25; he received another 20 percent markdown.

At the time, the NCAA was investigating Mississippi State. It soon got word
of the transactions, along with a tip that the discounts could be a rules violation:
after all, athletes are not allowed to receive benefits that are not available to
nonathletes. A young investigator named Jim Delany—yes, the same Jim Delany
who would go on to become the powerful commissioner of the Big Ten (see
chapter 5)—was dispatched to interview the owner of the store, Howard Miskelly. Miskelly explained to Delany that he had indeed offered that discount to
Gillard—it amounted to about a $12 savings. Further, Miskelly said, he had
offered the same discount to a football player from Ole Miss. Other students
too could get the same markdown, Miskelly said. He later testified at the 1978
congressional hearings that he tried to give Delany the names of others who
received the discount, but the investigator declined the offer.

Instead, Delany went to see Gillard, who said he was unaware that he had
received any discount. Delany told Gillard he had already been to see Miskelly
and the store owner said Gillard received a one-third discount—even though
Miskelly claimed he had said no such thing. Not sure what all the fuss was
about, Gillard said he simply paid what he was told.

When the NCAA later levied sanctions against Mississippi State, it included a charge against Gillard: accepting an unauthorized one-third discount from Miskelly. The penalty was astoundingly harsh: a three-year suspension, essentially ending Gillard's college career. Miskelly, meanwhile, was ordered to sever ties with Mississippi State without so much as the chance to utter a word in his defense. (Delany does not recall the specifics of the Gillard allegations today, but says any loss of eligibility was "over the top.")

Although Gillard's sentence was reduced to one season after he appealed, he still felt so aggrieved that he sued the NCAA. A lower court allowed him to keep playing. But the Mississippi Supreme Court ultimately decided the case in the NCAA's favor, ruling that engaging in college football afforded Gillard no due process rights.

But that was not the end of it. After Director of Enforcement Warren Brown was summoned to Starkville to testify in the trial, he fired off a memo to one of his staff members, Dave Berst, instructing the enforcement staff to take another look at Mississippi State. He wanted to know who had paid for Gillard's lawyer and suggested that the NCAA should charge Mississippi State with breaking NCAA rules by participating in the suit. "I believe we should pay strict attention to the penalties imposed upon the University and even do some checking on the institution during the course of its probationary period," Brown concluded.

Brent Clark, the former NCAA investigator, put it this way: "In later conversations, I was told by Brown and Berst to switch gears and attempt to generate any damaging information I could against Mississippi State supporters, enrolled student athletes, and athletes who had signed to go to Mississippi State, with a view to uncovering violations of rules to be used against them when the institution came up for review. In the process, it became clear to me that information regarding Ole Miss was worthless to my superiors because they had set their sights on Mississippi State for having refused to submit to NCAA authority. Once again the NCAA would have its pound of flesh."

And after its victory in court, the NCAA, citing its noxious restitution provision, stripped Mississippi State of nineteen wins from the 1975, 1976, and 1977 seasons, when Gillard was on the team.

"I never saw so much hell raised about two shirts and two pairs of pants, but for a total of $62, $12 of which was supposed to be a discount," Gillard's lawyer said.

# CHAPTER 3

# "SOMEBODY OUGHT TO FILE A LAWSUIT"

O n Saturday, January 2, 1999, the University of Florida Gators
crushed the Syracuse Orangemen in the Orange Bowl, 31–10, ending their season 10–2 and ranked fifth in the country. It was
another great year for the Gators, which under Coach Steve Spurrier, a
Florida alum and former Heisman Trophy winner, had won five SEC championships since 1991 and a national championship in 1997. Not surprisingly, the same year the Gators won the national championship, Spurrier
signed a six-year contract extension that was poised to make him the first
college football coach to break the $2-million-a-year barrier.

At some point during the telecast, Brad Nessler, the announcer calling
the game for ABC, mentioned Spurrier's lucrative contract. It may be an
exaggeration to say that this offhand remark would lead to a decade's
worth of antitrust litigation against the NCAA. But it's not much of one.

One of the people watching that game was Ernie Nadel, a garrulous
fifty-five-year-old former economics professor at Berkeley who worked at
a consulting firm called LECG. (It was originally named the Law and Economics Consulting Group.) LECG was in the business of providing expert
economic witnesses for lawyers bringing complex lawsuits, often revolv-
ing around antitrust issues. Nadel, who grew up in Canada a hockey fan,
had never paid close attention to college football and hadn't realized that

the compensation of top college coaches was now in the millions. "I was staggered by how much Spurrier made," he says now.

When he got to work the following Monday, still mulling Spurrier's $2 million salary, Nadel mentioned his puzzlement to one of his office mates, Dan Rascher. Rascher, who was thirty-one, had a PhD in economics and taught sports management at the University of San Francisco as an adjunct. Their offices were just a few doors apart, and they had become friends in the two years since Rascher had joined the firm; Nadel was notorious at LECG for wandering into people's offices just to shoot the bull for a while. Rascher enjoyed his company, which was not true of everyone at LECG.

Rascher explained: simply put, the NCAA was a classic cartel. Amateurism was merely a high-minded word meant to disguise the fact that the cartel suppressed the wages of its labor force—that is, the players. At the same time, big dollars were pouring into college sports as it became ever more commercialized. Spurrier made the kind of money he did because all that money had to go somewhere, given that the players weren't getting any of it. ("Rent-seeking behavior," in economic terms.) And since success in college football was impossible without the ability to recruit good high school players, it made perfect sense that a smooth-talking recruiter like Spurrier would make a lot of money.

His curiosity aroused, Nadel began peppering Rascher with questions about the NCAA over the ensuing weeks and months. Rascher's tutorials became more extensive. He gave Nadel a book from his bookshelf entitled *The National Collegiate Athletic Association: A Study in Cartel Behavior*, published in 1992. The book's three authors, including Robert D. Tollison, a former economist at the Federal Trade Commission, compared the NCAA to such formidable cartels as OPEC, and suggested that even though university athletic departments were nonprofit entities, the NCAA's members "engage in classically defined restrictive practices for the sole purpose of jointly maximizing their profits."

Rascher also suggested that Nadel take a look at a recently decided case, *Law v. NCAA*. In 1991, after repeated efforts to control what it viewed as the spiraling costs of college athletics, the NCAA passed a rule that both limited the number of coaches a team could employ and fixed the salary of the most junior assistant coach at no more than $16,000. (Football coaches were exempt.) The so-called restricted-earnings coaches sued, saying that the NCAA had no legal right to restrain their pay—that it amounted to price fixing. Seven years later, after a jury trial, the assistants were awarded damages of $22.3 million, which were tripled because that is what the law calls for when the antitrust laws are violated. And the NCAA was permanently enjoined from setting coaches' salaries. (It was also held in civil contempt for refusing to pay the attorneys' fees. The two sides settled in 1999 for $54 million.)

Nadel, whose areas of expertise included maritime economics, was quite familiar with congressionally mandated cartels, which are legal in the shipping lanes between the lower forty-eight states and Hawaii, Guam, Alaska, and Puerto Rico. But he was stunned to learn from Rascher that no such legislative authority existed for the NCAA's cartel. Indeed, the more Nadel learned, the more astounded he became—and the more outraged. Its cartel nature, its exploitation of its workforce, its blunt power: he had a hard time believing that the way the NCAA operated was even legal.

By this time, a third LECG consultant had joined Nadel and Rascher's discussions about the NCAA. His name was Andy Schwarz, and he was thirty-two, a year older than Rascher. A hyperkinetic workaholic, at once blunt and endearing, Schwarz was the case manager for a nasty lawsuit in which LECG's client, the National Football League, was pitted against the Oakland Raiders and its litigious owner Al Davis, who was seeking $1.2 billion from the league. (The NFL ultimately won the suit.) When Rascher was hired, he was also assigned to the case, which is how the two men became friends—and realized that not only were they both sports fans, but that they had an abiding interest in the economics of sports.

At some point in the summer or early fall of 1999, Nadel and Rascher placed a call to a lawyer named Dennis Cross, who had brought the *Law* case against the NCAA. What came out of that phone call was a suggestion that Rascher write a paper about the NCAA for a special sports-themed issue of *Antitrust*, a magazine published by the American Bar Association, that would come out the following spring and that Cross was editing. Rascher agreed, and quickly enlisted Schwarz to cowrite it with him.

All through the fall of 1999, the two men worked on the paper, with Nadel kibitzing from the sidelines. When it was published in the spring of 2000, the paper had the geeky title "Neither Reasonable nor Necessary: 'Amateurism' in Big-Time College Sports." If the phrase meant nothing to a layperson, it was instantly recognizable to antitrust lawyers and economists. That headline was Schwarz and Rascher's way of saying that from an antitrust standpoint, the NCAA's legal rationale for the restrictions it placed on players did not pass muster: the restrictions were "neither reasonable nor necessary."

Nadel, for his part, thought it was a fine paper, and he was happy to be credited in a footnote for his help. But it was just a paper. It wasn't going to change anything. It did, however, firm up in his mind a thought he'd had for some time about the NCAA.

"Somebody ought to file a lawsuit," he said.

When Andy Schwarz was eleven years old, his father moved his family from California to the Boston suburbs. In Newport Beach, John Schwarz had been the assistant commissioner of World TeamTennis, the gimmicky coed professional tennis league that attempted to take advantage of the tennis boom of the 1970s. The move was made so that Schwarz's father could take the post of general manager of the Boston Lobsters, the WTT franchise owned by Robert Kraft—the same Robert Kraft who would later own the New England Patriots. Schwarz remembers hanging out with Martina Navratilova, working the scoreboard, and generally enjoying the access that comes of being the son of a sports executive. Even if it was only World TeamTennis.

As he got older, his twin passions were the Larry Bird–led Boston Celtics and history. He largely gave up playing sports, partly because he wasn't very good, but also because, as he puts it today, "I had a comparative advantage in the classroom." The one varsity letter he got at Wellesley High School was for being on the sailing team. He enjoyed history so much that one semester he took European history in the morning and then skipped lunch so he could go to a second history class he wasn't registered in. It wasn't until the first exam that the teacher realized there was a pupil who didn't belong in the class and tossed him out. Schwarz started high school as a high-strung kid who was excessively anxious; by the time he graduated he was the high-strung, excessively anxious valedictorian and class clown.

At Stanford, where Schwarz majored in history—early modern European diplomatic history, to be precise—he was a regular at virtually every football and men's basketball home game, and found himself growing more passionate about college sports, even as his interest in pro sports waned. After a year at Johns Hopkins, where he got a master's degree, he came back to California and took a job in public relations, where he was miserable. ("I was afraid to make phone calls," he says.) He escaped a few years later by going to UCLA and getting an MBA. After another miserable year in the workforce, this time at Hewlett-Packard, UCLA called him and asked if he wanted to join its economics PhD program.

He wasn't cut out for that either. The math required for an economics doctorate was daunting, but just as important, since he was a student of history, Schwarz's approach to academics—and indeed to life—was fact-oriented, whereas economics at that level is highly theoretical. He spent a year at UCLA and another year and a half at Berkeley before throwing in the towel. At that point, he was a married thirty-year-old man who wanted to start a family—and needed to find a real job, the kind that could lead to a career. He went to his favorite professor, a well-known antitrust economist named Richard Gilbert, and told him, as Schwarz puts it now, "that it wasn't working out." Gilbert said that if that were really the case, then Schwarz should come work for him. A former deputy assistant attorney general in the antitrust division of the U.S. Justice Department, Gilbert was also one of the cofounders of LECG.

Started in 1988 by four Berkeley economics professors, LECG had helped transform the practice of using expert witnesses in trials. Prior to the rise of litigation consulting firms, a lawyer bringing an antitrust suit would call a brand-name economics professor, who, if he agreed to serve as an expert witness, would do his research and work on his testimony with the help of his graduate students, all in their spare time. LECG, a publicly traded company with around seven hundred employees at its peak and offices scattered around the country, made it possible for economic experts to take on many more cases at any one time. It was teeming with smart economists; Schwarz remembers the Emeryville, California, office, where he, Rascher, and Nadel all worked, as a place that had more economics brainpower than most Ivy League schools. Berkeley allowed its professors to work one day a week on outside consulting work, so the rest of the week the work had to be done by the full-time staff economists like Schwarz.

Almost immediately after joining the firm, Schwarz was assigned to be the assistant case manager on the NFL-Raiders case, a lawsuit in which Gilbert was going to testify as the NFL's economic expert. Although Schwarz lacked a PhD—an impediment at a firm full of them—it didn't take Gilbert long to realize he had made an exceptionally good hire. "A big chunk of the work was taking real-world facts and fitting them into the framework that economics teaches," says Schwarz. That's exactly how his mind worked. He liked working collaboratively, which meshed well with Gilbert's own style. He worked crazy long hours—and not only didn't complain but actually seemed to enjoy it. He was the kind of person who had trouble sleeping because his brain was always "on"; the kind who, when stumped by a question, couldn't move on until he had found the answer; the kind who would work twenty-hour days for days on end rather than miss a deadline; the kind who would race from the shower to his computer, still in his towel, because while showering he had thought of five e-mails he needed to write.

"Andy was somebody who always wanted to get something done," says Gilbert now. "Frenzied and productive" is how Rascher describes his friend's working style. Nadel says that Schwarz is the only person he ever met who learned to use a mouse with his left hand. (Nadel thought he did it so that he could write with his right hand while using the computer. In fact, it was because Schwarz had shoulder problems, which an ergonomic nurse told him would be eased if he learned to vary his mouse hand.) It wasn't long before Gilbert promoted Schwarz to case manager in the NFL suit.

Which was also where Schwarz got to know Dan Rascher. Born and raised in St. Louis and then Worthington, Ohio, a suburb of Columbus, Rascher was a fan of both the St. Louis Cardinals and the Ohio State Buckeyes. After graduating from the University of California, San Diego, he and some friends made a cross-country trip, the purpose of which was to watch a baseball game in every major-league stadium. As an academic, he found himself drawn to the study of sports, even though his professors sometimes frowned on it; sports economics lacked the cachet as a discipline it would later develop. When Rascher got his PhD from Berkeley, his thesis tackled, among other things, a subtle form of racial discrimination that existed in the NBA: marginal white players, he discovered, had much longer playing careers than marginal black players.

Rascher spent a year at the University of Massachusetts teaching sports management. But realizing, as he puts it, "that I only knew what went on inside a classroom," he quit to return to California, where he too was hired by his former professor, Gilbert. At LECG, he worked on a handful of mergers involving concert promoters, and an antitrust case in which microbrewers were suing Budweiser because they could not gain access to the independently owned trucks that shipped Bud. His involvement in the NFL case was not as full-time as Schwarz's, but they were two offices apart from each other, and they often worked together on other cases as well. They made a good team: Schwarz was the excitable one, Rascher the unflappable one. More important, Schwarz's mind-set was to seek out facts that illustrated the point they were trying to make, while Rascher worked at fitting those facts into an overarching framework.

What neither man had done was spend much time grappling with the structure of the NCAA—not until they wrote their article for *Antitrust* magazine.

Working on that article galvanized them. Although Schwarz and Rascher came at it in an entirely different way than Sonny Vaccaro—with cool legal reasoning rather than a lifetime in the trenches—that article marked the beginning of their own quest to take on the NCAA.

In retrospect, "Neither Reasonable nor Necessary" stands as a kind of foundational document, serving both as a road map for potential antitrust litigation against the NCAA and a framework for the radical-sounding ideas Schwarz and Rascher would propound over the next decade and a half.

Because of their work on the NFL case, the two economists had a deep understanding of how professional leagues worked, and why they weren't "per se" violations of the nation's antitrust laws, which forbid collusion among competitors. Collusion, however, is a critical component of any sports league—how else could the various teams (a.k.a. the competitors) jointly agree on a schedule and rules? "There is a line in one of the Raiders decisions, that if you don't have a league, you just have a bunch of teams barnstorming around the country" like the Harlem Globetrotters, Schwarz says. "That resonated with me." He adds, "A league creates a better product— a season in which there are standings, and a championship." That's why, using the "rule of reason"—the antitrust version of legal common sense—courts have viewed the kind of collusion teams engage in by forming a league as procompetitive: it was both *reasonable and necessary* to create a product that fans would want to see. Although wages are suppressed in many of America's sports leagues—think salary caps—this too does not violate antitrust laws because those caps have been negotiated at arm's length with the various players' unions. (Major League Baseball has no salary cap, precisely because the players' union has never agreed to it.)

The essential point Schwarz and Rascher made in their article was that unlike the legal collusion that took place in the professional leagues, the collusion that took place under the umbrella of the NCAA—to force athletes to remain "amateurs" in order to play college sports—did not pass the "rule of reason" test. "The NCAA," they wrote, "has long maintained that amateurism is an essential component of the product it sells and that its rules regulating the compensation of athletes are procompetitive because they preserve amateurism and thereby maintain competitive balance."

But, they continued, "if amateurism is what college sports fans demand, there ought to be no need to collude to preserve it." In layman's terms, if fans won't show up to watch paid college athletes, then you would hardly need to pass a rule that forbade such payment; schools would not pay athletes of their own volition. If instead there was something else that fans valued rather than amateurism, then "concerted action to preserve amateurism was mere wage fixing."

"The NCAA has done a great job of convincing everybody that 'college' and 'paid' are opposite," Schwarz would say years later. "But students get paid all the time." In Schwarz and Rascher's view, what made college sports unique—what truly differentiated it from professional sports—had nothing to do with the fact that the athletes received no financial compensation. Rather, it was that the players were also students attending the university. "We love seeing young men who go to our school—for real—representing the school," says Schwarz. "We don't really care whether or not they are playing for free."

In a later e-mail, Schwarz wrote, "I see no evidence that the pay level of the athletes affects the popularity of the product. I see lots of evidence that the connection between the team and the university in a holistic way matters a lot. . . . I think in the long run, if the connection between school and athlete were severed such that the athletes were no longer legitimate students, demand for the product would go down."

While acknowledging that the NCAA was necessary to "set rules regarding scheduling and safety and the like," Schwarz and Rascher argued in their paper that "an agreement among all its members not to compete for its most important resource, the athlete, is unnecessary and unreasonable. It lowers the quality of the game and exploits the athletes." What's more, they said, the courts should stop simply accepting at face value the NCAA's arguments in favor of amateurism, and should instead scrutinize it "rigorously." Of course, there was really only one way for that to happen: someone had to bring an antitrust suit against the NCAA.

Most of "Neither Reasonable nor Necessary" laid out a variety of legal arguments that a plaintiff might make in such a case. But Schwarz and Rascher had a few other beliefs they put on the table as well. One was that the conferences, rather than the NCAA, were the natural entities to engage in the kind of legal collusion that the courts viewed as procompetitive. Coming out of their work for the NFL, they firmly believed that a league, with some sort of round-robin schedule leading to a championship, adds value and that the college sports equivalent was each conference, not the NCAA. In their view, conferences should compete with each other not just on the field but in the kind of deals they were willing to offer players. If one conference wanted to pay athletes and another did not, so be it. But they assumed that the conferences would wind up using money as a means to compete for players.

They believed that players should be able to have agents, who could negotiate on their behalf. (Current NCAA rules state that a player becomes immediately ineligible if he has dealings with an agent.) And the negotiations didn't have to strictly be about money. A player might agree to stay for at least three years under the terms of his contract. He might negotiate a scholarship for life so that he could come back to school if he failed to graduate. He might insist on the right to transfer without having to sit out a year.

"Every cartel cheats," says Rascher. "In college sports, cheating is called recruiting violations." If money were to legitimately change hands, there would be far less incentive for coaches and boosters to cheat—or for the NCAA to write hundreds of pages of rules that controlled every aspect of an athlete's college experience. Boosters who now paid players under the table could contribute to an athletic department fund to pay players, for instance. There would no longer be any need for no-show jobs. And so on.

Education could also be part of the negotiation. It was undoubtedly true that many college athletes, especially in football and men's basketball, did not arrive prepared for the rigors of the classroom. This has been true for as long as there has been college sports. Schwarz believed that athletes should be able to go, say, half-time while they played and finish up their degree after their eligibility had ended. Or they could insist that the schools provide them with the remedial education they needed. "I think that if the NCAA got out of the business of hyper-regulating the money, and allowed agents to bargain, schools would quickly realize that it was cheaper to guarantee educational value than money, and to trade that off," he says. "Once the market kicked in, athletes and their parent would demand the sorts of variety of educations that work best, and schools would love to provide them," he wrote in an e-mail.

How much should players get paid? Nadel says that he tried to get Schwarz to write a paper that estimated the value of a college athlete playing various positions in football or basketball. But Schwarz never did so, and at least part of the reason was that he believed that that value couldn't really be ascertained until the amateurism rules were abolished and the free market was able to finally work its will. Indeed, his and Rascher's real advocacy was less that the players should be paid than that the NCAA and the universities should stop colluding to *prevent* them from being paid. What happened after that, well, the market would figure it out. That's what markets do.

"Although there would be mistakes from time to time," Schwarz says, "we wouldn't expect to see athlete pay get so sky-high that college sports bankrupts itself. Basically if pay gets unsustainably high, it will come down until it is sustainable again. Unlike sports leagues that might go bankrupt before they adjust, schools have a huge cushion because most universities are orders of magnitude larger than their sports programs and can help soften the adjustment period."

The NCAA rulebook, he thought, could be reduced to three fundamental rules: Players had to be students in good standing, using the same criteria as any other student on campus. They couldn't play for more than four years. And they couldn't have played professionally in their college sport—that is, they couldn't quit a professional basketball team to play on a college basketball team.

Even before Rascher and Schwarz wrote their paper, Nadel had been agitating that they do more than simply talk about the NCAA—that they try to do something about it. Indeed, that was the original purpose of the call to Dennis Cross: they wanted to see if he was willing to file an antitrust suit against the NCAA. (He wasn't.) Rascher, who had been a full-time university professor before joining LECG, was taken aback. "I had always been geared to thinking about something you could submit to academic journals, which is the currency of academia," he says. "I had never thought about trying to influence policy." But Nadel would not be deterred. He nudged and then nudged some more—and after the publication of "Neither Reasonable nor Necessary," he became nudgier yet, although, as he says now, "It didn't take all that much to get Andy and Dan fully engaged."

In truth, Nadel's sudden passion for taking on the NCAA was a little out of character for him as well. His father, a Polish immigrant who came to Montreal in 1936, was a furrier who was also a devout Marxist, in part, Nadel says, "because of the Communist promise, which he naively believed to be nondiscriminatory against Jews." By contrast, Nadel studied at that bastion of conservative economics the University of Chicago, where one of his teachers was the free-market icon Milton Friedman ("A wonderful, smart, and practical man"). Nadel was considered a big talent in economics, and had his pick of job offers. He chose Berkeley, just in time to be swept up in the counterculture. "I wasn't really suited for a professorship," he says now. "It was too political and you had to kiss too much ass." Though extremely popular with students—"I enjoyed showing off and telling jokes"—he was denied tenure, and resigned from the Berkeley faculty after seven years. Upon leaving academia, he worked at a series of consulting firms before landing at LECG. He wasn't someone you would go to if you needed a quick answer, says Schwarz, but if you had some patience he'd give you a slow, deep answer.

"Ernie was obsessed, and so he figured we would be just as obsessed," recalls Schwarz. Nadel viewed Rascher and Schwarz's paper as a kind of legal query letter, a way to interest a lawyer in suing the NCAA. So that became the goal: use the paper to find a lawyer willing to sue the NCAA. Though it was hardly the sort of thing most legal consultants did, Gilbert didn't have any problem with it. So off they went.

Their original plan was to go straight at the NCAA's amateurism defense, using the arguments they had put forth in "Neither Reasonable nor Necessary." This became known in house as "the nuclear case," because if they won, the current system of college athletics would be blown to smithereens. The damages could potentially be in the billions.

But there were two problems with the nuclear case. First, were there really plaintiffs' lawyers out there who *wanted* to blow the NCAA to smithereens? Or judges, for that matter?

The second problem went all the way back to the Supreme Court's 1984 decision in *Regents*. Although the NCAA had lost the case, there was one paragraph in Judge John Paul Stevens's decision that had long given the NCAA great solace: "The identification of this 'product' with an academic tradition differentiates college football from and makes it more popular than professional sports to which it might be comparable, such as, for example, minor league baseball," Stevens had written. "*In order to preserve the character and quality of the 'product' athletes must not be paid, must be required to attend class, and the like.* And the integrity of the 'product' cannot be preserved except by mutual agreement; if an institution adopted such restrictions unilaterally, its effectiveness as a competitor on the playing field might soon be destroyed." (Italics added.)

These three sentences were what lawyers call "dicta," digressions that depart from the issue that is being decided—in this case, whether college football teams had the right to negotiate their own television deals. Because dicta are not central to the issue being litigated, they do not necessarily have the force of law in the same way that the main body of the decision does. Ever since Stevens's decision, however, the NCAA had been waving around that paragraph as proof that amateurism was so essential to the character of college sports that even the Supreme Court thought it had to be preserved.

Years later, Nadel would concede that "I didn't know enough to realize how strongly believed—by academics and consultants and especially by attorneys—was the Supreme Court's *Regents* dicta." He would find out soon enough.

Although LECG was a firm that mainly did defense work for big companies, Nadel had a few contacts on the plaintiffs' side of the bar, and he reached out to them. The first law firm the three economists approached was Cotchett, Pitre & Simon, a big plaintiffs' firm in San Francisco. (The firm is now known as Cotchett, Pitre & McCarthy.) Name partner Bruce Simon, an antitrust lawyer, had been a student of Nadel's, and Nadel had also served as his economics expert in a big class action case. And Joe Cotchett, the firm's cofounder, had been one of the lawyers who had brought the assistant coaches' lawsuit against the NCAA. During one of his early meeting with the economists, Simon asked them if the lawsuit meant he would be suing his alma mater, Berkeley. Nadel said yes. Simon was horrified at the idea of suing his beloved Cal. That took care of that.

A second lawyer they approached asked how the economists expected to get past Justice Stevens's view that amateurism was essential to college sports. "It's just dicta," replied Schwarz. "It's pretty fucking strong dicta," replied the lawyer. He sent them packing as well.

One lawyer who expressed interest was Max Blecher, the founding partner of Blecher Collins Pepperman & Joye—and someone who had been described to Nadel as a lawyer who was "smart, has deep pockets, has balls and is a mensch," which was pretty much what he was looking for. Blecher's specialty, the *Wall Street Journal* would write years later, "was underdog antitrust battles against powerful figures, including the NFL and the NBA." Indeed, he had represented Al Davis and the Oakland Raiders in an earlier case against the NFL, and had won. Blecher was intrigued, but his staff was united in its opposition to his taking the case. Some of the lawyers feared that such a case would undermine Title IX, the 1972 law that called for gender equality for "any education program or activity involving federal financial assistance"—and that had led directly to the rise of women's athletics on college campuses. Another objection was that the nuclear case was simply unwinnable. Many judges were college sports fans, after all, unlikely to want to upset the college sports applecart. And even those who weren't would surely feel uncomfortable upending a system that had been in place for over fifty years, no matter how powerful the antitrust argument.

Nadel, Schwarz, and Rascher shopped the nuclear case for nearly three years with no success. By the middle of 2003 the three men had basically given up; it appeared that taking on amateurism was just too high a mountain for most plaintiffs' lawyers to climb. Late that October, though, they discovered another route they could take to sue the NCAA.

Jeremy Bloom was one of America's best skiers—and was also a starting wide receiver for the University of Colorado football team. (He would eventually both play pro football and ski in two Olympics.) Like many well-known Olympic athletes, Bloom took endorsement money as a skier, which he used to pay his trainer and support staff—and which the NCAA said he had to forgo to play football for the university as an amateur. After his sophomore season, he decided to defy the NCAA and accept the endorsement money. The NCAA wasted little time in ruling him permanently ineligible to play college sports of any sort. Bloom sued. After he lost in federal court (he eventually lost at the appeals court level as well), he wrote an angry opinion article for the *New York Times* blasting the NCAA. It was entitled "Show Us the Money." Bloom noted, among other things, that "no Division 1 student-athlete will receive a dime of the $6 billion contract between the NCAA and CBS" for the March Madness tournament.

The article was reprinted in the *Denver Post*, where it came to the attention of Myles Brand, the former president of Indiana University, who had become president of the NCAA in 2002. In response, Brand wrote a lengthy letter to the editor of the *Denver Post* defending the NCAA. His letter included these two sentences: "Ideally, the value of an athletically related scholarship would be increased to cover the full-cost attendance, calculated at between $2,000 and $3,000 more per year than is currently provided. I favor this approach of providing the full cost of attendance."

What Brand was referring to was that full athletic scholarships covered tuition, room and board, and books but provided no money for living expenses. For athletes from poor families, it often resulted in abject poverty, with players struggling to pay for basic necessities. Indeed, a study in 2012 by a group called the National Colleges Players Association found that more than 80 percent of top-level college athletes on full scholarship lived below the poverty line. It had not always been thus: there was a time when college athletes received a small monthly allowance of $15—laundry money, it was called. But the NCAA did away with it in the 1970s in a move to cut costs.

When Nadel saw Brand's words, he immediately understood that they could be used to sue the NCAA without having to take on amateurism—or grapple with Justice Stevens's dicta. If Brand was saying that athletes would still be amateurs if they got the full cost of attendance, then why was the cartel refusing to allow them that money? How was this not a form of price fixing—just like the assistant coaches' case that the NCAA had lost a few years before? Schwarz helped frame it within the "rule of reason": if a higher level is "ideal," then it couldn't possibly be reasonable or necessary to choose a lower cap. Even if you accepted the validity of the NCAA's amateurism defense, forbidding the full cost of attendance—something the NCAA president was now on record as saying would be a good thing—violated the antitrust laws because it created a cap that was lower than necessary.

"A class action like this has never been brought against the NCAA," Schwarz, Rascher, and Nadel wrote in a lengthy memo that they hoped would induce a lawyer to take the case. "In past lawsuits against the NCAA ... the NCAA has always fallen back on its mission of defending 'amateurism' as sanctioned by *Board of Regents*. With Myles Brand's statement—that raising [of the scholarship amount] to the [cost of attendance] would not alter the amateur status of college sports—the NCAA has undermined its most likely (and, until now, only) defense."

The economists estimated that the annual damages were more than $29 million a year. It wasn't the billions they had once envisioned, but when you added it up over the four years of an athlete's stay in college, and trebled the damages, it wasn't peanuts either. And it would establish the principle that the NCAA had to follow the antitrust law just like any other sports business.

By early 2004, the three of them had reengaged with Blecher, who agreed to take the case, along with a lawyer from the well-known plaintiffs' firm of Susman Godfrey. His name was Stephen Morrissey. Schwarz, Rascher, and Nadel had their case. They had their lawyers. Now they needed someone who could serve as the face of the lawsuit. They needed to find a college athlete.

# The Confessions
# of Dale Brown

**DALE BROWN COACHED AT LOUISIANA STATE UNIVERSITY FROM 1972**
until 1997. A hyperkinetic man with a slight penchant for paranoia, Brown was
the target of numerous NCAA investigations. He was also one of its most vehe-
ment critics at a time when most people in college sports were paralyzed with
fear in the face of the all-powerful NCAA. In 1989, Brown gave a series of interviews to Don Yeager, the author of *Undue Process,* one of the earliest and most
biting accounts of NCAA hypocrisy, with an emphasis on the absurdity of many
of its amateurism rules. In talking to Yeager, Brown detailed a laundry list of
rules violations he had committed, many of them involving food and medical
care that his players and their families badly needed, but that NCAA rules forbade. His view seemed to be that if a coach had even a smidgen of compassion,
he had no choice but to violate NCAA rules.

The stories are numerous and often heartbreaking. He bought dinners for
players' families, had LSU pay for eyeglasses for his team when the NCAA only
allowed contact lenses to be covered (glasses weren't basketball-related), and
once got a dentist to waive a fee for a player who needed emergency work done
but didn't have the money to pay for it (and of course it was against NCAA rules
for LSU to pay).

One LSU player, Brown told Yeager, a Yugoslavian named Zoran Jovanovich, went home over Christmas break with a teammate and popped his knee
out while they were working out. Jovanovich was rushed to the hospital and

Brown was called about insurance. He told the doctors Jovanovich was covered by LSU and to go ahead with any necessary procedure or surgery. He later learned that because the injury occurred on the player's own time, LSU could not cover the operation under NCAA rules. "His knee did not pop out in practice; it popped out while working out," Brown said. "There's a rule that makes one a violation and the other not. But I had told them to work out over Christmas. I told them to run in the morning and shoot in the afternoon. They were doing exactly what I told them to do."

Brown asked a trainer to type up a letter spelling out the workout instructions so he could make the workout look official. It worked: LSU covered the operation. "What were we going to do, let him lay in a hospital room?" Brown asked.

But no anecdote was more gut-wrenching than the one about Mark Alcorn, a reserve guard who was diagnosed with cancer in December 1980. He left the team and returned home to St. Louis to undergo chemotherapy. The bills for his treatment were bankrupting his parents, so Alcorn's high school coach organized a fund-raising banquet. Bob Costas agreed to serve as master of ceremonies, and Brown promised to be there.

Soon after, Brown got a call from Mark's mom, Sheila. She told him that Mark didn't have much time left and he had a request—a dying wish, really. He wanted his three best friends from the team, Joe Costello, J. Brian Bergeron, and Andy Campbell, to attend the banquet.

Sheila Alcorn also needed a favor from Brown. Mark's medical bills had put her deeply in debt, and she couldn't afford to pay for his teammates' airfare. Would LSU cover the cost? Of course, Brown said. Soon, news of the benefit spread to the governor's office; Governor Dave Treen offered to lend the state airplane to take Brown and the players to St. Louis. He also wanted to present Alcorn with a special commendation for courage.

As he was preparing for the trip, Brown remembered he needed to run the plan by the NCAA. The answer that came back was unambiguous: absolutely not. Transporting college athletes to an off-campus function was illegal entertainment. Brown was furious, but swore he would not let Alcorn down. The night before the benefit he pulled the blinds in his office and called the three players in one by one. He handed each of them a brown envelope with $300 inside. It was enough to cover a red-eye flight, a shared motel room, and a couple of meals.

"I felt like I had to take a shower or something," Brown said to Yeager. "Here I was doing this nice act by giving them the money, but I felt almost like there were cameras peering down on me."

Steve Morgan, the NCAA's associate director at the time, explained the rules to Yeager: "The public sees—they see this terminally ill kid and ask what kind of heartless people are involved in the NCAA. That's the general perception of it. And unfortunately, those of us on the staff who have the responsibility of trying to answer these questions as to how the rules apply to given situations and providing advice, unfortunately a part of our job is to provide the hard answers to those questions."

Brown put it this way: "Just because it's a rule doesn't make it right."

For all the times the NCAA investigated LSU, it only handed down sanctions against the basketball program once, in 1998, right after Brown had left. A player named Lester Earl, who had transferred to the University of Kansas, told the NCAA that he had received money from three people: Brown, assistant coach Johnny Jones, and an LSU booster, Dr. Redfield Bryant. Brown and Jones were ultimately cleared by the NCAA, although the twenty-one-month NCAA investigation and the sanctions, especially cutting the number of scholarships for three years, took a toll on the LSU basketball program (Jones is now the head coach of LSU).

But seven years after the NCAA handed down its ruling against LSU, Earl wrote a public apology, saying that he had been pressured by the NCAA to give them "dirt" on Brown and Jones. "They said, 'If we don't find any dirt on coach Brown, you won't be allowed to play but one more year at Kansas,'" he wrote. "'If we do find out wrongdoing by coach Brown, you will be able to play two and a half more seasons.'"

"I was 19 years old at that time," Earl continued. "The NCAA intimidated me, manipulated me into making up things, and basically encouraged me to lie, in order to be able to finish my playing career at Kansas."

"Coach Brown," he concluded, "I apologize to you for tarnishing your magnificent career at LSU. The second apology I owe most is to coach Johnny Jones. Coach Jones, I never imagined you would have suffered so much because of the few supposed 'little things' I told the NCAA that you did."

# CHAPTER 4

# "VOLANDATORY" PRACTICE

When Ramogi Huma was a freshman linebacker at UCLA in 1995, one of his teammates, an All-American linebacker named Donnie Edwards, told a local radio station that he didn't have enough money to buy food. A few days later, an agent left a bag of groceries, worth about $150, on Edwards's doorstep. When the NCAA found out, Edwards, who would go on to have a long and successful pro career, was suspended for one game. The suspension had a profound impact on Huma: UCLA could sell Edwards's jersey in the campus bookstore for $50 a pop, he thought, but he couldn't have dinner? It didn't seem right.

Unlike most college athletes, however, Huma didn't just let the thought pass. The following year, as a sophomore, he founded a group whose goal was to put public pressure on the NCAA to improve the lot of the athletes. It was called the Collegiate Athletes Coalition; over the course of the next decade, from a borrowed cubicle next to the Torrance airport, Huma had since built an organization that had chapters at universities from the Pac-10 to the SEC.

For years, Huma had railed to anyone who would listen about the inequities of big-time college sports. He'd even persuaded the United Steelworkers of America, a union, to join his cause, leading the *Wall Street Journal* to christen him the "Norma Rae of jocks." This, of course, drew the ire of the NCAA and the college sports establishment. Longtime CBS announcer Billy Packer once called to berate him about the perils of associating with the Steelworkers. Mostly, though, Huma was brushed aside by the powers that be, as he canvassed the country trying to spread his message.

The NCAA may not have taken the Collegiate Athletes Coalition terribly seriously, but Schwarz and his fellow economists did. Huma had something they needed—college athletes, thousands of them, who were members of the CAC and could potentially serve as the lead plaintiff for the lawsuit they were trying to gin up. It would be asking a lot of a young athlete to face off against the legal and public relations machinery of the NCAA, but surely one of them would be willing to step forward. And surely Ramogi Huma would find him.

Huma grew up in Covina, California. His father was a Kenyan immigrant who met his mother at Cal State–Los Angeles. He was teaching Swahili; she was a student. They married and named Huma after the founding chief of his father's tribe, the same tribe Barack Obama's father hailed from. Huma learned to play football from his older brothers and became a star at nationally ranked Bishop Amat Memorial High School in nearby La Puente. He earned scholarship offers from schools all over the West Coast, but settled on UCLA partly because it was close to home, and partly because Coach Terry Donahue, nearing his second decade at UCLA, told him, "I've been here a long time. I'm not going anywhere." Huma's parents had divorced when he was twelve and the prospect of stability appealed to him. Donahue left the next year for a TV job.

The summer after his freshman year, Huma's coaches recommended that he participate in summer workouts with the team, but also told him that because they were voluntary and didn't occur during the school year, NCAA rules prohibited UCLA from providing health insurance (schools around this time actually defeated two legislative proposals that would have allowed them to pay for surgeries needed from summer workout injuries and to cover care for any nonathletic injuries or illnesses). Huma was stunned. He was quickly learning that the free ride he had heard so much about wasn't so free after all. "It was very clear that something wasn't right," he says today.

Huma's brother, Miregi, was involved in student government at Idaho State University and suggested that he start a student group. Huma spoke to UCLA coach Bob Toledo about how he hoped to advocate for athletes and give them a voice in the way the system worked. He earned Toledo's blessing, but even after signing up a number of UCLA athletes, organizing proved difficult, if not impossible. In the pre-Internet age, he didn't know how to reach out to other schools. Even on his own campus, he would call meetings, expecting dozens of athletes, only to have three or four show up.

With his new Collegiate Athletes Coalition treading water, Huma got a lesson in activism in 1998 that would help shape both his and his group's future. Proposition 209, a highly controversial California ballot initiative, had passed a couple years earlier. Although it used the language of civil rights in banning discrimination on the basis of race, sex, or ethnicity, critics contended its true purpose was to roll back affirmative action at state schools. It had sparked a string of legal challenges and heated debate across California that fall. John Carlos, one of the American Olympians who raised his fist on the medal stand at the 1968 Olympics in a show of black power, was an outspoken critic of Prop 209, and the UCLA Black Student Union arranged for him to speak to African American members of the football team.

During a clandestine meeting in the student union one night after practice, Carlos told Huma and the players about what he had done, the importance of his message, and the abuse and death threats he suffered afterward. Huma was riveted at the social power athletes possessed. The players agreed to wear black wristbands during their next game at Miami to protest Prop 209.

But word quickly leaked to Coach Toledo, who called a meeting of his own with the team, strongly suggesting players not wear the wristbands. UCLA was undefeated with one game left in the season and the Bruins had the inside track for a berth in the national championship game. As Huma recalls, Toledo said there were southern writers who might not appreciate a team speaking out about race. It could hurt them in the polls. If they wanted to make a statement in the national championship game, he added, he might reconsider. The team stood down, but lost to Miami anyway.

Two things about the experience stuck with Huma. The first was the realization of the untapped potential of the athletes' voice, given the stage that came with playing in front of a television audience of millions. The second was how easy it was to stop a movement in its tracks. "You can't cede the discretion to a coach who has a conflict of interest," Huma says. "I always tell that to players now."

When Huma's playing career was cut short by a hip injury, UCLA honored his scholarship, and he earned a sociology degree. By 2000, he was pursuing a master's in public health, though his concerns about college sports never waned and his awareness grew. He read two books that offered their own blistering critiques of the NCAA: *Unpaid Professionals*, by Smith College economist Andrew Zimbalist, and Walter Byers's memoir. "It was a good feeling to know I wasn't alone," he says.

That summer, Huma redoubled his organizing efforts, but he understood that he needed help to build a stronger organization that could gain a large membership and truly speak for players. So he sent e-mails to a handful of unions, as well as a number of lawyers across the country, laying out inequities big-time college athletes faced. He got exactly one reply. It came from the United Steelworkers, based all the way across the country in Pittsburgh. Huma's e-mail had been forwarded to Tim Waters, a passionate, old-school organizer in his thirties, who had recently helped college students mount a campaign against sweatshop labor.

The son of a deeply conservative Church of Christ minister, Waters had grown up in tiny Wabash, Indiana, a sports nut and huge fan of Indiana University basketball and its coach, Bobby Knight. Huma's e-mail shocked him. Some cursory research corroborated much of what Huma had written, and Waters was intrigued. The Steelworkers had some sports history; Marvin Miller was their top negotiator before he went on to become the trailblazing leader of the Major League Baseball Players Association, the man who engineered the era of free agency in the 1970s. With the go-ahead from the Steelworkers' top brass, Waters flew out to California to meet Huma. He returned to Pittsburgh impressed and with a message for his bosses: the cause was worthy.

"Everyone asks me why we got involved," Waters says. "The answer has always been it's the right thing to do. No one understood it then, but these guys were being exploited and they weren't going to get anywhere without help." Huma and Waters were clear about one basic tenet from the start, though: players were not forming a union, which they viewed as a nonstarter. Legally, they were not employees, so they had no labor rights. Huma didn't want to go in that direction anyway. His goal was to speak for players, not to strike. What the Steelworkers did deliver was legal support to turn the CAC into a 501(c)(3) nonprofit. Then came the money to help

Huma organize. "It was the basics," Waters says. "How do you set up a conference call? How do you pay for a cell phone bill?"

On January 18, 2001, Huma held a press conference at the UCLA student union to announce the CAC to the world. He was joined by fifteen members of the UCLA football team, Waters, and Daylon McCutcheon, his high school teammate and member of the Cleveland Browns. The CAC's platform was simple and straightforward: better health care, life insurance, higher monthly stipends, and the removal of NCAA rules that barred athletes from holding down jobs during the school year.

"We appreciate the athletic gifts that we possess and we appreciate the opportunities that are available to us that are not available to others as a result of those talents," Huma said that day. "But we also put our bodies on the line for what we do. As a result of our effort and hard work, we bring tremendous resources to both the NCAA and our respective individual institutions. Stated simply, we only want what is right for college athletes."

The press conference was well covered, and was billed as a groundbreaking organizing attempt by college athletes. When Huma was pressed on the question of whether the players might someday strike, he adamantly said there would be no player walkouts. "They stood together in a brightly lit conference room, these athletes without a coach, labor organizers without the legal basis to form a union," J. A. Adande wrote in the *Los Angeles Times*. Still, some college officials understood Huma's nascent movement as a direct challenge to the long-held relationship between athletes and their schools. "It puts the smell of employee on this—employee vs. student athlete," said Syracuse president Kenneth "Buzz" Shaw. "Whether it's a union without a union, it doesn't matter. What matters, though, are these student-athletes, or are they employees?"

Huma may not have been meaning to, but he was scratching the surface of an issue Walter Byers had tried to put a padlock on nearly half a century earlier. In 1955, Ray Dennison, a member of the Fort Lewis A&M Aggies football team, injured his head on a kickoff and died two days later. His widow sued for workers' compensation benefits, first raising the issue of whether college athletes, paid with a scholarship, were college employees like their peers in the bookstore, or whether they were students who happened to be engaged in an extracurricular activity. The Colorado Supreme Court decided the latter, declaring that the school was "not in the football business." But the case shook Byers. With injuries to players competing in sports rather common, hundreds of schools didn't want to be on the hook for workers' compensation payments. To fight the prospect that a court might someday view playing football or men's basketball as a job, Byers worked to make scholarships four-year grants instead of a single year, which could look like a contract. (The four-year scholarship was eliminated in favor of the one-year renewable alternative around the same time as the laundry money was taken away. The move was billed as a cost-cutting measure, but it gave coaches and schools far more control over their players. They could be cut from the team and lose their scholarships for anything from poor play to an injury.) Dennison's case also moved Byers to coin the term "student-athlete."

"We crafted the term," Byers wrote, "and soon it was embedded in all NCAA rules and interpretations."

The label, intended to convey that players were first and foremost students, helped inoculate the NCAA from legal claims. Fred Rensing, an Indiana State football player who was paralyzed during practice in 1976, brought a case similar to Dennison's. After he lost a decision with the state workers' compensation panel, an Indiana appellate court ruled that Rensing was a school employee and entitled to benefits. Ultimately, however, the state supreme court overturned the ruling. A more prominent challenge came from Kent Waldrep, a running back at Texas Christian University. Waldrep took a handoff during a game against Alabama in 1974 and sprinted for the sidelines, where he was met by a crush of Crimson Tide defenders. When he awoke, he was in a hospital bed, paralyzed. His neck had snapped. For nine months TCU paid his medical bills, but then stopped, leaving the Waldreps to get by mostly on charity. When Division I schools began carrying disability insurance for football players in 1990, Waldrep sued and won $70 a week from the Texas workers' compensation board. The decision was appealed by TCU's insurance carrier and later overturned by a state district court. Not until June 2000—less than a year before Huma announced the CAC—did the Texas Supreme Court confirm the lower court's ruling. Waldrep wasn't an employee because he had not paid taxes on the financial aid that he could have kept even if he quit football, the court ruled.

Soon after Huma's press conference at UCLA, Jim Hill, a local sportscaster, put him in touch with Vaccaro, who opened his network to him. Later that summer, Tim Waters, his Steelworkers ally, flew out to Los Angeles and, with Huma by his side, met Vaccaro over breakfast at Gladstone's on the Pacific Coast Highway, overlooking the ocean. Though Vaccaro was still in the sneaker business, he promised to help Huma however he could. "I bought into what they were doing," Vaccaro says. "Their cause was pure."

Huma and Waters made an unlikely pair. Huma was a California football player, complete with a tattoo and hoop earring. Waters enjoyed a cigarette and a pint of Guinness. With Huma buried in his organizing work, Waters often had to keep him up to date on sports. "I'd always have to tell him which teams had won and lost," Waters says. But the two men connected immediately. Huma saw Waters as a mentor, one of the few who shared his zeal for his cause. Waters recognized in Huma an ability to lead a movement. "Ramogi is a leader and an organizer and an agitator in the purest sense of the word," Waters says. "Not mean, not abrasive, but constantly pushing for change." In the early days, they had a standing call each night at midnight to strategize. The message needed focusing; Ramogi needed to get to more schools; how could they find players to lead on each campus they visited?

Huma's plan was to organize, school by school and team by team, building the CAC's network and gradually increasing its clout so the NCAA would have to pay attention. Not long after his press conference, though, his timetable got a major jolt.

At its 1991 convention, the NCAA passed new rules to limit how much time coaches could spend with their players. For the first time, the NCAA capped how long and how often a team could practice. The new restraints limited team activities to four hours per day. During the season twenty hours per week was the maximum; the off-season cap was eight hours each week. At the same convention, schools voted to cut football scholarships from ninety-five to eighty-five. Administrators had costs in mind, but they were also under pressure to refocus on academics, and the new rules were meant to reinforce what college sports were all about: the student-athlete. Coaches, predictably, were not thrilled. "The quality of the game will be affected; how much, only time will tell," said Oklahoma coach Gary Gibbs. "It disturbs me."

Soon, though, a loophole emerged. Just because a coach wasn't present and it wasn't an official practice didn't mean a team couldn't work out. And so a new phrase entered the NCAA lexicon: "voluntary practices." These were organized by team leaders to help players get in shape, run plays—essentially many of the things they would do at an official practice, but without coaches' supervision. Though they may not have been present, coaches often encouraged attendance and got reports on who was there and who wasn't. Huma and his UCLA teammates coined another name for them: "volandatory." "They were mandatory in everything but their name," Huma says.

Between February and August 2001, three college football players died while working out with their teams at Florida State, the University of Florida, and Northwestern, respectively. Two of the deaths occurred during summer voluntary workouts that sometimes did not have the same medical personnel available as at official practices; the other came at an off-season conditioning workout that was also considered "voluntary." "It was almost incomprehensible," Huma says.

In February, Florida State freshman Devaughn Darling collapsed and died one morning during the Seminoles' famous mat drills—a Coach Bobby Bowden staple since he took the job in 1976 that involved an array of high-intensity tumbling and agility exercises. Darling, a native of the Bahamas who attended high school in suburban Houston, was eighteen and one of the younger players on the team. During the workout he began to wheeze and told teammates he was having trouble breathing. When a coach yelled to hit the mat, he obliged. After he crumpled to the floor, he was rushed to Tallahassee Memorial Regional Medical Center, where he was pronounced dead of an apparent cardiac arrhythmia. The Darlings received a death benefit from Florida State of $10,000 that didn't even cover burial costs, according to the Los Angeles Times. (The family later reached a $2 million settlement with Florida State, but to this day has received only $200,000 of it because the Florida legislature, which must approve large settlements with state institutions, has not done so.)

Five months later, Eraste Autin, an eighteen-year-old incoming freshman fullback at Florida, collapsed while jogging off the practice field. It was an 88-degree day with a heat index of 102 in Gainesville and Autin had run a series of 150- and 200-yard sprints. But as he jogged away from the field, he didn't look right. Tim Garvey, a local dentist who was driving by the campus, noticed Autin running "like a puppet on a string" and jumped out of his car to help. Autin collapsed in his arms, mumbling, "I've got to run . . . got to run." "No, big guy, let me put you down," Garvey said, as he dialed 911.

Autin's body temperature had reached 108 degrees. He suffered a massive heart attack and spent the next six days in a coma before he passed away. "You have to tell players, 'Give it your best shot. If you feel like you can't make it, you have to use your discretion,'" said Florida coach Steve Spurrier, who was not present at the practice. Florida State coach Bobby Bowden suggested that the ubiquitous use of air-conditioning could be blamed for players being unprepared for the heat, or perhaps they were eating too much fast food. "We are looking at our program," he said. "How did this thing slip up on us? We are not doing anything different than we have done for the last twenty-five years." But there was still more tragedy to come.

Rashidi Wheeler was a twenty-two-year-old sociology major at Northwestern and a starting strong safety on the football team. The senior from Southern California had started all twelve games during his junior season in 2000. He made 88 tackles and recovered a fumble. He dreamt of playing on Sundays in the NFL one day.

On the afternoon of August 3, Wheeler and his teammates were on Northwestern's field hockey field, attempting to complete Coach Randy Walker's fitness test. It was a voluntary workout; Walker was not there. Temperatures were in the low eighties and Wheeler had already completed ten sprints of 100 yards, eight of 80 yards, six of 60 yards. He had four 40-yard sprints left when he fell to the turf.

Wheeler was an asthmatic and had suffered attacks before while playing. He had an inhaler with him just in case. But on this day he was not the only player in trouble. Around ten of his teammates also keeled over from the workout, so trainer Tory Aggeler could not attend to Wheeler alone. Wheeler was placed on a bench to recover, but he couldn't sit up. He looked up at teammate Kevin Bentley and said, "K.B., I'm dying." Within the hour, Wheeler would be dead.

As players continued the fitness test, trainers tried to resuscitate Wheeler. Someone tried to call 911 from a nearby emergency phone, but it was broken, apparently inoperable after a recent flood. A cell phone call was finally placed to paramedics, but by the time Wheeler arrived at Evanston Hospital he was without a pulse.

"I think Tory did the best job he could in the situation," Bentley said. "But he was the only one who knew everybody's medical history and maybe we were a little undermanned for that situation." A coroner determined Wheeler's death was a "classic case of exercise-induced bronchial asthma."

No one knew at the time, but later—after Wheeler's parents filed a wrongful death suit—it was learned that in the days after the death, long-time Northwestern director of health services Mark Gardner had burned Wheeler's medical records. In sworn testimony he said he took them to a wooded area near campus and destroyed them, before checking into a hospital for treatment for emotional distress. Gardner later quit, and Northwestern settled the suit for $16 million.

As questions swirled around Wheeler's death, his family reached out to Huma for help. Huma flew to Chicago and held a press conference with the Steelworkers and the Reverend Jesse Jackson Sr. at the Allegro Hotel. Huma announced a new platform, which he called "The Critical Safety, Catastrophic Injury and Death Initiative." Its goals were to end the voluntary workout loopholes, require schools to provide health coverage for all sports injuries (including summer activities), and increase the $10,000 death benefit.

From Chicago, Huma's next stop was Seattle to support the family of Curtis Williams, a Washington safety who had been paralyzed while making a tackle. He was now a quadriplegic and his insurance benefits were set to run out if the NCAA and its insurer didn't agree to lift the cap. (Eventually they did, though Williams died at age twenty-four.) "It all happened right away," Huma says. "We moved so much faster than we planned."

Word of the CAC spread almost entirely by word of mouth in the early years. Huma and some teammates connected mostly with players who had UCLA connections and wanted to learn more. When a call came in, Huma hopped in his Toyota Camry or caught a flight to visit with the curious players. He traveled to schools across the West Coast, addressing teams in locker rooms and on practice fields—always away from the eyes of coaches. Summer health insurance, stipends, and scholarships that could be canceled on a coach's whim resonated most with players. When Huma finished his pitch to the new team, he passed around a sign-up sheet for a new chapter, and asked players to put a star by their names if they were willing to be leaders in the movement. "It wasn't a hot topic then," says Matt Strohfus, then a Boise State fullback. "The first time I spoke to Ramogi, it was like a light bulb. He was the only one taking action."

By the end of the first summer, the CAC had chapters at the University of Southern California, the University of Washington, and Boise State. Huma earned support from some high-profile players too, including Southern California quarterback Carson Palmer and Stanford basketball player Casey Jacobsen. When the USC athletes joined the CAC, Palmer lent a quote to the press release. "These issues are so powerful that it even brings traditional rivals such as USC and UCLA together to fight for a positive change," he said. Huma had most of the Pac-10 signed up by 2002 and the men's basketball team at St. Louis University, before moving farther east to Alabama, the CAC's first school in the SEC.

Coaches had mixed reactions to Huma. When he visited the University of Washington campus, a former coach at UCLA now with the Huskies saw him on campus and invited him to speak with head coach Rick Neuheisel. Huma was wary of coaches and had actively avoided involving them, preferring to speak to players without the interference of higher powers. But he agreed to meet with Neuheisel, who surprised him by inviting him to speak to the entire team. He also spoke to Washington State's football team, with the blessing of head coach Mike Price after getting an invitation from a player there. The player was Devard Darling, Devaughn's brother.

Buoyed by the support, on Huma's next organizing trip to Arizona's campus he decided to change tactics and visit football coach John Mackovic. Mackovic agreed to see Huma and his co-organizer and former UCLA teammate Ryan Roques. He listened to Huma's pitch for Arizona to join the CAC, but wouldn't allow Huma speak to his players. "You've got the wrong guy," Mackovic said, and sent them on their way.

Huma got his biggest publicity break in early January 2002 when *60 Minutes* featured him in a segment entitled "Where's Ours? College Athletes Band Together to Insist on a Cut of Profits Made from Their Sporting Events." The reporter, Leslie Stahl, noted that bowl games produced roughly $150 million for universities that year, that Notre Dame took in $3 million in ticket sales for every home football game, and that Spurrier earned

$2 million a year. And, she added, CBS had just agreed to pay $6 billion to televise the NCAA basketball tournament for the next eleven years.

Huma compared taking on the mighty NCAA to a prep school team playing against the pros. And he'd had little luck getting a sit-down with the NCAA. But on national television Stahl put some of his questions to college leaders. "Why have the—the idea that—that a kid can't get a death benefit or health coverage if he's playing in a voluntary workout, which everybody knows is part of the program?" Stahl asked Ohio State president William "Brit" Kirwan, who was also chairman of the NCAA board of directors. "Well, I—they should," Kirwan said. "I think this is a—clearly a—a flaw in our system and it's something that needs to be addressed." At the end of the piece, Stahl announced the NCAA had agreed to meet with Huma.

Not everyone was impressed. CBS analyst Billy Packer vented to the *Los Angeles Times* after the story aired. "Haven't they ever heard of Title IX?" he said. "If you pay male football and basketball players, you're also going to have to pay women soccer players. . . . And someone should have asked the guy from the steelworkers union how many workers are left in the steel business. I'm from Bethlehem, Pa., and know all about the steel industry and how the union cost people their jobs."

Days after the *60 Minutes* piece ran, the NCAA announced from its convention in Indianapolis that the meeting with Huma was off. NCAA president Cedric Dempsey said the association would hear from its athletes through its Student-Athlete Advisory Committee, a nonvoting body that gave players some input on rules and policies. Michael Aguirre, the leader of the Division I SAAC and a former football player at Arizona State, was also wary of the CAC. "We're not comfortable with their association with the steelworkers," he said.

Huma would not get another shot at a meeting with the NCAA for more than a decade. Still, he pressed on. That November he passed out leaflets outside Buckeye Stadium before Ohio State hosted Michigan in front of more than 105,000 fans. "Attention, Buckeyes fans. The players you will watch today are at risk!" the flyers read. They included the telephone number of NCAA executive Ron Stratten, who later said he received about twenty-five calls after the game. Huma also got more financial help from the Steelworkers, who started hosting fund-raisers for him. Players from the Cleveland Browns and Pittsburgh Steelers signed autographs to help raise money.

But the going was slow and the NCAA was powerful. Huma sent letters to the CEOs of Coca-Cola, one of the NCAA's biggest sponsors, and CBS, its broadcast partner, asking for meetings. They turned him down. He tried to start an internship program for players, but the NCAA refused to grant a waiver to allow it. "Ramogi was a little naive," Vaccaro says. "He thought because he was right—because his cause was just—that he would win. But that's not how it worked."

Around the same time Huma began to realize he needed more than just a voice to make change, a state senator from Los Angeles named Kevin Murray contacted him. Murray was an entertainment lawyer and had been a strong advocate in Sacramento for recording artists. He had read about Huma and the CAC and was interested in legislation to address the cost-of-attendance issue. He didn't understand how schools could offer scholarships that knowingly left players short of basic necessities. With Huma's help, Murray introduced Senate Bill 193, the Student-Athletes' Bill of Rights. "Nobody's asking for them to be made rich, but the kids that play the big sports should get a decent lifestyle," Murray said at the time.

There had been other efforts to introduce an athletes' bill of rights, most notably by the Drake Group, which had been organized in late 1999 by Jon Ericson, a former professor and provost at Drake University. But this was different—this was an actual bill that offered up the potential of becoming California law.

The bill bordered on revolutionary. It would permit California four-year colleges to pay the cost-of-attendance differential to its athletes. They would also be able to offer more health benefits and allow a player to transfer without having to sit out a year if a coach left a school. Because the NCAA explicitly didn't allow colleges to give players any of these benefits, Murray's bill was going to either force the NCAA to adapt to California's new rules or force the California universities to leave the NCAA. Either way, the bill was a serious threat to the governance structure of college sports.

Murray held a hearing in April 2003 for his bill and Huma needed a current player to testify in Sacramento. He surveyed his network and asked a Stanford defensive back named Jason White if he was willing. Huma had visited Stanford in 2001, and his presentation to a handful of Stanford players resonated with White. A good friend of his had known Rashidi Wheeler, the Northwestern player who had died during a voluntary workout, so White knew that tragic story only too well. He had long been concerned about health insurance at summer workouts. "If something happened to you, you paid out of pocket," he says. White also lived with three other roommates in a run-down three-bedroom house. The stipend, he believed, was crucial for athletes. He agreed to testify.

Also speaking before lawmakers that day was Dan Rascher, who offered an economic theory in support of the bill. White's testimony focused on the gaps in health insurance and the meager monthly checks he and his teammates struggled to get by on. During his testimony, Rascher put forward what was then a radical view on college sports:

> The NCAA and its member schools generate billions in revenue and hundreds of millions in economic profit, comparable to professional sports leagues. Division IA college football profit margins are around 40 percent, the equivalent number for basketball is 50 percent. Accounting methods used by athletic departments understate the true economic profitability of college sports. . . .
>
> . . . The current system is often discussed as other sports or departments "needing" the money generated by football and basketball to stay afloat. In truth, it is a major cross-subsidy, a highly regressive redistribution of income, where revenue generated by a small group of relatively low-income minority athletes is given to predominantly white, higher-income coaches, athletic administrators, university administrators, faculty, and the rest of the university community. It serves as a form of reverse affirmative action against African-American athletes, lessening their economic opportunities.

The bill passed the senate in May, but was never voted on in the assembly. The NCAA mobilized athletic directors and its own political machinery to speak out against the bill, which they blamed on Huma, the CAC, and the Steelworkers. "If we are disallowed to conform to the rules of the NCAA, we can't be in the NCAA," Cal State San Bernardino athletic director Nancy Simpson said. "And if we can't be in the NCAA, we can't go to championships. And if we can't go to championships, then we really can't have a program. It's that drastic."

Over time, this became a recurring theme for Huma—a series of small victories, but certainly nothing to shatter the NCAA's stranglehold on power. Among the accomplishments: the NCAA loosened restrictions on athletes having jobs during the school year, and the death benefit was raised from $10,000 to $25,000. Most important, in 2004, schools were finally able to provide health insurance for summer workouts. They didn't have to, mind you, but should they want to, they now could.

Huma, meanwhile, took a job coaching high school football at Discover Charter Prep School north of Los Angeles in 2004. He did his CAC work out of his home and he tried to travel most weekends to visit players and spread the organizing message. That proved difficult, and momentum lagged. "It was getting to a point where I was going to have to work full-time on organizing or I was going to have to let it go," he says.

Everything changed one night in 2006 when Huma's wife got a call that her parents had been killed by a drunk driver in a car accident. She had younger siblings—a sixteen-year-old and an eighteen-year-old—who were still living at home, and it fell to her and Huma to pick up the slack. So they moved to San Bernardino to essentially raise the family.

The move forced Huma to reconsider the future of the CAC. He decided to change its name to the National College Players Association to more clearly state the group's mission. "We existed to represent players and we wanted everyone to know that." He opened an office in Redlands and would soon become a full-time employee of the NCPA. Another break came in the form of a phone call from Dave Meggyesy, a former professional football player who had become an activist. Nadel knew Meggyesy, and reached out to him as he and the other economists began their search for a lead plaintiff in the lawsuit they wanted to bring against the NCAA. Meggyesy explained to Huma that the suit was going to focus on the cost-of-attendance issue. Did Huma know anyone who might be willing to join the litigation? Huma instantly thought again of White. Again, White agreed.

The labor organizer and the economists had joined forces, and they were suing the NCAA. They were off and running. Or so they thought.

# Rulespalooza

**NCAA RULES CAN FEEL ALL-CONSUMING, AND WHILE SOME HAVE BEEN**
loosened over the years, their spirit has remained: monitor as much of an athlete's life as possible, denying them everything from the smallest perk to sometimes basic human decency—all in the name of competitive balance. Here are
just a few examples:

The 1983 North Carolina State men's basketball team is renowned as one
of the greatest champions in the history of college sports. Coached by the lo-
quacious Jim Valvano, the Wolfpack were a number six seed in the NCAA tournament, and pulled upset after upset until they reached the championship
game, where they met the top team in the nation: Houston's famous Phi Slamma
Jamma squad with future NBA Hall of Famers Clyde Drexler and Hakeem
Olajuwon.

On a miracle final play, Dereck Whittenburg threw up a desperation shot
that was caught at the rim by Lorenzo Charles, who scored the game-winning
dunk. The next day, President Ronald Reagan invited the Wolfpack to the White
House. Valvano happily accepted, only to discover that the university could not
pay for the team to travel to Washington; that would be—what else?—a violation
of NCAA rules, which stipulated the school couldn't pay for travel more than a
hundred miles from campus. North Carolina State appealed, and the NCAA
denied that too.

So Capitol Broadcasting Company, a Raleigh company, stepped up, offering to pay the team's way. Still a violation, decreed the NCAA. Instead, Capitol arranged for a ten-minute satellite feed for the players to greet the president. The expenses were covered by Capitol Broadcasting and cost $6,000—or about $4,300 more than it would have cost to buy round-trip plane tickets for the team.

In 1994, when Aaron Adair was fourteen, he was diagnosed with brain cancer. Adair's whole life was baseball; his father owned an indoor baseball facility in Dallas, and also coached baseball at Trinity Christian, where Adair went to high school. Adair beat that cancer and returned to baseball, winning a scholarship to the University of Oklahoma. But then the disease struck again; this time he had stomach cancer. After surviving that second bout with cancer, Adair wrote a book, called *You Don't Know Where I've Been,* that detailed his struggles with the disease and how they brought him closer to God. . . When he promoted it, however, the Oklahoma compliance department informed him that he was engaged in a commercial activity, which the NCAA doesn't allow, viewing it as "profiting" from his status as an athlete. For writing the book, he lost his eligibility—and his baseball career.

Between 1987 and 1993, a wonderful organization called Track Florida recruited some of the poorest athletes in South Florida and helped them compete in state, regional, and national meets by covering travel, uniforms, food expenses, and coaching. "Half of the kids came from sugar cane fields or the inner city, and most were very poor," John Citron, the former Track Florida director, was quoted as saying in promotional materials released by the McIntosh Foundation, which started Track Florida with a $95,000 grant. "Track Florida gave them an opportunity not only to see all of Florida but to visit all parts of the country. It also gave them exposure to college coaches and scouts they would not have normally had. Many went on to colleges with full scholarships."

But in 1993 a Track Florida coach was contacted by the NCAA and warned that the organization was compromising the students' amateur status. Why? Because the NCAA had learned that the organization was providing tutoring to help its athletes do well on their college entrance exams. It had also given some of its athletes emergency cash for phone calls and cabs during a competition in

Venezuela, and had taken a sick student-athlete to the hospital during an out-of-town meet.

"On a trip to Baltimore, one of our young women, 16 years old, came down with severe dental problems," Mike McIntosh, director of the McIntosh Foundation, wrote in an e-mail. "She had to have an operation, spent several days in the hospital and was released just in time to accompany us on our return to Florida. It happened to be the first time she'd ever been to a dentist because her parents couldn't afford it."

But to the NCAA, this emergency medical care was an improper benefit. "They called me and said, 'Did you take a student to the hospital in the middle of a meet?'" Richard Melear, a former coach, recalled to the McIntosh Foundation. "I said that she had an abscessed tooth, the poison was going through her body, she was in a great deal of pain. They asked if we paid for the visit. I said, 'Hell, yes. How could she have paid for it herself?'"

In an effort to preserve the program—and his athletes' amateur status—McIntosh took the NCAA to court. Though they won at the district court level, that decision was reversed on appeal. As a result, Track Florida was shuttered. The McIntosh Foundation has tried to resurrect the club in the ensuing years, but with no luck. If Track Florida's student-athletes are ineligible for college scholarships because they receive financial aid and study help from a nonprofit organization, then what's the point?

In January 1990, Marquette University sophomore Mike O'Hara attended a Loyola University basketball game in the Chicago suburbs. O'Hara, a runner on Marquette's track team who was home for the Christmas holidays, was chosen to participate in a halftime contest. Though he had been cut from his high school basketball team, he made a series of layups, three-pointers, and even two half-court shots. His prize was a case of Pepsi, a Loyola sweatshirt, airline tickets, and a $20,000 car—a red Ford Mustang convertible.

The next morning the O'Haras got a call from Marquette's compliance officials. They had read about Mike's big night and had some bad news. He was now ineligible to run at Marquette—unless he gave everything back. Why was it a violation for O'Hara to compete in a contest at Loyola when he was an athlete at Marquette? Because having won the contest, O'Hara might now transfer to Loyola, making him a "prospective" Loyola athlete, NCAA officials said, according to author Don Yeager.

O'Hara, who was only on partial scholarship, had to choose between his new Mustang and the rest of his track career. "I love to run," O'Hara told Yeager. "I know it sounds crazy, but it's pretty simple."

The next day O'Hara went back to Loyola. He turned over the car keys, the airline tickets, and the sweatshirt. He and some friends drank half the case of Pepsi, but he even returned what was left of that. He was still suspended for a week from the track team. Just by participating in the contest he had violated NCAA rules.

And then there are rules that are so confusing, so ambiguous, so utterly pointless that nobody actually knows what's a violation and what's not. Consider, for instance, the sport of women's rowing, which the NCAA added to its portfolio in 1997.

One of the long-standing traditions in rowing is that after a race, the losers give their shirts to the winners. As former Olympic rower Gardner Cadwalader, whose daughter later rowed for Radcliffe, put it in an e-mail, "In the sport of rowing . . . we have always 'bet our racing shirts' on the outcome of the race. The loser in high school and college races gives his shirt to the winner. Been that way for ages. It is a nice tradition. It is not gambling on the race and no one has ever thrown a race to win a stupid T-shirt. It is tradition."

But after the NCAA took control of women's rowing, the tradition stopped. One former top rower said, "We were always told we were not allowed to exchange shirts after races with the winners/losers because the NCAA didn't allow betting." A rowing coach said, "It *is* true, we cannot race for shirts. I remember the year the trading [betting] ended on the women's side. I was a sophomore, and it was right when rowing became an NCAA sport."

Here's the strange part. If you ask the NCAA about whether betting the shirt is a violation of NCAA rules, the response is no. According to spokeswoman Stacey Osburn, the NCAA specifically wrote a rule allowing the practice, precisely because it was such a long-standing tradition in the sport.

But try telling that to anyone in the women's rowing community. Will Porter, the women's rowing coach at Yale, said, "There is an NCAA rule that forbids betting on shirts, because it is a form of betting." Upon being informed that the NCAA specifically allowed betting on shirts in rowing, he was dumbfounded.

A former college rower named Cristina Mulcahy, who is now in law school, had rowed at William Smith College. "My first two years," she recalled, "we bet shirts on almost every race." The first year, the team had done so openly; the second year, more furtively, because they had begun hearing that it violated NCAA rules. By her junior year, betting the shirts had stopped. The school's athletic director by then had begun giving the rowing team a quiz, which included a question about whether it was okay to bet shirts. "The entire team failed that question," she said. The athletic director said that the practice was not allowed under NCAA rules. Even now, Mulcahy said, it still bothered her that this tradition had been taken away from women's rowers.

It wasn't long before Will Porter was back on the phone. "I looked up gambling in the NCAA rulebook and I did not see that there is an exception for rowing," he said. "The language is very vague, and doesn't mention rowing. I stand by my previous statement. I don't think it is legal."

Thus it appears that everyone in women's rowing believes that betting shirts is a violation of NCAA rules. Except the NCAA itself.

# CHAPTER 5

# THE CASH KING OF COLLEGE SPORTS

Jack Swarbrick, the athletic director at Notre Dame, likes to divide college sports into three distinct eras. For the first half of the twentieth century, he says, athletics were mostly controlled by the universities themselves without much national oversight. Then Walter Byers seized control and the NCAA ran the show for the next thirty years. But in the aftermath of the *Regents* decision, control of college sports—or at least its economics—moved to a handful of powerful conferences that had the clout to sign their own multimillion-dollar TV contracts. Thanks to those TV contracts, they are still dominating college sports today.

The paradigmatic example is the Big Ten, the conference that spawned the modern NCAA. In 1989, at a time when its revenues were $20 million, the Big Ten presidents hired Jim Delany to be its commissioner. In his previous job, as commissioner of the much smaller Ohio Valley Conference, Delany had cobbled together television deals that no one else had thought to do. As commissioner of the Big Ten, he began turbocharging the economics of college sports. He helped bring down the College Football Association, which had a momentary rise to prominence after the *Regents* decision—and whose schools competed with Big Ten schools for television deals. He started the first conference television network. His expansion moves forced every other conference in the country to scramble to keep up. He helped ensure that the big conferences like his got most of the financial spoils—despite the constant complaints of smaller conferences that they deserved a bigger piece of the pie. By 2013, the Big Ten was bringing in some $318 million, most of which was distributed to its member schools. Even the mighty SEC often found itself chasing Delany's latest financial moves.

Delany is now sixty-seven years old. He earns around $3 million a year. *Forbes* magazine once called his conference the "cash king" of college sports. Shrewd, visionary, and cutthroat, Delany is beloved in the Big Ten, and feared most everywhere else. He has become such an institution that *Sports Illustrated* once described his "gimlet eyes and gleaming pate" as being "as iconic . . . as the Horseshoe and 'Hail to the Victors.'"

A former basketball player at the University of North Carolina, Delany professes to harbor an abiding belief in the virtues of amateur college sports. "I don't know how I would have paid for college without my basketball scholarship," he says. Yet not since Byers has anyone clung so tightly to the romantic notion of college sports while creating a reality unrecognizable from that supposedly glorious past. Former Big East commissioner John Marinatto once compared Delany to Gordon Gekko, the character from the 1987 film *Wall Street*, who coined the phrase "Greed is good." *Washington Post* columnist John Feinstein has likened him to Darth Vader. Scott Cowen, the former president of Tulane University, puts it another way: "Power conferences led by long-serving and outspoken commissioners such as Jim Delany have adversely transformed intercollegiate athletics, including the NCAA, to the detriment of many Division I universities and student athletes. This trend . . . appears to be motivated, consciously or unconsciously, by an almost insatiable appetite for power and resources."

James E. Delany is an unlikely businessman. Growing up in Newark and South Orange, New Jersey, he was one of the few white kids who was a regular at Newark's public basketball courts. He wasn't a flashy player, but he was tough and had a good feel for the game. He was recruited by schools in the Northeast—Seton Hall, Fordham, Villanova, and Boston College—but he impressed an assistant coach from North Carolina at a recruiting camp and received a scholarship offer to Chapel Hill. There, he learned from basketball royalty: Larry Brown, later the coach of NCAA and NBA championship teams, guided the freshman team, and Dean Smith, among the winningest coaches in college basketball history, coached the varsity. As a junior, Delany cracked the rotation; he was named a captain in his senior year. He went to two Final Fours with the Tar Heels.

For Delany, the idea of education through athletics was sacred; his family, in fact, was built on the concept. His dad was the first in his family to go to college, where he played basketball at Seton Hall, while his older brother played at Niagara. His father taught him from an early age to use basketball as a means of social mobility. "Growing up, education and sports were always present, together," Delany says. "The lesson was use sports, don't let sports use you."

Going to college in the late 1960s, Delany was much more than an athlete; he was a political animal, whip-smart and unafraid to speak his mind. At North Carolina, he challenged Smith about playing time, and was the only Irish Catholic in a Jewish fraternity. (He was asked to join after he came to the aid of some friends in a fistfight that broke out between two Jewish fraternities following a football game. The frats fondly called the game the Nose Bowl.) His brother fought in Vietnam, and Delany was often more sympathetic to the war effort than his housemates when debates broke out.

After he graduated in 1970 with a political science degree, Delany found himself at a crossroads. His father had pleaded with him not to pursue a career in sports. "Because I think he wanted something more for his kids," he says. So Delany enrolled in law school at North Carolina, and then went to work for the North Carolina senate judiciary committee and later the state justice department. But by 1975 he had left North Carolina for a job as an NCAA investigator.

At the NCAA, Delany believed in his work, though he quickly learned that he was not cut out to be a foot soldier in any organization. Once during a pickup basketball game at NCAA headquarters in Kansas City, he nearly came to blows with his boss, Warren Brown, over a foul call. "I work for you upstairs, but I don't fucking work for you down here," Delany screamed at Brown on the court.

Like many other NCAA investigators of that era, Delany was accused of playing fast and loose. During the 1978 congressional hearings, a Mississippi State attorney claimed that Delany boasted to Mississippi State lawyers that as an investigator he had the power to make or break the futures of NCAA schools. (Delany denies he said anything to that effect. Of his time with the enforcement staff, he adds, "You might not like the process, but that doesn't mean people were acting with bad intent. They might have been young and inexperienced, but they weren't bad people. There were no conspiracies.") In those same hearings, it also came out that while investigating Mississippi State, Delany had befriended a high school student named James Jordan who was recruited by Mississippi State but signed a letter of intent to play at the University of Mississippi. Delany had let Jordan set him up on a date with a woman he then became involved with. (Delany was single at the time.) Later, when Delany found out a school he had investigated initiated a background check on him to see if he was involved in drugs or gambling, he told a fellow investigator that if anyone really wanted to embarrass him they could find out a high school student arranged a date for him.

After Delany was passed over for a promotion, he interviewed in 1979 for commissioner of the Ohio Valley Conference, a small conference nestled between Appalachia and the Mississippi River and made up of a series of small-profile schools like Morehead State, Murray State, and Eastern Kentucky. Delany, only thirty-one years old, with zero management experience, offered to take the job for one year and at a discounted salary of $30,000 (it was still a healthy raise over his NCAA pay). His final pitch was simple: "If you make a mistake, you should make a young mistake," he told the OVC presidents. As Delany readied to board his plane after the interview in Nashville, a message came over the loudspeaker. He had a phone call; he was hired.

Delany took over at the OVC the same year a fledgling twenty-four-hour cable channel called Entertainment and Sports Programming Network, or ESPN, went on the air. There is no event in the modern era that would have a more profound effect on college sports. Founder Bill Rasmussen, a former communications manager for the NHL's Hartford Whalers, paid $91 to incorporate it in 1978 in Bristol, Connecticut. At the time there were only around fourteen million cable homes across the country, with limited programming available. HBO had gone on the air in 1975; the following year, Ted Turner had launched his TBS "Superstation." CNN, Turner's twenty-four-hour news network, didn't follow until 1980.

Rasmussen originally conceived of ESPN as a regional cable channel to show sports in the Northeast. But even before it launched, its business model became much more ambitious: ESPN would be a twenty-four-hour national sports network, with 8,760 hours of programming to fill each year. Rasmussen began with sports like slow-pitch softball and Australian rules football until he signed his first big American sports contract with Byers and the NCAA to broadcast an array of sports, including the early rounds of the men's basketball tournament, which until that point were not seen on national TV. "Do you mean if Weber State and Lamar Tech are playing, you're going to televise it?" Byers had asked Rasmussen, according to *These Guys Have All the Fun*, a history of ESPN by James A. Miller and Tom Shales. "If they're in the tournament, yeah," Rasmussen answered. "Every game. We mean every game." (Weber State and Lamar Tech met, coincidentally, in the 1980 tournament.)

By a stroke of luck, two weeks after the ink dried on the pact, Magic Johnson and Michigan State met Larry Bird and Indiana State in the NCAA tournament championship. Broadcast on NBC on March 26, 1979, the game remains the highest-rated college basketball game in television history, with a live audience of thirty-five million (nearly one in four television sets were tuned to the game) at a time when the NBA Finals were still shown on tape delay. That game marked the beginning of a golden age for college hoops and made Rasmussen look awfully smart.

By the middle of the 1980s, ESPN was regularly broadcasting weekday basketball games, and in 1987 branded its Monday night showcase as Big Monday, featuring a prime-time doubleheader with teams from the Big East and the Big Ten. Indeed, the Big East, a collection of basketball schools from the Northeast, was founded precisely to take advantage of ESPN's unquenchable thirst for college sports programming—and was ESPN's first major deal with a conference, which helped legitimize the new network. Nearly thirty years later, Big Monday is still a staple of ESPN's lineup, as is another weekly doubleheader called Super Tuesday. ESPN also inked a Thursday night deal in 1987, putting college football regularly on weeknights.

"At first Thursday was a hard sell for schools," says Len DeLuca, a TV executive with CBS who later worked at ESPN. "They were worried coaches would complain, that the citizenry would complain about the weeknights. Then they realized how lucrative it was—how much ESPN would pay and how many people were watching."

A young Delany carefully observed television's new role and concluded that it was the way to separate the OVC from other small conferences around the country. In the summer of 1980, he drove throughout
Ohio and Kentucky to Youngstown, Akron, Hazard, Paducah, and elsewhere with a pitch to local television executives to put a weekly conference game on television. He found no takers. But he retraced his steps after
a meeting with Ralph Hacker, a Kentucky radio announcer. Because of
NCAA sanctions against Kentucky's basketball team in the early 1950s,
Hacker reminded Delany, the games were not shown live but on tape delay
after the nightly news. The light bulb went on; Delany would offer TV sta-
tions live sports at 11:30 at night.

The broadcasts became known as Friday Night Live (they replaced
*M\*A\*S\*H* reruns in some markets) and eventually reached some five million homes. After several seasons, ESPN acquired the rights to air the
games nationally. OVC teams were on television around the country more
than any other small conference. Soon the secret was out: live late-night
college basketball drew better ratings than sitcom reruns.

The Big Ten had always been close to Byers. His first employee and
longtime right-hand man Wayne Duke was commissioner from 1971 until
1989, and the conference had refused to join the CFA, staying loyal to the
NCAA when others revolted. Byers first pushed for one of his senior executives, Tom Jernstedt, to replace Duke. Jernstedt preferred to stay in Kansas
City, but he had a suggestion for someone else: a little-known commissioner from the Ohio Valley who seemed to have a knack for television.
"Everyone realized that, in Jim, we had one of the bright young minds in
intercollegiate athletics," says E. Gordon Gee, the president of Ohio State
from 1990 to 1997 and then again from 2007 to 2013.

Soon after Delany got the job, he and Jernstedt were in Colorado
Springs for a USA Basketball meeting. Afterward, they took in a round of
golf. As Delany prepared to tee off, Jernstedt noticed his socks and couldn't
suppress a chuckle—they were mismatched. He informed his friend that
he would have to look the part in his new job. "I told him he wasn't at the
Ohio Valley anymore," Jernstedt recalls.

Delany got another lesson early in his tenure when he went on a meet-
and-greet tour around the conference. In Bloomington, Indiana, he had
breakfast with a longtime Indiana sports columnist named Bob Hammel.

Hammel wrote to him after the meeting, reminding him of the conference's rich history and all who had come before him: Red Grange, Gerald Ford, Otto Graham, Jesse Owens, Jim Abbott, Branch Rickey, George Sisler, Herb Brooks, among so many others.

"Look down on Memorial Stadium and realize the place was dedicated 65 years ago with Grange running wild against Michigan, which would be the biggest thing that ever happened in a Big Ten stadium if they hadn't split the atom under the (former conference member) University of Chicago's," Hammel wrote. "This league's been around awhile, and you're the pilot now, Jim. There's no other job like yours." Twenty-five years later, Delany still has the letter framed in his office at Big Ten headquarters in suburban Chicago.

It did not take Delany long to embrace the stature of the Big Ten. At the OVC, he had served on the College Basketball Committee that selected the teams for the basketball tournament. He had been a fierce advocate for OVC schools, supporting them for at-large bids to the tournament whenever possible. That soon changed. "At the Big Ten, he's grumbling about the automatic qualifiers for the smaller conferences," says Roy Kramer, the commissioner of the Southeastern Conference from 1990 to 2002. "I've always been an advocate for the people I work with," Delany says, adding he has always been in favor of automatic bids for all conferences.

One of Delany's first acts as commissioner was to extend an invitation to Penn State, a previously independent football powerhouse coached by Joe Paterno—and part of the CFA. Penn State quickly accepted the invite. The Big Ten schools were all in the Midwest, which Delany viewed as his "territory"; adding Penn State extended its geographical reach. More important, the move added several million television homes to the Big Ten's footprint—and weakened the CFA, from which Penn State defected to join its new conference. "The goal is to make sure we're the number one conference in the country, not just on the field but in terms of revenue and a force in intercollegiate athletics," Gee says. "Jim thought it was very important strategically."

Not long afterward, Notre Dame shocked college sports by jilting the CFA and signing its own TV deal worth millions more for the Fighting Irish. If even priests were chasing TV money, it truly was a brave new world.

Notre Dame has long had a unique position in college football. A Catholic school located in South Bend, Indiana, it seems an unlikely candidate for the sport's most recognizable program, but Coach Knute Rockne helped the Fighting Irish assume the role by building a dynasty during the 1920s. Rockne coached players like the Four Horsemen—Notre Dame's 1924 backfield of Harry Stuhldreher, Don Miller, Jim Crowley, and Elmer Layden—who were covered glowingly by early sportswriters such as Grantland Rice. Notre Dame's national radio broadcasts—it gave away its broadcast rights for free to the big radio networks—also gave the program unrivaled exposure around the country, earning it fans from coast to coast. In 1940, the Hollywood movie *Knute Rockne All American* (starring Ronald Reagan) immortalized Rockne's "Win One for the Gipper" halftime speech and elevated Notre Dame even higher in the national consciousness.

But Notre Dame's mystique grew for another reason too. It was the university of all of Catholic America, and it stood for a different set of values than the "football factories" around the country. The Fighting Irish, for instance, declined bowl invitations from 1925 until 1969, on principle, because the administration believed it distracted from players' studies. Notre Dame's vast popularity made it the single most important university in the CFA.

It had also played a key role in holding the CFA together. In the immediate aftermath of the *Regents* decision, the CFA became the negotiating agent for its schools, signing a deal with CBS. But with a glut of games now available, the price the networks were willing to pay actually went down—as did the ratings. ABC, seeing the discontent among CFA members with their CBS contract, attempted to lure the SEC away with a four-year, $24 million deal. Notre Dame's representative on the CFA board was the Reverend Edmund P. Joyce, who was the chairman of Notre Dame's faculty athletics board. He had turned down lucrative TV packages offered to Notre Dame in the years since *Regents* because he believed in the unity of the CFA. As the SEC deliberated in 1986, he dispatched athletic director Gene Corrigan to pledge Notre Dame to the CFA and plead with the conference not to take ABC's money. The SEC agreed, in exchange for more exposure in the CFA's TV package.

By 1990, ABC was ready for another push, this time for the entire CFA. They offered a whopper of a contract: $210 million over five years, a 50 percent raise on the CFA's CBS deal. On a conference call that January, the CFA voted to accept ABC's offer, with the Reverend E. William Beauchamp, who had recently replaced Joyce, agreeing to the deal too.

But just two weeks later, Beauchamp and Notre Dame athletic director Dick Rosenthal called a meeting with CFA executive director Chuck Neinas at the Denver airport, where they dropped a bomb: Notre Dame was out of the CFA. They were planning to sign their own jaw-dropping deal with NBC, a $38 million pact that covered thirty home games between 1991 and 1995. Neinas begged the priest to reconsider, just as Notre Dame had once done with the SEC. But Notre Dame was unmoved. Gene Corrigan, by then the commissioner of the Atlantic Coast Conference (ACC), was crushed, along with the rest of the CFA, which had to renegotiate its deal with ABC for millions less. "It was heartbreaking," he says.

The SEC was next.

Of all the conferences, only the SEC, with its great southern sports schools like Alabama, Auburn, and Kentucky, had the means, the heft—and its football-laden tradition—to go toe to toe with the Big Ten. And its commissioner, Roy Kramer, was Delany's only true rival.

While Delany had his law degree, Kramer's background was as a football coach—he won the Division II national championship with Central Michigan in 1974. Kramer came from a well-known Tennessee family of lawyers, and he landed as athletic director at Vanderbilt in 1978. With Delany in Nashville at the Ohio Valley, the two shared a city for much of the 1980s before they entered the national spotlight (their wives also happened to be cousins). And like his counterpart in the Big Ten, Kramer proved a savvy businessman. "There were new rules for commissioners: the only thing you're trying to do is create money for your schools," says Corrigan. "Jim and Roy were the leaders, and the rest of us worked to keep up."

Kramer decided that what the SEC needed to extend its financial might was more schools. In May 1990, he turned his attention to the Southwest Conference, which had long been a football power, with schools like Texas, Texas A&M, and Arkansas. Kramer put feelers out to see if any would jump to the SEC. This was uncharted waters—never before had one conference so openly targeted another league's members. Suddenly, it was every school for itself. As the uncertainty grew, the Pac-10 and Big Eight made their own inquiries. Pac-10 commissioner Tom Hansen told Keith Dunnavant, the author of *The Fifty-Year Seduction*, "It's all one big grab of television homes—that's all."

With the exception of Notre Dame, universities could no longer hope to remain independent—not if they wanted a share of the television money the conferences were generating, which was now a necessity if they hoped to be able to compete with the big boys.

By the fall of 1990, the SEC had added Arkansas from the Southwest Conference and independent South Carolina. The ACC, long a basketball powerhouse but realizing it needed bigger and better football schools, took aim at Florida State, which Bobby Bowden had turned into a rising football power. Landing Florida State also meant adding millions of Florida television homes, as well as fertile recruiting ground.

The Big East, meanwhile, quickly saw that it needed to become a football conference as well as a basketball conference or face extinction. Its new commissioner, Mike Tranghese, soon reeled in Miami, where Coach Jimmy Johnson had turned the Hurricanes into a football juggernaut, along with Virginia Tech, Rutgers, and West Virginia (Pittsburgh, Syracuse, and Boston College also became full members of the Big East, bringing their previously independent football teams to the conference). The Big East was saved—for the moment.

The Southwest Conference wasn't so lucky. In 1994, the Big Eight peeled off its four remaining powerhouses, Texas, Texas A&M, Texas Tech, and Baylor. Its remaining members—Rice, Houston, Texas Christian, and Southern Methodist—scattered among lesser conferences. Within two years, the once mighty Southwest Conference was no more.

With the addition of South Carolina, the SEC had twelve teams, allowing Kramer to split the conference into two divisions. That move, in turn, gave rise to a groundbreaking revenue generator: the first-ever conference football championship game. While critics called the game a gimmick, Steve Spurrier's Florida Gators lost to Gene Stalling's Alabama team in a classic. Kramer soon moved the game to the Georgia Dome in Atlanta, generating $40 million in its first five years and spawning imitations around the country.

The growing power of the conferences doomed the CFA. Once it opened the door to a free market, it ceased to be useful, a victim of its own success. In 1994, the SEC signed a five-year, $85 million contract with CBS, doubling the amount of television money it had been receiving from the CFA. The ACC, Big East, and Big 12 followed the Big Ten and SEC and signed their own five-year deals, in the $50 million range, with CBS, ABC, and

ESPN. The CFA voted itself out of existence during the summer of 1996. Few sports fans even noticed.

By the mid-1990s, ESPN's dominance as a sports network was unquestioned. Acquired by Disney in 1996, it had vastly increased resources—and it could also combine forces with ABC, which Disney also now owned. With its insatiable need for "product," ESPN signed up smaller conferences like the Mid-American and Conference USA to help fill weeknight time slots. Those schools, desperate for the publicity, were more than happy to sign on—and to play games midweek, even late at night. But ESPN also had to find new ways to market college football to earn a return on its investment. In 1989, *SportsCenter* covered a young high school prospect's college commitment decision in Gainesville, Florida. The running back, future NFL Hall of Famer Emmitt Smith, held a press conference to announce he would attend Florida. Today, "national signing day" is a staple of the network's programming.

Beginning in 1993, ESPN began broadcasting its flagship Saturday morning pregame show, *College GameDay*, live from the site of one of the best games around the country each week—games that were likely as not on ABC or ESPN itself. Hosts Chris Fowler, Lee Corso, and Kirk Herbstreit would become household names, and the excitement generated by their live shows helped propel college football into a new stratosphere.

Corporate sponsors were moving into college football too. Jim Host, who had negotiated the first corporate sponsorship deal with the NCAA, was expanding his marketing business into schools and conferences. One of his earliest clients was the University of Texas, where his firm, Host Communications, had begun a radio network, selling ads for stadium programs, and eventually did deals for stadium signage and direct sponsorship. One day he walked into Texas athletic director DeLoss Dodds's office to find the AD on the phone trying to negotiate a contract with a Coca-Cola distributor. "What we need to do is make them the official soft drink of the Texas Longhorns," Host recalls telling him.

When Kramer introduced the SEC championship game, Host arranged for Golden Flake potato chips to sponsor it. He also helped Dr Pepper slap its name on the Red River Rivalry, the annual showdown between Texas and Oklahoma. And he helped funnel more money to coaches, through sponsors of their radio shows and other appearances. When Rick Pitino was hired as Kentucky's basketball coach in 1989, his salary was announced at around $150,000; Host paid him an additional several hundred thousand dollars each year.

There was some resistance, Host remembers, though it never lasted. Once, he visited a school—which he won't name—that didn't have any ads on the scoreboard of its football stadium, but had businesses sponsoring other campus buildings. Why not the scoreboard? he asked. "We just don't want to be commercial," came the reply. Today, Host says, the scoreboard has plenty of ads. Another time, at an NCAA basketball committee meeting, Tom Butters, the athletic director at Duke who hired Mike Krzyzewski, wondered what the NCAA tournament would be like without corporate sponsors. Host gently reminded him that that would mean getting get rid of all TV commercials too. "They wanted the money, but they didn't want to be seen as commercial," Host says.

Others were joining Host in the marketing and licensing business, like the Collegiate Licensing Company, which was founded by former Alabama football player Bill Battle in 1981. Battle convinced university clients to license the school's logo on nonsports products like fountain pens. Alabama eventually even had a Crimson Tide line of caskets.

In 1985, the Fiesta Bowl sold its naming rights to Sunkist, starting a trend that soon gave us the Sea World Holiday Bowl, Mazda Gator Bowl, and USF&G Sugar Bowl, named after a Baltimore insurance company. It was not long before bowls were outright named for companies, like the Blockbuster Bowl, which debuted in 1990.

As the money flowed through college sports, the beneficiaries were coaches and, as Delany likes to note, women's sports. Scholarship money for women and sports offered by schools increased dramatically—though it still represented a tremendous wealth transfer from the football and men's basketball athletes generating the money to others on campus. By the mid-1990s, two coaches cracked the million-dollar salary mark: Florida State's Bobby Bowden and Florida's Steve Spurrier. Spurrier signed his deal after the Tampa Bay Buccaneers tried to lure him to the NFL. "Some folks say it's too much money," Florida athletic director Jeremy Foley said, adding, "Our competition for his service is the next level, professional football. We recognize that. Therefore, he is compensated fairly."

In 1994, Cedric Dempsey became executive director of the NCAA. An athletic director at the University of the Pacific, San Diego State, Houston, and Arizona for nearly three decades, he had gained over his career an appreciation for the financial struggles of the smaller Division I schools, the ones that stood outside the power conferences (as they were coming to be called). They couldn't rely on the same TV money to fund their sports, and had to spend beyond their means to keep pace. Searching for ways to help such schools now that he was in charge of the NCAA, Dempsey concluded that they could get a boost from a college football playoff—a playoff that would preempt the bowl system, but also put the NCAA in charge of postseason football just as it was for basketball with its highly successful March Madness tournament. Nike founder Phil Knight had previously pushed the NCAA to adopt a playoff, and the CFA had discussed plans too, though neither proposal gained much traction. Dempsey figured that with all the money flowing in from the basketball tournament—the NCAA's first $1 billion March Madness contract with CBS kicked in in 1991—there was little reason football couldn't copy it. Before he was officially installed in the job, he flew to California with Jernstedt for a meeting with UCLA chancellor Charles Young. Over a round of golf at Sherwood Country Club in Thousand Oaks, Dempsey gave Young the task of exploring a college football playoff.

Young enlisted his right-hand man, John Sandbrook, and soon a special committee was formed. In an NCAA press release dated December 7, 1993, NCAA president Joseph Crowley declared, "There are some very strongly held views held about a college football playoff. The research group will help us separate fact from fiction." In early 1994, the group held meetings with television executives from the major networks in New York, as well as several current players, including Derrick Brooks, a linebacker at Florida State. The special committee first convened in May 1994 at the Hyatt Grand Champions Resort in Indian Wells, California. It comprised a number of faculty members and athletic administrators, like Kentucky coach Bill Curry and Georgia athletic director Vince Dooley.

Young recalled that an initial straw poll in the room showed only three or four of the more than twenty committee members in favor of the playoff. But after a second set of June meetings in Kansas City and a presentation by Sandbrook that showed declining ratings for bowl games and indications that an eight-team playoff could be worth hundreds of millions of dollars in new revenue, the vote flipped. There were even discussions about sharing the increased money directly with players. "Playoff advocates find ammunition," read a headline in the *Kansas City Star*.

There is no question that as the number of bowl games increased, football postseason had devolved into a state of chaos, with few rules governing the bowl selection process. Some had agreements with conferences, such as the Rose Bowl, known as the "Granddaddy of Them All," which since 1947 had pitted the Pac-10 champion against the Big Ten champion, and was by far the most lucrative and highest-rated bowl game. But as the ACC and Big East gained stature, there was little to stop competing bowls from fighting to entice the country's top teams. As Dunnavant explains, in 1990, Virginia, an ACC team, began the season 7–0 and accepted a too early—and secret—bid to the Sugar Bowl in the middle of the season. Virginia then lost three of its last four games and was unranked by the time it played Tennessee on New Year's Day. ACC champion and undefeated Georgia Tech was stuck in the less prestigious Citrus Bowl. "The selection process was out of control," said Corrigan.

But chaotic as it may have been, the major conference commissioners like Delany and Kramer had no intention of allowing the NCCA to regain even the tiniest bit of control over football. What Dempsey wanted—a way to share more revenue with the "have nots"—was exactly what they opposed, since it would be money out of their conferences' pockets. Commissioners were also learning to turn the current bowl system into additional guaranteed revenue streams by pledging more of their teams to more bowl games. As usual, Kramer and Delany led the way. Beginning in 1992, the Big Ten and SEC each promised its runner-up to the Citrus Bowl. As more bowls entered the market, the conferences created more alliances and more paydays.

In response to the formation of the playoff committee, Delany sent a letter to Young. "While reasonable people can argue the financial merits of a playoff approach, our presidents believe the benefits of our relationship with the Pac-10 through the Rose Bowl are of paramount and continuing importance," he wrote. "Therefore, I think that it is fair to indicate the Big Ten plans to strenuously oppose any effort to initiate a playoff system."

Kramer, meanwhile, had set about putting together his own version of a football postseason. In 1992, he spearheaded what he called the Bowl Coalition. The SEC, Big Eight, ACC, Big East, Southwest Conference, and Notre Dame joined in an agreement with the Sugar, Orange, Fiesta, and Cotton Bowls to ensure that the top two teams outside of the Big Ten and Pac-10 would meet in a so-called championship game. The system worked when on New Year's Day 1993, number 2 Alabama defeated number 1 Miami in the Sugar Bowl to clinch the national championship.

Soon Kramer saw an opportunity for more cash, engineering a bidding war for the top matchups, ultimately won by the Orange, Sugar, and Fiesta Bowls for a hefty sum of more than $300 million over six years. The stunned Cotton Bowl was left to scrape for the Big 12's leftovers. "The commissioners realize that money is the only thing that matters in this process," Rick Catlett, the executive director of the Gator Bowl—which was shut out of the newly renamed Bowl Alliance—told Dunnavant.

In June 1994, Charles Young delivered his presentation on a football playoff to the NCAA's Presidents Commission, which included university presidents from Divisions I, II, and III. It didn't take him long to realize that he didn't have much support, even among the smaller schools that might benefit from such a system. The conference commissioners and several presidents had run a vocal campaign against the playoff, and the members of the Presidents Commission, fearing criticism over growing commercialism in college sports, were reluctant to support a playoff. One ACC president, Sandbrook recalls, railed against commercialism even though his athletic department had signed a multimillion-dollar apparel contract with Nike the year before.

Young was so upset he stormed out of the meeting before the vote was even taken. When it was tallied, further study of the football playoff, which was all Young was really asking for, was tabled by a vote of 19–9. But defeating the playoff did little to curb commercialism. Conference championship games were added, lengthening the season. Realignment meant more time spent away from school; as conferences expanded geographically, traveling to and from games took up more time. Weekday games became a staple of fall schedules too. All the vote did was keep the major conferences in charge of a system in which they reaped the financial rewards. "The arguments about commercialism turned out to be a little ironic," says Eamon Kelly, then the president of Tulane and a member of the commission.

Sandbrook believes the commissioners duped the presidents. "While we were going on with this ad hoc committee, there was this backroom secret dealings with the commissioners," he says. "Conference commissioners didn't want to lose the power and control of postseason football. They won, and they're still in charge."

Delany insists there was no political viability for the playoff at the time, noting that even Young's own conference, the Pac-10, opposed the playoff. "I wasn't thinking about control as much as I was thinking about the Rose Bowl," Delany says. "The NCAA wanted to get its nose under the tent because there was probably a lot of money there."

By 1997, the Big Ten had signed a record-setting deal with ESPN worth more than $500 million for ten years. And soon even the Big Ten's precious relationship with the Rose Bowl gave way to an even bigger TV payday. Kramer's Bowl Coalition, since renamed the Bowl Alliance, was proving successful. ABC, which had been broadcasting the Rose Bowl since 1989, began to grow concerned over the package that rival network CBS had with the Fiesta and Orange Bowls. Kramer met with ABC executives and conceived of a new plan: a championship game that rotated among the four top bowls, the Rose, Sugar, Orange, and Fiesta—all on ABC. Delany and the Big Ten presidents were promised the Rose Bowl would keep its beloved afternoon time slot on New Year's Day for the first three years, and they signed off. The Big Ten and Pac-10 were still earning $13 million each year from the Rose Bowl, more than the conferences in the Bowl Alliance, but ABC pledged $550 million for the first seven years of what would become known as the Bowl Championship Series.

Rose Bowl executives resisted the new postseason, but the sanctity of the game, which had been "paramount," in Delany's own words, just a few years earlier, wasn't so important anymore. Rose Bowl football committee chairman Harriman Cronk told Sandbrook that one of Delany's closest allies, Penn State president Graham Spanier, put the screws to him, delivering an ultimatum: if the Rose Bowl did not join the BCS, the Big Ten would no longer be sending its champion to Pasadena (Spanier recalls the conversation as a "cooperative discussion"). Cronk relented and the BCS was in place for the 1998 season. The six largest conferences—the ACC, Big East, Big Ten, Big 12, Pac-12, and SEC—had automatic bids to the BCS bowls, which was fine by TV because they included all of football's top teams. But the rest of college football was shut out, from the games and from the money.

By 2011, the big six conferences took home 83.4 percent of the $174.1 million the BCS bowls earned. "That's not fair or equitable," says Gene Bleymaier, athletic director at Boise State and then San Jose State. "The commissioners have taken control, excluding the rest of us."

Says Kramer, "You had a responsibility to your constituency, to your members, to do the best you possibly could for them." Asked about pushing college sports into a bigger and bigger business, he called it inevitable. "Was it all for the best? Probably not," he says. "But it was the role you played." Delany puts it this way: "I've never gone to a place that's not connected to the fiduciary well-being of the Big Ten."

Unlike Kramer, however, Delany has no reservations about what college sports has become—nor does he see the influx of money as a reason to tinker with the amateur status of the athletes themselves. "Just because television revenue is $100 million and not $30 million, it doesn't change what is right or wrong with the value of a scholarship," he says, pointing to the millions of dollars in scholarship money the conference doles out and the thousands of athletes who earn degrees. "When I got here, sports were white and male. Look at the opportunities we've created for women! I'm not ashamed of anything I've done. The access to higher education is more important than ever. I know some people don't view it as a fair deal, but I personally feel like it is a fair deal."

In Delany's eyes, colleges have lost the battle against cost containment, and they should stop worrying about it. He remembers how the NCAA once tried to limit assistant coaches' salaries, but was sued for an antitrust violation. "It cost us a $55 million settlement," he says. Instead, he believes that since TV networks are willing to offer the money, his conference may as well have the most. "I'd rather have the problem of too much money than too little," he says.

In 1999, after the NCAA signed a new $6 billion, eleven-year contract with CBS for the basketball tournament, Cedric Dempsey broached the idea of giving some of the windfall directly to athletes to better reflect the full cost of attendance beyond just what the athletic scholarship covered. Dempsey says that his discussions, which were informal, took place with several college presidents and conference commissioners. Their response was cold: they weren't interested. (Delany insists that Dempsey never spoke with him.)

"I thought we should have given some of the money straight to the student-athletes," Dempsey says. "I couldn't get any traction."

# Ahab and the Booster

**IN MAY 1998, ROY KRAMER, THE COMMISSIONER OF THE SEC, RECEIVED** a fax from Tennessee football coach Phil Fulmer. "For your eyes only!!!" the cover page read. The subject of Fulmer's missive—one of several over a span of months—was a wealthy Memphis-based Alabama booster named Logan Young, a truly infamous character in SEC country who was said to have been close to the late, great Alabama coach Bear Bryant. As the story went, the two great loves of Young's life were liquor and Alabama football.

Fulmer had been fixated on Young for years, and detailed for Kramer a list of Memphis-area prospects he claimed Young had lured to Alabama by giving gifts to them or their high school coaches, usually either money or cars. He told Kramer that Tommy Tuberville, another SEC coach who was then coaching Ole Miss, was also fed up with Young. "This is not sour grapes . . . this guy is making a mockery of recruiting," Fulmer wrote to Kramer. "I can't operate my program with that jerk buying players from under our nose!"

Kramer, who was well aware of Young, forwarded the memos to Bill Sievers, a former FBI officer who did work for the SEC, dispatching him to meet with a handful of Tennessee boosters in Memphis about Young's tactics. Sievers also checked in with the FBI to see if they'd be interested in making a case against Young.

During the summer of 1999, Fulmer and Kramer caught a big break when Tennessee began recruiting a mountain of a defensive lineman named Albert

Means, out of Trezevant High School in Memphis. A *Parade* All-American, Means stood six foot five, weighed 310 pounds, and could bench press 400 pounds. Everyone in the SEC wanted him.

Tennessee assistant coach Pat Washington reported to Sievers that he had had a recruiting meeting with Means's coach, Lynn Lang. In exchange for signing Means, Lang asked to be paid $50,000; he later upped the ask to $80,000 thanks to a bid from a competitor. Was it Logan Young?

Sievers suggested to Kramer that Washington return to Trezevant and wear a wire. He thought catching Lang in the act would deter high school coaches from cashing in on their players. Kramer nixed the idea. And despite the warnings that his recruitment was tainted and trouble was looming for young Albert Means, no one thought to intervene on his behalf. Means was from a poor family of six children. His mother, Lisa, worked at a daycare center, and Lang had become a surrogate father—a man he trusted. Lang drove Means around, bought him underwear when he needed it, and let him sleep over when things were rough at home. "Albert doesn't have a father, so I'm Daddy," Lang once said.

But instead of busting Lang for soliciting a bounty, the bigger priority appears to have been Young, who Fulmer later learned was indeed in cahoots with Lang. Kramer insists today that he didn't intend to use Means as bait. Still, it remains difficult to see the case any other way. "It was like Ahab and the white whale," Alabama's former NCAA faculty rep, Gene Marsh, says. "Anything to get Logan Young."

Indeed, everyone, it seemed, was using Means: Young wanted him to play football at Alabama; Lang wanted cash; and Alabama's rivals wanted to use him to take out a rogue booster.

Means eventually signed with Alabama. Lang, meanwhile, began driving around town in a new truck. Rumors flew all over Memphis. The *Memphis Commercial Appeal* ran its first bombshell story in early 2001, claiming Young had paid Lang $200,000 to deliver Means to Tuscaloosa. The salacious story quickly gained national notoriety: Dan Rather covered it on the *CBS Evening News*; Lang was called a slave trader; the U.S. Attorney's Office began investigating.

Young was charged with—and ultimately convicted of—bribing a public official; he is believed to be the only man to be prosecuted and convicted for being a college booster. Lang testified during Young's 2005 trial that he received $150,000 from Young, routinely collecting the money in $9,000 installments, dispensed in $100 bills. Lang also testified that he was promised, and sometimes given, any number of things by other schools: Memphis coach Rip Scherer promised to get his wife into Memphis's law school and pay her tuition (Scherer denied it on the stand); he got $6,000 from a Kentucky booster when he took Means to Lexington for a campus visit (Kentucky was placed on three years' probation).

Lang also told NCAA and federal investigators that Danny Nutt, an assistant coach at Arkansas, took him to a strip club and he was later offered a coaching job with the Razorbacks; a Georgia assistant coach introduced him to a booster who met him at an Applebee's and told him he'd work on a payment between $50,000 and $75,000. (Means testified that Lang also arranged for his ACT to be taken by another student.)

Lang's plea deal included an agreement to cooperate with the NCAA's investigation of Alabama, and an NCAA enforcement staffer actually questioned Lang right alongside the FBI and the Tennessee Bureau of Investigation. This drove Young's lawyers crazy. They were furious that the NCAA could be so involved in a federal investigation. "It just showed the NCAA was driving the suit from the beginning," says Keltie Hays, one of Young's attorneys.

FBI agent Suzanne Nash, who worked the case, was disgusted by the entire sordid affair. "These schools would take the seniors on their recruiting trips out drinking," she says. "They would get prostitutes for them. It was sickening."

Kramer believes the episode helped clean up recruiting. "The consequences were very significant," he says. "In the long term, it probably did a lot to change the landscape in a lot of different ways that were good for the process."

Young's story had a macabre end. A federal judge had sentenced him to six months in prison, but allowed him to remain free on bond while he pursued his appeal. At home one day, Young fell down a flight of stairs and died from head trauma. Lang claimed that Lisa Means, Albert's mother, was in on the deal the whole time and that he gave her thousands of dollars during Albert's last years of high school. To this day, he bemoans the fact that he became the fall guy. Years after the trial, Lang resurfaced in Port Gibson, Mississippi, a few hours from Memphis, where, as of the time of this book's publication, he is the high school athletic director. On the wall of his office hangs a sign that reads "No Excuses."

Means, meanwhile, played only a single season at Alabama before his career was derailed by the scandal. He transferred to Memphis, but because he was out of shape and struggling academically, he had to sit out a season. By his senior season, he was named to Conference USA's all-conference second team, but he was not drafted. Asked once whether he got any money from Lang, Means responded, "Is a tomato a fruit or a vegetable? I don't know." (He has since said he knew nothing of the scheme.) Means managed to salvage his life, however; he teaches phys ed and coaches high school football in the Memphis area.

"It's sad what happened to him," Kramer says of Means. "He didn't deserve to get caught up in all that."

# CHAPTER 6

# THE BRANDING OF MYLES BRAND

By the turn of the new millennium, Cedric Dempsey's days as the executive director of the NCAA were numbered; the only person who didn't seem to realize it was him. Yes, he had negotiated that eye-popping new television contract for the March Madness tournament—and he'd also had the wit to trademark the phrase, so that the NCAA could license its use to sponsors while keeping it away from anybody who didn't pay for the privilege. By most other measures, however, his tenure was rocky. In 1997, he'd had to weather a brutal weeklong investigative series by the NCAA's hometown paper, the *Kansas City Star*. For days, it ran headlines like these: "Tradition of perks envelops NCAA"; "NCAA's tax-exempt jet carries foursome to Georgia for golf"; and "Athletes endangered by dearth of trainers." (Not long after the series ran, the NCAA announced that it would move its headquarters to Indianapolis.) A bureaucrat by temperament, Dempsey was unable to push back against the powerful commissioners, which infuriated all the other conferences and schools. And on practically a monthly basis, it seemed, the NCAA found itself announcing that it was levying sanctions at one university or another for major violations of its rules: Grambling State University in July 1997; UCLA in April 1998; Texas Tech, August 1998; University of Louisville, September 1998. And so on. The worst of these scandals, which took the NCAA completely by surprise, came in 1999 when, on the eve of that year's March Madness tournament, the *St. Paul Pioneer Press* reported that an academic adviser at the University of Minnesota had written some four hundred term papers, homework assignments, and take-home exams for eighteen Golden Gopher basketball players between 1993 and 1998. Minnesota was a Big Ten school, and the basketball coach, a former professional basketball player named Clem Haskins, was considered one of the "good guys" with "the right values." Although Haskins at first denied knowing what the adviser had done, it later emerged that he had paid her $3,000 for her ghostwriting efforts. And although the NCAA came down hard on the basketball program—and Haskins was essentially banned from college coaching—it was a huge black eye for the college sports establishment.

Perhaps the biggest strike against Dempsey, though, was something more mundane: he had come out of the ranks of athletic directors. From the time of Walter Byers, athletic directors had been the NCAA's primary constituents. They were the ones consulted on rules changes and television negotiations, and they cast the votes at NCAA conventions. When Byers retired, he was replaced by Dick Schultz, the former athletic director at the University of Virginia. But his tenure as executive director ended in disgrace in 1994 when the enforcement staff undertook an investigation into improper loans to athletes at Virginia that Schultz had almost surely known about. Although he was "cleared" by the investigators, he was quietly forced to resign. He was later named head of the United States Olympic Committee.

Even before Dempsey took office, however, the importance of athletic directors in the NCAA's governance structure had been slowly diminishing. In their place, university presidents began to assert control. If there's one moment you could point to that sparked this change, it probably came in May 1989, when Dexter Manley, the former defensive end at Oklahoma State and one of the biggest stars of the Washington Redskins, the capital's beloved hometown team, testified before a congressional committee that he had gotten through college without being able to read beyond the second-grade level. With a dozen television cameras pointed at him, Manley was reduced to tears as he tried, haltingly, to read his prepared statement. Finally, after a painful silence, he tossed aside his statement and spoke emotionally to the committee about his learning disability, and how he had been able to cover up his problem for so long. "I think that testimony embarrassed higher education," says Wally Renfro, the longtime NCAA executive. "The university presidents were just embarrassed by what they had wrought."

It wasn't just that one incident, of course. Graduation rates for big-time college athletes were abysmal; among a hundred major sports schools, thirty-five had graduation rates under 20 percent for their basketball players. A survey taken in the late 1980s suggested that a third of professional football players had accepted "illicit" payments while in college. Even as more fans than ever were watching televised college football and basketball—thanks to those rich new contracts being negotiated by the conferences—there was a gnawing sense that money was overtaking college sports, and that the academy was being corrupted as a result. As *Time* magazine put it in a 1989 cover story, "an obsession with winning and moneymaking . . . is perverting the noblest ideals of both sports and education in America." The sham courses athletes like Dexter Manley took to remain eligible, *Time* continued, amounted to "an educational travesty—a farce that devalues every degree and denigrates the mission of higher education." It was one of those times—not the first, and hardly the last— when the calls for reform reached a kind of public crescendo and morphed into conventional wisdom. *Something had to be done.*

Galvanized by the calls for reform, William Friday, the recently retired president of the University of North Carolina system, and a true believer in the old amateur ideal—went to the Knight Foundation, which was led by his friend Creed Black. Black agreed to fund a new group, called the Knight Commission on Intercollegiate Athletics, which Friday would cochair with one of the best-known and most respected names in both higher education and college sports: Father Theodore Hesburgh of Notre Dame. Its goal was to come up with recommendations for reforming college athletics, and in doing so reaffirm the primacy of academics, while getting commercialism under control so that athletic departments would no longer be the tail wagging the dog.

In March 1991, having spent eighteen months on its labors, the commission issued its first report. It was titled "Keeping Faith with the Student Athlete: A New Model for Intercollegiate Athletics." Although it listed dozens of recommendations, they all really boiled down to one thing:

university presidents should grab control of college sports. Presidents should ensure that athletic departments—and athletic directors—reported directly to them. They should call the shots at the NCAA. They should control those greedy conferences and conference commissioners. The Knight Commission went so far as to insist that presidents should even control "their institution's involvement with commercial television." Presumably that would mean an end to 11:30 p.m. games on Wednesday nights.

Almost a decade earlier, Walter Byers had established something he called the Presidents Commission, made up of, yes, university presidents. Up until then, the NCAA's management council—comprised mostly of athletic directors—had made most major decisions, in consultation with NCAA officials and the executive committee, on matters that did not require a membership vote during the annual convention. The members of the management council fully expected the Presidents Commission to be little more than a rubber stamp. "They were used to patting the presidents on the head and saying, 'Don't worry—we'll take care of it,'" says Renfro.

Instead, the presidents began making their own decisions, often in opposition to the management council. And in 1997—six years after the initial Knight Commission report, the blink of an eye in NCAA time—the association undertook a complete restructuring of its management structure. At the top was a new kind of executive committee, composed almost entirely of university presidents. Then each division, I, II, and III, had its own management structure that was again led by university presidents. (For Division I, it was called a board of directors; for divisions II and III, they were called presidents councils.) Under the board and the presidents councils was a management council, made up of athletic administrators and faculty athletic representatives. There was no doubt any more about who was supposed to be calling the shots—and that was also how it was portrayed in the press. "These changes were recognized as a shift from an emphasis on business interests to academic interests," wrote Joel G. Maxcy, a Drexel University associate professor who focused on sports economics. (He added that the true significance of the changes was not that university presidents were supposedly in charge, but that the major Division I football conferences "are mandated a majority on legislative issues.")

Dempsey, seeing which way the wind was blowing, helped bring about the restructuring. (He became an ex officio member of the executive committee.) But over time, the presidents came to see Dempsey as more hindrance than help. Although the NCAA stiffened its academic requirements for athletes under his watch, even reaching into high schools and dictating which courses were acceptable, the presidents always had the feeling he had to be pushed in that direction. They didn't think he was the kind of leader the NCAA needed. Most of all, he wasn't one of them—the fraternity of university presidents. In 2002, they got Dempsey to resign, and replaced him early the following year with a favorite son, a university president who had made a name for himself by firing perhaps the most famous coach in all of college basketball, and a man who said all the right things about the need to subsume athletics to a university's academic mission. His name was Myles Brand.

Little did they realize that they had just hired the fox to guard the henhouse.

And whom had Myles Brand fired? None other than Bobby Knight, the legendary basketball coach at Indiana University, revered by Hoosier fans and sports announcers, who over the course of nearly three decades at Indiana had won three national titles and become the most dominant figure on the Indiana campus—with far more clout than any mere university president. For the eight years before he became NCAA president (the title was changed from executive director after the 1997 restructuring), Brand was Indiana's president. Firing Knight had made him a hero to all those people who felt that college sports—and coaches like Knight—had gotten out of control. Nonetheless, people who knew Brand at Indiana were a little taken aback both that he was offered the NCAA job and that he took it. The reason was that Brand had never been much of a sports fan. "I was always surprised by how little Myles knew about sports," says the author Murray Sperber, who had been a professor at Indiana—and Knight's most public critic—and who used to have coffee with Brand from time to time.

Brand, who had grown up in Brooklyn and Long Island, was the first person from his family to graduate from college. Though he began as an engineering major at Rensselaer Polytechnic Institute, he "made the logical transition" to philosophy, as he would later joke, getting his doctorate from the University of Rochester. Although he did some important work in philosophy early in his career, he soon discovered that he had an aptitude for administration and fund-raising. Thus began his climb up the greasy pole of academia, as he hopped from the University of Arizona, where he went from head of the philosophy department to coordinating dean of the College of Arts and Sciences, to Ohio State, where he was the provost, to the University of Oregon, where he was the president and faced down the most severe financial crisis in that school's history.

By the time Brand arrived in Bloomington, Indiana, in 1994, Bobby Knight was already a legend, widely viewed as one of the greatest coaches in college basketball history, while staying on the right side of the NCAA rulebook and ensuring that his players graduated. (Sperber discovered that this latter claim was exaggerated.) Indiana legislators, who set the state budget for the university system, loved Knight, which made him all the more untouchable. But outside of Indiana he was a highly polarizing figure, a rude, volatile, mean-spirited man who was almost never called to account. In 1979, while coaching the American team in the Pan American Games in Puerto Rico, Knight was accused of assaulting a police officer; the university got the case delayed just long enough to spirit Knight out of San Juan, where he was convicted in absentia. In 1985, during a close game against Purdue, Knight became so incensed at a bad call that he picked up a chair and flung it clear across the court. The following year saw the publication of *Season on the Brink,* by the sportswriter John Feinstein, who spent the 1985 season with Knight and the Hoosiers and reported what he saw, warts and all. He portrayed Knight as a foulmouthed bully who nonetheless cared deeply about his players. A few years after that, Connie Chung, then a correspondent for NBC News, asked Knight during an interview how he handled stress. He replied, "I think if rape is inevitable, relax and enjoy it." His remark drew a stern comment from then Indiana University president Thomas Ehrlich, which so annoyed Knight that he spent a week publicly deliberating whether to take the coaching job at the University of New Mexico. The threat elicited pleas from newspapers, the governor, and finally even Ehrlich to stay, and he did. On a regular basis, Knight would threaten university employees who crossed him, scream obscenities at his players—he once kicked his own son during a game—and hang up on his supposed superiors. Clarence Doninger, who was Indiana's athletic director in the 1990s, and who was estranged from his basketball coach, says that it was impossible to control Knight—the best you could hope to do was "contain him."

Brand's initial strategy for dealing with Knight was to befriend him. Knight quickly learned to take advantage of the situation, going directly to Brand whenever he wanted something—raises for his staff, for instance—thus undercutting Doninger. Although there were the usual Bobby Knight dustups over the next few years, which Brand largely ignored, a true crisis emerged in 2000, when a former player named Neil Reed claimed that Knight had choked him during a practice in 1997. Knight denied the charge, but a few months later CNN aired a short videotape showing Knight walking angrily toward Reed, grasping him by the neck, and pushing him backward by the throat as he berated the player. Brand had already seen the video; it had been sent to the university anonymously. The initial view among the school's trustees and administrators was that this was the final straw—Knight had to go. Indeed, the trustees took a preliminary vote to fire him. But after a late-night meeting with Knight and his wife, during which Knight pleaded for his job, Brand decided that he would let his famous coach stay—so long as he agreed to a "zero tolerance policy." Knight agreed to change his behavior, and Brand sold the deal to the trustees. "I felt he was sincere and contrite about what had happened," said another Indiana administrator who attended that meeting.

That all transpired between March and May of 2000. Just four months later, an Indiana freshman told the campus police that Knight had grabbed him by the arm and gotten into a shouting match. The incident itself was ambiguous, and it is quite possible that Knight could have survived it, notwithstanding the zero tolerance policy. Brand called Knight, told him that he was awaiting a report from the campus police, and that Knight needed to be available to talk to him once he saw the report. Knight responded that he had made a commitment to go fishing in Canada the next morning.

"Coach," said Brand, "you need to be available."

"I'm going on a fishing trip," replied Knight. They went back and forth like this for a few minutes. In exasperation, Brand finally said, "You're giving me no choice. I'm going to have to fire you."

One last time, Knight told Brand that he would be in Canada fishing.

And that's what Brand did—he fired his famous coach—though it wasn't exactly the act of courage that it was portrayed as. Doninger, for one, was amazed at the press Brand got in the aftermath of the firing. "I kept reading in the papers that Myles had stood up to Bob Knight," he recalls. "In fact, Myles created this atmosphere and it turned on him. Myles was *forced* to stand up to Knight. He had no choice in the matter." (For his part, Sperber received death threats on his answering machine after the firing because of his history of publicly criticizing Knight.)

Not long afterward, Brand came to Doninger's office to discuss the various issues that were then swirling around college sports. He explained that he had been invited to make a speech about college sports at the National Press Club in Washington, D.C.—a speech that was bound to be well covered by the press, given the notoriety of the Knight firing. Brand needed to be briefed on the issues. "Suddenly he was the expert," says Doninger dourly. "And he parlayed that image into the NCAA job."

Brand spoke to the Press Club on January 23, 2001, four months after firing Knight. It was a luncheon speech, billed as an exploration of "the relationship between academics and athletics." The large dining room was packed with reporters and other Press Club members. Both NPR and C-SPAN recorded the speech, and other news outlets gave it significant play the next day. In introducing Brand, Dick Ryan, the Washington correspondent for the *Detroit News*, compared his firing of Knight to Harry Truman's firing of Douglas MacArthur. (Brand rolled his eyes at that remark.) Then Brand took the podium, and over the next half hour he made a speech that exactly parroted the concerns about college sports that were being voiced by all the modern critics—while also channeling the ideas of the Knight Commission. It was impossible to listen to that speech and not conclude that Brand was a dedicated reformer himself.

Brand began by contrasting two press conferences—the one in which he announced Knight's firing, which was overflowing with reporters and cameras and generated news stories for months, and a more recent press conference where he announced the largest private donation in Indiana University's history: $105 million from the Lilly Endowment to be used to start the Indiana Genomics Initiative. That, he said, had created a one-day story and was attended by six reporters. Clearly, priorities were askew.

Brand then complained about the athletic arms race, with coaches making millions of dollars and "Division I athletic budgets of up to thirty, forty, and fifty million dollars and more." He said that college sports had become "an entertainment industry" that had its own value system, which was "distorting the role and purpose of intercollegiate athletics." Indeed, he said, excessive commercialism was threatening "the essential academic mission." He decried the low graduation rate of basketball and football players at the Division I level. Athletic success, he said, was leading too many universities away from "our real purpose," and he labeled the reform he had in mind as "academics first." He called on his fellow presidents to make "a fundamental commitment to making the mission, the academic mission and integrity of the university the absolute first priority."

Brand's reform agenda began with presidential control over athletics. But he didn't stop there. He said that the NFL and NBA should have development leagues for players who didn't want to go to college. And he offered a list of reforms to curtail the growing commercialism: limit breaks for television commercials, thus making college sports less attractive to advertisers; limit stadium advertising; even ban the logos—like the Nike swoosh—worn by players and coaches alike; and so on.

"Would the consequence be a reduced revenue stream?" he asked as he concluded his remarks. "Yes," he said. "Is that good? Yes."

Thus it was that when the NCAA's board of directors—made up of Brand's fellow university presidents—began thinking about replacing Dempsey, Brand was an obvious candidate. Although some eleven candidates were interviewed, Brand was the odds-on favorite once he made it clear he wanted the job. After all, he had laid out his agenda—which aligned with the presidents' agenda—at the National Press Club.

Hadn't he?

# "The Whole Thing Is Ridiculous"

**AS MARK EMMERT PREPARED TO BECOME THE NEW NCAA PRESIDENT IN** the summer and fall of 2010, he received a series of brief memos from NCAA executives outlining the association's various departments and the issues facing each one. One such department is called the "Eligibility Center"—formerly known as the NCAA Clearinghouse—which wields surprising, and troubling, power over high school academics. Essentially, from the moment a potential college athlete enters high school as a freshman, he or she must take a total of sixteen core courses to be eligible to play right away in college. What's more, the Eligibility Center has taken it upon itself to approve, at every single high school in America, which courses count toward NCAA credit—and which don't.

It's easy enough to understand why high school academics would be a concern to the NCAA. "They're trying to guard against athletic diploma mills," said one high school guidance counselor who asked for anonymity because she regularly butts heads with the Eligibility Center. As the NCAA put it in one of those Emmert briefing documents, "The Eligibility Center is on the front line of academic reform, and seeks to ensure that the individuals who are certified are those who meet the spirit, intent and legislated parameters of the rules to ensure academic preparedness as the first element of academic reform."

If only.

In fact, high school athletes who breeze through underperforming urban schools—or are given a pass by teachers because of their athletic prowess—

generally have smooth sailing in getting their academic credentials approved by the Eligibility Center. But the prep school student, say, who wants to take interesting or unusual courses while in high school—he's in a heap of trouble. If you look at the curriculum at virtually any prep school, you'll see that some courses are "NCAA-approved" and others are not. For instance, at highbrow Deerfield Academy in Deerfield, Massachusetts, "Classic and Contemporary Literature" is NCAA-approved but "The Scholar's Craft" is not. "Topics in Western Civilization" is approved, but AP art history is not. "Advanced Math Tutorial" is approved; "Independent Study in Math" is not. One guidance counselor recalled that a prep school athlete took a course called "Principles of Chemistry." The NCAA disallowed it, believing that the word "principles" suggested it was not a college preparatory course. It took weeks to convince the Eligibility Center that it was.

And then there's the problem of students who repeat a grade. The Eligibility Center insists that ten of a high school athlete's core courses must be taken in his or her first three academic years. So if a student repeats a grade—which of course means repeating many of the same classes—that means that the student only has two years to take those ten core courses, a near impossibility. English 9 taken once as a freshman will count as a core course. But English 9 taken twice—the second time a repeat of the first—will count for zero courses, according to the impenetrable logic of the NCAA.

The way guidance counselors try to get around this is by making sure that the student takes English classes with different titles each year—that way the NCAA will count them, even if they are fundamentally the same class. The most likely repeaters are freshmen who had trouble at one school and are moving to a new school—"the fourteen-year-old boy not quite ready to be in high school," according to that guidance counselor. They are also the most likely to be repeating for academic, not athletic, reasons. Yet they are the most severely harmed by the Eligibility Center's rules. But an eleventh grader who repeats—which is almost always done for athletic reasons—will not have to worry about the Eligibility Center, because he will have completed most of his core courses. Another problem is that high schools are not allowed to file a formal appeal with the NCAA, since they are not NCAA members. Only colleges can do that. And since few coaches want to go through the hassle of appealing to get a player eligible, it means that that player is less likely to be recruited.

"The whole thing is ridiculous," said the guidance counselor. "Nobody is trying to pull the wool over the NCAA's eyes. Our graduation requirements should be enough."

While working on this book, we came across another bizarre example of the Eligibility Center at work. Sometimes it rules players academically ineligible, based on their high school transcript, even after they've spent several years in college. One example was Mario Austin, who played basketball for Mississippi State from 2000 to 2003. After completing a stellar sophomore season, the six-foot-nine forward opted to stay in school one more year rather than making the leap to the NBA. "I want to help my coaches and teammates compete for a national championship here at Mississippi State," he said. The Bulldogs earned a number 12 ranking in the preseason polls.

At the time, the NCAA was investigating Mississippi State football. For reasons that remain unclear, an investigator turned his attention to Austin's high school transcript, even though he had been cleared to play two years earlier. Since Austin arrived at Mississippi State, he had passed his classes and had fulfilled all NCAA and SEC eligibility requirements. No matter.

After Austin was mysteriously absent from the team's first exhibition game that fall, the Subcommittee on Initial Eligibility announced it had erred in clearing him two seasons earlier. Mississippi State held him out of action while he hired a lawyer to plead his case in Indianapolis.

According to Austin's lawyer, Don Jackson, the charge was not academic fraud or grade changes, but something far less sinister. "The NCAA believed the names of a couple of classes had been changed on his high school transcript," Jackson explained—which seems quite likely given the way the Eligibility Center operates. Austin missed the first six games of the season before the NCAA reversed course and Mississippi State reinstated him.

# CHAPTER 7

# THE COLLEGIATE MODEL

"What do you want to accomplish?" Wally Renfro recalls asking Myles Brand during one of their first meetings after Brand became NCAA president in January 2003. "I want to change the way people talk about intercollegiate athletics," Brand replied, according to Renfro. As it turns out, that was Renfro's agenda as well.

Renfro had been the NCAA's longtime head of public relations. He had expected to leave after Brand arrived, but instead the new president asked him to stay on and become a kind of minister without portfolio. In time, Renfro and Brand became philosophical soul mates, intellectual partners as they attempted together to redefine—or rather, reframe—college sports. An unwavering believer that the NCAA was a force for good and that amateur college athletics enriched university life, Renfro also saw nothing wrong with the rise of commercialism. Indeed, to him it made perfect sense. As college sports grew in appeal, it was only natural that revenues would grow, and corporations, wanting to show that they shared the NCAA's "values," would want to associate with college sports. He also held to the NCAA's dogma that amateurism was the sine qua non of college sports—not only because the athletes were students (though why this should prevent them from being paid was never really explained), but also because, just as Justice Stevens had expressed in the *Regents* dicta, amateurism is what sets college sports apart from the professional ranks. Purely as a function of entertainment, so this view went, amateurism was college sports' secret sauce. But how did one sell that to the critics and the reformers?

It is impossible to know now whether Brand truly meant what he said at the National Press Club, or whether he was simply serving up platitudes for public consumption that he never believed; he died of cancer in 2009, while still at the helm of the NCAA. Whatever the truth, what is evident from his time in office is that he walked into the job entirely uninterested in reducing commercialism or subsuming athletics to academics, no matter what he had said in Washington two years before. Rather, virtually all his reform efforts were fundamentally exercises in public relations. In this, he and his new special adviser were well suited.

Take, for instance, the graduation rates of college athletes, especially those who played football and men's basketball. Those rates, embarrassingly low at far too many schools, used the same equation that the federal government traditionally used to calculate the annual graduation rate of America's four-year universities: of the number of incoming freshmen, what percentage had graduated after six years? (In 2008, the graduation window expanded to eight years.)

How did Myles Brand fix this problem? Not by finding better ways to keep athletes on track for graduation. Rather, the NCAA simply changed the criteria, by eliminating from the equation all the athletes who transferred or dropped out of college—whether to turn professional or for any other reason—while still students in good academic standing. Not surprisingly, this adjusted number instantly caused the graduation rate of athletes to rise by a third; over the years, it would overstate the rates by between 12 and 25 percent annually. Indeed, with the use of this new "Graduation Success Rate," or GSR, as the NCAA called it, football and basketball players now appeared to graduate at a rate *higher* than the average college student. The NCAA had come up with its new measure, Brand said in his "state of the association" speech at his second NCAA convention, because "the federally mandated rate is an inaccurate graduation measure." And according to a paper published in the *Journal of Intercollegiate Sport*, Brand regularly "highlighted the GSR as evidence of the newly-instituted reform agenda's success." The author of that paper, Richard M. Southall, an associate professor at the University of South Carolina and a longtime NCAA critic, would later begin publishing his own annual study (coauthored by several academic colleagues) showing that the true graduation for college athletes in the big-money sports was far below that of the student body. And this was especially true for African Americans playing in the biggest and most powerful conferences, like the ACC and the SEC.

Second, instead of insisting that academics be placed squarely ahead of athletics in a university's priorities, as he had vowed to do in 2001, Brand instead began promoting the idea that, as Renfro later put it, "intercollegiate athletics was embedded in the values of the university." Renfro continued, "Myles started talking about it differently: there is educational value for all who watch it. It models educational values and life characteristics that we all make part of our lives. We talk about teamwork, pursuit of excellence, discipline. These are things that athletics teach." Thanks to this new definition, universities no longer had to be concerned about whether athletics took precedence over academics—because they were both now part of the same happy family! And if some universities fell down from time to time, as evidenced by the never-ending athletic "scandals," well, Brand had at least set down an "aspirational template" that schools should reach for. Thus did he reframe the issue of academics versus athletics.

Above all else, there were the ever-rising levels of commercialism, the omnipresent issue during Brand's six-year tenure at the NCAA. Clearly, commercialism wasn't going away—and rare was the university president who even contemplated purposely reducing revenues. Instead, college stadiums had begun selling naming rights, which had rarely been done before. Popular jerseys weren't just sold in the bookstores; they could be found in the downtown department stores. The *New York Times* reported that by January 2004, some two dozen coaches made over $1 million. Video game makers began paying licensing fees to use the names of college teams in video games. Marketers like Jim Holt were signing up ever more university athletic departments. In 2005, ESPN created yet another new channel, ESPNU, that was completely devoted to college games that weren't big enough to be shown on ESPN or the major networks. The licensing rights to those games funneled yet more money to schools and the NCAA.

Market forces had made college sports a multibillion-dollar industry, and yet the athletes who played the games that made all this income possible still received nothing beyond their scholarship. How could this continue to be justified? Here came Brand's masterstroke. With Renfro's eager assistance, he coined a phrase in 2004 that was meant to square the circle: "the collegiate model," he called it—a term he contrasted to "the professional model." If the phrase "student-athlete" had been Walter Byers's great propagandistic coup, then "the collegiate model" was Brand's.

"The collegiate model" incorporated, first of all, Brand's notion that athletics had educational value, and that was its primary reason for existing on university campuses. But the collegiate model also not only condoned commercialization—it *insisted* upon it. After all, commercialism had been part of college sports practically since its beginnings. And so it had to remain if college sports was to continue to be financially healthy. Here is how Brand rationalized it in his 2006 "state of the association" speech: "Athletics, like the university as a whole, seeks to maximize revenue. In this respect, it has an obligation to conduct its revenue-generating activities in a productive and sound business-like manner. . . . That is, on the revenue side, the input side, athletics, like the university itself, must follow the best business practices."

But, he continued, on "the expenditure side, the output side as it were, athletics must follow its non-profit mission. Like the university as a whole, athletics must maximize the best experiences for the students, including maximizing the number of participation opportunities." Athletes, of course, were the students whose experiences were being maximized, and giving them a share of the spoils would disrupt the entire rationale. Renfro put it more bluntly in a speech he gave at the University of Santa Clara in 2012, shortly before he retired from the NCAA: "The principle of amateurism as applied to the student athlete should stand apart from the consideration of how commercial activity in intercollegiate athletics is governed." In short, this was the two men's philosophical justification for taking in every last dollar they could find, while the athletes had to play for "the feeling of pride in the competition itself," as Brand put it in another one of his early speeches.

The only problem—and it was not insignificant—was that there were long-established bylaws in the NCAA rulebook that forbade certain kinds of revenue generation. For instance, athletes were never supposed to be seen endorsing a product, even implicitly, and even if they were not being paid themselves. That was viewed as "exploitation," which the NCAA was supposed to be preventing. For this, Brand had no high-minded philosophical justification. Instead, he simply tried to change the rules.

In March 2003, just two months after Brand assumed office, the NCAA signed a new promotional deal with Pontiac. The new pact included a campaign called the "Pontiac Game Changing Performance," which allowed fans to go to the Pontiac website and vote for their favorite plays from the basketball and football seasons. Over the years, the promotion became a huge success, with fans voting for moments like Illinois's miraculous comeback to beat Arizona during the NCAA tournament (2005) or the fake field goal by LSU that helped the Tigers defeat South Carolina (2007). The winning plays earned their schools donations from Pontiac—$5,000 if they were the weekly favorite and $100,000 if they were the year's best. A video of the moments ran alongside a Pontiac logo and pictures of Pontiac cars.

To Renfro and Brand, agreeing to the deal was a no-brainer. "When I first saw it, I thought it was awesome," recalls Renfro. "I wasn't even remotely disturbed by the proximity of the video of student-athletes in the game to the logo of that sponsor. Who on earth wouldn't want a great American corporation to stand beside it and say, 'This is good.' Pontiac saw values in the NCAA and college sports that were right, good, and marketable. And they found a way to activate that relationship with this game-changing moment."

Except that it clearly violated the NCAA rule that strictly prohibited athletes from promoting commercial products. What's more, the universities receiving the checks from Pontiac were directly profiting from their players' individual performances. "This is a line they have never crossed before," Peter Rush, the lawyer for the Olympic skier and Colorado football player Jeremy Bloom, said in 2005. "The real question is what right do they have to use players' images to sell Pontiacs?"

With the national exposure—and criticism—that the contest received, university presidents, who were leery of so blatant a use of their athletes' images, complained to Brand. Brand not only declined to scale back the promotion, he called together the NCAA's Subcommittee on Agents and Amateurism and asked them to rewrite the name and image guidelines.

"It made sense to change the rule," says committee member Elizabeth Altmaier (known as Betsy), then a graduate professor of psychology at Iowa. After all, the Internet was changing the way media was consumed; plus, schools already sold bobbleheads of players and jerseys with players' names on the back. An artist in Tuscaloosa had started a business selling paintings of Alabama football players. Iowa ran a promotion with a credit card that rewarded customers with visits to Hawkeyes practices. There needed to be some sense of where the line should be drawn.

"What I didn't know," adds Altmaier, "is that by changes, they meant they wanted to make more money off students."

At a June 2004 meeting, both players and athletic department marketers gave presentations to the committee as it worked on new guidelines. Altmaier recalls the athletic director from Miami of Ohio discussed the marketing campaign for Heisman Trophy candidate Ben Roethlisberger the season before. Several athletes asked what would happen if they found their image next to a product they didn't want to be associated with. In response, the subcommittee proposed rule 2005-25 that actually tightened restrictions rather than loosened them, proposing that names and images never be used with any for-sale ventures. Schools could give away bobbleheads, but couldn't sell them. Jerseys with players' names on the backs were out too. This was not what Brand had in mind.

The proposal was sent to the board of directors, which countered with a proposed rule of its own, 2005-26, and was backed by Brand. The board suggested names and images were fair game as long as there was no direct endorsement of a product—a player could not be pictured holding a can of Coke, for example. And as long as 75 percent of a promotional website was related to a nonprofit, educational, or charitable purpose, amateurism was still protected. When the subcommittee reconvened in September 2005, it rejected the board's proposal. "I can remember thinking I'm in a little trouble," Altmaier says. "It was really unheard of to oppose the board."

When the group wouldn't budge, an NCAA staffer let slip that the association was already operating under the rule the subcommittee had rejected. That's when Altmaier first learned of the Pontiac promotion. (Not being much of a sports fan, she hadn't seen the ads before, she says, and neither had other members of the subcommittee.) Committee members pulled up the "Game Changing Performance" campaign on a computer.

"They had written the legislation to match the ad and we were furious," Altmaier says. "It was deception. We didn't understand how they could sign the Pontiac deal without our permission in the first place."

Altmaier asked the NCAA staffers if one of the reasons the committee was reexamining the name and image rules was because there was an ad running that wasn't in line with current rules. "Eventually they said yes," she recalls. "I was dumbfounded."

It sometimes seemed in those days that Betsy Altmaier and her fellow sub-committee members were the only ones willing to stand up to Brand and face the darker realities behind the collegiate model head-on. The daughter of a Shell chemical engineer from New Jersey, Altmaier, who was raised in an Evangelical Christian household, graduated from Wheaton College in suburban Chicago before getting a PhD in counseling psychology in 1977 from Ohio State. Her first job was at the University of Florida, where she recalls being greeted by a culture of misogyny. Her office was equipped with only a chair and a wastebasket, and if she needed to type, she had to use the secretary's typewriter while the secretary was at lunch. Altmaier didn't stay long, and by 1980 she had found her way to the University of Iowa.

At Ohio State, she had taught a life-planning class that many athletes took, and she introduced it at Iowa, getting to know a number of football and basketball players there too. Soon she joined an athletic advisory board that helped hire Iowa's athletic director, and future Big 12 commissioner, Bob Bowlsby. (Altmaier held another position that handled professorial misconduct, and dealt with a number of professors who had affairs with students. "I got rid of one predator a year, I think," she says.)

Altmaier was asked by Iowa president Mary Sue Coleman to become the faculty athletic representative in 2001—meaning that she was the faculty's liaison to the athletic department and the NCAA—and she readily accepted. "It would give me some of my highest highs and lowest lows of my life," she says. She had her first taste of the lows the next year when she got a call from a university attorney alerting her that an incident had taken place, but she didn't need to know the details. Altmaier later learned that star basketball player Pierre Pierce had been accused of raping a women's basketball player.

Coach Steve Alford vocally defended his player's innocence, even allowing the unofficial team chaplain to arrange an uncomfortable prayer meeting between the victim and Pierce. But police reports stated that Pierce held the victim's arms over her head and covered her mouth when she tried to scream. Pierce, who was eventually charged with third-degree sexual assault, escaped with a misdemeanor after the victim agreed to mediation, and he returned to the team only to be kicked off for good following another domestic violence incident with a different woman. "I never let anyone tell me there was something I didn't need to know ever again," says Altmaier.

On the NCAA's Agents and Amateurism subcommittee, Altmaier found herself at odds with the NCAA's efforts to dictate the group's decisions, and the hypocrisy stunned her. "Maybe it was more naiveté on my part," she says. But she stood tough, and her committee's proposal, with its toughened standards on names and images, was adopted by the full association in 2006, while Brand's board-backed proposal was withdrawn. The Pontiac promotion was now even more overtly on the wrong side of the line.

In response, Brand formed a new commercialism task force to reexamine the issue. The task force, he felt, needed to better understand the NCAA's corporate sponsors, so he summoned its members—including Altmaier—to Orlando in January 2007 for meetings with reps from EA Sports, Cingular, State Farm, and others. Nike wanted to run more ad campaigns using footage of current athletes to celebrate "its" college teams; Cingular wanted to show clips of athletes on its cell phones for a March Madness promotion; EA wanted access to players' names for its video games, rather than mere avatars that didn't use actual names. All promised to honor the "values" of the NCAA. According to an NCAA memo, Brand said after the meeting, "We can not exploit individual student-athletes, but it is not clear what exploitation is."

"The whole trip was meant to soften us up, so we'd write a different rule," Altmaier says.

Altmaier vividly remembers a constant theme in Orlando: telling the good stories of college sports. Sponsors showed examples of promos with soft background music and athletes overcoming long odds. Altmaier didn't mind the stories; what bothered her was that they needed corporate sponsors. "Here they were trying to counter the bad press about the NCAA with these 'good stories,'" she says. "Except they had to be sponsored, they had to make the NCAA money. It didn't make any sense."

Brand repackaged his ideas into new legislation in 2007, but still couldn't force it through the membership, which infuriated him. The rules were already being broken, he knew, and companies were practically begging to hand over millions of additional dollars to the NCAA. In an e-mail to three of his top executives, Dave Berst, Kevin Lennon, and Greg Shaheen, Brand wrote, "The presidents have been professing that they do not want [to] support commercialism, most especially when student-athletes' images are involved. Of course, the conferences and the schools are already doing that—for example the Pontiac ads that they complain about are a staple in the fall football season, which they control. The presidents want it both ways: they want to be able to rail against commercialism and they want the revenue that comes with corporate ads."

He continued, "The presidents delegate the responsibility to the commissioners to produce revenue from corporate ads, but at the same time they want the conferences and their schools to be 'pure.' The way they all handle this cognitive dissonance is by blaming the national office. By pointing the finger at the national office, they relieve both the commissioners and themselves from the responsibility of dealing with this set of issues."

Brand had still another idea, though: he would handpick his own group of presidents to sponsor the legislation. "The normal governance structure will not work," he wrote. "I predict at the beginning such a group would scream about commercialism. After that noise, and if we pick leaders among the presidents, they will come (to) grips with reality. We will get to where we want to go."

In January 2008, Brand e-mailed Altmaier, inviting her to be an adviser on the new presidential task force, which would be chaired by Penn State president Graham Spanier. Brand came armed with numbers to show just how commercial college sports already were. In a fact sheet distributed to the task force, it was noted that during the previous year's BCS championship game there were 6,913 commercial exposures shown simultaneously to athletes on the field. The national office had done surveys too, and found that a number of schools were running a hundred or more promotions each year trading on athletes or their names. Seventy-four institutions had eight or more corporate partners. The Big Ten, meanwhile, was bringing in more than $50 million a year in royalties, licensing, advertisements, and sponsorship dollars. "The NCAA national office is not aware of an ongoing effort or existing systems in place at Division I schools/conferences to regularly police and approve corporate activations," the memo read.

During one of the group's meetings, Altmaier suggested to Brand that if the NCAA was going to earn more money off players' images, it ought to share the proceeds with them. She suggested putting money into a continuing education fund for former athletes or creating a nationwide concussion monitoring program.

"That's a slippery slope, Betsy," Brand told her.

"Myles, we're surrounded by slippery slopes," she answered.

She then took her idea about sharing the money with the players directly to the presidents. "I remain committed to the idea of having some return (financial) to the student athletes themselves," she wrote to the group. "Falling short of at least suggesting that . . . is a mistake, I believe."

Spanier responded to Dave Berst, "For the record, Dave, I disagree strongly with her idea that we compensate athletes for the use of their images. I wouldn't put this in the report at all—not even a hint of the possibility."

Christine Plonsky, the women's athletic director at the University of Texas, wrote back to Altmaier, "I am opposed to ANYTHING remotely associated with s-a's 'deserving' something from this."

When Berst released the final proposal to the task force, which read much like Brand's previous attempts to remake the rules on using players' images, he didn't e-mail one to Altmaier. She had to ask for a copy.

Still, in the end, even the presidents couldn't push through Brand's package. How, then, had the Pontiac ads continued to run? How were schools allowed to dress their websites in corporate sponsorship?

In 2012, during a deposition, Berst offered an explanation. The board of directors, as far back as 2005, allowed the NCAA to interpret the commercialism rules as it saw fit, which it happily did following Brand's recommendations. "The board authorized us to live in limbo until we get it solved, and we haven't done it yet," Berst said. "And that continues to today?" asked the lawyer who was questioning him. "Today, yes," Berst answered, adding, "I don't think our members paid one whit of attention to whether or not they could do it, it just made sense, sure, we can have another logo on our website." The NCAA had essentially pretended that legislation had passed.

It was not the only time the NCAA willfully failed to enforce its own rules. Through the years, *Sports Illustrated* often ran promotions for national championship football and basketball teams, offering free commemorative yearbooks and later DVDs for new magazine subscribers. The NCAA had rules against using players' names and images to promote a commercial product, of course, and someone at LSU raised questions about the practice after its 2008 BCS title. The response came back from the NCAA: schools "are advised to send a cease and desist letter which preserves the eligibility of the student-athletes. SI ignores the letter and we all go on about our business." One college administrator echoed what *Sports Illustrated* thought of the letter, writing, "My recollection is that they use those letters to line bird cages."

A month before she retired in the spring of 2015, Altmaier sat in her office in Iowa City, reflecting on her years fighting the good fight against Brand and the NCAA. It was a warm and sunny no jacket sort of day, and Altmaier wore a chartreuse sweater that matched her green eyes. To understand the NCAA and what commercialism really means, she said, you have to see it up close. "You have to see everything from the eyes of a recruit," she said.

She had arranged a tour of Iowa's new football facility, just opened the year before thanks to $55 million in private donations and athletic department funds generated through public support. Altmaier pulled up to the Stew and LeNore Hansen Football Performance Center in her Hyundai SUV. The facility looked bigger than an airplane hangar. "Un-fucking-believable the size of it," she said. The new building had a full-size indoor practice field, a palatial weight room—the machines were Iowa's colors, black and yellow—and a players' lounge equipped with a PlayStation and Xbox, Ping-Pong, pool, shuffleboard, and a few flat-screen TVs. There was a video room reserved for NFL scouts who visited campus, and innumerable tributes to the NFL players Iowa had produced through the years. "You can be nineteen years old and not worry about signing away your name and image for your entire life because you look around and it's like oh my God," Altmaier said.

Despite her distaste for so much of the world of big-time college sports, she also treasured her time as faculty athletics rep, from the intellectual challenges to being around students. Altmaier served on the search committee that brought longtime football coach Kirk Ferentz to Iowa in 1999, and she appreciated the volunteer work his players did in the community at schools and hospitals. During the tour, she stopped by his office for a goodbye hug. Over the years, she had heard from hundreds of athletes about their lives and their sports. "When they were given the opportunity to speak, they had amazing things to say," she said. And, once, she recalled being presented with a new concussion management plan at a Big Ten conference meeting. As administrators patted themselves on the back for the new plan, Altmaier noted that one of the doctors involved wasn't board certified. The proposal was dropped. "The room went silent when I said that," Altmaier says. "It was one of my all-time favorite shocked silences."

She was asked why she thought Brand had put her on the commercialism committee, when she disagreed with him at every turn. Was it because he valued her opinion? Or was it because she was the token dissenter, there to speak her mind and inevitably be ignored?

"Passionately, I thought I could change their minds," she said.

She pointed to the bulletin board next to her desk where a postcard read "Sometimes you've got to put on your big girl boots and prove that you can use the pointy end."

"At the very least," she said, "you always have to try."

On Christmas Eve 2008, Brand was diagnosed with pancreatic cancer. The next day, he asked Renfro to visit him, and he broke the news. "He looked bad," Renfro recalls. Brand had a request: he didn't feel well enough to deliver his "state of the association" speech, which had become a staple of the NCAA's annual convention, held each January. He had already written out his speech, and he asked Renfro to deliver it.

Entitled "The Challenges of Commercial Activity," it amounted to Brand's final justification for the collegiate model. Athletes were students, and could not be paid, and must not be exploited. Commercial activity was both proper and necessary, especially as expenses continued to rise. The educational value of athletics had to be central. And while athletes could not endorse products, their images could be used in a variety of other commercial ways by other entities. How this did not constitute exploitation was something Brand never explained—not then, nor at any of his previous defenses. He did acknowledge, however, that "if this issue has not yet already reached a crisis, it is certainly approaching it." Of course, the harsher truth was that no one in college sports had done as much to create that crisis than Myles Brand, who had pushed the line of what was acceptable further than anyone ever had—including conference commissioners like Jim Delany.

Myles Brand continued to serve as president of the NCAA until September 16, 2009, the day he died.

# A Mind Is a Terrible Thing to Waste

**ANDREW JOLLY ARRIVED ON HAMPTON UNIVERSITY'S CAMPUS IN THE** summer of 2007, a wide-eyed freshman looking forward to college—and to football. The big lineman had a late growth spurt as a teenager; he shot up to six foot six and made the all-district team at T. C. Williams High School, the same school that once helped bridge racial divides in Alexandria, Virginia, and was depicted in the movie *Remember the Titans*. Jolly was thrilled to be offered a scholarship to Hampton, which was just a few hours from his home. He was also going to be attending one of the nation's historically black colleges, whose mission was to educate African Americans; indeed, for decades the United Negro College Fund, the fund-raising arm for the nation's historically black colleges, had used the famous slogan "A mind is a terrible thing to waste."

After his high school graduation, Jolly enrolled in summer school at Hampton, a Division I-AA, or Football Bowl Subdivision, school, and began working out with the team, hoping to become a freshman starter. When he began practicing, he asked about his scholarship paperwork—he had only signed a letter of intent—and was told everything would be taken care of when fall practice started. But Jolly never made it to fall practice; he tore his Achilles tendon during a workout, a devastating injury that required surgery and months of rehab. Hampton paid for the surgery, but while he was home recovering Jolly was told there was no scholarship for him because he had not been academically cleared by the NCAA's Clearinghouse.

To this day, Jolly remains confused about what exactly happened—why was he allowed to practice if he wasn't eligible to play?—but back then he shook off his doubts. His mother had recently received a retirement settlement from a job and was able to cobble together the money to pay for his freshman year at Hampton. He became interested in graphic design and got good grades, he said. A cubist self-portrait he drew was featured in an art show at a local gallery. Jolly also recovered from his surgery and Hampton's new football coach offered him a scholarship for his sophomore year—he signed the paperwork this time. Everything was looking up.

But once again he was seriously injured during a practice that took place before the season started. This injury was even worse than the previous one: he tore his ACL and PCL in his right knee and suffered damage to his peroneal nerve. And this time, Hampton abandoned him. He had to phone his mother, Joan, to come pick him up from the hospital.

"It felt like we were very alone," Joan Jolly says.

Because he had signed his scholarship papers, Jolly returned to campus later that year and hoped he'd be able to graduate from Hampton—"the student part of the student-athlete was just fine," he says. Even though it was obvious that his career was over, coaches insisted he participate in team workouts and conditioning. At one morning practice, he got in a spat with a coach. "They treated me like I was a player recovering from an injury," Jolly says. "But everyone knew that wasn't true."

Hampton then hired another head football coach—Donovan Rose, a former player at Hampton—who informed Jolly there would be no scholarship for his junior year. Jolly asked about a medical scholarship, something the NCAA had instituted to help critically injured players, so he could still receive aid and go to school. Rose said no, according to Jolly. There were cost issues, Rose said, and he brought up the altercation with the coach.

Bills soon started arriving at Joan's house for the knee surgery, as she continued to seek answers from Hampton. Eventually she forwarded news stories she read about the mistreatment of athletes and the NCAA's health insurance policies, and got Hampton to schedule an appeals hearing. She also contacted the NCAA, which covered much of the medical costs under its catastrophic injury insurance.

Joan attended the appeals hearing, but wasn't allowed to speak on her son's behalf. The school denied the appeal, and later, when Joan asked for a copy of the transcript, she was told she would have to subpoena it.

A similar story unfolded halfway across the country at the University of Oklahoma, where Kyle Hardrick, a six-foot-eight forward, suffered a knee injury during his freshman season in 2009. Team doctors told him it was not serious and he should play through the pain, but it persisted into his sophomore year. Another MRI taken showed a torn meniscus, but Oklahoma refused to authorize the surgery. Hardrick's family paid for the surgery themselves, while Oklahoma canceled his scholarship.

Kyle's mother, Valerie, and Joan Jolly traveled to Washington, D.C., in 2011 to participate in a roundtable discussion on Capitol Hill about college athletics hosted by Congressman Bobby Rush and moderated by ESPN's Jeremy Schaap. "I want Andrew's story to be told," Joan says. "He deserves that."

Hardrick now works for Halliburton on an oil field and still has severe knee pain. Jolly, meanwhile, moved to Colorado and handles paperwork for Kaiser Permanente. He suffers from foot drop and struggles to get around. Neither he nor Hardrick graduated from college.

Jolly says he tries not to think about what happened to him at Hampton anymore, but when he does it is not his football career that bothers him.

"I wonder 'what if' about school," he says. "I'm not stupid. I made the dean's list. I could have a degree of some kind, and that's what hurts. That's what they took away from me."

# CHAPTER 8

# THE DEPOSITION

The NCAA had a long history of winning court cases brought by aggrieved athletes. In the mid-1970s, when it faced a series of lawsuits brought by players the NCAA had ruled ineligible, it countered that playing a sport in college was not a right that an athlete could sue over. It either won these suits outright or wore down the plaintiffs until they gave up. Those were the lawsuits that led to the passage of the noxious Restitution Rule, which said that any player or institution that sued the NCAA—and ultimately lost—would be *retroactively* punished from the point at which the litigation began. But still the lawsuits came.

In the early 1990s, a Notre Dame football player named Braxston Banks sued to remain eligible—he had one year left—even though he had attended an NFL tryout camp. Banks lost. In 2001, a star soccer player at the University of Southern California, Rhiannon Tanaka, sued USC and the NCAA because the university would not allow her to transfer to UCLA unless she agreed to sit out two years—and lose those years of eligibility. (Tanaka wanted to transfer, she said, because USC was arranging for athletes to receive fraudulent academic credit for sham classes.) She lost. In 2004, a former University of Washington football walk-on, Andy Carroll, attempted to bring a class action suit against the NCAA, arguing that the restrictions on the number of scholarships—and the fact that walks-ons weren't entitled to them—amounted to "classic cartel behavior." The judge declined to certify the class, mooting the lawsuit. Plus there was the Jeremy Bloom case and plenty of others.

In cases against the NCAA in which the plaintiffs were grown-ups—such as the *Regents* case, or the assistant coaches' class action lawsuit over their wages being fixed—the judiciary could be pretty clear-eyed about what did and did not constitute an antitrust violation. That is, even if the judge was a big fan of college sports, his rooting interest didn't interfere with how he saw the law. But when it came to cases involving teenagers—athletes who had no recourse within the college sports system—judges usually found for the NCAA. Indeed, they often fell back on Justice Stevens's dicta as an important part of their reasoning.

But the association had also never faced an athlete's lawsuit quite like *White v. NCAA*. The argument Nadel had devised, and then developed with Schwarz and Rascher, was cleverly and narrowly drawn. It did not contest the *Regents* dicta. It involved not just one athlete or a handful of athletes, but, potentially, every player in the nation who played football or men's basketball. This lawsuit simply asked the NCAA to allow schools to pay the full cost of attendance, which, you'll recall, Myles Brand had said was "ideal," along with athletic scholarships. The notion that depriving athletes of the full cost of attendance was somehow necessary to the popularity of college athletics was a much harder argument for the NCAA to make than arguing that amateurism itself was the critical element.

The NCAA had a well-earned reputation for dragging out lawsuits as long as possible, but that didn't happen with the *White* lawsuit. Filed in February 2006, it was granted class action status a mere eight months later—the first lawsuit by college athletes to achieve that status. By the standards of the federal judiciary, that was lightning speed. The original judge in the case, known for his "rocket docket," insisted on a speedy pace and squashed efforts to delay it.

Schwarz, Rascher, and Nadel had worked hard to find lawyers who would take the case; once it was filed, they revved into action again, helping to frame the arguments that the plaintiffs' economic experts would put forth. The lawyers had hired Bobby McCormick, a well-known economics professor at Clemson, to serve as the plaintiff's economic expert; the three LECG economists were supposed to provide him "support," as they did with testifying experts on many different kinds of cases. But with just days to go before the expert had to turn in his declaration, as it was called, the team was still unsatisfied with his draft, including the lawyers who had hired him. The weekend before the declaration was due, one of the lawyers called Schwarz and told him to take over the draft. "I could have kissed him," Nadel said of the lawyer. "Nobody knew the subtle arguments better than Andy." Schwarz redrafted key sections of the report over the course of a weekend, the expert adopted the ideas and signed on, and that deadline was met. But once the case achieved class action status, the three economists stopped hearing from the lawyers.

For Schwarz at least, that was just as well. He had separated from his wife in 2004, during the time he and the others were shopping the case, and was divorced two years later. Even as he was frantically trying to complete work on the *White* case, he began dating Melodi Dewey, a psychologist he had met through an online dating service. He was also deeply involved defending Oracle in a lawsuit brought by the federal government to block its merger with PeopleSoft, a smaller competitor (the merger eventually went through), as well as a number of other big cases. He was in charge of the junior staff at his firm, LECG, with whom he met once a week, doling out their assignments and overseeing their work. One year, he recalls, he billed twenty-six hundred hours ("which probably means I worked three thousand"). This was partly because work was a respite from his marital problems, but it was more because that's just who he was. "Andy is the hardest-working person I know," says Melodi, who married him in 2013. "He naturally likes working and wants things to be done the way they should be done." That was a quality that the partners at LECG had long ago discovered and had come to not only appreciate but depend on. Though he had his eccentricities, Schwarz had become an important figure at LECG.

Which, as it happens, was falling apart. Back in 1997, around the same time Schwarz joined LECG, the firm had issued stock to the public, an unusual move for a consulting firm, and one that put it under a lot of financial stress. Almost immediately, recalls Schwarz, "it was clear they were having trouble making their numbers"—that is, meeting the earnings projections they had encouraged Wall Street to expect. "We were all told to work more in June, and take vacation days in July, which was a sign they were worried about second-quarter revenue," he adds.

Over the next half dozen years, LECG was bought and sold several times, finally winding up in the hands of a Berkeley economist named David Teece, who purchased it for pennies on the dollar. A native of New Zealand—indeed, he is reported to be one of the richest men from that country—Teece had been one of the original cofounders of LECG. He quickly proceeded to take it public again, but this time his way of "making the numbers" was to steadily buy up other firms and use their revenue to prop up LECG's. Eventually, though, the firm started missing its earnings again, the stock started tanking again, and the board of directors pushed out Teece (who went on to start a competing firm, BRG, which he runs to this day). Alas, the new chief executive seemed to know very little about the dynamics of litigation consulting.

By 2007, Schwarz had had enough. Rich Gilbert, his old mentor, had bailed out several years earlier. Rascher had left too, to focus on getting tenure as a professor of sports management at the University of San Francisco. That December, Schwarz persuaded Rascher (who by then had tenure) to join him and several others who were ready to break away and start their own firm. They called it OSKR, the first letters of the last names of the four principals. Nadel, who was older than the others, went into semiretirement, but they all remained friends. As for LECG, it collapsed four years later. (Today, OSKR and BRG, David Teece's firm, share the same building in Emeryville, California.)

It was in the middle of these machinations that Schwarz, Rascher, and Nadel learned that Max Blecher and Stephen Morrissey, the lawyers to whom they had entrusted the *White* case, had sold them—and, more important, the players—down the river.

The NCAA had vowed early on that it would never settle the *White* case because it was such a "threat" to amateurism. It had the track record to back up that promise. Yes, it had settled *Tarkanian*, but only after two decades of litigation that went all the way to the Supreme Court. Mostly, its strategy of refusing to settle lawsuits had worked well for it over the years. The plaintiffs fully expected the NCAA to contest every motion, seek delays at every turn, and take the case as far as it could be taken—even if it took years.

The lawyer managing the *White* case on a day-to-day basis was a young antitrust attorney named Tibor Nagy, who had only recently gone to work for Susman Godfrey. Nagy had joined the firm in no small part because he wanted to be a part of the case. His primary responsibility was to find witnesses he could question under oath in a deposition. Some of these witnesses might later testify at the trial itself—assuming there was a trial—but even if they didn't, their words would become part of the lawsuit's record. As part of his research, Nagy had read Walter Byers's book; it occurred to him that deposing Byers could be key to unlocking the case. Despite the dozens of lawsuits against the NCAA since Byers's retirement, he had never been deposed.

Nagy tracked down Byers to a ranch in Emmett, Kansas, a small town a hundred miles west of Kansas City; Byers had become a cattle rancher after leaving the NCAA. When Nagy first approached him, Byers turned him down, but Nagy was persistent. Relying on Byers's daughter as an intermediary, he finally wore down her father's resistance. And so it was that on three separate days in late July and early August 2007, the lawyers for both sides in the *White* litigation took Walter Byers's deposition. The questioning took place at Byers's ranch.

He was eighty-five by then, but to judge by the transcript of the deposition, he was as ornery as ever. Under questioning by Nagy, Byers noted that players used to have something called "laundry money"—$15 a month for incidental expenses. It was taken away in 1975, during an NCAA convention that was held for the express purpose of reining in supposed out-of-control costs.

"Did you have any indication, sir, that laundry money somehow lessened the popularity or demand for football or college basketball?" asked Nagy.

"No," replied Byers.

"Do you believe that the NCAA needs to restrict grants-in-aid so that they do not cover incidental expenses in order for amateur college athletics to exist?"

"No."

"Do you agree, sir, that providing incidental expenses to a student athlete in the form of a grant-in-aid constitutes pay for play?"

Although this was meant to be a softball question, Byers practically exploded. "Well," he began, "it doesn't constitute any more than the grant-in-aid itself. The grant-in-aid is basically a one-year contract. It used to be four years and they cut it back to one. And a one-year contract sets up a one-year tryout, and the one-year tryout gets rid of all the players that aren't good enough to play and the coach brings up a whole new group." He was rolling now. "So the contract, itself, is a contract for athletic performance . . . and I hold that to be self-evident and true. . . . And when you tinker around with, is it $15 a month, is it in or out, is an irrelevancy to the whole question of pay because one year is a paid contract, period."

Byers described the NCAA's various defenses for not paying the full cost of attendance as "nonsensical" and "defying belief." He said the NCAA was a monopoly that exploited athletes. When asked whether paying players $15 or $100 a month would impact athletic budgets, he again couldn't contain himself. "Look at that deal that Alabama made with the coach, the one from LSU and the Miami Dolphins and brought him back in with a no-cut contract, millions and millions and millions of dollars," he said. (This was a reference to Nick Saban, whose compensation at Alabama was $5 million a year.) "And they're talking about $15 a month or $100 a month of financial aid for students? Come on. This is the real world out there and they're living in an ivory tower with no relationship to the facts."

The NCAA, he concluded as his first day of testimony wound up, "is a cartel that's restricting things, which is a violation of the antitrust laws."

Nagy could not have been happier with Byers's testimony. In addition, he had taken the deposition of Dave Berst a month after taking Byers's deposition. Berst by then was the head of Division I athletics, making him one of the NCAA's highest-ranking executives, and had been designated by the NCAA to give testimony on behalf of the organization. The NCAA had built its defense on two planks. First, it argued that giving players additional money to cover the full cost of attending college amounted to "pay for play," and was therefore a violation of amateurism. And its second "procompetitive" justification was that not allowing cost of attendance helped maintain "competitive equity"—that is, an effort to level the playing field among all the Division I football and men's basketball programs. These two justifications were what Berst was supposed to defend.

During his deposition, however, Berst completely undercut the NCAA's defenses, claiming that the competitive equity justification was "not real" and that the only real issue was pay-for-play. After any deposition, the person deposed has thirty days to correct the record—which usually means correcting a misunderstanding by the court reporter (such as using the word "know" instead of "no"). In this instance, however, the NCAA's lawyers attempted to change the substance of Berst's testimony, by cutting the words "not real," which is a blatant violation of the rules. Nagy of course quickly filed an objection.

By then, however, the two sides were in settlement talks. For all its bluster, the NCAA rationale for settling was obvious: thanks in no part to Byers and Berst, the lawsuit was going badly. The surprise was that White's lawyers, who clearly had the upper hand, also wanted to settle. They could offer their reasons: a new judge had been assigned to the case, and they feared she would be pro-NCAA. Trials can be a crapshoot, no matter how much the evidence favors your position. The *White* lawyers worried that the *Regents* dicta might still pose a stumbling block. Blecher, in particular, feared that despite the clear-cut nature of the case, the amateurism defense might still carry the day. But there was also this: the settlement the two sides quickly drew up called for the lawyers to be paid $8.5 million. For less than a year's work, it was an awfully nice payday.

And what did the athletes who made up the members of the class get? Practically nothing. The NCAA promised to put up $10 million, which could go toward "bona fide educational expenses" for athletes who could show financial need. They would be allowed all of $2,500 in such aid. This small pot of money would disappear after four years, however. As written, the settlement proposed that an additional $218 million would be made available for schools to use on behalf of athletes for other "purposes allowed under the current guidelines." In fact, this was money that was already being distributed to schools to use as they saw fit and the settlement basically renamed the funds without changing much else. (Much of this money wound up being spent by universities on athletic equipment.) In addition, the universities would be allowed to provide insurance to athletes—though they were not required to, and most did not. The upshot was that the NCAA, which as part of the settlement was able to deny all wrongdoing, was not forced to change its behavior or bylaws in any way whatsoever. "The athletes did get something out of *White*, but it was small potatoes compared to what *White* was all about," says Roger Noll, a Stanford University economist who worked with the plaintiffs. Less than

$6 million of the $10 million was ever spent. In 2012, the NCAA quietly distributed the remaining money to some of its member schools.

Schwarz, Rascher, and Nadel were devastated by the settlement. "Ernie was close to tears," recalls Schwarz. He and Nadel flew to Houston and confronted Stephen Morrissey, the partner at Susman Godfrey who was managing the case, and "told him the settlement was a joke," Schwarz says. "It was the first time an athlete class action had been certified against the NCAA and they got rid of it with $10 million and a wave of the hands." Nadel recalls having several loud arguments over the phone with Blecher: "You're selling out the athletes," he told the lawyer. Nadel even proposed filing suit to block the settlement, though Rascher and Schwarz quickly dismissed the idea: it would be suicidal for a brand-new litigation consulting firm to gain a reputation for opposing negotiated settlements. A lawyer on a later NCAA case would remark that the three economists seemed "scarred" by their experience in the White case. It was true; they were. They thought they had devised a lawsuit that would put the first real dent in the NCAA's antitrust armor, perhaps paving the way for other cases that more directly took on its amateurism defense. Instead, it was settled for a piffle.

Jason White, who hadn't been consulted by the lawyers and learned about the settlement from the news media, was furious. The named plaintiffs were all supposed to get $5,000, but with Ramogi Huma's help White and another named plaintiff, Brian Pollack, a former football player at UCLA, tried to oppose the settlement (they reengaged their lawyers and were able to ensure that at least the accounting for the $10 million settlement would be public). Years later, White would express ambivalence about the case; he was never interested in the notoriety that came with being the lead plaintiff and wasn't looking forward to participating in a high-profile trial. His wife was at business school, and he was working at Google; he was far removed from his day-to-day struggles as a college athlete. (In fact, Google's general counsel, David Drummond, played football at Santa Clara University, and has strong pro-athlete views about the NCAA's exploitation of athletes.) In retrospect, he said, "I think our case opened the door to other cases."

Huma, who had found White in the first place, was every bit as outraged as the others. "I scoured through the settlement," he later recalled. "It was awful." But he refused to publicly display his anger; that wasn't his nature. And like White, as time went on, he began to see the glass as half full.

"We weren't happy with the $10 million," he would later say. "But it set a precedent. A class had been certified and that had never happened before. And it showed that football and men's basketball players could be treated differently from other athletes on campus. We finally got the NCAA to admit that they played different roles, and had different needs."

In retrospect, the *White* case was the greatest missed opportunity to loosen the NCAA's stranglehold on big-time college sports. But Huma was right too; the precedents it set would, in just a few years, turn out to be important.

# "Intent to Professionalize"

**ALL MUHAMMED LASEGE WANTED TO DO WAS GET TO AMERICA TO PLAY** college basketball. It wasn't that he was especially talented, but he was six foot eleven with a decent shooting touch. And he knew that basketball could be his ticket out of Lagos, Nigeria—and could lead to a better life if he got a chance at an American education. He was also, however, sixteen years old, with no idea how to go about getting college coaches interested in him, or even how to obtain a visa to the United States.

So in 1997, when a Nigerian coach told Lasege he could help him find an American college that would give him a scholarship, Lasege was immediately interested. The only hitch, the coach continued, was that he would first have to go to Russia, where it would take maybe a month to get a travel visa, during which time he would be able to practice with college-level players.

Instead it was a scam. Lasege did indeed go to Russia with three other Nigerian basketball players—where they were forced to sign professional contracts guaranteeing them $9,000, though they were also told they would never see the money. According to an article in the *Louisville Courier-Journal* by Eric Crawford, "When he questioned [the contract], he was told that he was not good enough to play for a U.S. college team and he would need to play more in Russia."

"I felt I had no choice," Lasege would later say.

So play he did, for more than a year, for a professional junior team in Moscow. He and the other Nigerians were constantly monitored by bodyguards.

(According to Crawford, the NCAA would later describe the bodyguards as an impermissible benefit.) When they tried to call home, their phones were disconnected. When they protested by boycotting practice, they were physically threatened.

Finally, in November 1998, Lasege managed to obtain a Canadian visa; after landing in Toronto, he made his way to the United States thanks to the auspices of a middleman who often guided foreign players to American colleges. The middleman paid for Lasege to visit UCLA and Louisville (another impermissible benefit), where then coach Denny Crum offered him a scholarship.

Lasege's troubles with the NCAA went far deeper than some mere recruiting rules violations, however. It quickly concluded that he could never play college basketball, because in traveling to Russia and signing that contract, he had shown an "intent to professionalize." When Louisville tried to have him reinstated, arguing that the papers he'd signed were not true contracts—for one thing, he'd never been paid the money—the NCAA refused to bend. At one point, the NCAA Clearinghouse (now known as the Eligibility Center) declared him academically ineligible, concluding that one of his Nigerian exams had been forged, even though by then he was carrying a 3.8 grade point average as an economics major at Louisville.

So Lasege hired a lawyer named Jim Milliman and sued in Kentucky state court. Much to Milliman's—and the judge's—amazement, Louisville filed a brief supporting the NCAA, not its player. During the trial, which took place in late 2000, Milliman questioned the NCAA's "Reinstatement Committee director," a twenty-six-year-old woman named Julie Roe Lach. This was the same Julie Roe Lach whom Mark Emmert made director of enforcement in 2011—and then fired in the aftermath of the Miami scandal (see chapter 12).

According to an account Milliman gave to the sportswriter Dave Kindred, "I asked her, 'If a contract is put in front of a student, and if he had a gun held to his head, and if he's told, "If you don't sign this, I'm going to pull the trigger," and then he signs the contract, is he then ineligible for NCAA competition?'"

"Her answer, without a second's hesitation: 'Yes.'"

The circuit court judge hearing in the case wrote a scathing decision describing the NCAA's ruling against Lasege as "an injustice." The Kentucky appeals court unanimously upheld that decision. But the Kentucky Supreme Court voted 4–3 in favor of the NCAA. Several observers noted that the four justices who ruled against Lasege were all graduates of Louisville's in-state rival, the University of Kentucky.

This is one *Indentured* story that has a happy ending, however. By the time the Kentucky Supreme Court issued its ruling, Rick Pitino had replaced Denny Crum as coach of the Cardinals. The new coach took Lasege under his wing, making him a graduate assistant, allowing him to work out with the team, giving him private basketball tutorials, and even helping him pay some of his college expenses. The goal was to improve Lasege's skills to the point where he could play abroad after graduation and make enough money to get an MBA. That's exactly what happened: after playing in Europe and Iran for a few years, Lasege got an MBA from Wharton. He is now a financial executive for ExxonMobil, based in Houston.

"This is an incredible young man," said Milliman. In the end, basketball did make it possible for Lasege to attain that better life he yearned for. No thanks to the NCAA.

# CHAPTER 9

# "DUDE, YOU'RE ON A VIDEO GAME!"

I n 2006, the NBA and its players' union, the NBA Players Association, negotiated a new contract that included a provision setting the minimum age for joining the NBA at nineteen. What's more, even if the player was nineteen or older, he had to be a full year out of high school. The purpose, quite obviously, was to prevent high school players from entering the draft without spending at least a year in college. (Thus was born the "one and done" college freshman.) NBA commissioner David Stern, in applauding the move, said it would help keep pro scouts—and sneaker executives— away from promising players at high school gyms. "Their presence there is unseemly," said Stern.

Though Sonny Vaccaro was on the verge of leaving Reebok, and thus didn't really have an economic interest in the issue, he was nonetheless furious. How could the basketball establishment deprive young men, most of them black and poor, from being able to make a living when they wanted to? Why was it always black athletes who were targeted? So many of the NCAA's rules surrounding amateurism discriminated against players who lacked money and means. Black athletes from disadvantaged neighborhoods were the ones most likely to struggle in college, because they had gone to subpar high schools—and they were also the ones most often accused of academic fraud. And of course they received no remuneration, even as they were making everyone around them rich. Allen Sack, a former Notre Dame football player who had become a professor at the University of New Haven and was a founder of the Drake Group, an early effort to advocate for college athletes, once got into an argument with Vaccaro about the right way to compensate athletes. Like the Knight Commission, the Drake Group strongly believed that the right way to reform college sports was to refocus it on sound academics. "We want to compensate athletes with a real education," he said. Vaccaro replied, "Allan, you're an intellectual. These kids don't want what you are offering. They want cash."

Even after leaving his job at Reebok, Vaccaro mentored one final athlete: Brandon Jennings, who was widely considered the best basketball player coming out of high school in 2008. Jennings had no intention of going to college. "I knew I wanted to go straight to the pros from high school from the time I was in the eighth grade," he told an ESPN documentary crew. After all, he said, he grew up in a single-parent household where he was expected to be the man of the house. "We needed money," he said. Vaccaro helped Jennings sign with a team in Italy, where he played for a year until he was eligible for the NBA draft. (He now makes around $8 million a year with the Detroit Pistons.) Well, that was one way to get around the NBA's new minimum age requirement.

Not long afterward, Vaccaro appeared on HBO's *Real Sports* show. The host, Bryant Gumbel, asked Vaccaro why this issue mattered so much to him. "You can't just write a rule saying you can't earn a living or"—and here he stumbled for a moment as he tried to find the right analogy—"you can't go to this drinking fountain, Bryant. Not in America."

Vaccaro's new career as an NCAA nemesis had begun in earnest in the spring of 2007, when he accepted an invitation to speak at Duke University's law school. He hadn't really figured out *how* he was going to take on the NCAA, but he knew he wanted to start by speaking on college campuses, especially to law schools, business schools, and journalism schools. Those audiences, he felt, were the most likely to be receptive to his message and—who knows?—might someday be in a position to do something about the NCAA.

His talk was videotaped, and would be posted on YouTube. You can see Vaccaro, standing in front of a lecture hall, wearing an open-collared shirt and a blue sweater. There are at most thirty people in attendance, including his wife and Pam Valvano, Jim Valvano's widow, who lives nearby. The first four or five rows of desks are empty. He has no notes.

He organizes his speech around his own career, starting with the Roundball Classic, and ending with his decision to quit Reebok and begin speaking out about the NCAA. Vaccaro tells the old stories about convincing Nike to give money to coaches, persuading the company to bet it all on Michael Jordan, and signing Kobe Bryant to a $1 million Adidas contract. He mentions the time he tried to get the NCAA to solicit money from the shoe companies to send the parents of athletes to the Final Four. He is entertaining, though hard to follow for anyone who doesn't already know details of the Sonny Vaccaro story. But he is so animated and passionate—his hands in constant motion, his voice rising as he speaks—that nobody seems to mind his bewildering digressions. In between his narrative is biting commentary, not just about the NCAA but about the NBA, about agents, about virtually everyone involved in college and pro basketball. Like a reformed sinner who freely admits his sin, he is quick to acknowledge his own role in the commercialization of college sports.

His theme, to the extent he has one, is the distinction between laws and rules. "The law," he tells the Duke students, "we know what the law is. . . . But rules are something that people make arbitrarily in a small group, without any electoral situation, and they directly influence that part of society or the workforce that they control. They very seldom venture out into the wider world. Otherwise make a rule that says you can't go back to your dorm after 11 p.m. That may be fair or unfair or whatever. But the people who made it said that's what it is. And you have no legal recourse whatsoever."

Is there any doubt that he is talking about the NCAA? Of course not. "[Basketball players] get discriminated against more than any athletes in the world," he says a little later in his speech. "Most of them are minority kids. . . . People use discriminatory words: thugs, street agents." But, he adds, "those kids gave me a platform to do things. And I have to do this. Whether I am received or not is not my concern. I need to say that I tried.

"I don't think the people at the NCAA are bad people," he continues, suddenly changing direction. "I think they are so closeted by the enormity of their institution that they are blinded. The money in sports is fantastic. They receive all these benefits off the backs of kids. I don't understand why their only interest in life is making things hard for athletes. Because of their *rules*. I can't believe they sit up there . . . and make these rules."

In the fall, Vaccaro was invited to make three more speeches—to the law schools at Harvard and Yale, and the business school at the University of Maryland. His approach never changed—he always spoke without notes, built his talk around his own career, went on lengthy digressions, made allusions to incidents that the audience couldn't possibly under-stand, veered occasionally into incoherence—and yet it didn't matter. One blogger, upon hearing him at Harvard, described him as "mesmerizing." Another called him "an amazing storyteller." The *New Republic*'s Jason Zen-gerle wrote a lengthy article after his Maryland talk. He noted Vaccaro's rambling style and his list of grievances against the NCAA. "The NCAA," he quoted Vaccaro as saying, "is the most fraudulent organization that ever lived."

He wondered, though, whether Vaccaro was the right person to be leading this burgeoning movement. "At one level," he wrote, "Vaccaro could harm the cause of reform by sullying it. Is the man who boasts of having 'written a check to everyone' really the person best suited to clean-ing up college athletics? At the same time, Vaccaro, more than anyone else in the movement, knows the nature of the enemy—having once been the enemy. Vaccaro used his undeniable talents to help build college sports into the corrupt behemoth it is today. The question now is whether he can use those same talents to tear the whole thing down."

After the speech, according to Zengerle, Vaccaro and some others went to an Italian restaurant for dinner. The person Vaccaro paid the most attention to during the dinner was a staffer for the House Judiciary Com-mittee. "'I want to testify,' he told the staffer between slurps of soup," wrote Zengerle. "'I want to put my left hand down, put my right hand up and say I'll tell nothing but the truth so help me God. I'm begging you.'"

One of the people who attended Vaccaro's Maryland talk was a Washing-ton lawyer named Rob Ades. He had known Vaccaro for years; indeed, he was the intermediary who had brokered the deal between Nike and the University of Miami in the 1980s, in that first all-university deal. He was also a college basketball aficionado who threw a gala dinner every year at the Final Four; everyone in college basketball knew him. After the speech, he approached Vaccaro and said he would love to get together if Sonny were ever back in D.C. A year later, Vaccaro came back to the East Coast to give several speeches, including one at Howard University in Washington. Before the Howard speech, Vaccaro and Ades had lunch.

Vaccaro pitched Ades on the idea of suing the NCAA. He had a half dozen different thoughts about what someone might sue over, including the fact that the NCAA was licensing those old games on ESPN Classic without giving any of the money to the former athletes who had played in those games. Ades (who died in 2013) had no interest in bringing such a suit himself, but he sent Vaccaro to see Kenneth Feinberg, the famed lawyer who had headed the 9/11 compensation fund. Feinberg heard him out and then sent him to see Michael Hausfeld, a prominent Washington, D.C., antitrust attorney who had recently been forced out of his longtime firm and had started a new one, called Hausfeld LLP.

Hausfeld, a thin, soft-spoken man in his late sixties with a fussy, precise manner, is one of those plaintiffs' lawyers who likes to think of himself not just as an attorney representing a client but as a crusader for social justice. He first made a name for himself by suing Texaco in the mid-1990s for discriminating against minority employees, a case, he liked to say, "that resulted not just in a monetary judgment"—of $176 million—"but a restructuring of the company's relationship with minorities." He has sued Exxon on behalf of Native Alaskans after the *Exxon Valdez* spill; Union Bank of Switzerland to reclaim assets belonging to Holocaust survivors; and German industry for its use of slave labor during World War II. (Although Hausfeld's Polish father emigrated in time to escape the Holocaust, one of his uncles was taken into a field and shot by the Nazis.) A 2000 *Wall Street Journal* profile of him led with this question: "Is there a hot social issue that Michael Hausfeld hasn't turned into a lawsuit lately?" What Hausfeld usually seeks in a big case is precisely what Jason White's lawyers failed to get: injunctive relief. That is, whether he goes to trial or settles a case, what he is seeking as the outcome is not just money, but terms that force the defendant to change its behavior. "If you can reach the right resolution," he says, "you can develop a new framework for all the parties involved."

He had his share of critics, of course. According to a 2014 article on ESPN.com, Hausfeld could be "imperious" and "condescending," and "frequently fought with lawyers on his own side." And his high-mindedness was a source of ongoing friction between him and his former partners at the boutique plaintiffs' firm of Cohen, Milstein, Hausfeld & Toll, where he was the chairman. As the *Wall Street Journal* put it in that same 2000 article, "To the chagrin of some of his partners, he handles certain cases for free, and has invested millions in others that have flopped." The final straw came when Hausfeld insisted on opening a lavish London office, even though the British system frowns on the kind of aggressive plaintiffs' suits that are common in America. Hausfeld thought he could import American-style lawsuits to Great Britain. But he was wrong, and the office cost the firm millions. The partner delegated to tell him he'd been fired couldn't find him—Hausfeld was at a settlement conference—and so left a note on the chair in his office.

Hausfeld knew nothing about sports or the NCAA; tales would later circulate that he had to be told what a touchdown was. What he knew was that he needed a big, headline-generating case that could establish his new firm's bona fides. Not surprisingly, he didn't know quite what to make of Vaccaro, who was not only immersed in the world of sports but could not have had a more different personality. But when Hausfeld mentioned during a conference call with the firm's other lawyers that he had been put in touch with Vaccaro, one of his partners, a man named Jon King, spoke up. King had played a little college basketball, and he used to read Vaccaro's column in *Basketball Times*. "I knew exactly who he was," King recalls, "and after I explained his importance in the apparel business, I was deputized to meet with him."

King, who worked out of San Francisco, flew to Los Angeles, where Vaccaro and Pam were then living. They met in a conference room at the Ritz-Carlton Hotel in Santa Monica. Vaccaro had come prepared: he brought several large boxes of clippings and documents, contracts and files.

Vaccaro had a list of things the NCAA did that he felt were wrong, but he didn't know for sure whether they were legitimate legal claims or simply moral wrongs. The lack of due process. The one-year scholarship. The eligibility rules. The draconian hold over any athlete wanting to play college sports. "He couldn't get over the fact that the NCAA had been able to operate the way it had for so long," recalls King.

When they got to talking about image rights—why former players didn't have the right to their own images even after leaving college—Vaccaro showed King the release forms athletes had to sign, giving those rights away, in perpetuity, before they could play a college sport. The NCAA was exactly the kind of powerful, even untouchable organization that Hausfeld liked to sue. As Hausfeld and King began their research into the NCAA and its history of litigation, they gradually realized that the NCAA's licensing of the name, likeness, and image of former players could be the basis for an antitrust lawsuit.

"It dawned on us how unique this would be," says King. "The NCAA has never had to face a lawsuit involving former players. Our guys would have real staying power. And the issue—that these guys were being deprived of the right to their own image—is a very easy-to-understand symbol of all the ways the NCAA deprives athletes of their rights."

There was another reason why a lawsuit built around image rights was the right way to attack the NCAA, though Hausfeld and King didn't realize it at the time. The NCAA had known for years that this was an area where it was vulnerable.

In the late 1980s, for instance, NCAA corporate sponsor Oldsmobile came to Jim Host, the marketer, with an idea for a promotion. The company wanted to use old footage of former UCLA star Kareem Abdul-Jabbar in a new TV ad. After the NCAA approved the ad, Abdul-Jabbar's agent called Host and asked how much he was planning to pay Abdul-Jabbar. Host answered nothing, and the agent threatened to sue. The NCAA told Host he was in the clear, but he wasn't so sure. Using the image of Abdul-Jabbar without paying him for it struck him as a legal land mine. "We didn't want to go there on legal grounds," he says today. "It's common sense that individual rights for a person will always prevail." Oldsmobile didn't run the ad.

During the Myles Brand era, there was constant back-and-forth between the NCAA staff and others over how far companies could go in using a player to help promote its products. The line was constantly being redrawn to allow companies to do things that had previously been considered exploitation.

One example was fantasy football. In 2008, the NCAA debated allowing CBSSports.com to start a college football fantasy game. In an internal e-mail David Berst argued it would violate the association's rules because

CBS would be using the names and images of players to sell advertising. The response, from the NCAA's managing director of corporate and broadcast alliances, David Knopp, spoke volumes: "To say CBS is using names and stats to sell advertising to make money and is therefore against the rules seems to cast a blind eye on all the other ways CBS and ESPN and NCAA.com etc all use student-athlete images, footage, stats, names, news on TV, online etc to sell advertising." Fantasy college football was greenlighted, though it would later be discontinued.

For that matter, the NCAA had wrestled with the same issue regarding video games—and landed in the same see-no-evil place. When EA Sports bought the rights from the NCAA and member institutions to produce video games based on college football and basketball games, it specifically agreed not to use the actual names of any players. There were to be no names on the backs of jerseys, for instance. However, as a 2008 NCAA legal memo pointed out, the avatars clearly corresponded to individual players, including jersey number, position, stats, skills, physical appearance—even their hometowns. Any sports fan would know exactly who each player was.

What's more, third-party software developers had come up with software that allowed video game players to upload the actual names to the rosters. To combat this third-party software, EA Sports had devised its own add-on that allowed for the same thing—which the NCAA had approved for EA's 2009 version of its football game.

A legal memo, written by three attorneys from the Chicago law firm of Foley & Lardner, concluded that the NCAA was stepping into dangerous legal waters with these deals. One risk, they wrote, was that "a company that wants to use student-athlete names or other aspects of identity could successfully argue that NCAA has acquiesced to the exploitation of student-athletes' identities." Second, they said, "The fact that these uses are tolerated also can be used to lessen the impact of the unique characteristic of college athletes." In other words, it would be harder to argue in court that college sports was distinct from professional sports on the grounds that its athletes were unsullied amateurs. Of course, there was also a third possibility, which the lawyers didn't mention: that the NCAA's refusal to allow athletes the rights to their own images while in college would ultimately be found to be a violation of the nation's antitrust laws.

Meanwhile, as Hausfeld and King were getting up to speed, "Sonny kept connecting us to people and sources," King says. "He was like an educator, teaching us about the NCAA." King, in fact, came to greatly admire Vaccaro during the years the two men worked together. He would later write a long e-mail about Vaccaro that included this paragraph:

> When meeting with him and Pam to prepare to produce documents to the NCAA in response to their subpoenas of the Vaccaros, he showed me folders he had compiled... about the process by which now famous civil and human rights leaders had worked to change people's perceptions of what is acceptable conduct.... To me it was kind of a mind-blower to see this physical documentation of just how serious and committed he was. And to me, there was a broader message in it about the thinking that is needed to try to effect major change. To be clear, he was never in the slightest way comparing himself to those figures. But I can see now looking back that there were times as lawyers that we might have been tempted to take "the low road" on issues (as lawyers can tend to do), and Sonny would steer us to "the high road." I think he was again miles ahead of us on... persuading people on issues that are as much moral and ethical as legal. When I saw his files, I felt like it really explained a lot about where he was coming from.

For Hausfeld, the NCAA suddenly loomed as the perfect antitrust challenge. "It was a cartel right out in the open," says King. "It got his intellectual juices going. It was like taking on OPEC."

Still, you can't file a lawsuit without an actual plaintiff, and neither Hausfeld nor King knew any athletes. But Vaccaro sure did. He called many of his old basketball friends, former players like Pearl Washington of Syracuse fame and Jimmy King, who had been one of Michigan's Fab Five. Then, one day, more or less out of the blue, he got a call from Ed O'Bannon, the former UCLA basketball star who had led his team to a national championship in 1995. O'Bannon's pro career had been a disappointment, and he was now working at a Las Vegas car dealership. In a story that would be recounted endlessly, the son of one of O'Bannon's friends had been playing a college basketball–based video game created by EA Sports. One of the teams was O'Bannon's old UCLA championship team. Although there

were no names on the jerseys, the avatars' features—and even their signature moves—resembled unmistakably the players on that team.

"Dude, you're on a video game!" the boy said. O'Bannon and the others
gathered around to watch the game. "It was definitely me," says O'Bannon.
"A left-handed black guy." His friend turned to him and said, "You know
what is crazy? EA Sports is getting all that money, and you're not getting
any of it."

O'Bannon says that similar thoughts had crossed his mind when he
was at UCLA. "When you're in college," he says, "you go into the student
bookstore and see jerseys being sold with your number on them, and you
can't help but wonder why you're not being compensated. But you don't
know how to approach it, or even how to express your displeasure. You
just wind up thinking there is nothing you can do."

O'Bannon and his mother had been close to Vaccaro when he was in
high school and beyond. And though they hadn't spoken in years, Vaccaro
was the obvious person for him to call about the video game. Maybe even
the only person.

Vaccaro put him in touch with Hausfeld and King, who quickly realized that O'Bannon, a poised, mature man with no skeletons in his closet,
was the perfect lead plaintiff. (Eventually more than a dozen other former
players would join the case, including basketball greats Bill Russell and
Oscar Robertson.) Having landed the plaintiff, Vaccaro signed on as a consultant to the lawsuit, which was filed in July 2009. He refused to accept
compensation, which amazed Jon King. "For the work he did, he could easily have commanded $800,000 to $1 million," says King. Once again, Vaccaro didn't want to do anything that might allow the NCAA to cast
aspersions on his motives.

Andy Schwarz went into a funk after the deep disappointment of the
*White* case settlement in 2008. OSKR, the new firm he had started with
Rascher and two other colleagues, hit a dry spell after the financial crisis,
which didn't help his mood. He took up drumming as a hobby, and began
having long talks with his fiancée, Melodi, about whether he should take
his career in a different direction, maybe even get out of consulting entirely.

The day after *O'Bannon v. NCAA* was filed in 2009, Schwarz and
Rascher dashed off a lengthy memo to Hausfeld, outlining the work they had

done on the *White* case, their views about how to beat the NCAA's amateurism defense, and why their expertise made them the right firm to serve as Hausfeld's economic experts. Hausfeld responded politely, but didn't make any immediate move to sign them up.

Then, in March 2011, Schwarz was interviewed by Tom Farrey, an ESPN reporter who often did stories about the NCAA. Farrey was doing a long segment on *Outside the Lines,* ESPN's newsmagazine show, about whether college athletes should be paid. Although Schwarz had no public profile outside a small circle of sports and antitrust economists, Farrey had met him during the *White* case and knew that he was likely to give a provocative quote or two on camera.

Schwarz was thrilled for his first national exposure—he desperately wanted his views to be more widely known. And truth be told, he wanted himself to be more widely known too. With the cameras rolling, he delivered for Farrey. "I personally think it is the greatest injustice in American sports that we have these people that everyone loves to watch on TV and in person, and we adore them, adulate them, but we don't let them benefit from all of the money that they generate in any way near to what we would if there was a market system in place," he said, offering a succinct summary of his core belief. Later in the segment, which was entitled "Selling the NCAA," Schwarz expressed another contrarian view that few sports fans had likely ever thought about. Among the many reasons the college sports establishment gave for not paying football and men's basketball players was that the revenue they generated was needed to subsidize all the non-revenue sports, like golf, tennis, women's softball, and so on. "Is that the way we want the subsidy to go," Schwarz asked, "from a lot of inner-city minority kids to suburban white kids playing nonrevenue sports?"

On camera, Mark Emmert scoffed at Schwarz's argument, and the pushback continued after the broadcast; an NCAA blogger named David Pickle, whose official title was "director of digital communications"—and who was gaining a reputation for making ad hominem attacks on NCAA critics—described Farrey's piece as "a terrible piece of journalism" and "junk." For Schwarz, Pickle's blog post was the equivalent of a player taunting his opponent the day before the big game, giving the other team that much extra motivation. Suddenly he was energized about taking on the NCAA in a way he hadn't been before, not even during the *White* case.

Over the next month, he spent almost every nonworking, nonsleeping moment writing a long paper entitled "Excuses, Not Reasons: 13 Myths About (Not) Paying College Athletes." Though heavily footnoted, it was not exactly a piece of dispassionate scholarship; Schwarz used the paper to aggressively demolish every rationale the NCAA put forth for refusing to compensate college athletes. The paper dripped with disdain. For example, in responding to Myth 1—"It's too hard to figure out how to pay players fairly"—he noted that it was assumed that committees would have to be set up to establish a pay scale for college athletes. "It makes you wonder," he wrote, "how the Software Industry Wage Commission ever decides how much to pay computer programmers, and how the Law Firm Pay Commissariat decides on associate and partner compensation each year." In the fall, Schwarz delivered the paper at a sports law symposium held by the Santa Clara University law school.

A few months after writing the "13 Myths" paper, Schwarz started a blog called *Sportsgeekonomics*, which he thought of as a place where he, and occasionally Rascher, could lay out their controversial views and let readers respond to them. His visibility continued to rise. At the suggestion of Ramogi Huma, he was invited to speak at a "congressional forum" held by Bobby Rush, an Illinois Democrat. It wasn't a full-fledged hearing—Rush couldn't convince the Republicans, who controlled the House of Representatives, to hold one—but he gathered a group of NCAA critics for a daylong session that was well covered by the media. In his opening statement, Rush compared the NCAA to the Mafia. ("I think they're one of the most vicious, most ruthless organizations ever created by mankind," he said.)

The day before the forum, as he was driving to the airport to fly to Washington, Schwarz got a call from his thirteen-year-old son telling him that his ex-wife, Jennifer, had died suddenly. He turned around to go back, but then, thinking that maybe his son was mistaken and that Jennifer, who was only forty-three, was instead in a deep sleep—or *something*—he asked Melodi to go to her house and see for herself. When Melodi got there, she confirmed that Jennifer was dead; she had died of an aneurysm. Schwarz and Jennifer had not been especially close after their divorce, but they hadn't been estranged either, and they had successfully coparented their son with a minimum of conflict. Schwarz drove back home to comfort his son and put him to bed. But he also called his parents in Boston and asked them to take the red-eye to San Francisco, so that they could be with his son when he woke up, while Schwarz took the red-eye to Washington. That's how badly he wanted to testify.

"I think other people would have cancelled," he later wrote in an e-mail. "But as I sit here now trying to justify to myself . . . about leaving my son . . . he loves my parents more than anyone other than he loved his mom, so I don't know. It just seemed the efficient (I use that word with all of the dripping irony a half-Vulcan can muster) thing to do. I think I would do it again. But I also think that other people would think this makes me a cold person." At the least, it was not his finest moment.

The "13 Myths" paper had been a big enough hit at the Santa Clara symposium that its organizers asked him to write another paper for its 2012 event. At the same time, a sports lawyer and entrepreneur named Jason Belzer had approached Schwarz about writing something together. What the two of them came up with was a paper entitled "National Letter of Indenture: How College Athletes Are Similar To, and in Many Ways Worse Off Than, the Indentured Servants of Colonial Times."

"Like many of today's college athletes," they wrote,

Daniel Dulany, a Queens native, came from family of modest means. His father had recently run into financial troubles, so Daniel was forced to transfer from an expensive private school. The free ride he received to Maryland was a blessing for his family. Daniel had always aspired to be an attorney, and promised himself that he would work hard and eventually get into law school.

John Noblin, on the other hand, was a Norfolk native and grew up a Cavalier at heart. A young man from a family of little means, the prospect of four years in Virginia with the opportunity to practice his craft, and a free education along with room and board was a dream come true. Sure, the days would be long, especially during the summer grind preparing for the fall season, but he would take to the field in search of glory.

Dulany finished in three years, and went to work for George Platter II, a successful lawyer. He traveled to London, and upon finishing law school returned to Maryland and was admitted to the bar. He became a prominent attorney in Annapolis, and later a major land developer....

Noblin was not as fortunate as Dulany, and eventually entered the construction business. Maybe Noblin was not to blame for his lack of success; maybe it was the fault of his agent, David Warren, for getting him a raw deal in the first place. Whatever the reason, Noblin would become just another statistic in a system where unpaid labor was exchanged for the promise of success that often was out of reach.

Among today's college athletes, for every Daniel Dulany there are many John Noblins. Yet for all the similarities, neither John nor Daniel ever played college sports. In fact, when Dulany immigrated from Queens County, Ireland, in 1703 and Noblin from Norfolk, England, in 1655, it would be more than a hundred years before the University of Virginia or Maryland would be established.

Dulany and Noblin, of course, were indentured servants who "lacked the resources to pay their way to a better world and thus faced a hard bargain—stay behind in their old lives with little prospect of advancement or else spend several years working only for room and board and training in the hope of bettering themselves." The comparison to college sports was obvious—and in some ways even eerie. "Modern-day college athletes ... face similar challenges—low prospects of turning professional in their sports after their college days are over and a system in which a good deal of their value is transferred to others." The contracts that indentured servants signed was akin to the "letter of intent" heavily recruited high school athletes sign when they decide which college they'll attend. Both athletes and indentured servants faced significant penalties if they tried to abrogate that contract (such as transfer to another school). Although indentured servants got room and board—just like college athletes—the former were often paid a small wage while the latter were not. Eventually, indentured servitude faded away, in part because a stronger European economy provided jobs that made ambitious young men less willing to spend years in the shackled employ of a man of means.

"As the history of indentured servants has shown," Schwarz and

Belzer concluded, "with economic competition there is economic justice, even for those choosing short-term bondage. As the history of college athletics has shown, without economic competition, there is not."

That was the last paper about college sports that Schwarz would write on his own time. Hausfeld had attended the 2011 Santa Clara symposium, and had heard Schwarz's "13 Myths" presentation; soon thereafter he had finally hired OSKR. He had already hired Roger Noll of Stanford, with whom he had worked in the past, to serve as the *O'Bannon* plaintiffs' other economic expert. Even as Schwarz was working on the "National Letter of Indenture" paper, he and Rascher, along with Noll, were also hard at work on something far more important: the economic report that made the case for certifying the class of plaintiffs in the *O'Bannon* lawsuit. Rascher filed that report in November 2012.

They were climbing the mountain again.

# The "Our Way or the Highway" Bylaw

UNLIKE FOOTBALL AND BASKETBALL PLAYERS, WHOSE ONLY REAL ROUTE to a professional career is through college, baseball and hockey players have real choice when their high school playing days are over. That's because unlike the NFL and the NBA, baseball and hockey have extensive minor-league systems, so a baseball or hockey player who wants to skip college can sign a pro contract and start playing for a minor-league team immediately.

Most players—and their parents—need advice to make such an important decision at such a young age. As a result, a cottage industry has sprung up, with lawyers, agents, and others who advise these players while purporting to stay within NCAA rules. Whether they do stay within the rules is questionable, given the way NCAA rules attempt to keep players away from agents. Mostly the NCAA has chosen to look the other way at this widespread practice.

Andy Oliver, a pitching phenom out of Vermilion, Ohio, was in precisely this situation in June 2006. He had signed a letter of intent to go to Oklahoma State University, but he had also been drafted by the Minnesota Twins, which hoped to sign him to a professional contract. To prepare to make this decision, Oliver and his father had retained the services of Robert and Tim Baratta, two brothers in the sports advisory business. There was no signed contract between the Barattas and Oliver, and no talk of a fee. The unspoken assumption was that Oliver would hire the Barattas whenever he signed a pro contract.

At the end of the summer, well after Oliver had committed to Oklahoma State, a representative from the Twins met with Oliver and his father and offered the pitcher $390,000 if he would sign with the team instead. Oliver declined the offer and decided to stick with his plan to attend college. In his capacity as Oliver's lawyer, Tim Baratta also attended the meeting.

Two years later, by which time he had become the ace of the Cowboys' pitching staff, Oliver fired the Barattas. Furious, the lawyers sent him a bill for over $100,000—and threatened to turn him in to the NCAA if he didn't pay. Sure enough, when Oliver declined to pay, they sent a letter to the NCAA with numerous allegations of improper benefits, most of which were false. But in the course of its investigation, the NCAA discovered that Tim Baratta had been in the room when Oliver and his father were talking to the Twins. NCAA rules state that a lawyer or adviser for a player cannot directly negotiate with a pro team on behalf of a client—or even be in the room when such discussions are being held. Oklahoma State quickly declared Oliver ineligible. Indeed, under pressure from the NCAA, it was forced to do so literally hours before Oliver was supposed to pitch in an important postseason game.

Oliver retained a Cleveland attorney named Richard Johnson and sued to force the NCAA and Oklahoma State to allow him to play. Like virtually every lawyer who sees the NCAA up close for the first time, Johnson was horrified at how it operated. Oliver had been rendered ineligible without any finding of wrongdoing, or a hearing of any sort. The NCAA claimed that he had no standing to sue because he wasn't actually a member of the NCAA; only the universities were members. The idea that a college athlete couldn't use an adviser while negotiating with a potential employer struck Johnson as not only repugnant, but a violation of Ohio law—and that of every other state. What possible legal authority did the NCAA have to promulgate a rule—bylaw 12.3.2.1 in the NCAA rulebook—preventing a lawyer from competently representing his client?

But the NCAA rule Johnson found most infuriating was bylaw 19.7, the infamous Restitution Rule. That was the rule that said that if a player or an institution brought a lawsuit against the NCAA and won a temporary injunction restoring a player's eligibility, the NCAA could retroactively punish the player and the school if it eventually won the case. The alleged rationale was that opponents needed "restitution" because they had played a team with an ineligible player. To Johnson, though, it appeared that the NCAA was placing itself above the American court system, giving institutions the Hobson's choice of either ignoring a court order—and facing a potential contempt charge—to placate the NCAA, or risking punishment by the NCAA by following the dictates of the court. As Johnson later wrote in a lengthy—and angry—law review article, "Why does a rule like this even exist, and why is it called *restitution* when, more appropriately, it might be called the *it's our way or the highway* rule?" He asked for a permanent injunction that would render both bylaws unenforceable.

After a two-week bench trial in January 2009, Judge Tygh M. Tone issued his ruling in February. It was a slam dunk for Oliver. "For a student-athlete to be permitted to have an attorney, and then to tell that student-athlete that his attorney cannot be present during the discussion of an offer from a professional organization, is akin to a patient hiring a doctor but the doctor is told by the hospital board and the insurance company that he (the doctor) cannot be present when the patient meets with a surgeon because the conference may improve his patient's decision making power." He added, "No entity . . . can dictate to an attorney where, what, how or when he should represent his client."

As for the Restitution Rule, Tone was equally harsh. "Student-athletes must have their opportunity to access the court system without fear of punitive actions being garnered against themselves of the institutions and teams of which they belong," he wrote. "The old adage that you can put lipstick on a pig but it is still a pig is quite relevant here. The Defendant may entitle Bylaw 19.7 'Restitution' but it is still 'punitive' in its achievement and it fosters a direct attack on the constitutional right of access to the courts."

One result of Tone's decision was that Oliver was able to pitch again for Oklahoma State, though he had a poor season, winning no games and losing five. Another was that the NCAA, realizing that both its "no advisers in the room" rule and its Restitution Rule were in real jeopardy if the case was ultimately upheld, paid Oliver a $750,000 settlement, thus mooting the trial judge's decision.

Although Johnson would be forever proud of having beaten the NCAA, at least at the trial court level, the sad result of the settlement is that both bylaws remain on the NCAA's books to this day.

# CHAPTER 10

# "MAGNIFICO EXCELENTISIMO"

There was never any question after Myles Brand died that the NCAA would choose another university president to lead it. Whatever his conflicts with his fellow presidents during his tenure—mostly over commercialism—Brand had many qualities that appealed to them. He was an intellectual. He spent a lot of time conducting "shuttle diplomacy"—as Wally Renfro would later put it—between the powerful conferences and the smaller ones, smoothing over some of their disagreements. He was a far better public face of the NCAA, and college sports generally, than any of his predecessors—a man who could make college athletics sound like the quintessence of all that was good and right about American life. Although criticism of college sports was on the rise, thanks in part to the publicity the *O'Bannon* case was generating, Brand's reframing of college athletics as "the collegiate model" was something many college presidents applauded. The days when an athletic director could become the head of the NCAA were long over.

The man the search committee landed on was Mark Emmert, the fifty-seven-year-old president of the University of Washington. After six years in office—years in which he led a $2.6 billion fund-raising effort, but also lost bitter battles with the legislature over the state's funding of higher education—Emmert had wanted out; he considered a number of university presidencies before landing at the NCAA. In many ways he seemed the perfect choice. Most of his academic experience had been spent on campuses that stressed big-time sports; in addition to running the University of Washington, he had served as chancellor of the University of Connecticut and president of Louisiana State University. And unlike Brand, he knew a great deal about college sports; he regularly attended games, and at LSU in 1999 he had hired Nick Saban to coach the football team. Under Saban, LSU won the BCS championship in 2003, shortly before Emmert moved to Washington. "Success in LSU football is essential for the success of Louisiana State University," Emmert once said.

Telegenic, with an easy smile and a head of well-coiffed gray hair, Emmert was a popular figure on most of the campuses he presided over. He put on midnight pancake breakfasts during finals, kissed pigs, and scuba dove in the shark tank of the New Orleans aquarium to raise money. He was also a huge believer in the collegiate model—which is not to say there weren't changes that he wanted to make. Indeed, upon taking office in November 2010, he barnstormed the country, making speeches in which he decried the NCAA's outdated and absurdly long rulebook and stressed the need to give players the cost-of-attendance differential, the very issue the NCAA had fought just a few years earlier in the White case. He cast himself as a reformer.

"I was hired to be the face of a nameless, faceless bureaucracy," Emmert says. That is certainly what he became, though not quite the way he—and the people who chose him for the job—expected.

Mark A. Emmert grew up in Fife, Washington, a "farm town," as he calls it, thirty miles south of Seattle. His father was an optics technician in Tacoma; his mother a teacher's aide and a homemaker. The only college graduates he knew as a boy were his teachers and a doctor. As for sports, he played some basketball and football, and ran a little bit of track, but he was never a standout.

The most formative experience of his youth came in eighth grade, when he took a field trip to the University of Washington. After touring the campus, he told a cousin that he wanted to be president of the university one day. "I don't think I understood exactly what it meant, but there was something about running something that big," he says. "I had never been on a college campus, and it just struck us both that this would be a really cool place to be."

After high school, Emmert spent a year at community college before transferring to Washington and earning a political science degree. He supported himself by working at a garage. He had already developed a love of sports cars; he drove an Austin-Healey around campus, sometimes racing it around the Seattle area. According to friends, he was always one of the fastest drivers.

Emmert went to graduate school at Syracuse University, where he got a master's degree in public administration, and then landed his first job in higher education—student aid director at Central Wyoming College, a community college that had a branch on a Native American reservation. When he married his wife, DeLaine, also a Fife native, their first home was in a trailer on the reservation, where conditions were spartan and the drinking water had to be treated with lye.

By 1980, after a short stint at the University of Northern Colorado, Emmert was back at Syracuse, where he got a doctorate in public policy. His academic interest was well suited for the leadership roles he would take on, even foreshadowing the work he would do at the NCAA. "One of the notions that fascinated me is how do you hold together organizations? How do you get people committed to and attached to an organization, when that's not the natural predilection of our species?" he later told the University of Washington alumni magazine.

After teaching political science at Northern Illinois for three years, Emmert joined the faculty at the University of Colorado's Graduate School of Public Affairs in 1985. Seen as bright and eager, and a rising star in academia, he was soon tabbed as the assistant dean in the public affairs school, where he caught the eye of the university's president, E. Gordon Gee. Gee, who was a bit of a prodigy himself, having been named president in his thirties, was struck by Emmert's ability to rally various constituencies around his vision. "He knew that in an academic leadership role he had to connect with the public and in the political arena," Gee says.

From there, Emmert job-hopped from the University of Colorado Denver (associate vice chancellor) to Montana State University (provost) to the University of Connecticut (chancellor) to Louisiana State University (president).

It would be hard to overstate the importance of big-time athletics at LSU. The entire state, it can sometimes seem, obsesses about Tigers football. In a good year its athletic department revenue can be as much as a quarter of the entire school's revenue. (By contrast, at a large public university like the University of Michigan, athletic department revenue is a small sliver of the university's overall revenue, often in the low single digits.)

Emmert arrived in Baton Rouge in 1999. That year, the football team had a dismal 3–8 record. After the season ended, Emmert fired the coach, Gerry DiNardo, and spearheaded the search to find a replacement. One of the coaches he sought out was Nick Saban, then the head coach at Michigan State.

They met in Memphis, where Saban's agent lived. With several board members as well as his athletic director, Joe Dean, in tow, Emmert flatly told Saban—without having consulted the others—that he was the man LSU wanted. On the plane ride home, he asked Dean how he would handle the salary negotiations. Dean said he would make a competitive offer. Emmert replied that Dean should ask him what it would take to get him to LSU—and then give it to him.

Saban signed a contract worth more than $1 million annually to coach the Tigers. The next year, the team went 8–4 and won the Peach Bowl. In 2001, LSU won the SEC championship. And in 2003, when Saban delivered a national championship, Emmert was named Man of the Year in Baton Rouge. Emmert later doubled Saban's pay, making him the highest-paid coach in the nation. "He is absolutely the best boss I've ever had," Saban would tell a Baton Rouge newspaper. "He's the most significant reason I was interested in this job. Never once has he disappointed me."

Emmert's success went beyond the football field. He introduced the Flagship Agenda, aimed at raising the academic profile at LSU. When many states were investing less in higher education, LSU's funding increased 25 percent over his first four years, thanks in no small part to Emmert's persuasive lobbying. He also convinced people in Louisiana to accept tuition hikes that helped raise faculty salaries more than 20 percent and allowed for more academic programs. He lobbied the state legislature for a supercomputer and used it to recruit an astrophysicist from the Max Planck Institute in Germany. "He had a cultlike following like something

I've never seen," says Stanley Jacobs, a member of the LSU Board of Supervisors. "People would kill for him. He just had that way about him that people were drawn to."

If there was one discordant note, it was Emmert's own compensation. After the University of South Carolina tried to poach him in 2002, he was given a more than 70 percent pay increase to nearly $500,000 annually. A study at the time showed that he was paid around 40 percent more than similar executives in the South. At a Louisiana Board of Regents meeting at the time of the raise, faculty president and computer science professor Sudhir Trivedi distributed copies of "Infectious Greed," a critique of Emmert's pay written by two LSU professors. The faculty voted to condemn the new pay package.

Still, by 2004 Emmert was being wooed by his alma mater. Washington was in the midst of enormous upheaval, with a recent string of scandals that touched nearly every part of its campus: football coach Rick Neuheisel had been fired for gambling in a March Madness pool (he later reached a $4.7 million wrongful termination settlement with Washington and the NCAA); the medical center was accused of billing fraud; riots on Greek Row had strained relationships in the community; and a previous president had been asked to leave after he had an extramarital affair with a woman in his administration.

Emmert's first task was to restore Washington's tarnished image. Washington sports were not quite as successful as LSU's, but he was praised for hiring former Notre Dame football coach Tyrone Willingham. He also got credit for starting the Husky Promise, a scholarship program that paid full tuition for low-income students. In April 2008, the Dalai Lama visited campus.

Emmert's biggest impact, though, was in fund-raising. In 2007, Washington received from the state legislature a 15 percent increase over its previous two-year budget, marking the largest such bump in almost twenty years. He wrangled another $4.5 million in funding from the legislature for a laboratory to help lure scientist Gabriel Aeppli, a nanotechnology expert, to Washington from the University of London. Emmert's trick: he brought Aeppli with him to Olympia to lobby lawmakers. Though Aeppli would eventually turn down the job, it was another example of Emmert's skill at playing politics.

Over his six years in the president's office, he spearheaded a campaign that raised more than $2.5 billion. "With all respect to his predecessors, Mark Emmert is the best I have seen," Bill Gates Sr., a Washington regent and chairman of the university's fund-raising foundation—and father of Bill Gates, the Microsoft founder—once said. "The question is, do you emanate a sense of confidence, have an impressive and appropriate vision for the institution, and act like someone people would like to be nice to? Mark does all those things to a high degree."

Once again, however, Emmert's salary and benefits raised questions. Before he moved into the thirteen-thousand-square-foot president's mansion on campus, the home got a $540,000 makeover. His starting pay of nearly $600,000—other perks raised his compensation to more than $750,000—was almost double what the previous president earned. According to the Associated Press, he was the highest-paid president at a public university in the country at the time. At the end of 2007, he received a raise of more than $150,000.

When the recession hit the next year, Emmert's compensation became an even thornier issue. The presidents of Washington State University and the Evergreen State College voluntarily cut their own salaries; Emmert did not. And in a down economy, his continued pleas for more state funding were not well received; huge cuts squeezed his budget, as they did most other state agencies. His wife canceled her subscription to the *Seattle Times* after an editorial questioned her husband's salary. She wrote letters to lawmakers decrying the funding cuts. Washington "had bigger cuts than any University in the country, including in California! The state is starving your district's golden goose and yet you DON'T even mention it as a concern?!!!!" read one e-mail to House Speaker Frank Chopp.

Some in Olympia viewed Emmert's appeals for additional state funds, coupled with his own pay, as out of touch. As Emmert left Washington for the NCAA in 2010, state representative Mark Miloscia may have had the most prescient words about him. "Personally, he is a nice guy, but boy, he is the wrong messenger," Miloscia said.

Before accepting the NCAA presidency, Emmert spoke with his old mentor, E. Gordon Gee, who by then was on his second stint as the president of Ohio State University. Gee, who was also an athletics-savvy president, urged him to take the job.

"This was obviously a different task than leading a university," Gee says. "But it was very encouraging to have someone of Mark's abilities leading the NCAA. Looking back," he adds, "I don't think any of us fully grasped what he was getting into, including him."

There were hints, though, at what was to come. A month before he arrived in Indianapolis, Emmert received two memos that spoke of the greatest challenges he would face. One e-mail, dated October 4, was a strategic plan from Bob Williams, the NCAA's vice president of communications. "One of the most damaging criticisms we face is the hypocrisy in which we operate," it read.

The eleven-page document described in detail how Emmert would have to lead the campaign to change the perception that the NCAA was "cold and faceless." He would have to be active on social media and visit campuses around the country. The NCAA, in turn, would help tell the stories of its student athletes, from producing online "Day in the Life" features to approaching Turner Broadcasting, which owned the rights to March Madness, about partnering on a national student-athlete town hall. "We have both a significant need and a unique opportunity to change the public discourse related to intercollegiate athletics," Williams concluded.

Two weeks later, Emmert received another e-mail, this one from Wally Renfro, who laid out other key issues Emmert would face. Again the issue of hypocrisy was at the top of the list.

"There is a general sense that intercollegiate athletics is as thoroughly commercialized as professional sports," wrote Renfro. "Some believe that athletics departments study how to emulate the pros on marketing their sports (primarily football and basketball), and sometimes lead the way. And the public would generally agreed [sic] that has all taken place at the expense of the student-athlete whose participation is exploited to make another buck for a bigger stadium, the coaches, the administrators or for other teams who can't pay their own way. It is a fairness issue, and along with the notion that athletes are students is the great hypocrisy of intercollegiate athletics."

Later in the memo, Renfro called student-athlete well-being a "really big question" and asked Emmert to think about how he would tackle it. "What is your commitment? How important is this compared to competitive equity? A former commissioner, whose name I will not mention but whose initials are Roy Kramer, would often stand before the NCAA Convention during the debate on legislation and proclaim that this or that proposal was good for student-athletes or bad for student-athletes. I'm confident Roy believed the position he advocated, but it was relatively easy to figure that whether it was good or bad for student-athletes was almost always related to whether it was good or bad for the SEC. If the well-being of student-athletes is your No. 1 focus, it will be important to define with some precision what that means and where the boundaries are."

Emmert had no interest in the kind of radical reform being advocated by Sonny Vaccaro, or that was implicit in the *O'Bannon* case—reform that might allow the athletes to share in the riches being generated by the games they played. "If we move towards a pay for play model, that would be the death of college athletics," he said to one interviewer early in his tenure. "Then they are employees, subcontractors. Why would you even want them to be students? Why would you care about their graduation rates? Why would you care about their behavior? This is exactly why the NCAA was created—to stop such nonsense." He maintained, as his predecessors had, that in contrast to the NFL and the NBA, "we are a voluntary association whose primary function is education." And he talked constantly about the NCAA's "core values." At a retreat he held for college presidents in August 2011, he asked if there was anyone in the room who didn't believe in the collegiate model. It was clear from the way he asked the question, says someone who was there, that he was not looking for a robust debate, but rather an expression of solidarity.

Emmert's idea of reform was to make things somewhat better for the athletes without doing anything that might truly upset the applecart. He was in favor of multiyear scholarships, for instance, instead of allowing a coach the authority to renew the scholarship each year. He set up a committee to examine the enforcement process, and another to look for ways to shrink the rulebook, which he believed should be a quarter of the size it was. He raised the academic progress rate teams needed to meet in order to play in the postseason. (One of the first teams to be punished under that rule was the University of Connecticut.)

Sometimes, in those early speeches he made during his barnstorming tour, Emmert could sound as if he were the NCAA's biggest critic. He openly mocked the NCAA rulebook, for instance. He liked to tell audiences that athletes were allowed to receive a bagel, but that if they got cream cheese too, it was a rules violation. "Stupid, picayune rules," he said, shaking his head in dismay.

His first big reform push, which he says came out of that presidents' retreat, was to provide scholarship athletes with a $2,000 stipend, as well as allow schools to offer four-year scholarships. The stipend, Emmert said, was not "pay for play"; rather, it was his way of helping scholarship athletes close the cost of attendance gap. To Emmert, the stipend would show that the NCAA was willing to change and modernize, and that student-athletes were indeed at the center of his agenda.

The NCAA's executive committee approved both measures later that year. The changes were made outside of traditional NCAA legislative channels, meaning compliance officers and athletic directors were mostly bypassed. In athletic departments across the country, the blowback was harsh—particularly among smaller schools who worried they, too, would have to pay stipends to keep up with schools with more resources.

"The money has to come from somewhere," Akron athletic director Tom Wistrcill said at the time. "Where do you get it from? I can't go out and raise $500,000 a year to pay for this."

University of Minnesota women's basketball coach Pam Borton also voiced concerns. "I think you'll see more sports cut because of this, more opportunities taken away from other student-athletes in other sports," she said, adding that she believed that college athletes would likely just waste the money anyway. "Kids are spending the money going shopping and buying shoes and tattoos and buying mopeds," she said. "Things they don't need instead of using the money for things that they do need."

Schools complained about four-year scholarships too, even though the new rules simply allowed rather than mandated them. Indiana State wrote to the NCAA that a team could be "locked in" to a contract "potentially with someone that is of no 'athletic' usefulness to the program."

By December, more than 160 schools opposed the stipend measure, overriding the board's edict, and Emmert and the NCAA were forced to retreat. The four-year scholarships, meanwhile, remained, though barely. More than 60 percent of Division I schools voted against them as well. The force of Emmert's personality, so tried and tested in his previous jobs, had fallen short in his first big moment at the NCAA.

If coaches and university athletic administrators were quickly becoming Emmert critics, there was another constituency that was also troubled by the NCAA's new leader—the NCAA's staff. Even as Emmert officially took over the president's post, he fired a number of top executives. Among them were general counsel Elsa Cole, senior vice president Dennis Cryder, and executive vice president Tom Jernstedt. Greg Shaheen, who was named interim executive vice president for championships, would later be fired too. Jernstedt, a longtime and well-respected staffer known throughout athletic departments around the country, was let go over the phone—without a face-to-face meeting. By September, another seventeen employees had been laid off. ("It's not the way it should have been handled, but the way I had to do it at the time," said Emmert of Jernstedt's telephone firing.)

The reshuffling rubbed many the wrong way—inside the building and around the country. "These were people you had long-standing relationships with," one athletic director says. "There was a trust factor that was lost."

The harsh rhetoric Emmert used to describe the NCAA in his public remarks was off-putting to some of the staffers who remained. David Pickle, the "director of digital communications," who used to send out nasty tweets mocking opponents of the NCAA, grew concerned over Emmert's use of what he called his "bully pulpit." Emmert, he complained, was criticizing the NCAA with such seeming relish that it was demoralizing to the staff. (Pickle left the NCAA in 2013.)

There were other worries too. Former enforcement staffer Dave Didion recalls the day Emmert was introduced to the staff as the new president. Emmert told a story about traveling to Spain with a group of college presidents. Before one of their meetings, Emmert was asked his title and he said he was a college president, an important position in the United States. When he arrived at the meeting, his placard, as Didion recalls Emmert's telling of the story, read "Magnifico Excelentisimo." Although Emmert would later claim the story was meant as a joke, nobody laughed.

"Of all the stories he could have told that first day, why this one?" Didion says. "You could tell he thought very highly of himself." It was true; Emmert was not a modest leader. He drove a Porsche with a license place that read "Boxster," the make of his sports car. He and other higher-ups in the NCAA had special parking places near the entrance to the building;

many saw the Porsche parked next to the Maserati driven by the new general counsel, Donald Remy, on their way in to work every day.

Emmert owned a second home on the posh Whidbey Island off the coast of Washington. His salary was more than $1.5 million. Staffers gossiped over reports of how much money he spent on the NCAA's private jets. Rumors circulated—which he later flatly denied—that he spent thousands of dollars on a Persian rug for his executive suite. "He certainly loves the good life and sometimes the optics aren't exactly what you might expect," Pickle says. "He enjoys his trappings of being in a powerful position." Added another former staffer, "There was a feeling that this wasn't our mission, that Mark didn't stand for what higher education should be about."

Even Emmert's attempts to engage his employees backfired. Early in his tenure, he introduced a new slogan—"One Team, One Future"—to build morale inside national headquarters. He brought staffers to the JW Marriott, a short walk from the NCAA building in downtown Indianapolis, to unveil it. When they returned to work the new motto was emblazoned on the sidewalk outside their offices and on walls inside the building. Even their desktop computer backgrounds were changed to feature the new slogan. "You were just thinking what an utter waste of money and an utter waste of time," one former staffer said. "We had real work to be doing."

The stories of Emmert's self-importance went beyond Indianapolis. One year, he was invited to the Kentucky Derby by Kentucky governor Steve Beshear. When he arrived in Louisville, Emmert asked for his own private police escort from the hotel to the track. He showed up at the race with a detail of two bodyguards who hovered near him the entire time— the governor had only one security person with him, according to a person who attended the function. "Like he was being protected from something," the person says. "The governor didn't even want to sit with him." ("I have no memory of being flanked by bodyguards," says Emmert. "They had people escorting folks all over the place.")

Longtime employees couldn't help but compare Emmert to their old boss, Myles Brand. Brand also used a private jet and was paid well, but he didn't flaunt it. He drove a Chevy Blazer, "and not a new one," one staffer says. In many ways, the two presidents were polar opposites. Brand was often shy and reserved. Aside from his annual "state of the association" speech each year, he was a low-key presence at NCAA conventions, while Emmert liked to interview student-athletes after they won awards, "talk-show style," as Pickle described it. Emmert was in front of the media so often that he was nicknamed "King of the Press Conference" by some staffers. When a series of favorable stories were written about him after the presidents' retreat, he forwarded the clippings to his wife so she could note the good press he was getting.

Emmert to this day remains mystified that his salary could engender so much animosity. "It is somewhat ironic that people say this guy is hypocritical because he's well compensated," he says. "Well, I am well compensated, but I've never understood compensation in America. A basketball coach in America oversees thirteen people whether it's an NBA coach or a college coach and might make five, six million dollars. A high school teacher overseeing thirty-five people in the inner city makes $60,000. I don't understand that. I think I know what's more important to society, but I don't know what's more important to the marketplace. The marketplace seems to think a coach overseeing thirteen kids is worth a lot more."

The topic of his car also ruffles him. "Just so you understand, I have a $50,000 Porsche Boxster," he says. "I've got friends with SUVs that cost more than my car."

As the NCAA faced greater threats, it would need better from its leader.

# An Excess of Tutoring

**THE BIGGEST ACADEMIC SCANDAL EVER TO HIT COLLEGE SPORTS TOOK** place at the University of North Carolina, where for almost two decades the chairman of the African and Afro-American Studies Department, along with the department administrator, created fake "independent studies" classes that never met and required almost no work, in an effort primarily aimed at helping athletes remain eligible. As noted in chapter 12, the scandal unspooled slowly, beginning in 2011, thanks to the investigative reporting of Dan Kane, a reporter for the *Raleigh News and Observer*. Although the NCAA eventually charged the school with violating its rules, it averted its eyes for almost four years, seeming to wish it away because it had only recently sanctioned the school for a completely different scandal, one having to do with football players consorting with agents (heaven forbid!).

Yet well before the broad outlines of this truly horrific academic scandal became known, the NCAA had no trouble severely punishing two Tar Heel football players, on allegations of academic fraud, for what should have been no more than traffic violations: they sought "improper" help from tutors. The NCAA has rules limiting how much assistance an athlete can get from an academic counselor; that's part of its pretense that players don't get special treatment due to their athletic stature. Among other things, a tutor not only can't edit an athlete's paper, he or she isn't even allowed to make specific suggestions to improve it. Also, a tutor can only interact with an athlete during special tutoring hours, and not via e-mail at other times.

Thus it was that in the course of investigating that earlier North Carolina consorting-with-agents scandal in 2010, an athletic department official came across a November 2008 e-mail exchange between a tutor named Jennifer Wiley and Devon Ramsay, a junior fullback with pro potential. Looking through Ramsay's old e-mails—yes, athletes at most schools have to give athletic department officials access to their e-mail accounts—the official discovered that the fullback, who was then a freshman, had sent her a three-page sociology paper, and she had made a series of edits, including rearranging the first paragraph, adding a three-sentence conclusion, inserting five commas, making four tense changes, and adding a period at the end of a sentence. The e-mails also made clear, however, that Ramsay understood the material and had written the paper himself. The university's Honor Court found the help Ramsay got from Wiley to be so within the bounds of normalcy that it declined to even hold a hearing.

The NCAA didn't bother to hold a hearing either, but for a rather different reason: after reviewing the e-mails, and without even bothering to talk to him, it declared Ramsay permanently ineligible on the grounds of academic fraud, thus seeming to end his college career four games into his junior season.

Up to this point, Ramsay had been navigating this problem on his own, without a lawyer. That's something college athletes often do, especially when the alleged offense appears to be a misunderstanding that they think (usually wrongly) will be cleared up once they explain the situation. Ramsey also assumed that the university would have his back, which is almost always a mistake. Most of the time, a university's main concern when it runs into trouble with the NCAA is its own welfare, not that of its athletes.

Ramsay finally found a lawyer in Robert Orr, a former state supreme court justice. Or rather, Orr found him after reading a story about his plight in the *News and Observer*. Ramsay's mother, Sharon Lee, had driven to Chapel Hill from New Jersey; upon arriving, she asked to speak to a reporter from the paper. They met in a local coffee shop, where Lee poured out her anger, bewilderment, and hurt at what had happened to her son, before driving back to New Jersey.

By then, UNC had been granted a reinstatement hearing by the NCAA. Orr, who had never handled an NCAA case before, was horrified to learn that such a hearing requires that the player acknowledge his guilt, and that university officials were pressuring Ramsay to do so. Orr insisted that the university cancel the hearing, and shrewdly pointed out to the NCAA that there was no evidence that Ramsay ever used Wiley's suggestions; his two-year-old paper had been tossed by the professor long ago. On that grounds, the NCAA restored one year of Ramsay's eligibility. After a journalist from the *New York Times* began looking into the case, the NCAA gave him back his second year as well.

Sharon Lee, though happy with the outcome, still fears for her son's future. "Devon is always going to have to answer questions about his ethics," she said. "The NCAA has done far more damage to my son than deprive him of the chance to play football games."

The second North Carolina football player to be accused of academic fraud by the NCAA was Michael McAdoo, a linebacker; his problems also stemmed from an e-mail exchange with Wiley in November 2008, when he was a freshman. Needing to finish a paper for his Swahili class, McAdoo reached out to Wiley (who had officially left her tutoring position, but was still helping athletes when they asked). He had never learned in high school how to write citations for a paper, and now he had a paper that was due the next day. Wiley wrote the citations herself. When the North Carolina athletics department came across the e-mails two years later—again, as part of the investigation into the agent scandal—it turned the evidence over to the Honor Court and the NCAA. The Honor Court ruled that McAdoo should be suspended from UNC for a semester. The NCAA ruled that the linebacker was finished as a college athlete.

Unlike Ramsay, McAdoo was unable to get his eligibility restored, so he sued the NCAA and the university. The suit was tossed out of court, but before that happened, McAdoo's lawyer submitted as evidence the Swahili paper that had caused all the trouble. Fans of rival North Carolina State quickly—and gleefully—discovered that much of it had been plagiarized. At the *News and Observer,* Dan Kane, who had just been assigned to cover the tail end of the agent scandal, noticed that the professor for McAdoo's Swahili class, who had failed to catch the plagiarism, was Julius Nyang'oro, the head of the African and Afro-American Studies Department. In fact, McAdoo had taken three courses from the department. He later said that the Swahili course had been "assigned" to him by an academic counselor. "You sign up. There's no class. You write the paper. I'd never seen anything like it," McAdoo said. But he did as he was told.

Then, in August 2011, Kane obtained a transcript for Marvin Austin, a former UNC defensive end who had been drafted by the New York Giants. It showed that during the summer of 2007, before he was even officially enrolled in the school, Austin had taken a senior-level course from the African and Afro-American Studies Department—and got a B-plus. His professor? Julius Nyang'oro. Thus began Kane's investigation into the sham courses in the department, which three years later resulted in an internal report that acknowledged, finally, that their main purpose was to help athletes retain their eligibility.

Sadly, Devon Ramsay was seriously injured in his first game back, dashing his hopes of playing in the NFL. McAdoo, meanwhile, went undrafted in the NFL's supplemental draft, but signed on with the Baltimore Ravens in 2011, the year the Ravens won the Super Bowl. But after suffering a torn Achilles tendon, he was cut by the Ravens in 2013, and most recently was playing Arena football.

McAdoo and Ramsay have both filed class action lawsuits against UNC, claiming they were robbed of the first-class education they had been promised when they were being recruited. Ramsay is being represented by his old lawyer, Robert Orr, who has become something of an NCAA activist, along with Michael Hausfeld, the mastermind of the *O'Bannon* suit.

For his part, McAdoo can still recall the humiliation he felt after being banned from college football by the NCAA. "I had days when I was so depressed I had trouble getting out of bed," he said.

Then he added, "I would still like to get a college degree someday. Just not at the University of North Carolina. They just wasted my time."

# CHAPTER 11

# "THE WAY YOU WERE TAUGHT TO PLAY"

A delegation from ESPN flew to Chicago and Big Ten headquarters in the spring of 2004 to meet with Jim Delany. Although the Big Ten's decade-long deal with the cable giant still had three years to run, at more than $500 million, Delany and ESPN's head of programming, Mark Shapiro, were about to start negotiations on a new deal.

Ratings had been somewhat flat in recent years, and some believed that it was because there was a glut of college sports on the air. Shapiro delivered ESPN's offer: an inflation-based raise, which amounted to a nominal bump on the previous pact. Delany didn't bother to consider whether it was an opening bid and not meant to be taken too seriously or a hard-line proposal. He felt insulted. "They said if you don't accept, you're rolling the dice. The offer might not be here in a year," Delany recalls. "I said, 'Consider the dice rolled.'" Still, his options were limited. With all-sports cable networks like NBC Sports Network and Fox Sports 1 still years away, ESPN was the only game in town. And it was playing hardball.

"College presidents were happy to accept modest growth," Delany says. "I thought we could do better." Spurning ESPN, he decided that the Big Ten would start its own all-sports network. And so it did: in 2007, the Big Ten Network, or BTN, a joint venture between Fox and the Big Ten, went on the air, with programming rights selling for a staggering $2.8 billion for twenty-five years. Not for the first time, a Delany move forced everyone else in college sports to race to catch up. As they did, they triggered a wave of commercialism that dwarfed anything that had come before it.

Delany had been thinking about a Big Ten network for years. He took note when the New York Yankees started the YES Network in 2002, and former ESPN honcho Steve Bornstein launched the NFL Network the following year. (The Mountain West Conference started a channel the year before the BTN, but retained no equity.) Around the time of his meeting with Shapiro, Delany broached the idea of a Big Ten network to Dave Brandon, a University of Michigan regent who was also the CEO of Domino's Pizza. Brandon assumed at first that Delany was bluffing. "The business model was believable enough that I said to him, 'This is a brilliant strategy,'" Brandon recalls. "'You're going to head-fake ESPN into believing that you have an alternative.'"

In fact, Delany was so serious that he never had a second meeting with ESPN. And when the network doubled its offer, he still said no. To see his vision through, he needed two things: a green light from the Big Ten's presidents and a partner to build and launch the network. For years, Delany had been a master at working with school presidents; he spoke in academic terms rather than sports, and his professorial style and law school background endeared him to them. And of course he had always delivered financially, so they trusted his business acumen.

His pitch to the presidents was that the channel would be a way to showcase less visible sports like wrestling and women's lacrosse. To appease their fears that this might be a bridge too far, he vowed that the network wouldn't accept beer advertising. "In a way, I don't think it was a departure," says then Northwestern president Henry Bienen. "We were already in the TV business. You already had your big-time athletics." Besides, Bienen adds, "Northwestern was interested in more revenues and Jim was a great negotiator."

Delany found a partner in News Corp.–owned Fox, which was hungry for college sports programming, and had recently outbid ESPN for the BCS. (The network began to broadcast the games in 2006.) Delany's tenure and record of financial success also appealed to the president of Fox Sports,

Bob Thompson. "Jim was always at the forefront and that's one of the reasons we wanted to work with the Big Ten," Thompson says.

Why was Fox so determined to land more college sports? Because with technology like the DVR and the Internet allowing people to skip advertisements and watch TV shows at their convenience, sports was being perceived—correctly—as the only form of programming that consistently drew live audiences. Which in turn meant bigger advertising dollars. Late in 2004, the NFL announced a series of new five- and six-year TV deals worth a total of $11.5 billion. Major League Baseball would announce new contracts in the summer of 2006 for $3 billion over seven years. In a memo he wrote to the Big Ten presidents in 2005, Delany noted that college sports stood to gain as well. In addition to ESPNU, ESPN's all-college-sports network, CBS was buying the nascent College Sports Television cable channel. "All of this creates some uncertainty and real opportunity for this conference," Delany wrote to the presidents. At the World Series in Chicago that year, he ran into Len DeLuca, the ESPN executive. "We're in a very advantageous situation," Delany told him.

In June 2006, the Big Ten announced the creation of the Big Ten Network, with Fox owning 49 percent and the conference 51 percent. The new network would only televise the lower-tier football games, meaning that the marquee matchups like Michigan–Ohio State were still up for grabs. This time, ESPN didn't take any chances: it paid $1 billion over ten years to acquire the rights. It was a new record for a college conference. By 2008, all but two of the Big Ten's eighty-eight football games were televised nationally, while no other conference topped 70 percent.

According to a doctoral dissertation written by then University of Pennsylvania student and now Drexel University professor Karen Weaver, when the agreements were finalized Delany reported to Big Ten presidents that the Big Ten was the fifth most valuable sports entity in the country, behind only the NFL, Major League Baseball, the NBA, and NASCAR. "They're like General Electric," says former Big 12 commissioner Dan Beebe. "They're the biggest." For his efforts, Delany was given a $1.5 million bonus.

Having trumped ESPN, Delany now took on the big cable companies like Comcast and Time Warner. Their view was that the BTN amounted to niche programming that belonged on a sports tier. Delany wanted the network on basic cable in the eight states where the Big Ten schools were located—which would mean an additional seventeen million cable subscribers, and more than $200 million a year in subscriber fees.

Comcast put up the biggest and most public fight. It poured money into an advertising campaign and issued a press release claiming, "Indiana basketball fans don't want to watch Iowa volleyball, but the Big Ten wants everyone to pay for their new network." For their part, Delany and Big Ten schools urged their fans to drop Comcast for DirecTV, which was also owned by News Corp. and was more than happy to carry the BTN.

As the BTN launched in 2007 without agreements with Comcast and other major cable companies, millions of fans in Ann Arbor, Columbus, Madison, Iowa City, and other Big Ten cities couldn't watch their favorite football teams. Delany took a beating in the press. Editorials referred to the "Big Ten tax" Delany wanted to impose. Representative John Dingell, a Democrat from Michigan, asked why the conference was taking games off free TV and making fans pay for them. An op-ed in the *Wisconsin State Journal* wondered if the Big Ten was "becoming a publicly funded sports franchise with classrooms."

But it was Comcast that ultimately folded. With the stalemate threatening to drag into a second football season, Comcast lost customers by the droves. So the cable giant relented, agreeing that summer to put the BTN on basic cable in the Midwest. Reflecting today on the land mines he navigated to launch his network, Delany can't help but explain it with a sports metaphor. "We're the Big Ten, we're the big guy, so they say we're not supposed to scrap for loose balls, we're not supposed to draw the charges," Delany says. "But the answer is we're in an environment of competition and you do it because that's the way you were taught to play."

That "environment of competition" meant, of course, that the other big conferences weren't about to allow themselves to be lapped by the Big Ten. And they weren't. In 2008, the SEC signed a fifteen-year pact with both CBS and ESPN that paid out around $3 billion. Two years later, the ACC signed a deal with ESPN that paid nearly $2 billion over twelve years. In 2010, with its March Madness deal up for renewal, the NCAA signed a fourteen-year agreement with CBS and Turner Broadcasting worth $11 billion. In 2011, the Pac-10—which by then had been renamed the Pac-12—announced the formation of the Pac-12 Network. The next year, the ACC signed an extension with ESPN worth $3.6 billion over fifteen years. The Big 12 nabbed a thirteen-year deal worth $2.6 billion with Fox and ESPN. In 2013, ESPN and the SEC announced an extension of their deal and the formation of a new SEC Network. Months before the network launched on August 14, 2014, a Baton Rouge newspaper, *The Advocate*, estimated the SEC Network would soon be worth $500 million for the conference—or more than $35 million annually for each of its schools.

Those TV deals, in turn, sparked a new round of conference realignment that was astonishing in both its scope—by the time the dust settled one in four major football programs had swapped conferences—and its naked display of greed. From a business perspective, it made perfect sense: the big conferences wanted to add good football schools in important television markets, which would increase their value in the marketplace, expand their footprint, and enrich all their members. Universities that weren't already in a "power conference," as they were now being called, clamored to join one: not only would they play in a more prestigious conference, but they would share in the television spoils. That longtime rivalries would be severed; that the time college athletes spent on the road and away from the classroom would increase dramatically; that one storied conference would even be destroyed—all these considerations paled in comparison to the money to be made from switching conferences. And that's all that mattered.

Once again, a Delany move started the dominoes falling. In 2009, he said that the Big Ten was considering its expansion options—an announcement that sent shudders through the other conferences, which knew that few of their members would be able to resist the lure of the Big Ten's revenues. The Big Ten considered twelve-, fourteen-, and sixteen-team league models before finally deciding to invite Nebraska, a longtime Big 12 football power, in June of 2010. Needless to say, Nebraska said yes. (Delany called Nebraska's addition exciting "academically and athletically," though no one was fooled.) A few days later, the Pac-10 added Colorado, another Big 12 school. The rush was on. The Pac-10 later lured Utah from the Mountain West—that's when it renamed itself the Pac-12—while the ACC plucked Syracuse and Pittsburgh from the Big East. The SEC nabbed two Big 12 schools, Texas A&M and Missouri, thus destroying two great rivalries in one fell swoop: Texas–Texas A&M, and Missouri–Kansas.

Schools dreaming of striking it rich pitched themselves like used-car salesmen. Hawaii wanted to join the Pac-12; Memphis made overtures to the SEC; Southern Methodist flirted with the Big 12. For those schools that couldn't find their way into a top conference, TV still offered a path toward greater visibility. The Mid-American Conference, desperate for exposure, signed a deal with ESPN putting more games in the middle of the week. Louisville built its football program around one central tenet: get more games on ESPN—and it proved successful when the Cardinals got an invite to the ACC.

Having lost four schools to other conferences—and on the verge of losing Texas and Oklahoma to the Pac-12—the Big 12 was near collapse. It persuaded Texas to stay, but it wasn't loyalty that motivated Texas; it was money. To keep Texas, the Big 12 had to promise that it would get a larger share of the conference's TV package and that it could even start its own network. By 2012–13, the Longhorns led the nation with $110 million in football revenue. (The next closest school was Alabama with $88 million, according to Dan Rascher.) To replenish its ranks the Big 12 grabbed Texas Christian University, which scrambled aboard, reneging on a pledge to join the Big East. Then the Big 12 reached halfway across the country for West Virginia from the Big East.

The Big East wasn't so lucky. For nearly two decades, commissioner Mike Tranghese had feared this moment. "I was commissioner for nineteen years and I never spent one day in which I didn't worry about losing members," he says. Founded as a basketball conference, the Big East had always been a step behind in football, which is why most of its football schools were so quick to seek out greener pastures. In a last-ditch effort to survive, the Big East invited three schools with football programs from the other side of the country: San Diego State, Boise State, and Houston. Except that didn't last either, as the core basketball schools of the traditional Big East—Catholic schools like Georgetown, Marquette, St. John's, and Providence—announced that they planned to start a new conference of their own. The Big East, first imagined by Dave Gavitt to harness the power of television, was destroyed by television thirty-five years later. Gavitt had picked the wrong sport.

Connecticut, a longtime football-playing member of the Big East, was the biggest loser of all. With the Big East gone, and its football program not strong enough to get into one of the power conferences, it found itself in a geographic hodgepodge called the American Athletic Conference with a motley collection of schools like Tulane, Temple, and East Carolina—schools whose only commonality is that they had no place else to go. Connecticut's plight pained Tranghese. "It sickens me and angers me that you have this program with unbelievable accomplishments—national titles in men's basketball, an unprecedented run of excellence in women's basketball—and now they're out of the Power 5, they're left on the outside because of football," he says.

Multibillion-dollar TV deals and conference realignment weren't the only examples of how college sports had become big business. Take, for instance, licensing and marketing. By the early 2000s, Jim Host had plenty of competition as the marketing arm for university athletic departments. One competitor, Learfield Sports, had deals with nearly a hundred schools and estimated annual revenues of around $300 million by 2014. Learfield handled, among other things, stadium concessions and hospitality services, ticket sales, and online streaming. One of its most successful marketing campaigns was to help Allstate introduce a field goal net bearing the insurance company's logo. Allstate started with the few Learfield-affiliated schools in 2004 and soon had its name on the nets at some seventy-five college stadiums.

Host, meanwhile, sold his company to the global entertainment giant IMG in 2007 for $74 million. A few months earlier, IMG had bought another company, the Collegiate Licensing Company, and had started its own powerhouse college sports marketing division. (Its founder, Bill Battle, joined IMG before he was hired as Alabama's athletic director.) By 2013, IMG College's revenues hit $375 million. Just how much were the deals worth to schools? Kentucky left IMG for a start-up, JMI Sports, in 2014. The Wildcats' marketing rights sold for $210 million over fifteen years.

Or take coaches' salaries. Bill Curry had made $42,500 as the football head coach at Georgia Tech in the early 1980s; by the mid-1990s, he was at Kentucky, where he made upward of $350,000. "It seemed like an awful lot of money to me," he says. "But really it was just the beginning."

By 2014, the nation's twenty-five highest-paid football coaches at public universities earned an average of $3.85 million a year. In many states, college football or basketball coaches were the highest-paid public employees. After winning three national championships, Alabama's Nick Saban was courted by Texas; Alabama kept him by delivering a $1.5 million raise, which put his 2014 salary above $7 million. When Ohio State hired Urban Meyer in 2011 at a base salary of $4 million a year, university president E. Gordon Gee described the contract as "a mark of our dignity and nobility." On the basketball side, Duke's Mike Krzyzewski was king. He pocketed nearly $10 million in salary and bonuses in 2011, according to *USA Today*. Schools even paid coaches millions just to go away, just like the pros did. When the University of Illinois fired its football coach in 2011 and its men's and women's basketball coaches in 2012, the school was on the hook for around $7 million in buyouts.

College coaches were now represented by the same superagents who represented professional athletes and pro coaches. One such agent was Jimmy Sexton, whose client roster included both professional and college coaches, a number of whom went back and forth between the two ranks, getting raises with each move. When athletic directors complained about Sexton—and they did—he had a simple response: "We *are* responsible for driving up prices," he once told *USA Today*. "What else are we supposed to do? Drive them down?"

Administrators did just fine too. Ohio State athletic director Gene Smith had a clause in his contract that called for an extra week's pay—around $18,000—for any individual national championship won by an Ohio State athlete. The clause had been in place for years, but it only became widely known when the bonus kicked in after wrestler Logan Stieber won a title in 2014. The question raised was a simple one: why could an AD cash in on an athlete's success but not the athlete himself? (By the next year, the clause was eliminated for individual athletes, though it remained for titles won by the football and men's basketball teams.)

Along with their expensive coaches, universities now needed state-of-the-art facilities that usually came along with massive fund-raising drives—how else could they attract the top-rated recruits? A sampling of activity from 2005 to 2013: Arizona spent $72 million on its football stadium, while Baylor dropped $250 million and Colorado $170 million; at Illinois, $116 million was tabbed for its football stadium and another $11 million on new basketball locker rooms, training rooms, and other arena improvements; the price tag for Iowa's football stadium upgrades was

$89 million; Georgia Tech and Kansas State treated their basketball facilities to $50 million and $18 million makeovers, respectively. The most opulent of them all was Oregon's palatial $68 million football training facility. Opened in 2013, and largely funded by Nike founder Phil Knight (Knight donated so much to Oregon that his alma mater was dubbed the University of Nike), it included such luxuries as hand-woven rugs from Nepal, couches made in Italy, and wood imported from Brazil.

Schwarz and Rascher had long argued that it would make much more sense—and be much more cost-effective—to spend money *on* the recruits rather than on all the excesses designed to attract recruits. Of course this argument held no sway over the college sports establishment. South Carolina president Harris Pastides gave one of the more novel rationales, saying, "We don't want to have collegiate superstars getting large incomes, living in luxury housing, driving a luxury car and having luxury jewelry."

Athletic directors were now supposed to have the skills of a CEO, managing all the facets of a growing—if nonprofit—business enterprise. In the case of Michigan, its athletic director between 2010 and 2014 *was* a former CEO; Dave Brandon, the Michigan trustee, had stepped down as the chief executive of Domino's Pizza and taken the reins of the Michigan athletic department. Brandon saw the completion of a $226 million renovation of the university's famed football stadium, the Big House, and spent nearly $100 million on the basketball stadium and millions more on other athletic facilities. He started a marketing department, ramped up fundraising, increased coaches' salaries, and raised ticket prices at the Big House.

He viewed his job like any of those he'd held in the business world. "Capital investment in this business is more than any for-profit New York Stock Exchange–listed company I've ever worked for," he says. "I have to raise revenue, deploy capital, manage costs, market to a broad group of stakeholders. I have to be stand-alone and be accountable to a lot of people who care about what I do. All that reminds me of the work I did as a CEO for twenty-two years. The way the model works, what I'm running now is a $150 million business, only our products are eighteen- to twenty-three-year-old kids who are student-athletes." (Brandon resigned in disgrace in 2014 after a Michigan quarterback returned to a game after sustaining a concussion, although the football team's 18–16 record his last three seasons certainly didn't help his cause. He was replaced by an interim athletic director, Jim Hackett, the former CEO of Steelcase Inc., an office furniture company based in Michigan.)

What did universities gain by chasing revenue that it could then spend on its athletic department? One rationale was that there was no better way to market a school in the twenty-first century. Presidents had a favorite saying: the athletic department is the front porch of the university. It is the shiny façade that makes potential students take a closer look. The theory that a successful athletics program can attract students is also known as the "Flutie effect," dating to 1984 when Boston College quarterback Doug Flutie threw a last-second Hail Mary pass to defeat defending champion Miami on national TV. After Flutie won the Heisman Trophy, applications at BC jumped 30 percent the next two years.

There have been studies over the years reflecting this theory, showing bumps in applicants, class sizes, and even higher SAT scores for incoming freshmen after a school reaches a top-tier bowl game or makes a deep run in the men's basketball tournament. Texas A&M commissioned a study that found that when its quarterback Johnny Manziel won the Heisman Trophy in 2013, it carried $37 million worth of media exposure. And winning teams were also said to help schools land big donations. But not everyone agrees. A 2004 Knight Commission examination found the "Flutie effect" to be minimal, and the commission has also noted that even if such gains are real, they are often short-lived. Still, it hasn't dissuaded university presidents. "When you have a team that does well, applications soar," says Maryland president Wallace Loh. "Your athletic program is how most people get to know you. Whether you like it or not, that's the reality."

But another supposed rationale was that universities had no choice: they needed the additional revenue to keep pace with their ever-growing expenses. "People talk about the marketing and growing commercialism in college athletics," Wisconsin athletic director Barry Alvarez said when the Big Ten Network was formed, "and it's true. I fully understand the expenses in running a program like ours, trying to fund twenty-three sports while giving our coaches the wherewithal to compete at this level. That costs money." Without more money, athletic departments couldn't build the glistening facilities they needed to attract the best athletes, couldn't hire the brand-name coach, couldn't pay for the chartered jets to get to games halfway across the country that would be televised nationally in prime time—*they just wouldn't be able to compete.* In the messaging prepared for Big Ten presidents in the 2007 rollout of the network, PR firm Hill & Knowlton wrote that "being able to show the *need* for new revenue versus the *want* for new revenue will be important."

Andy Schwarz, for his part, had no problem with conferences and schools chasing multimillion-dollar deals—it was the market at work, which he fiercely believed in. But he thought the explanation offered by the college sports establishment got it exactly backward. "College sports broadcast rights are not expensive because it costs a lot to hire coaches," he says. "Coaches are well paid because college sports broadcast rights sell for good money and a good coach helps get those broadcast contracts—and the fund-raising that comes with a good team." Schools wanted the money, says Schwarz, and then blamed the market they themselves created.

One reason for the increasing popularity of college football during these years was the Bowl Championship Series, that postseason system designed by the commissioners in the late 1990s to pit the nation's top two teams against each other in a championship game. During the season, weekly computer rankings announced the BCS's top two teams and the potential number 1 versus number 2 matchup that had been absent from the sport for decades. And while the rankings were almost always controversial, that was actually a marketing plus; it meant increased attention and intrigue with every passing week of the football season. SEC fans paid closer attention to the Pac-12 and the Big Ten—and vice versa—because games all across the country each Saturday affected the BCS rankings.

Unlike the NCAA-run men's basketball tournament, where the proceeds were shared by all NCAA schools, the BCS was controlled by the top football conferences. The leaders of that group, the ACC, Big East (and after its demise the American Athletic), Big Ten, Big 12, Pac-12, and SEC, had designed the system to reward their members with most of the money and almost all the prime spots in the top bowl games each year—the Orange, Sugar, Rose, and Fiesta.

The terms of the BCS made it extremely difficult for a team from one of the smaller conferences to appear in the best games and collect the big payouts. The money reflected the divide too. In the 2003–04 postseason, the sixty-two BCS universities collectively earned about $90 million for the four bowl games; the fifty-five teams from the other conferences split $6 million. The big schools created the wealth and they intended to keep it. "The Mid-American Conference and Mountain West and those conferences received some money from the BCS, but they really weren't a part of the thing," acknowledges Roy Kramer, the former SEC commissioner.

But the BCS also created an enormous backlash. The smaller schools vocally and passionately campaigned against it—and they found sympathy from a public that was clamoring for a postseason playoff. Tulane went undefeated in 1998 and didn't merit a BCS invite; Marshall did the same the next year. Utah and Boise State each finished the 2004 season unblemished, but there was only room for one in the BCS and neither got a shot at the national title. (The Utes beat Pittsburgh from the Big East, 35–7, in that year's Fiesta Bowl.) "This is classic cartel behavior," William Greiner, president of the University at Buffalo, said of the BCS in 2003.

The BCS engendered so much animosity that Congress hauled college sports leaders to Washington three times to discuss it. In 2003, Tulane president Scott Cowen testified, calling for an eight- or sixteen-team playoff. After his home-state Utah Utes went undefeated again in 2008—and were again passed over for the national championship BCS game—Republican senator Orrin Hatch called a hearing to examine whether the BCS violated antitrust law. Utah's attorney general appealed to the Department of Justice. The next year, Yahoo Sports' Dan Wetzel, Josh Peter, and Jeff Passan published a scathing book, *Death to the BCS*, that derided the series as a malignant, money-hoarding cartel. They referred to Delany as "the ayatollah" because of his insistence on protecting the Big Ten's relationship with the Rose Bowl and the larger conferences' lion's share of the payouts.

Around this time, a lawyer with ties to the Big South Conference reached out to Schwarz and Rascher looking for help. The economists responded by writing a letter with a number of other economists and legal professors to the Justice Department, calling for an antitrust investigation into the BCS, which they called a "cartel that controls distribution of competitive opportunities and benefits."

"These smaller conferences thought of the cartel differently than we did," Schwarz says. "They didn't want to blow it up, they just wanted in on it. But finally they were using the right vocabulary."

When Emmert called his presidents' retreat in 2011, he addressed the widening financial gap between the BCS schools and the other football programs. Briefing materials for the presidents included a report that noted that over the previous two years, median-generated revenues in the non-BCS conferences declined by 5 percent, while expenses grew by 6 percent. "This is where the real pressure on sustainability comes into question," the report read. One of the options to address it was a greater redistribution of wealth, including the football TV dollars.

Needless to say, the idea went nowhere. The BCS added a fifth big bowl game and two more teams in 2006, but it went no further. At a college sports conference in December 2010, a panel of commissioners discussed the state of the BCS, among them Delany and Karl Benson, then the commissioner of the Western Athletic Conference (WAC). As Benson spoke of wanting more access to the "big stage" for his schools, Delany cut him off. "The problem is your big stage takes away opportunities for my teams to play on the stage they created in 1902," he said, adding that there was no more give in the revenue structure either.

Benson had watched Delany operate for as long as anyone. He became commissioner of the MAC in 1990, then moved to the WAC in 1994 and finally the Sun Belt in 2012. In all their years as conference commissioners, one conversation sticks out for Benson. Fifteen or so years ago, he asked Delany what he might like to do after he was done at the Big Ten. The answer surprised him. "Jim said he'd like to be an athletic director at a Division III school," Benson recalls. No TV money, no hundred-thousand-seat stadiums, no athletic scholarships, no million-dollar coaches. Just pure college sports.

Two schools on the East Coast watched the conference musical chairs from very different perspectives. Rutgers, New Jersey's flagship state school, was never much of a sports powerhouse. Although the Scarlet Knights are reputed to have played the first-ever college football game (against Princeton, in 1869), Rutgers spent most of the modern era in the Atlantic 10, with schools like the University of Massachusetts, Xavier, and Dayton. A new football stadium helped it score an invite to the Big East for the 1995 season, but as the Big East crumbled during conference realignment, Rutgers needed an exit plan.

Maryland, some two hundred miles south, was a founding member of the ACC in 1953 and had been a stalwart member of one of the top conferences in college sports for six decades. The Terrapins had sent Super Bowl quarterbacks to the NFL, like Boomer Esiason and Neil O'Donnell, and in more recent years the basketball program, under Coach Gary Williams, competed successfully with Duke and North Carolina, even winning a national championship in 2002. Maryland appeared to be very comfortably on the right side of college sports' divide.

But the two schools did share one thing: red ink. Neither had a tradition of football success, but given football's growing importance, each invested heavily in the first decade of the twenty-first century. After Rutgers went 11–2 in 2006 and finished the season ranked twelfth, best in school history, the athletic department went all-in, giving coach Greg Schiano a big raise (at $2.3 million, he was the highest-paid football coach in the Big East), increasing stadium capacity, and adding more luxury seating. But fund-raising fell short and the team regressed. Schiano eventually left for the NFL, and the athletic department racked up an incredible $190 million deficit between 2004 and 2012. To offset the losses, student fees were raised and state funds diverted.

At Maryland, new coach Ralph Friedgen led a renaissance when he arrived in 2001. In his first season, the Terrapins won the ACC for the first time since 1985, earning an invite to the Orange Bowl. In the ensuing years, the athletic department spent millions to upgrade its football stadium, increasing capacity to more than fifty thousand; a new $125 million basketball arena was also opened in 2002. But when both the basketball and football teams faltered, so did donations. Annual deficits reached $7.8 million. Seven varsity sports were cut in 2012. Maryland needed money, badly.

From his perch in the Midwest, Delany was also watching the shifting landscape. He was especially bothered when the ACC grabbed Pittsburgh and Notre Dame (Fighting Irish football remained independent, however) and the SEC crept north to annex Missouri. In Delany's view, his rivals were encroaching on Big Ten territory. "We felt threatened," he says.

Population across the Rust Belt, the heart of Big Ten country, was stagnant, while other parts of the country saw increases. In 1960, Michigan had twice the population of Georgia; today they're close to even. With population the key to TV markets, Delany worried about the long-term viability of his iconic conference.

In Rutgers and Maryland, Delany saw opportunity. Rutgers offered access to the biggest media market in the country, New York, while Maryland was in another important market, Washington, D.C. Between the two markets there were ten to fifteen million TV homes, a half a million of whom were Big Ten graduates. In November 2012, Delany extended the two schools invitations to join the Big Ten. It was his coup de grâce. "Our assessment was the world had changed around us," he says. "There was more risk in staying where we were than in changing," His own role in the change went unmentioned.

For Rutgers, the decision was easy. Toiling away in the American Athletic Conference after the Big East's collapse, the school was thrilled to have a chance to play with the big dogs. "It's a coup," says Tom Pernetti, Rutgers's athletic director at the time. "No one did better than Rutgers in conference realignment." Rascher agrees. "They made an investment and it paid off," he says. "Ten years from now they're going to be identified with the Big Ten and they're going to get the money and the status that comes with that." Indeed, soon after announcing its move to the Big Ten, Rutgers inked a huge marketing deal with IMG College worth $65 million over eleven years. (Pernetti resigned in 2013 after a video surfaced showing Rutgers's basketball coach verbally and physically abusing his players. In early 2015, Pernetti was appointed president of multimedia for IMG College.)

There are some at Rutgers who remain unconvinced, like economics professor Mark Killingsworth. Even as the Big Ten payouts come rolling in, he notes Rutgers is still projected to run a $183 million deficit between 2013 and 2022. The library recently had its budget cut by $500,000, while the football coach received a $200,000 raise to lift his salary to $1.25 million. And there are calls from alumni and a state senator to spend as much as another $100 million to upgrade facilities to better compete with the likes of Michigan and Ohio State. "If Rutgers is in the Big Ten, and they want to be competitive in the Big Ten, those are the things they are going to have to do," said New Jersey governor Chris Christie.

"Spending money to make money in athletics has never worked at Rutgers," Killingsworth counters. "It's the football version of supply-side economics. We heard the same thing when we joined the Big East, so Big Ten or no Big Ten, we need to stop using academics as a reserve fund. It's a simple question of resource allocation."

Maryland's story was more complicated, though it ultimately came down to the same thing: money. The ACC had lots of TV money coming in and it was used to doing the poaching, rather than being poached. But the Big Ten simply had more financial resources than even a powerful conference like the ACC. Seeing Maryland's losses pile up, Delany approached the university and opened secret negotiations with Maryland president Wallace Loh. Maryland was projected to make as much as $100 million in six years by jumping ship; the windfall was too much to resist. But that didn't mean the Maryland community was happy about it. When the news broke, ACC fans were outraged—and so were the other ACC schools, which felt blindsided. Internal Maryland e-mails published by the *Chronicle of Higher Education* painted a stark picture. "How ugly is it getting?" Maryland chancellor William "Brit" Kirwan wrote to a colleague. "We have 80 emails against, 2 for," came the answer.

Pat Forde of Yahoo Sports wrote a tough-minded column decrying the moves. He called collegiate athletics "College Sports, Inc.," writing, "Avarice and ego are what drives realignment, at further cost to college sports' soul." In the press conference announcing Maryland's move, Loh didn't necessarily disagree. "Number one, by being members of the Big Ten Conference, we will be able to ensure the financial sustainability of Maryland athletics for decades to come," he said.

Julie Hermann, who took over at Rutgers for Pernetti, also understood that it was all business. "We have to make our contribution to the Big Ten," she says, "and get cable companies to pay for the Big Ten Network out here."

Delany was in a reflective mood one morning in the summer of 2013, as the Big Ten was holding its annual football media days in Chicago. These were annual kickoff parties for the upcoming season: players and coaches met the media and talked up their teams, and die-hard fans turned out and got revved up. Commissioners also used the occasions to deliver "state of the conference" addresses.

Hours before he delivered his keynote, Delany sat on the twenty-third floor of the Hilton, high above the hustle and bustle, looking over a pile of notes. His communications director and former Michigan basketball player Diane Dietz sat by his side. Delany's room stood at the end of a marble hallway lined by crystal light fixtures that offered a sweeping, panoramic view of Lake Michigan. It was a perfect July morning; sailboats dotted the horizon. Delany later made sure to note that the room had been comped by the hotel.

Staring out at the lake, Delany defended his two and a half decades at the Big Ten. He stressed the education that came with a college scholarship—which could change the life of Big Ten athletes, just as it had changed his life. There were ten thousand student-athletes in the Big Ten who were getting $150 million in aid so they could go to school, he said.

Delany understood the criticism. He earned nearly $3 million in 2011. Federal graduation rates around the country hovered at 50 percent. Calls to pay players had never been louder. With so much money rolling around—money he helped generate—it was getting harder and harder to defend amateur college sports. Delany agreed that players deserved more; he wanted them to have a stipend of a few thousand dollars—similar to the laundry money he had. "Kids deserve to have pizza and beer," he said. In a lot of ways, in fact, he seemed to wish that he could roll back the clock, back to the days when he was an athlete at North Carolina. "You can't take at-risk students and put them into our environment and not expect there to be an element of exploitation," he said.

But Delany also knew that the more money that poured into college sports—which he was as responsible for as anyone during his years at the Big Ten—the harder it was to go back. "There's no doubt about it, it's more difficult the more commercial you are," he went on. "It's more difficult the more national you are, the more global you are. There's conflict all the time there."

Delany delivered his "state of the conference" speech that afternoon. It focused on his own roots and how schools could better keep faith with their athletes. They could promote education by adhering to the NCAA rule that was supposed to prevent athletes from spending more than twenty hours a week on their sport, he said. They could offer scholarships that covered the full cost of attendance. They could provide lifetime education trusts so if an athlete turned pro he could always return to complete his degree.

"I believe in the opportunity for young people to go to college through intercollegiate athletics who otherwise wouldn't have an opportunity to go there," Delany said during his speech. "And I believe in the equal opportunity of players and students to achieve that opportunity. These in some ways seem like maybe quaint ideals, but they're more than a quaint ideal to me, I've experienced it."

The next morning, Delany put on his other face, his business face, as he hosted a breakfast at the Hilton for Big Ten athletic directors and bowl executives. The Big Ten was now affiliated with around a dozen bowls, from the Rose Bowl in Pasadena to the Pinstripe Bowl in Yankee Stadium. Delany schmoozed the crowd and posed for photos. A video played, recognizing the academic achievements of Big Ten athletes. Then Delany welcomed everyone to Chicago—and welcomed Maryland and Rutgers to the conference. With the Big Ten now covering nearly 30 percent of the country by population and more than 15 percent geographically, he was practically giddy about the possibilities of his new empire. "Our footprint is Colorado to the mid-Atlantic, Canada to the mid-South," he said to the group. "We wanted to have a national slate of bowls because we're the closest thing to a national conference."

During the summer of 2012, Delany traveled to Tanzania to climb Mount Kilimanjaro with several Rose Bowl executives. One day he went on a tour of Arusha, a town near the mountain. He saw a building with a satellite dish on it, approached, and found it was the local cable operator. In the door, he left his card with a note on it.

"Call if you're interested in Big Ten sports," it read.

# Scholarship Blues

**JOHN ROCK WAS IN HIS SOPHOMORE SEASON AT GARDNER-WEBB, A** small Baptist school located in the foothills of the Blue Ridge Mountains, when he began seriously contemplating life after football. It was 2010. Rock was the starting quarterback for the Runnin' Bulldogs, but he knew he wasn't an NFL prospect; Gardner-Webb is a tier below the top programs, and Rock's education was important to him. When he accepted his scholarship, he agreed to redshirt for a season, in part because it would give him a chance to begin a master's degree during his final year of football eligibility. Rock, in other words, was exactly the kind of "student-athlete" the NCAA purports to exalt.

By his third year on campus, the Ohio native had grown interested in a politics degree. He applied and was accepted to an internship program that fall that would send him to Raleigh for the spring semester to work for state senator Debbie Clary. He would get to see the political process unfold up close and be back on campus for summer football practice. "One of the majors I was considering required an internship, and this was how I could play football and make the most of college," he says today. "It seemed perfect."

Rock was wary of NCAA red tape and understood his year-to-year scholarship wasn't guaranteed, so he talked to the compliance department, his coach, and the athletic director, Chuck Burch. Everything was fine, they said. His scholarship would be waiting for him. It was, they agreed, a great opportunity. Rock happily went off to Raleigh.

But while he was away during his internship, Gardner-Webb's football coach was replaced by Ron Dickerson Jr. Rock first met his new coach when he made a trip from Raleigh for a team banquet. When he introduced himself to Dickerson, he recalls, his new coach was gruff. "I thought you transferred," Dickerson told him. "I was about to draft your release."

Confused, Rock explained the internship and that he would be back for summer workouts. He was happy to compete for the starting job, he said, but he had been assured of his place on the team—and of his scholarship. Still, nervous about the scholarship, he went back to the athletic director. "It's between you and your coach," he was now told.

At another meeting with Dickerson the next day, Rock pleaded to remain on the team, while insisting on finishing the internship. He believed he and his coach came to an understanding: he would regularly call to check in from Raleigh for the remainder of the semester and the coaches would reassess the situation over the summer. Slightly relieved, he returned to the state capital, but soon he got a disturbing call from a teammate. His nameplate had been removed from his locker and an equipment manager had cut the lock. All his notes on opponents from the previous season were gone and teammates had scavenged through his equipment. Rock called Dickerson, who flatly told him he was done. His scholarship had been given to another player. "It was like a punch in the stomach," Rock says.

After a series of follow-up calls and e-mails to Dickerson and the athletic department went unanswered, Rock returned to campus seeking answers. He found his coach in the stands after the team's spring game and begged for his scholarship. The best Dickerson would offer was the chance to walk on the next season. Rock didn't know what to do. "Where do we go from here?" he asked. "I don't know where we go," Rock recalls Dickerson saying. "But I'm going to watch film."

In the summer, Rock received the official paperwork canceling his scholarship. In an appeal hearing, the university found no evidence that he should keep it. And because the process dragged out across the entire summer, his transfer options were limited. Even enrollment at a new school would be difficult without taking off a semester. Backed into a corner, he took out around $40,000 in loans for tuition, room, and board so that he could stay at Gardner-Webb and graduate. He is still paying off the debt.

In 2012, Rock sued the NCAA over its one-year scholarship policy—and limits on total scholarships—on antitrust grounds. If there was competition in the marketplace, his lawyers argued, athletes could choose schools that offered more secure financial aid. He isn't alone. Two years earlier, Joseph Agnew, a former Rice cornerback whose scholarship was revoked after he sustained a back injury, sued the NCAA over the one-year scholarships. Durrell Chamorro, a kicker who arrived at Colorado State in 2005, was cut from the team, stripped of his scholarship, and went into debt trying to pay for his education. He filed a lawsuit in 2014, but did not meet statute-of-limitations requirements. Agnew's case was dismissed. As of publication, Rock's case was still winding its way through the courts.

Rock graduated from Gardner-Webb, but still has the football bug. After playing in German and Italian leagues, he tried a semester of law school, but went right back to Germany to be quarterback and offensive coordinator for a new team. "I'm just not ready to give up the game," he says.

# CHAPTER 12

# "THE WHIFF OF THE PLANTATION"

Sonny Vaccaro's favorite movie is *The Insider*, starring Russell Crowe and Al Pacino. The 1999 film tells the story of a former cigarette executive named Jeffrey Wigand, played by Crowe, who becomes the first whistleblower from inside the tobacco industry. Pacino plays Lowell Bergman, a renowned television producer who relentlessly pursues and cultivates Wigand as a source as he prepares an exposé of Big Tobacco for *60 Minutes*, the CBS newsmagazine show.

"I must have seen the movie three or four times," Vaccaro says. "I was mesmerized by it. It inspired me."

By 2010, Bergman was gone from *60 Minutes* and had moved to *Frontline*, the PBS weekly documentary show, where he was an on-air interviewer as well as a behind-the-scenes producer. He had also joined the faculty of the UC Berkeley Graduate School of Journalism, where he organized a conference on investigative reporting every spring.

Vaccaro was by then some four years into his crusade against the NCAA. He'd had one important early success, helping to convince Michael Hausfeld to file the *O'Bannon* lawsuit. But that litigation would surely take years to get to trial, assuming it wasn't settled first. From time to time, Vaccaro would get invited to make a speech on a college campus, and while he was getting larger crowds than he had at the beginning, his talks were not making much of an impact on the wider world. Not long after he left Reebok, he had lunch with James Gandolfini, the star of *The Sopranos*, who was considering playing him in an HBO film. That would certainly put his cause on the map, but while Gandolfini agreed to play the part, the film was still years away. When Gandolfini died suddenly of a heart attack in the summer of 2013 at the age of fifty-one, the movie still hadn't been made.

Then, in the spring of 2010, during one of his occasional forays to New York, Vaccaro had lunch with Armen Keteyian, an investigative reporter for CBS who specialized in sports stories and had done work over the years for *60 Minutes*. Vaccaro asked Keteyian if he knew Lowell Bergman; Keteyian said he not only knew him, he would soon be heading to Berkeley to attend Bergman's conference. "Can you make contact with him for me?" Vaccaro asked. Keteyian came back from Berkeley with permission to give Vaccaro Bergman's e-mail address.

In June, Vaccaro e-mailed Bergman, requesting a meeting. He responded by asking Vaccaro to send him "something in writing" that would give some details about what he wanted to talk about. ("Saves a tremendous amount of time.") Vaccaro ignored Bergman's request, and instead sent Bergman a second e-mail: "Currently I am involved with the O'Bannon lawsuit as an unpaid advisor," he began. "It is this case and many other things I have witnessed over the years in sports at the highest corporate levels that are inconsistent with the ideals of amateurism in America on the collegiate level. I would like to meet with you not necessarily with a specific agenda but to discuss thoughts I have had over the years pertaining to the mix of amateurism and professionalism and to share my thoughts with you on the moral and ethical solutions."

He continued, "I know what you have done and who you are and what you stand for. Over the past four years I have been following a different path in my continuing fight against what is called today amateur athletics."

Intrigued, Bergman set up a meeting for later that month. On the appointed day, Vaccaro and Pam made the two-and-a-half-hour drive from Carmel, where they were then living, to Berkeley—only to be told that Bergman didn't have a lot of time, twenty minutes at the most. Instead, they spoke for two hours.

It didn't take Bergman long to realize why Vaccaro hadn't tried to put his thoughts down on paper. That approach would never work with Sonny Vaccaro; he neither spoke nor thought in a linear fashion. No matter. What Vaccaro told Bergman shocked him—just as it had Hausfeld and Jon King. "This guy is telling me that athletes only get one-year scholarships, so coaches can cut them. He's telling me about all the money being made in college sports and the athletes aren't getting any of it. He's telling me that they don't get workers' comp if they get injured, and that the NCAA gets around that by calling them 'student-athletes,'" says Bergman. "I was dumbfounded."

Largely on the basis of that meeting, Bergman decided to do something about the NCAA for *Frontline*. The story didn't run until March 2011—timed, naturally enough, to air just as the NCAA's March Madness tournament was getting under way. Titled "Money and March Madness," it was only twenty-one minutes long. But it covered all the bases—bases that were all too familiar to people like Andy Schwarz and Ramogi Huma, but were a revelation to the millions of people, even dedicated sports fans, who didn't follow the ins and outs of the NCAA.

On camera, Andrew Zimbalist, a Smith College sports economist and author of *Unpaid Professionals*, his stinging critique of the NCAA, explained to Bergman the unfairness of the one-year scholarship. Bestselling author Michael Lewis, who had written *The Blind Side*, about an offensive lineman at the University of Mississippi, described college athletes as "indentured servants," echoing Schwarz and Jason Belzer. O'Bannon told Bergman about his lawsuit, while Vaccaro, in his usual excitable fashion, explained that he had left Reebok to "go after the complete fraud of amateurism in America."

Vaccaro had persuaded Chicago Bulls star Joakim Noah, who had played at the University of Florida, to speak to Bergman. "There is a whole lot of exploitation going on," said Noah, who told him about the sense athletes had that the NCAA's real mission was to nail them for something. ("Oh, this kid's dirty," he said, recalling things players would hear.) Noah had loved playing college basketball, he said, and he loved his coach, Billy Donovan, whom he was still close to. "Kids giving everything they've got, and doing it for their schools—that's a beautiful thing," he said. "But who are these people making all this money, and shouldn't the kids get a piece of it?"

Watching "Money and March Madness," one gets the sense that the NCAA never saw it coming. And why would it have? March Madness usually brought it glowing press. The worst criticism the NCAA got in the nonsports press was that the graduation rates were low—something that Mark Emmert claimed to be addressing with the new ban on postseason play for schools that didn't score above a certain number in their academic progress rate.

Emmert himself went on camera to defend his institution. He came across the way corporate spokesmen often do when confronted by a tough television interviewer: defensive, cautious, wedded to his talking points—and a little shell-shocked at the questions he was being asked. No doubt, he expected Bergman to ask him about the NCAA's $10.8 billion contract with CBS and Turner Broadcasting to televise the tournament. But he seemed surprised when Bergman asked him about his own salary, which he refused to divulge. (Instead, Bergman noted that Brand had been making $1.7 million when he died.) He bridled when Bergman asked his response to Michael Lewis's contention that the way college sports treated its athletes was unjust. He seemed taken aback when Bergman handed him the document that athletes had to sign in order to play—and asked whether this was why they didn't control the rights to their own images. When Bergman asked him why the NCAA wouldn't use some of its riches to fly players' parents to the Final Four—something Noah had complained about, noting that many parents couldn't afford the trip—Emmert huffed, "The NCAA doesn't provide travel benefits for families." Over and over, he kept insisting that "student-athletes are students, not employees." Maybe in a friendlier forum this answer might have sufficed. But on *Frontline*, it sounded hollow.

Vaccaro contends that Bergman's story was important not just because of its content but also because of its audience. A journalist completely outside the realm of sports, working for a media organization that was aimed at an elite, educated, nonsports audience, had looked closely at the NCAA and found it wanting. Issues of due process, injustice, and exploitation would resonate with this audience. Just a few years before, the *White* case had gotten almost no publicity. Yet the *O'Bannon* lawsuit was now getting exposure on PBS. "Things really started to feel different," says Vaccaro.

If Bergman was one of the first important nonsports journalists to delve into the inequities of the NCAA, a second one was right behind him. Taylor Branch, the Pulitzer Prize–winning historian best known for his three-volume history of the civil rights movement, had accepted an assignment from the *Atlantic* magazine to examine the NCAA. Branch knew a lot about sports, which was why the NCAA intrigued him; he had been a football star in high school, and had also coauthored Bill Russell's fine autobiography, *Second Wind*. One of the first people Branch sought out was William Friday, the cofounder of the Knight Commission, who had spent some thirty years as the president of the University of North Carolina system; the two men had known each other since the days when Branch was a student at Carolina. A passionate believer in amateurism, Friday "positively exhorted me to take on The Atlantic project and rescue colleges from the NCAA's money trap," Branch later recalled in an e-mail. "His charge was literally to 'give the university back to Socrates,' which I took to mean restoring the primacy of academics." That was Branch's starting point.

As he worked on the story, however, "the scales fell from my eyes," and by the time the article came out in the October 2011 issue of the magazine, Branch had arrived at a very different place. The cover image showed the sweaty torso of a muscular African American athlete with a tattoo on his arm that read "Property of NCAA." The story was titled "The Shame of College Sports."

The real scandal in college sports, Branch wrote, "is not that students are getting illegally paid or recruited, it's that two of the noble principles on which the NCAA justifies its existence—'amateurism' and the 'student-athlete'—are cynical hoaxes, legalistic confections propagated by the universities so they can exploit the skills and fame of young athletes. The tragedy at the heart of college sports is not that some college athletes are getting paid, but that more of them are not." In an online video accompanying the article, Branch said, "There is absolutely no justification, in principle or law or reason, why the people who are generating all of this money, these hundreds of millions of dollars, shouldn't be entitled to a piece of it."

Branch was struck by the way the NCAA punished athletes for selling their university-branded football paraphernalia for tattoos (there was just such a case with a handful of Ohio State players in 2010), yet these same football players wore corporate logos of companies that were paying millions for the privilege. "Last season, while the NCAA investigated him and his father for the recruiting fees they'd allegedly sought," he wrote, "Cam Newton compliantly wore at least 15 corporate logos—one on his jersey, four on his helmet visor, one on each wristband, one on his pants, six on his shoes, and one on the headband he wears under his helmet—as part of Auburn's $10.6 million deal with Under Armour."

It also did not escape Branch's notice that the majority of athletes who played college football and men's basketball were African American. "Look at the money we make off predominately poor black kids," Dale Brown, the former basketball coach at Louisiana State University, told him. "We are the whoremasters." In the most incendiary line in his article, Branch wrote that the NCAA lets off "the unmistakable whiff of the plantation."

Walter Byers had used that same word in his 1995 autobiography, but the country hadn't been ready to hear it. Now it was. In the months after his article came out, Branch was the country's most visible NCAA critic. He was invited onto television shows and college campuses to detail his critique. His article was tweeted and talked about. Inside the NCAA, executives passed it around like samizdat. If Bergman's Frontline story had caused tremors, "The Shame of College Sports" was more akin to an earthquake.

As the earth began shifting under the NCAA, Emmert and his staff seemed completely unprepared to deal with the new tougher scrutiny they were facing—scrutiny that was suddenly coming not just from one-off magazine articles, but from the community of sportswriters who covered the NCAA, most of whom had always before accepted its version of reality. Sportswriters like Dennis Dodd at CBSSports.com, Andy Staples of Sports Illustrated, and the blogger Patrick Hruby became relentless critics of the NCAA. Longtime NCAA practices—practices that had rarely been the subject of press coverage, much less criticism—were now being held up to ridicule: the Harvard freshman women's basketball player who lost a year of eligibility because the NCAA misunderstood the significance of a standardized test she had taken while living in England. The graduate student with a year of eligibility left who went to a different graduate school and couldn't play because the NCAA refused to grant him a waiver from the rules that transfers had to sit out a year. The two years' probation meted out by the NCAA to the University of Nebraska because the athletic department had violated a rule covering, if you can believe this, textbooks. Nebraska had mistakenly covered the cost of athletes' books that their professors recommended for their classes rather than only the ones their professors *required*, which was what the NCAA allowed.

The deference the sports press used to accord the NCAA was replaced by withering commentary. Pat Forde at Yahoo.com started using the phrase "College Sports, Inc." whenever he wrote about commercialism. Staples's articles, often dripping with sarcasm, stressed the NCAA's inconsistent application of its rules, many of which he clearly found to be idiotic. ("Welcome to the maddening world of the transfer athlete at the mercy of the NCAA, where the rules apply as written—unless they don't," he wrote in one of his stories.) Dodd went straight at Emmert himself, even calling for him to resign in February 2013.

Writers who had never before thought to take on the NCAA began to see the sports beat differently. One such journalist was Jon Solomon, a college football writer for a relatively small newspaper, the *Birmingham News* in Alabama (he has since moved to CBSSports.com). In 2011, he wrote a six-part series examining how college athletes were treated, a series that flowed from one central idea: "There was a lot of new money flowing into college sports," he says, "and the paper wanted to know what the athletes thought about it. Who was speaking for them?" He wrote stories about health insurance for college athletes, Ramogi Huma's efforts to build an organization that would advocate for players, and the NCAA's commercialism committee. When he learned that a former Duke basketball star named Jay Williams had once authored a paper documenting how the Duke jersey with his number 22 had generated more than $1 million in sales for apparel companies and Duke, Solomon wrote about that too. By 2013, he was writing almost exclusively about the NCAA, with an emphasis on the *O'Bannon* case and other NCAA-related litigation, about which he was one of the acknowledged experts among the press corps.

Sportswriters were not the only ones piling on. Coaches used to live in fear of the NCAA, yet in December 2012, John Calipari, the controversial

Kentucky basketball coach known for recruiting "one and done" freshmen—
players who leave for the NBA after a single season in college—felt embold-
ened enough to write a blog post harshly critical of the NCAA for its rules
about food. Athletes were only allowed to eat university-provided food the
three times a day they were at the training table—and couldn't even bring
snacks from the training table to their rooms. "We're signing billion-dollar
agreements and moving teams across the country for money, and we're
worried about a kid eating a sandwich at night," he wrote. (Calipari later
wrote a book in which he described the NCAA as a crumbling empire, comparing it to the Soviet Union just before the Berlin Wall fell.)

At *USA Today*, a reporter named Steve Berkowitz created a database of
coaches' salaries and athletic department revenue, which became a much-
covered annual event. Brad Wolverton of the *Chronicle of Higher Education*
began to write deeply reported stories that burrowed far inside university
athletic departments. One of his most memorable articles, published in the
summer of 2012, was about the culture of academic counseling, which had
grown enormously since the NCAA stopped requiring minimum SAT
scores in 2003. Wolverton built his story around a University of Memphis
football player named Dasmine Cathey, who could barely read when he
got to college, struggled academically throughout his four years, and, despite badgering from the academic support staff, remained several courses
short of graduating by the time his eligibility was up. He was working as a
deliveryman.

In North Carolina, an investigative reporter for the *News and Observer* in
Raleigh, Dan Kane, who had never covered sports, began to slowly unravel
an unprecedented academic scandal at the University of North Carolina.
With the help of a key source, former UNC academic counselor Mary Willingham, Kane exposed the fact that for nearly two decades, the university's African and Afro-American Studies Department had allowed athletes
and other students to enroll in sham classes that never met, required almost
no work, and for which they were given high grades. Academic counselors
regularly steered athletes to these classes, especially those who were in
danger of losing their eligibility due to poor grades. The scandal would re-
verberate for years, humiliating UNC, embarrassing the NCAA, and impli-
cating the department head, Julius Nyang'oro, and the former department

manager, Deborah Crowder, who had been the prime mover behind the fraud. (Ultimately, Julius Nyang'oro was indicted but the indictment was dropped when he agreed to cooperate with an internal UNC investigation.)

All of this was bad enough. What made it worse was that even as the NCAA was facing more scrutiny than at any time in its history, its top executives, starting with Emmert, presided over a series of self-inflicted debacles. The most prominent of them were these three:

**Penn State, July 2012:** In the wake of the Jerry Sandusky sexual abuse scandal—in which the former Penn State assistant coach was accused (and ultimately convicted) of sexually molesting young boys, sometimes in the Penn State football shower room—Emmert held a nationally televised press conference to announce the sanctions the NCAA was imposing on the school. The punishment was severe: a four-year postseason ban; the erasure of all victories going back to 1998 (which meant that Penn State's legendary coach, Joe Paterno, who died several months after the scandal broke, would no longer be college football's winningest coach); a loss of ten scholarships for the next four years; and a $60 million fine, among other things. Penn State football players would also be able to transfer without having to sit out a year. Throughout the press conference, Emmert repeatedly denounced Penn State for putting football above "academic values"—as if that problem were unique to the university. The sanctimony was palpable.

Critics were quick to note that Emmert had completely sidestepped the NCAA's own enforcement process: it had done no investigation of its own, had given Penn State no opportunity to defend itself, and had essentially strong-armed the school into accepting its harsh penalties by threatening to impose the "death penalty"—banning the school from playing football altogether. Critics also questioned whether the Sandusky scandal was even within the purview of the NCAA. Wasn't this something law enforcement should handle? Indeed, as horrible as the scandal was, what NCAA rules had been violated?

Given the enormity of the scandal, no one inside the college sports establishment dared to publicly criticize Emmert. But many insiders seethed. To them, it appeared that Emmert had stepped outside the boundaries of his authority in an effort to make himself and the NCAA more powerful. Their resentment would soon bubble over.

(After a Pennsylvania state senator sued the NCAA over the Penn State sanctions, e-mail evidence was made public that showed a number of top NCAA executives were wary of what one described as Emmert's attempt to "bluff" Penn State into accepting the penalties. The lawsuit, which was settled in 2015, resulted in the NCAA repealing some of its sanctions.)

**Shabazz Muhammad, November 2012:** Widely thought to be the best player coming out of high school, Muhammad was declared ineligible before playing his first game for UCLA. The issue was that a white benefactor, with a long history of friendship with his family, had paid for several of his recruiting trips. The NCAA, unconvinced that the friendship was real, ruled that the money was an improper benefit. Muhammad, after missing a half dozen games, appealed.

Shortly before the appeal was supposed to be heard, the *Los Angeles Times* published a remarkable story. Florence Johnson Raines, a Memphis lawyer, told a reporter that three months earlier, literally days after Muhammad's family had turned over hundreds of pages of documents to the NCAA, she had been on an airplane and heard a man bragging that his girlfriend, "Abigail," was going to bring down Muhammad. "My girlfriend's investigating him, and he's dirty," she recalled the man saying. His girlfriend was Abigail Grantstein, the NCAA enforcement official investigating Muhammad.

Offended, as she later put it, "in the delight he seemed to take in something that . . . could ruin this man's life," Raines sent an e-mail to Dennis Thomas, the commissioner of the Mid-Eastern Athletic Conference—and at the time the head of the Committee on Infractions, which would be ruling on Muhammad's case. Thomas didn't even bother to respond. So Raines forwarded her e-mail to Robert Orr, the prominent North Carolina attorney-turned-NCAA critic, who was representing Muhammad. He, in turn, leaked the story to the *Los Angeles Times*. "They have prolonged this investigation, trying extraordinarily hard to find some basis to rule Shabazz ineligible," Orr told the newspaper.

The next day, without even hearing the appeal, the NCAA reversed itself and declared Muhammad eligible. Orr said, "I have been continually stunned by what I have learned about the system." Two months later, Grantstein was fired.

**University of Miami, January 2013:** For two years, the NCAA had been investigating the University of Miami football team, ever since Yahoo Sports published a story alleging that a Miami booster named Nevin Shapiro had spent millions providing all sorts of improper benefits to dozens of Miami football players, including cash, jewelry, prostitutes, entertainment in his multimillion-dollar homes and yacht, bounties for on-field play (including bounties for injuring opposing players), "and, on one occasion, an abortion." He was a modern-day Sam Gilbert.

Shapiro, who pled guilty in 2010 to running a Ponzi scheme—and angry that the university turned its back on him—was cooperating fully with the NCAA. But other potential witnesses were not. So two NCAA investigators paid Shapiro's bankruptcy lawyer to ask questions relating to their investigation during depositions of two such witnesses—depositions that were supposed to be about Shapiro's bankruptcy, not the NCAA investigation. Although this was clearly unethical, the investigators saw nothing wrong with getting information this way; indeed, a former NCAA enforcement official says the staff had paid lawyers to help them gather information in the past, with no repercussions. Their attitude had always been that, lacking subpoena power, they had to get their information by whatever means possible.

But when the attorney, Maria Elena Perez, sent a $20,000 invoice to the NCAA for her troubles—and Emmert discovered what had happened—he blew the whistle on his staff, describing what the investigators had done as "shocking" and "an embarrassment." He vowed that the NCAA would investigate "the overall enforcement environment, to ensure operation of the program is consistent with the essential principles of integrity and accountability." Although the NCAA fired the two investigators involved—and Emmert eventually fired the head of enforcement, Julie Roe Lach, whom he had promoted to the post two years earlier—the damage to the NCAA's reputation was enormous. It wasn't just Jerry Tarkanian or Sonny Vaccaro saying that the NCAA played dirty. Emmert himself was essentially acknowledging it.

By the time the 2013 Final Four rolled around in early April, Emmert was under siege. Internally, NCAA officials were furious at him for what they saw as his holier-than-thou handling of the Miami investigation, his firing of a number of top officials, his ham-handed dealings with the press, and his ubiquitous public presence, which stood in such contrast to his predecessors. Employees had become so suspicious of his motives that at least one of them questioned whether he had intentionally torpedoed the case against Miami to curry favor with his former contemporary, Miami president Donna Shalala, who had been Bill Clinton's secretary of health and human services.

Coaches were angry with him for pushing for new bylaws that would hold them responsible for any violation of NCAA rules—even if they hadn't known about the infractions. Athletic directors? In April 2013, Pat Haden, the highly respected athletic director at the University of Southern California, organized a two-day conference of his fellow Division I ADs to discuss all the turmoil taking place in college sports. During the conference they held a private meeting to talk about the NCAA and Emmert, whom they felt was shutting them out and only dealing with university presidents. Several of them had also had a stern private talk with Emmert during the Final Four, which had taken place a few weeks earlier.

Conference commissioners were no happier. With the legal issues presented by the *O'Bannon* case, conference realignment, and a great deal of uncertainty about the future, college sports needed someone to lead the way—and more and more, they were concerned that Emmert was turning out not to be that leader. His PR staff picked unnecessary fights with critics, while the NCAA itself seemed to have adopted a bunker mentality. "What are you doing throwing digital grenades at people?" an annoyed Jim Delany recalls, referring to the NCAA's strategy of sending out snarky tweets after the publication of an article it didn't like. "It was stupid." He added, "We were under a lot of pressure and there was tension with Mark." Recalls one former NCAA executive, "It had become an us-versus-them mentality. The membership had turned against the national office."

The extent to which the criticism had gotten under Emmert's skin became clear at a press conference he held at the Georgia Dome, the site of the Final Four. The run-up to the Final Four had been unlike any that an NCAA president had ever faced. Emmert appeared on *Face the Nation* and *Meet the Press*, where he was peppered with tough questions. Days before the Final Four, *USA Today* had published a harsh story about his career as a college administrator. The story suggested in painful detail that he had mismanaged a multimillion-dollar construction project while he was president at Connecticut, and had minimized what was later alleged to be widespread academic fraud in Nick Saban's football program while he was at LSU. The article infuriated Emmert, which he saw as impugning his integrity. "Nobody likes it when their family's reading nasty things," he would say later.

As he walked onto a raised dais—the same spot from which athletes and coaches would be interviewed after each game—he spotted Dennis Dodd, the writer who had called for his resignation six weeks earlier. "By the way, thanks for the career advice," he said snidely. "Kept my job anyway." After a long opening statement in which he described himself as "an agent of change," he opened the floor to questions. There were no softballs. Dodd asked him if the NCAA was still relevant. Other reporters asked him about the lawsuit that had been filed over the Penn State sanction, the botched Miami investigation, and all the other problems the NCAA was facing. Emmert's responses were testy and defensive: "If you're not getting sued, you're not doing anything," was his answer to a question about the Penn State litigation. Finally, as he walked off the podium, he looked at Dodd once again. "I'm still here," he said. "I know you're disappointed, but here I am."

"I lost my composure," Emmert later said.

# Actual Malice

**SCOTT TOMPSETT HAS SEEN IT ALL. A LAWYER BASED IN KANSAS CITY,** he has spent close to a quarter century representing clients who have been accused of violating NCAA rules. Most of his clients have been coaches, who, Tompsett says, have the most at stake when they go up against the NCAA, because they can lose their livelihood as the result of an NCAA finding against them. "When a coach calls me, he is going through the most serious professional crisis he'll ever go through," he says. "I've seen coaches' careers destroyed. They're dealing with people's lives here." He spends most of his time defending his clients before the NCAA's Committee on Infractions, which decides cases brought by the enforcement staff. It can be frustrating work. (Tompsett also represented Ryan Boatright's mother, Tanesha, whose story was told in the prologue.)

"I've been doing this work a long time, and I'm invested in the process," he says. "I would like to see the system work. When I get a client who is in trouble with the NCAA, I want to be able to tell him that this is a fair process, a fair system." But he can't. "There often seems to be an inappropriate presumption that the coach is guilty," he says, speaking of the Committee on Infractions' bias. "To overcome that is hard. You have to almost blow them away with overwhelming evidence refuting the allegation. The Committee on Infractions usually resolves conflicts or inconsistencies in favor of enforcement staff. And other times they just get the facts wrong."

Case in point: his client Todd McNair.

McNair, a former running back in the NFL, was an assistant coach for the University of Southern California Trojans from 2004 to 2009. At the point at which he hired Tompsett, in September 2009, he'd been interviewed twice by the NCAA, in September 2006 and February 2008, part of a long-running investigation into USC athletics. (The basketball program and the women's tennis program were also eventually hit with sanctions.) On the football side of things, the NCAA investigation centered on Reggie Bush, one of the greatest USC running backs ever, who won the Heisman Trophy in 2005. The central allegation was that two hustlers who knew Bush and were hoping to become his agents had put up his mother, brother, and stepfather in a house in San Diego, rent-free. This violated two NCAA rules: players are not supposed to have dealings with agents while they are in college, and their relatives are not supposed to accept benefits that are given because of the player's status as a college athlete. When Bush went pro and didn't hire them as his agents, they leaked word of their relationship with Bush and his family to the NCAA.

With Bush leaving college to join the NFL, he was beyond the reach of the NCAA. (He did have to return his Heisman Trophy to the Heisman Trust, however.) But unless the NCAA could show that someone in the USC athletic department or on the football coaching staff knew about the impermissible benefits, it would only be a case of two wannabe agents trying to lure Bush away from USC. The worst USC could have been accused of was failing to uncover the scheme—that is, not keeping closer tabs on its superstar running back.

The person at USC the NCAA investigators decided to target was McNair. Their sole source was Lloyd Lake, one of the men hoping to enlist Bush as a client. According to the June 2010 report issued by the Committee on Infractions, Lake made a two-and-a-half-minute phone call to McNair in the wee hours of the morning on January 6, 2006, asking him to convince Bush "either to adhere to the agency agreement or to reimburse Lake . . . for money provided to Bush and his family." The committee went on to say that despite McNair's categorical denial of the allegation, it found Lake's version of events to be "credible."

The penalties the Committee on Infractions meted out to the USC football team were some of the most severe any college team has ever faced: a loss of thirty scholarships over a three-year period—an astonishing number compared to penalties handed out to other schools for similar infractions—a two-year postseason ban, the stripping of its 2004 national championship by the BCS, and the erasure of all of its wins in 2005.

What's more, the committee declared that McNair was guilty of unethical conduct, and that he was forbidden from recruiting for a year. It also issued a "show cause" order, meaning that if USC—or any other institution that might employ him—did not abide by McNair's recruiting restriction, it had to "show cause" why it shouldn't be penalized as well. A "show cause" order almost always renders a coach unemployable, and so it was for McNair. His contract with USC wasn't renewed, and he hasn't worked as a coach since.

There was only one little problem with the Committee on Infractions' report, at least as it concerned McNair: it bore almost no relation to the particulars of the actual investigation. To find McNair guilty of unethical conduct, the committee members had to "change and mischaracterize" what Lake had told the investigators, as Tompsett would later write in appealing the findings. This they did with abandon.

To begin with, when Rich Johanningmeier, the chief investigator, interviewed Lake, his questions suggested that McNair had called Lake, and not the other way around. Rather than correct him, Lake agreed. Lake then told Johanningmeier that McNair had said he would try to resolve Lake's problem, and he didn't want the university implicated. For this to be true, McNair would have to have known much earlier about the relationship between Lake and Bush—yet there was zero evidence to support that, not even from Lake himself. The committee also claimed that "[Lake] said he also told [McNair] that he did not intend to lose the money he had given [Bush]." But Lake had given no such testimony—this was completely made up. The committee claimed that Lake's girlfriend supported his version of events, though she had done no such thing. And so on.

"They based a career-ending finding on demonstrably false statements," Tompsett later said.

Tompsett's clients rarely went to court to contest an NCAA finding against them; the lawyer knew full well how challenging such a case would be thanks to the Supreme Court's 1988 *Tarkanian* ruling. But this was different. McNair was able to sue not on the grounds that the NCAA's rules were unfair but on the grounds that he had been defamed by the NCAA.

Defamation suits are also challenging, of course, and that's particularly true for someone like McNair, who the NCAA claimed was a public figure under the law, which would require him to prove that the NCAA defamed him with "actual malice." In other words, the NCAA made the allegedly defamatory statements knowing they were false, or with "reckless disregard" for whether they were false or not.

McNair and his lawyers felt they had a strong case from the start: after all, in appealing the Committee on Infractions' decision Tompsett had pointed out the false statements chapter and verse. Yet the appeals committee had completely ignored them in affirming the career-ending penalty imposed on McNair. Then, during the initial discovery process, he got internal NCAA documents relating to the Committee on Infractions' deliberations. They were astounding. They included a series of e-mails between the voting members of the committee and a handful of others that amounted to whispering in committee members' ears. The first revelation was that this ex parte communication had taken place at all—it was plainly unethical since the defense didn't have the same access to the committee members. And second, what they had whispered was beyond the pale.

Shep Cooper, an NCAA administrator whose title was director of the Committee on Infractions (i.e., liaison), wrote in one e-mail that McNair was "a lying, morally bankrupt criminal . . . and a hypocrite of the highest order." A nonvoting member of the committee, Roscoe Howard, wrote that "McNair should have all inferences negatively inferred against him. . . . As with all tribunals and fact finders, we need not say why we disbelieve him, we need only let the public, or whomever, know that we disbelieve him." A second nonvoting member, Rodney Uphoff, compared the McNair case to the trial of Terry Nichols, one of the Oklahoma City bombers—saying, incredibly, that the evidence against McNair was stronger than the evidence against Nichols. At the same time, several of the actual voting members of the committee acknowledged that the evidence against McNair was paper-thin.

In the fall of 2012, more than two years into the case, Los Angeles County Superior Court judge Frederick Shaller ruled on the NCAA's motion to dismiss. Not only did he deny it, but he went on to write that the NCAA had operated "maliciously" toward McNair, and he described the e-mail evidence as tending "to show ill will or hatred" toward the former USC coach. Shaller concluded that despite being a public figure, McNair "has shown a probability of prevailing on the defamation charges."

The NCAA quickly asked that all the e-mails be placed under seal, claiming that their public release would harm future investigations. Shaller declined. "I think the public has a right to know," he said. But he stayed his order to unseal the documents while the NCAA appealed to the California Court of Appeal. In February 2015, the appeals court ruled against the NCAA, and the damning e-mails were unsealed.

As of this writing, the NCAA's appeal of Shaller's denial of its motion to dismiss has yet to be ruled on.

# CHAPTER 13
# CLASS IS IN

On June 20, 2013, halfway through the NCAA's annus horribilis, as 2013 was fast becoming, a hearing took place in a standard-issue federal courtroom in Oakland, California. The question on the table was whether the *O'Bannon* plaintiffs should be granted class certification, and it was probably the single most important hearing in the four years since the lawsuit had been filed. If the federal judge hearing the case, Claudia Wilken, ultimately certified the class, *O'Bannon v. NCAA* would become a class action lawsuit, meaning that the "class" of people suing the NCAA would grow to include not just the twelve former college athletes who had joined the lawsuit alongside Ed O'Bannon, but every college athlete, current or former, who had played football or men's basketball. The damages were potentially huge; one of the plaintiffs' economic experts, Stanford economist Roger Noll, had submitted a preliminary report to the court estimating that damages for just two years for two conferences was over $300 million. (Much later, Dan Rascher submitted a final damages report that showed the money owed to the former players could be as much as $3 billion.) At least as important, if the *O'Bannon* side won an eventual trial, the NCAA would likely be forced, at a minimum, to end its ban on paying college athletes for the rights to their names, images, and likenesses—"NIL" in legal shorthand—something it had vowed never to do. And there was at least the possibility that the remedy could blow up the "collegiate model" entirely. If, on the other hand, Wilken ruled against certifying the class, the case would effectively be over. Although individual plaintiffs could continue suing the NCAA, it would be pointless, because no one player was going to be awarded enough money to justify the expense of bringing a lawsuit. Denying class certification meant victory for the NCAA.

There was little doubt by then that Judge Wilken was none too happy that the case had dragged on for as long as it had. A sixty-five-year-old former public defender, private attorney, and law school professor, with wire-rimmed glasses and salt-and-pepper hair, Wilken had been appointed to the federal judiciary by Bill Clinton in 1993. On the bench, she came across as engaged and unpretentious but extremely businesslike, the kind of judge who wants to move things along at a brisk pace, especially once she feels grounded in the issues. Yet unlike in the *White* case, the NCAA had reverted to form in *O'Bannon*: contesting minor issues as if they were life-or-death, burying the judge and the plaintiffs in long-winded motions and briefs, seeking endless delays, and generally dragging things out as much as possible. Andy Schwarz compiled a timeline of all the motions filed in the case: for instance, thirty-two in January 2011, thirty in February, all the way up to seventy in October 2012 when the two sides were filing their briefs and motions for and against class certification.

Although the hearing was mostly a civil exchange between Hausfeld, Greg Curtner, the NCAA's lead lawyer, and Wilken, she had trouble hiding her annoyance from time to time at the NCAA's tactics. For instance, Hausfeld had only recently added current college athletes, not just former athletes, to the class he hoped Wilken would certify. As the hearing opened, Wilken asked whether the *O'Bannon* lawyers needed to file a new "amended complaint" that included current players, while making it abundantly clear that she saw no need, because it would just delay things further and allow the NCAA to file another motion to dismiss the case—a motion she would undoubtedly deny as she had done several times already. It might even push back the trial date, which had been set for the following June.

"What would be served," she asked Curtner, "by forcing them to file another 500 pages and perhaps have another round of motions to dismiss?" Curtner told her he had "maybe" five legal points to back the NCAA's position that a new complaint was required. He wasn't even two sentences into his first argument—that the famous Supreme Court *Regents* decision precluded paying current athletes—when Wilken broke in. "Could you make it more of a summary?" she asked. "You said you had five points. Could you just make them in, like, a sentence?"

She broke in again after another minute. "One way or another, I'm not going to deny class certification or strike it because of this new theory," she said. "And I'm not going to dismiss the case or anything else." And *still* Curtner forged ahead, seemingly oblivious to what Wilken had just told him. He seemed at that moment as tone-deaf in dealing with this judge, who was handling the most important NCAA lawsuit since *Regents* and *Tarkanian,* as Mark Emmert had been at his Final Four press conference two months earlier.

(At the end of the ninety-minute hearing, when she asked if there was anything further to discuss—judge-speak for "I've heard enough"—Hausfeld and two other lawyers immediately replied no. Speaking last, Curtner said, "We have a few more points if the court's interested." The spectators burst out in laughter. "That was a joke, right?" said Wilken.)

Irritating the judge is never a smart move, especially when it is as avoidable as it was in this case. But the NCAA's foot-dragging had at least two other consequences. Although Wilken knew even less about sports than Hausfeld—she once joked that she associated the acronym SEC with the Securities and Exchange Commission, not the Southeastern Conference—she became during those four years thoroughly versed in the procompetitive arguments that the NCAA put forth to defend the collegiate model. And the more she understood them, the more skeptical she became of them. In one hearing not long before the *O'Bannon* trial, for instance, she said that "amateurism" was not a useful word because the NCAA could—and did—define it any way it saw fit. Given that the NCAA's core defense was precisely that amateurism made its practices procompetitive under the rule of reason, her statement presented a big problem for the defense.

She also ruled that the NCAA's second big argument—that the Supreme Court "explicitly endorsed its rules prohibiting student-athlete compensation" in the *Regents* decision—did not apply. "Board of Regents," she wrote, focused on a different set of competitive restraints than the rules challenged in this case. Indeed, the Supreme Court never even analyzed the NCAA's ban on student-athlete compensation under the rule of reason nor did it cite any fact findings indicating that this ban is the type of restraint which is "essential if the [NCAA's] product is to be available at all." More importantly, the Court never examined whether or not the ban on student-athlete compensation actually had a procompetitive effect on the college sports market.

In other words, those famous three sentences from Justice John Paul Stevens that the NCAA had relied on for so many years was just dicta after all. And not even "pretty fucking strong dicta"—as a lawyer had once told Schwarz. Her ruling was exactly what Schwarz, Rascher, and Ernie Nadel had first contended thirteen years earlier when they tried, unsuccessfully, to gin up their "nuclear" case against the NCAA. Schwarz would later write in an e-mail that he viewed that ruling as "the biggest victory in the entire [O'Bannon] process. A judge had finally stated that the NCAA wasn't immune to scrutiny in the way it treated college athletes." It was also, he later said, "the most exhilarating moment prior to the trial."

"It turns out that the worst thing the NCAA could have done was give Judge Wilken all that time to learn about them," he said.

The other consequence of the NCAA's foot-dragging was that the O'Bannon case became a constant drumbeat in the sports press—*for five years!* In O'Bannon, the plaintiffs had a sincere, admired former athlete who could well articulate why college athletes deserved to be compensated for their names and images, just like anybody else would be; he became the perfect foil for Emmert. Journalists instinctively sided with the O'Bannon team, the plucky Davids up against college sports' lumbering Goliath. This was especially true of Internet sports websites, such as SB Nation, Deadspin, Grantland (an ESPN site), and later Vice Sports, with their instinctive antiauthoritarian bias. Eventually, the O'Bannon case became part of the larger NCAA narrative: every time the NCAA botched an investigation, or persecuted hapless athletes, or made one of its commonsense-defying rulings, there was the O'Bannon case, hovering in the background, with its implicit suggestion that maybe—just maybe—the NCAA might one day be held to account and even forced to change.

Thus it wasn't just the lawyers who understood the importance of the *O'Bannon* case becoming a class action lawsuit; sports journalists understood it too. Charlie Pierce, writing for Grantland, described the possibility of an *O'Bannon* class action trial as "the meteor they never saw coming." Patrick Vint at SB Nation: "If the class is certified, the NCAA would be faced with the difficult decision to either cave on their entire business model of 'amateurism' in a settlement or go to trial and face a potentially crippling award of damages." Jon Solomon called the class certification hearing a "pivotal moment," and added that nothing less than "the current model of college sports" was at stake. The longer the case lasted, the more "it opened people's eyes," as Jon King would later put it.

A few months after the class certification hearing, another event took place that helped shape the public perception of the *O'Bannon* case. It was a simple, eye-opening prank played by Jay Bilas, the prominent college basketball analyst for ESPN.

Bilas was a star at Duke University in the early to mid-1980s. A lawyer by training, he had been thinking about the NCAA for a very long time, ever since he was a "student member" of an NCAA committee. When he first got on the committee, he recalls, one of the issues he wanted to raise was the NCAA's transfer rule—the rule that forces an athlete to sit out a year if he transfers to another school, unless he can get a waiver from his coach and the NCAA. "Coming out of high school, one of the coaches who had recruited me had left by the time I got to college," he says. "But when I brought it up in a meeting, I was shot down. I was told that 'you choose an institution not a coach.' I tried to explain that that's not how it works—it's the coach who picks you up at the airport, not the institution—but they didn't want to hear it. You quickly realized that they wanted you to keep your mouth shut, and you got rewarded for parroting their perspective."

The idea of paying athletes wasn't always at the top of Bilas's mind; his early concerns were about making the rules fairer for them. In large part, this was simply because there was so much less money in college sports when he was going to Duke. "My coach"—Mike Krzyzewski—"was making less than $100,000," he says. But as the money rolled in and coaches like Krzyzewski began making millions, the disparity between what the players got and what everyone else in college sports got became too large to ignore.

Joining ESPN in 1995, Bilas felt secure enough in his role with the network by the mid-2000s that he began to speak out about the NCAA. Not while he was broadcasting a game, to be sure, but at other times, during ESPN roundtables, or in interviews with newspaper reporters. By 2013, he had become one of the most prominent critics of the NCAA. "I don't think money and education are mutually exclusive," he says. "No other student is restricted in what they can do and how much money they can make. They only police that with athletes."

Bilas believed that college sports should be deregulated, and that athletes should be able to make whatever the market would bear. Whenever he was asked how exactly a school would go about paying players, he would reply that schools and athletes would sign contracts, as people do in every other sphere of economic life. He would say this with a nonchalant shrug, as if nothing could be more obvious.

One of the means by which Bilas voiced his criticism of the NCAA was via Twitter, where he had over half a million followers. (It's now close to a million.) One day in August 2013, someone told him that if you plugged the name of an athlete in the search engine on the NCAA's shopping site, a team jersey with that player's number would pop up for sale. His name wouldn't be on the jersey, of course, since that was something the NCAA didn't allow, allegedly as part of its concern about "exploitation." But just as with avatars on NCAA-themed video games, any sports fan would know exactly whose jersey it was. And the NCAA knew it too. Indeed, that was precisely the reason why people were willing to pay cold hard cash for those particular jerseys.

"I didn't believe it at first," says Bilas. But he typed "Manziel" in the search box on the NCAA site—Johnny Manziel, nicknamed "Johnny Football," had been Texas A&M's freshman sensation in 2012—and sure enough, a series of Manziel's Texas A&M jerseys, with his number 2, popped up. He posted a picture of the jerseys on Twitter and wrote, "Go to ShopNCAAsports.com, type in Manziel in the upper right search box, hit enter. This comes up."

Then he did it again, putting in the name Jadeveon Clowney, the

University of South Carolina's star linebacker. And again, with Clemson quarterback Tajh Boyd. And Teddy Bridgewater, the quarterback of the Louisville Cardinals. Again and again he did it, each time using a different college star's name. The NCAA reacted by disabling the search engine.

The tweets quickly went viral, with one writer after another noting that Bilas had just made a shambles of the NCAA's insistence that it was protecting athletes from exploitation. Several explicitly linked Bilas's Twitter prank to the *O'Bannon* case. How could the NCAA refuse to allow athletes to profit from their own likeness when the NCAA was doing exactly that itself? Bilas, in fact, had just proven that the NCAA absolutely understood that the jerseys of star players had monetary value. "The NCAA maintains that it can't pay athletes or consumers will vanish" because college sports would lose its special sauce, Andy Schwarz would later note. "Video games and jerseys presented clear evidence that the opposite was true. Selling the players was key."

To make matters worse for the NCAA, Bilas's tweets came just days after it had begun an investigation into whether Manziel had been paid to sign some autographs. This time, though, instead of portraying Manziel's alleged offense (which he denied) as an example of an athlete breaking the rules, most of the sports press focused on the absurdity of the NCAA's rule against signing autographs for money. Embarrassed, Emmert announced that the NCAA would stop selling jerseys with university logos. "I can certainly understand how people can see that as hypocritical," he said. The NCAA preferred to exit a profitable market rather than—to quote Schwarz again—"pay the players for the right to serve consumer demand."

Even after the NCAA shut down its search engine, Bilas got in one last jab. "Go to ShopNCAAsports.com and type 'Mark Emmert' in upper right search box, then hit enter," he tweeted. "This comes up." It was a picture of a man from the neck down, wearing a shirt and tie, holding sacks and sacks of money.

Judges rarely render their decisions on the spot, and that was certainly going to be true in a case as contentious and high-profile as the *O'Bannon* lawsuit. June turned to July, July to August, August to September—and no ruling from Judge Wilken about whether the *O'Bannon* plaintiffs would be certified as a class or not.

For the lawyers involved, three months in the course of a big lawsuit was a blip on the radar screen. There were many judges who took far longer than that to render an important ruling. But for Sonny Vaccaro, who had never before been involved in a major piece of litigation, and who was impatient by nature, it was an eternity.

From where Vaccaro sat, the case was like being on a never-ending roller coaster. The judge would do something—or say something in court—that gave encouragement to the plaintiffs, and he would be happy, joyous even. Then she would say something that appeared to offer encouragement to the NCAA, and he would be downcast for days. But the delays, the constant delays, were what drove him around the bend. "They were terrible to live with," he says. "The first time the case got extended," he adds, "it felt like a death sentence."

One of the worst moments for him came in January 2013, when Jon King, the lawyer who had first met him on Hausfeld's behalf, filed a lawsuit against Hausfeld. Though few outside the firm had known about it, Hausfeld and King had had a bitter split the previous October. In Hausfeld's view, King, despite his enthusiasm for the case, was making critical legal mistakes, so much so that he had largely turned his role over to two other lawyers on his staff. King was also feuding with several attorneys in Hausfeld's Washington office. Hausfeld fired King in San Francisco, shortly after they appeared together at a hearing on the case with the magistrate judge, Nathanael Cousins. (A magistrate judge conducts hearings and rules on a variety of logistical concerns and disputes between the parties that the district judge hearing the case appoints him to oversee.)

The complaint King wrote in filing his lawsuit combined extraordinary pettiness—he accused Hausfeld of not letting him get his personal belongings from his office—with the occasional serious charge. He said that Hausfeld had taken on "immediate and crushing debt obligations" in setting up his firm, and that as a result he was cutting ethical corners, including secretly wiring "millions of dollars in disputed money to his London office to generate cash." He also said that the firm's spending was out of control; that Hausfeld was obsessed with monitoring his old firm; that King had been instructed at least once to create a false billing record; and that Hausfeld routinely had other lawyers in the firm listen in surreptitiously on what were supposed to be private phone calls.

Perhaps his most serious allegation, though, was that Hausfeld had settled a name, image, and likeness case involving former NFL players for $50 million—a pittance compared to what the former players believed their case should have been worth. King said that he did so because the Hausfeld firm badly needed its share of the $8 million in legal fees the plaintiffs' lawyers stood to reap from the settlement. Indeed, former NFL quarterback Dan Pastorini went so far as to file a malpractice suit against Hausfeld, though it was soon dismissed.

Hausfeld denied King's charges; indeed, he would later say that the $50 million set aside for the retired players was a triumph because he eventually realized that they had a weak case. And King's lawsuit went nowhere. Nonetheless, Vaccaro was shocked when he first heard about it. For one thing, selling out the players was exactly what had happened in the *White* case—and what some in the *O'Bannon* camp most feared might happen in their case as well. Besides, King had long been his primary point of contact with the firm. He trusted Jon King, and worried that his departure would hurt the cause. It took some doing for Hausfeld to reassure Vaccaro that King's lawsuit wouldn't affect the case.

It truth, it was important to ensure that Vaccaro understood what was going on with the litigation, not just that one time after King was fired, but with every important legal twist and turn. Vaccaro, after all, had brought them this lawsuit in the first place; even though he was not an official adviser, and was not being paid, there was a sense among the lawyers that they owed him that. Second, he was a participant: he had spent eight hours in a contentious deposition—the first question he was asked by the NCAA's lawyer was whether he had ever committed a felony—and there was some talk that he might testify if a trial took place. (He never did.)

Most important, Vaccaro had a huge network of people in the world of college sports—including most of the journalists who were covering the litigation. Anytime something happened, Vaccaro would be inundated with calls from reporters and others. Sometimes his primary role was to assure journalists that the case was still on track; other times he was called on to comment for the record, such as when Jim Delany made a laughable declaration to the court contending that if schools had to start paying players, the Big Ten might have to deemphasize athletics and move to Division III. Describing Delany's declaration as "insane," Vaccaro added, "It's the most irrational statement I have ever seen from a person who's in power to do something for the players."

"A lot of people got their information from Sonny," says a lawyer named William Isaacson, a partner at Boies, Schiller & Flexner, who was among the outside attorneys working on the case. Isaacson recalls going to see *A Streetcar Named Desire* in Washington with two high-profile sports journalists, Tony Kornheiser, the cohost of the ESPN show *Pardon the Interruption*, and John Feinstein, the author of *Season on the Brink* and an occasional columnist for the *Washington Post*. Feinstein, in particular, had been a fierce critic of Vaccaro during his sneaker pimp years. "They cornered me," says Isaacson. They wanted to be sure that the lawyer understood Vaccaro's story, and how ironic it was that he had become a college sports reformer. And they wanted Isaacson to know how important Vaccaro was to the case. This was something, however, that Isaacson well knew already.

The day finally came when Wilken issued her ruling. It arrived at the lawyers' offices on November 8, 2013, late in the afternoon, some four months after the June hearing. It was not what anyone had been expecting. Just two weeks before, she had denied the NCAA's final motion to dismiss—the one that Curtner had insisted on at the class certification hearing.

When she did that, the O'Bannon lawyers were convinced that Wilken was going to grant them their class-action lawsuit. And up to a point, she did: Wilken indeed certified the O'Bannon plaintiffs as a class—but only for the purpose of injunctive relief. That is, if the O'Bannon team won at trial, the result would be some kind of ban on the NCAA's strictures against paying players, at least for their names, images, and likenesses. In other words, the plaintiffs could seek a system that would pay *future* college athletes. But Wilken denied what's called the "damages class." That meant that plaintiffs could not ask for money for all the tens of thousands of *former* players who made up the O'Bannon class, other than the handful of named plaintiffs. So much for the potential $3 billion windfall.

Suddenly the case was much less valuable to the lawyers. With a damages class, they could claim a percentage of the damages, which could have run to the hundreds of millions of dollars. They estimated how much the damages might be for the named plaintiffs only, the twelve former athletes and five current athletes who had been added to the case: the total amount for all of them ranged between $265,000 and $908,000. That barely covered the copying costs for the case. Without damages, the best the lawyers could hope for if they won was to have their attorneys' fees paid for by the NCAA. That sum would be in the millions, for sure, but not the hundreds of millions.

Schwarz, for one, was nervous that the lawyers might decide it wasn't worth moving forward with the case. King would later say that part of his motivation for filing the suit was to help ensure that Hausfeld didn't sell out the *O'Bannon* plaintiffs. But if Hausfeld had second thoughts, nobody ever saw them. Forcing an institution to change motivated him enormously— just like the old Texaco case he'd won many years earlier. "Yes, financially it was less valuable," he later said. "But from a commitment standpoint, nothing had changed. There was never a moment of wavering."

After Hausfeld told Vaccaro about the ruling—and promised him they were not dropping the case—Vaccaro called O'Bannon, something he always did after talking to the lawyers. He explained to him that although the case was moving forward, there would be no pot of money for plaintiffs like him.

"That's okay, Mr. Vaccaro," O'Bannon replied. "We're still alive."

# Block That Transfer!

ST. JOSEPH'S UNIVERSITY DOES NOT FIELD A FOOTBALL TEAM, BUT that does not mean the small Jesuit-run school in Philadelphia is immune to the one-sided power dynamics of college sports. Its basketball team, coached by Phil Martelli since 1995, has flirted with the big time, even reaching the Elite Eight of the NCAA tournament in 2004. Four years later, a seven-foot center named Todd O'Brien transferred from Bucknell to St. Joe's after his freshman year. He sat out the requisite season required by the NCAA and then was a contributor for the Hawks, though his production slipped and he barely played by his senior year, averaging 1 point per game.

O'Brien graduated that year with a major in economics, but because he had sat out for a season after he transferred, he still had a year of eligibility left. He intended to play one more year of basketball; he also wanted a graduate degree in public administration. St. Joe's didn't have a program that matched his academic needs (he said academic advisers there suggested he delay graduation and fill his schedule with classes like pottery), so he found one at the University of Alabama at Birmingham. The basketball team would also welcome him for a season.

Yet when O'Brien announced his plans to Martelli, the coach delivered an expletive-ridden, threat-filled tirade. Martelli would block him from finishing his classes, or even sue him, he screamed. In another meeting, Martelli was clear with O'Brien: he would "be playing at St. Joe's next year or not playing anywhere."

In truth, there was no NCAA rule against O'Brien transferring to UAB. The NCAA, in fact, specifically allows players who earn their degree but have remaining eligibility to transfer freely. The only catch is that the previous school must "release" the player. St. Joe's, clearly at the behest of Martelli, would not release O'Brien. And when O'Brien appealed to the NCAA, the NCAA denied him again, siding with his school and his coach. Although O'Brien did transfer and get his masters at UAB, he never got to play for the basketball team.

Coaches, as everyone knows, hold tremendous clout. They are the face of their programs far more than the players themselves. And they can break contracts and switch schools as they please. They also have the power to prevent their athletes from doing likewise. O'Brien is hardly the only athlete to run into this power struggle and lose.

Take, for instance, Wes Lunt, a quarterback at Oklahoma State. In 2013, when he tried to transfer, his coach, Mike Gundy, listed nearly forty schools he would not be allowed to transfer to.

Or take the case of Robert Marve, a quarterback at the University of Miami, who attempted to transfer in 2009. He started eleven games his sophomore season, but then lost his starting job and announced his plans to transfer. Marve's father, Eugene, an eleven-year NFL veteran, was battling prostate cancer in Tampa. Marve hoped to be closer to his father. But Miami coach Randy Shannon blocked him from moving to any schools in Florida. The list went on: Marve couldn't transfer anywhere in the SEC or the ACC. Marve wound up at Purdue. "It hurt our family," Eugene Marve says. "They had all the power."

After a series of debilitating injuries, including two torn ACLs, Marve went undrafted by the NFL and wound up playing in 2014 for the Winnipeg Blue Bombers in the Canadian Football League.

# CHAPTER 14
# ALL PLAYERS UNITED

On a below-zero January morning in 2014, Ramogi Huma and Tim Waters walked into the National Labor Relations office on West Adams Street in downtown Chicago. Huma, a Los Angeles–area native still living in Southern California, had bought his first-ever winter coat before making the trip, but he barely noticed the cold. He was carrying a package that represented something he and Waters had been thinking about for the last year: it contained union cards signed by almost all of Northwestern University's football players.

"We're here to unionize the Northwestern football team," Huma announced as he handed over the package. The clerk did a double take.

Fifteen miles away on Northwestern's Evanston campus, Kain Colter sat in a meeting with his coach, Pat Fitzgerald. Colter, then twenty-one years old, had been Northwestern's starting quarterback for the past two seasons. He was a team captain and in 2013 piloted the Wildcats to a Gator Bowl victory, Northwestern's first bowl win in six and a half decades. Fitzgerald, meanwhile, was an icon on campus, a former All-American linebacker who had led Northwestern to the Rose Bowl in 1995. Fitzgerald broke his leg and missed that game, and the pin and screw inserted to hold his leg in place after the surgery hang in his office, framed, next to his old number 51 jersey.

Colter had been in the office countless times for meetings over the years. But this time he wore a suit—he had to leave directly for a press conference to announce the union—and he wasn't there to talk football. Colter told his coach that he believed it was important to change college sports, that the power structure marginalized players, and that he had deep-seated concerns about such issues as long-term health care for college athletes. The team had signed union cards, he said, and they were being filed as they spoke. Fitzgerald leaned back in his chair and linked his fingers behind his head. "I'm proud of you guys for doing this," he said. "I think it's a great cause and you're bringing up great points." But, according to Colter, he added that before he could take a public position he would have to see how the school wanted to handle it (Fitzgerald denies this).

Later that morning, Huma and Colter held their press conference at the downtown Hyatt Regency to announce they had filed a union petition with the NLRB. Northwestern players sought employee status under the law, and with it the ability to bargain collectively through a new entity that Huma and Colter formed the same day: the College Athletes Players Association. In front of a bank of TV cameras and a room full of reporters, Colter said, "The current model resembles a dictatorship, where the NCAA places these rules and regulations on these students without their input or without their negotiation." He continued, "The NFL has the NFLPA, the NBA has the NBAPA, and now college athletes have the College Athletes Players Association."

Theodis Kain Colter grew up in Boulder, Colorado, with sports in his blood. His uncle, Cleveland Colter, was an All-American safety at the University of Southern California in 1988. His dad, Spencer, was a safety on the University of Colorado's national championship team two years later. A cousin, Steve Colter, spent a decade playing professional basketball, including part of a season with the Chicago Bulls during the Michael Jordan era. The son of a football coach and a paralegal, Colter played sports, lots of them, as a kid. But football was his favorite. He was undersized for a quarterback, standing just five foot ten, but he made up for it with quickness and smarts. He was good enough by his junior year at Cherry Creek High School that he was recruited by schools across the country, Texas Christian, Northwestern, and Stanford among them. Colter committed to Stanford. "That was my dream school," he says. "I loved the academics, loved Palo Alto."

But early in his senior season in high school, Colter suffered a torn labrum while reaching for a loose fumble. He tried to play through the pain and his performance suffered. The letters and phone calls from Stanford's coaches slowed to a trickle, even as he took all the AP classes they asked and kept his grades up. He was damaged goods; eventually Stanford told him he wouldn't be accepted. Crushed, he frantically looked for another scholarship. Northwestern was still in the market for a quarterback, so he headed east to the Big Ten.

In Evanston, Colter spent his freshman season on the bench redshirting, learning the system and saving a year of eligibility. Then, late in the year, starting quarterback Dan Persa ruptured his Achilles tendon. Fitzgerald asked if Colter would step in and play—in other words, sacrifice a full year of eligibility for the three remaining games, a practice known as "burning the redshirt." Colter agreed, and three games later, on January 1, 2011, he had his breakout moment in the TicketCity Bowl, rushing for two touchdowns against Texas Tech.

Colter had arrived at Northwestern with the hope of pursuing two dreams: he wanted to be an NFL quarterback and, after his playing days were over, a doctor. He began college on a premed track, but as a quarterback on scholarship, he needed to be at every minute of practice. He couldn't leave early to get to a class the way some walk-ons could. And with team activities conflicting with the science classes he needed, it became increasingly difficult to take them. He fell behind, pushed the classes to the summer, before finally switching his major to psychology. It wasn't so much that Northwestern's academic advisers pushed him away from the strenuous chemistry classes—Colter says they didn't—but rather that he felt he had to make a choice. "I had a chance to be a pro football player or I had a chance to be a doctor, but I couldn't do both," he says.

There were other aspects of college football life that bothered him. Stipend checks for off-campus living, which were part of his scholarship, were difficult to stretch from month to month, especially since the team mandated that players purchase meals from the athletic department. He spoke to friends and former high school teammates at other schools who were also struggling financially. And many of them, unlike Colter at Northwestern, were concerned about the lack of academic support they received.

Medical care was Colter's biggest concern, however. The way the system worked was that Northwestern and other athletic departments around the country provided a secondary health policy for players—but it was usually only used as a supplement to a player's primary insurance. Primary coverage was either provided by an athlete's parents, or they might have to pay out of pocket for the school's health plan if the family couldn't provide one. (Through the new cost of attendance scholarships— see epilogue—schools could pay for a primary policy if a player does not have insurance through his family.) What further troubled Colter was that once players left school, there were few guarantees. They were usually on their own.

Colter also had a very personal reason for caring about player safety. His uncle Cleveland had been considered a shoe-in to jump to the NFL from Southern Cal—he was considered the best athlete on a defense that included future NFL stars Junior Seau and Mark Carrier—until he suffered a severe knee injury. He never fully recovered. Instead of getting drafted, Cleveland never even graduated. Now he runs a catering business, and his knee still bothers him nearly three decades later. "Think about a twenty-year-old kid who's got all this pressure from his family—he's been an All-Star his whole life and is getting ready to be drafted in the first round and he tears his knee up," Kain Colter says. "Your whole financial life is based on sports. You're not thinking you're going to go to school and get a great degree and be a doctor. You're thinking, 'I've been working my whole life for one thing and now it's out the window.'"

During the summer of 2013, Colter enrolled in a class called "Field Studies in the Modern Workplace," taught by graduate student Nick Dorzweiler. Colter took the seminar with around fifteen students in conjunction with a finance internship at Goldman Sachs. The class was a social and historical look at how white-collar work developed in America— "essentially how we ended up getting office jobs," Dorzweiler says. There were field trips to the downtown Chicago offices of Groupon and then a steel mill just across the state line in Indiana, as well as discussions of important moments in the history of the labor movement, like the Haymarket Riots of 1886 and the Pullman railroad strike of 1894.

The trip to the steel mill sparked a class discussion about the role of organized labor—how it evolved, how it functioned, and why blue-collar workers had unionized. One rationale was health and safety protection. During the discussion, Colter raised his hand and drew a parallel to college football players. "Through my uncle, I had always known the system needed to change, but learning about the history of labor organizations and unions made a lot of sense," he says. "It was like the blueprint was already there for big-time sports business in the professional leagues. In the NFL, the NBA, and baseball they all have unions and the unions help protect the players. And without them, players would be at a disadvantage, they wouldn't be treated fairly."

Around the same time, Colter met Tregg Duerson, a graduate of Northwestern's business school who worked at Goldman Sachs and whose father, Dave, had played eleven years in the NFL, seven with the Chicago Bears. Dave Duerson killed himself in 2011 with a gunshot to the chest, and was later found to have a degenerative brain disease called chronic traumatic encephalopathy, or CTE, caused by repeated hits to the head. As they talked, Tregg Duerson helped Colter understand the dangers of football, well beyond his uncle's story. Colter had never been afraid of controversy—in high school he had helped lead a student protest when his father was fired as Boulder High School's coach ("Once a unionist, always a unionist," says Jim Delany)—and now he turned all these new ideas over in his head. Later in the summer he would write a paper for Dorzweiler, describing the NCAA as a cartel and raising the possibility of a union. He also sought out more information. Did college athletes have anyone looking out for them? he wondered. He searched the Internet: "Can College Players Have a Union?" He found the National Collegiate Players Association site—Ramogi Huma's site—and saw endorsements from pros like Hines Ward. In the comment box he poured out his frustrations and his ideas—all from his Goldman Sachs cubicle. He hit send. "I really didn't think I was going to hear back," he says.

When the Steelworkers agreed to back Ramogi Huma's Collegiate Athletes Coalition in 2001, questions of unionization naturally followed. How could they not? Here was a campaign for players' rights that was being backed by organized labor. But it was always a step that Huma and Waters had been reluctant to take. In the years after the *White* settlement, Huma continued on his soapbox, telling anyone who would listen about the cost-of-attendance issue and how players saw next to none of the spoils of a college sports industry that was generating billions of dollars. He had even helped get the NCAA's ban on multiyear scholarships removed by speaking to the Justice Department. It wasn't long after Justice officials questioned the NCAA about the policy that schools were given the ability, if they so chose, to offer four-year scholarships that were not contingent on a coach's approval after each season. In 2012, Huma worked on a study with Drexel professor Ellen Staurowsky that found the average scholarship fell short of what top-division football players needed by more than $3,000 each year, while more than 80 percent of athletes playing football on "full scholarship" lived below the poverty line. What's more, the study found that if a free market existed and revenue was shared between players and owners as in pro sports, Division I football players would be worth $137,357 a year; their basketball counterparts were worth $289,031.

But even some of Huma's successes were bittersweet. California governor Jerry Brown signed legislation in the fall of 2012 called the Student-Athlete Bill of Rights, which brought new scholarship and health protections for players at the state's biggest college sports programs (mandating health coverage for two years beyond eligibility was included). But it passed the legislature only after it was stripped of some of its strongest language, like allowing players to transfer schools without sitting out a year. "We were trying to be advocates," Huma says. "We wanted the NCAA to listen, to come to the table with us." But the NCAA did neither, and by the time Colter came calling, Huma was ready for bigger and bolder action, thanks to a new problem he never imagined back in 2001: concussions. "Head injuries were a game changer," Huma says.

Forensic pathologist Dr. Bennet Omalu first found CTE in the brain of the great Pittsburgh Steelers center Mike Webster, who died in September 2002, six months past his fiftieth birthday. The discovery was shocking: here was a relatively young former football player with dementia, depression, early-onset Alzheimer's, and a brain that looked like it belonged to a much older man. Over the next several years, more former players—Terry Long, forty-five, and Andrew Waters, forty-four—took their own lives, leaving their brains to science and confirmation that they too suffered from CTE. (Junior Seau, Cleveland Colter's former teammate, received the same diagnosis after he shot himself in 2012.) The repeated and violent hits to the head so elemental to the game of football were causing irreparable brain damage, and in some extreme cases were leading to death. By 2009, Congress had gotten involved, with the House Judiciary Committee calling hearings to examine head injuries, the dangers of football, and what safety measures were in place to prevent these tragedies.

The scope of the hearings went beyond the NFL, and included discussions about youth football, leading NCAA officials to wonder how exposed they were. In February 2010, NCAA government relations director Abe Frank wrote to David Klossner, then the NCAA's health and safety director, "Do you think this renewed emphasis on youth sports will increase the pressure on the NCAA to do more at the college level?" he asked. Klossner's response was telling. "Well since we don't currently require anything all steps are higher than ours," he wrote.

As early as 2003, NCAA research suggested problems with its concussion management. An article published in the *Journal of the American Medical Association* stated most college football players were back on the field less than five days after suffering a concussion. Returning to play that soon "may increase the risks of recurrent injury, cumulative impairment, or even catastrophic outcome," the study said. Internal NCAA calculations found that between 2004 and 2009, nearly thirty thousand NCAA athletes suffered concussions, more than half of them football players. In response to the growing research and concern over head injuries, the NFL adopted guidelines in 2009 prohibiting players from returning to play if they exhibited concussion signs. The same year, the National Federation of State High School Associations also required that players be removed from a game if they were suspected of suffering a concussion. The Committee on Competitive Safeguards and Medical Aspects of Sports recommended that the NCAA adopt a uniform concussion policy. It refused. Health and safety director Klossner asked that, at the very least, the NCAA send suggested guidelines to coaches and add those guidelines to the NCAA rulebook. "And, what about the NCAA? Would we be protecting/helping the organization by not providing the information?" asked Assistant Director of Playing Rules Administration Teresa Smith.

In April 2010, the NCAA held its first-ever concussion summit, during which it released a survey of athletic trainers. The results were troubling. Less than 50 percent of schools required a physician to see all athletes who suffered concussions; 39 percent did not establish guidelines on how long athletes should sit out before returning to play; nearly half said they allowed athletes to return to play in the same game in which they suffered a concussion. Finally the NCAA was moved to act—barely. It mandated that universities develop their own concussion protocols, but still did nothing to monitor them. As for whether anyone was ever disciplined for not following safety rules? "Not to my knowledge," Klossner later said.

The importance of stronger safety protocols only became clearer in the coming months. Owen Thomas, a junior lineman at the University of Pennsylvania, mysteriously hanged himself in his off-campus apartment that April. Five months later, doctors examined his brain and found early stages of CTE. In 2011, Adrian Arrington, a former safety at Eastern Illinois, sued the NCAA over its lack of concussion policies. Arrington had sustained five concussions during his career, some so bad he couldn't immediately recognize his parents afterward. After one hit, his father rushed from the stands to tell coaches that his injured son couldn't return to the game. By the time he was twenty-seven, Arrington was on welfare and couldn't hold a job because of seizures so violent one tore his rotator cuff. Derek Owens, a former Central Arkansas wide receiver, filed a second concussion suit. His symptoms were so severe he had to drop out of school. "I feel like a twenty-two-year-old with Alzheimer's," he told his mother.

(Just a month before the Northwestern players' union announcement, the NCAA put forward a jaw-dropping legal argument in filings for a wrongful death suit brought by the family of Derek Sheely, a former Division III football player at Frostburg State. Sheely collapsed after he began to bleed following repeated blows to his head during a preseason drill in 2011. He died six days later. "The NCAA denies that it has a legal duty to protect student-athletes," the filing read.)

Huma, desperate for a way to bring attention to college football's concussion crisis, traveled to Miami Gardens, Florida, for the 2013 BCS championship game between Alabama and Notre Dame. Along with Morgan Thomas, Owen's brother, he attempted to call a press conference at the media hotel for the throngs of press gathered for the game. But hotel staff wouldn't allow it—college football officials didn't want him there. Instead, he passed out flyers to the media. "It was a breaking point," Huma says. "When we couldn't talk about concussions, we had to change course."

Later that year, Huma finally got his long-awaited meeting with the NCAA. He met with the association's new chief medical officer, Brian Hainline, to talk about concussions and player safety. Hainline made it clear to Huma that he alone couldn't impose new safety regulations; they had to come from the membership.

Huma had heard from hundreds of players over the years about the NCPA. Sometimes they just wanted information; some joined the NCPA; others pledged to help the movement. There was an urgency to Colter's e-mail that made it feel different. When Huma called back—within the hour—almost the first words out of Colter's mouth were, "College athletes need a union." For several months, Huma had been wrestling with the same idea, but even on the first call with Colter he was reluctant to say he agreed. "Union" was a word he'd been running away from for nearly fifteen years. For starters, his backer, Waters, was opposed to an organizing effort. "A union was off the table and Ramogi knew that," Waters says. There were myriad reasons why, not the least of which was the immense undertaking it would require. From the lawyers to the organizing to the difficulty of finding the right player to lead the charge, Waters had never been prepared to take the leap. He also never thought it would be necessary. "College sports, to me, was a lift-up-the-rock issue and see what's underneath," he says. "Once people saw what was really going on, it wasn't going to take a union to change it." Still, the rock was up and nothing had happened.

Colter's arrival helped change the dynamics of the NCPA. Huma had been a one-man operation for so long, but now he had a fellow football player for a copilot. (Waters was always involved, but he had many other responsibilities with the Steelworkers.) Huma was not cut from the same cloth as Sonny Vaccaro, a man comfortable comparing himself to Che Guevara. He did not have the same gregarious personality and never sought the media spotlight the way Vaccaro did. Journalist Ivan Solotaroff, who profiled Huma for SB Nation in the spring of 2014, likened getting biographical details from Huma to "finding hair on a bald man's head." "There's nothing there for you," Solotaroff says.

No one—not Vaccaro, not Andy Schwarz, not Michael Hausfeld—would claim to have players' interests at heart as single-mindedly as Huma. But while Vaccaro was easily suited to be the face of the *O'Bannon* lawsuit—even though he wasn't the plaintiff—Huma's transition into a public figure was different. "Ramogi has a hard time trusting anyone who doesn't believe in what he believes in," says Vaccaro. "He can be very pure in that way." Vaccaro adds, "He doesn't know how to handle the press thing sometimes. I tell him, 'If someone beats you up, you got to let it go.' He's much more personal."

Colter was a three-time member of the Big Ten's All-Academic team. He was articulate, persuasive, and full of energy. As Waters says, "Kain was like the second coming of Ramogi. With Colter fully engaged, he and Huma talked often about a union over the summer, mostly in private. Meanwhile, Colter joined a conference call Huma had arranged a few times a month with a handful of other players around the country. Colter heard other athletes talk about the same things he noticed: too-small stipend checks, lack of medical coverage, watching teammates and friends fail to graduate. "It was cool because you realized we're all in this together," he says. He soon recruited a Northwestern teammate onto the calls, and pressed Huma and Waters to begin moving on a union. "He pushed our status quo," Waters says. "He wanted everything to be bigger, to be more public. He always wanted to know what was next."

That fall, Huma and the group of athletes on the conference calls devised a way to publicize their concerns: players would write "APU," short for "All Players United," on their wrist tape during games one Saturday in a nationwide show of solidarity. Colter and several Northwestern teammates displayed the acronym. So did Georgia Tech quarterback Vad Lee and several Georgia offensive linemen. The action was small but significant, perhaps more for the men who had been involved in the struggle for so many years than the players themselves. Waters watched Northwestern play Maine that afternoon in a game that was televised by—who else?—the Big Ten Network. When the camera focused on Colter, Waters took a photo with his phone, then zoomed in: sure enough, there was the "APU" in white capital letters on the black wrist tape. He tweeted the image, with the caption, "Northwestern Star QB (Colter) wears #APU logo on both wrists to join @NCPANOW national player solidarity action today."

Someone else noticed as well: Sonny Vaccaro. "Players had never taken it upon themselves before," he says. "It was a beautiful day."

The response to the APU protest was predictable. Fitzgerald told Colter he wasn't necessarily against players voicing their opinions, but a public display like that should have been discussed within the team beforehand. But Colter says when he asked if he could address the team about the "APU" movement, Fitzgerald said no. (Fitzgerald says Colter never asked him to address the team.) "It hit home that we had no leverage, no power," Colter says. "If a coach or AD or school wants to shut something down, they shut it down."

Colter and Huma were not the first to attempt a symbolic protest aimed at the NCAA, but their success—and growing momentum—was unlike anything that had come before it. Three decades earlier, an ex-Duke basketball player named Dick DeVenzio founded the Revenue Producing Major College Players Association and tried to persuade athletes to stand up for their rights. He sent pamphlets to teams across the country, urging players to speak out. "We know through painful experience that freedom is never voluntarily given by the oppressor. It must be demanded by the oppressed," read one flyer, quoting Martin Luther King Jr.

Advocating for any number of reforms, from a union to paid athletes, DeVenzio was willing to try just about anything to bring attention to the NCAA's treatment of athletes. He once sent out a hundred checks for $100 each to the top football players at more than sixty schools around the country. His hope was they'd cash them after the season in defiance of NCAA rules. The NCAA, he reasoned, couldn't make all those schools forfeit their seasons.

His biggest splash came in the fall of 1986 when he urged players at Nebraska and Oklahoma to stage a thirty-minute strike at the start of their nationally televised game. As the game approached, Sooners linebacker Brian Bosworth told reporters there was a fifty-fifty chance players would delay it. Yet when kickoff time rolled around, all that happened was a few players knelt in a prayer circle before the game started. DeVenzio tried again with players from Michigan and Southern California ahead of the 1990 Rose Bowl, with no luck. He died of colon cancer in 2001 without ever gaining much traction.

But others took up his cause. In the winter of 1989, the football team at Prairie View A&M University, a Division I-AA school forty-five miles northwest of Houston, boycotted practice, demanding that Coach Haney Catchings be fired. The reason? The players claimed their textbooks were withheld so they could focus more on football. "Last year, some of the guys didn't get their books until midterm," said Kevin Pierce, a member of the team. "This year, after the last football game, when we had two weeks until finals, he said, 'All right, y'all, now you can go work on your academics.'"

The monthlong strike drew national attention, forcing the school to undertake an internal investigation, though university president Percy Pierre ultimately decided not to fire Catchings, saying the coach could not be held accountable for academic problems. Soon enough, the players returned to practice, and the story faded and college sports went on as usual.

The next team to consider a strike was the vaunted UNLV basketball team, which had won the NCAA championship in 1990 and seemed a lock to make it back in 1991. Coached, of course, by Jerry Tarkanian, the Runnin' Rebels players had their own beefs against the NCAA, none bigger than star point guard Greg Anthony. Anthony had started a successful T-shirt business called Two-Hype with two friends; the company made enough money that Anthony tried to give back his scholarship after UNLV won the national championship—a value of $12,212. But that wasn't enough for the NCAA, which said Anthony had to drop ties to his business or put his eligibility at risk (the supposed concern was that boosters could use a player's businesses to funnel him money).

As Anthony and his teammates inched closer to an undefeated season and a championship in 1991, players talked about protesting the NCAA ahead of the tournament final, according to a person with knowledge of the discussions. They talked of perhaps delaying the start of the game by not taking the court. But their primary idea was to strike during the championship game itself. Alas, the point was rendered moot when Duke—whom UNLV had beaten by 30 points in the title game the year before—upset UNLV in the Final Four. No championship game, no protest.

Four years later, basketball players at schools across the country, from UCLA to Wake Forest to the University of Massachusetts, discussed a nationwide strike to draw attention to their plight. It was supposed to happen during the first day of March Madness; players planned to walk to the center of the court and just sit down. "It was going to be huge," said Rigo Nunez, a UMass guard. "Definitely change the way we operate from an NCAA perspective, the whole scope of amateur sports." But that action fizzled as well. The games went on just as scheduled.

By 2001, a group of college basketball players, led by Duke star Shane Battier, had formed the Student Basketball Council, meant to foster discussion about athletes' rights. The council held just one meeting. Battier later said he was "naive" to think a student group could lead the NCAA toward meaningful change.

Indeed, it was a common refrain. Athletes could plainly see the hypocrisy swirling around them, but could do little about it.

Until now. By the fall, Waters had come around; he quietly floated a college players' union to Steelworkers leadership, and discussed the idea with top labor minds. Whether Colter realized it or not, he was changing the NCPA. "When you work for something for so long, when you live it, you don't let yourself think about something happening like Kain Colter," Waters says. "You have to be born with this, to be a leader and to have a mental approach to know you're about to get attacked, but do it anyway. It takes a different kind of person to do this stuff. But here he was, the real deal. This wasn't a third-string safety; this was a quarterback of a Big Ten team at a pretty well-respected school." Waters and Huma flew to Evanston later that fall to visit Colter. If they were really going to start a union, Waters needed Colter to understand what he was signing up for. They sat around Colter's kitchen table and Waters, between sips from his Monster energy drink, gave him a crash course on the basics of organized labor.

As a private university, Northwestern was governed not by state law but by the National Labor Relations Board. (It also helped to have Barack Obama in the White House; the five-member federal board, which hears all appeals, was part of the executive branch and a majority would be aligned with Democrats and likely friendlier to labor.) Huma, Waters, and Colter needed 30 percent of the team to sign union cards to form the union, and then, after Northwestern refused to recognize them—a near-certain outcome—there would be a public hearing before the regional NLRB, followed by a decision. The Steelworkers would handle the legal questions, such as how they would represent the players. (The College Athletes Players Association would have to be incorporated, for instance.) They looked into who was eligible and what an employee designation would mean for players. Colter, meanwhile, handled organizing the team. They were off and running.

Colter had to slowly spread the word among his teammates without alerting the coaches. Some of the other players knew about Colter's interest in the All Players United movement, but now he was asking for their help. He gathered a small group of teammates one afternoon at a nearby house where several of the players lived and delivered the bombshell: he wanted to start a union at Northwestern. Some had questions about employee status—would they be able to play other teams of nonemployees? But most had many of the same gripes Colter did, and agreed they were in a unique position to put pressure on the NCAA. Coming from a Big Ten school like Northwestern, they felt they would be taken seriously and could speak for players around the country—and just maybe change things too. "Nobody said, 'This is crazy, screw you,'" Colter says. "So that's when I knew it was possible."

Huma and Colter organized a series of conference calls with what Colter called his "core group," the handful of players who were most enthusiastic about the idea. The union cards, they decided, would wait until January, after the season, but things would have to move quickly after that—they couldn't risk a coach getting wind of anything. How to present the cards to the team was another question. They considered a large auditorium to fit the whole team, but thought it would be easier to address smaller groups. The football facilities were out, of course; the meetings had to be secret.

Colter reserved a classroom for Sunday, January 26. Northwestern players received texts about an "urgent players-only meeting" and they arrived in groups of twenty throughout the afternoon. Colter began the sessions by talking about how he had gotten involved in the players' rights movement. He told his teammates to understand the gravity of the moment. This would be covered by ESPN and CNN, he said. He then introduced Huma, who talked about the NCPA, and how the Steelworkers were involved. He explained the cost-of-attendance issue, and promised that a union would not affect other sports on campuses. He had a packet of FAQs for each player. Huma promised total confidentiality for anyone who signed or didn't sign. For a decade and a half, this had been his life—speaking to groups of young men about their rights and their voice—and what they could do if they spoke together. "It was the most important day," Huma says. "I had an hour to tell them everything we'd been doing for fifteen years."

Colter then finished the pitch with a personal story. He played much of his senior season on injured ankle cartilage, and as he trained that winter for the NFL draft the injury continued to bother him. The ankle was part of his exit physical—meaning it was an injury from his time at Northwestern—but when he asked Northwestern to pay for an MRI, the school declined. He paid for it himself, and found he needed ankle surgery, a big hit to his draft prospects. And only after the MRI found that surgery was needed did Northwestern offer to reimburse him and then find a doctor to perform it. (Northwestern says Colter failed to properly notify the school about the MRI, and once the needed paperwork was filed the school was willing to pay for the MRI.)

Players had plenty of questions. NFL players had to pay dues; would the union cost them money? Huma assured them there would be no dues. Others asked about Fitzgerald, the popular coach. Colter said he would handle talking to him, but that Fitzgerald couldn't know about the union because he was part of the system. Colter didn't know what his reaction would be, he said, but he knew he had always supported his players. With every group, they passed out union cards. When the last of the players trickled out, Huma, Colter, and a few others sat at the desks and counted the cards. Almost every player had signed. They looked at each other, wide-eyed. "It was awesome," Colter says. "We knew we made history."

Two days later, Huma turned in the cards. It was indeed national news, just as he had predicted. And while not every commentator agreed with the idea of a college athletes' union, Colter drew praise from all corners of the sports world for raising issues of health care and NCAA intransigence. Northwestern athletic director Jim Phillips put out a statement that denounced collective bargaining, but said, "We love and are proud of our students. Northwestern teaches them to be leaders and independent thinkers who will make a positive impact on their communities, the nation and the world. Today's action demonstrates that they are doing so." Fitzgerald tweeted, "Kain and our student-athletes have followed their beliefs with great passion and courage. I'm incredibly proud of our young men! GO CATS!"

Not surprisingly, Northwestern refused to recognize the players as employees. So a hearing was scheduled for February, and when it was moved from a room inside the NLRB in downtown Chicago to a federal courtroom in the nearby Dirksen Building to accommodate the media, the new setting only added to the feeling that it wasn't so much Northwestern but the NCAA itself that was on trial. The central issue at stake was whether football players at Northwestern were students or employees—just as it had been decades earlier when Walter Byers came up with the term "student-athlete" to sidestep the question.

An employee, under the National Labor Relations Act as well as Supreme Court precedent, is usually quite easy to define: he or she is an individual who performs services for another, under the control of another, for compensation or payment. But the federal NLRB had dealt with a similar case in 2004, when it ruled that Brown University graduate teaching assistants were not employees because they were primarily students. The Steelworkers were unconcerned with that precedent. There was little reason, Waters thought, that the players could not be both students *and* employees.

The Steelworkers had spent months preparing its arguments and had lined up some legal heavyweights. Attorney John Adam, sporting a thick brown mustache faintly reminiscent of Mike Ditka, had argued more than a hundred cases before the labor board. (Adam gave Colter a copy of Byers's memoir when he first met him.) His partner was Gary Kohlman, a D.C. labor lawyer and a pit bull of a cross-examiner. "If anyone thought we were going to walk into that hearing without the best lawyers in the country for the job, they don't know the Steelworkers," Waters says today.

The gist of the College Athletes Players Association's case was rather simple: the players were already employees because they were paid with a scholarship to attend Northwestern, which the school valued as high as $76,000. In exchange, they were expected to put in huge amounts of work with the football team under the strict control of their coaches, who were effectively their bosses. And if they did not follow the rules, they could lose their scholarships.

Colter, who was completing his final two courses while rehabbing his ankle and training for the draft in Bradenton, Florida, flew in to testify first. He hoped to simply tell his story at Northwestern, demonstrating the time demands and the authority wielded by his coaches. On one level, his testimony was very straightforward. Colter said he spent sometimes as many as fifty or sixty hours a week with the team; team rules required him to accept all Facebook friend requests from coaches; he needed the team's approval to do mundane things like move out of the dorms and into an off-campus apartment. On another level, his testimony belied the simplicity of his description. Here under oath—with college sports and the NCAA under scrutiny like never before—was finally a public accounting of the life of a college football player.

Adam walked Colter through a detailed itinerary for a November 10, 2012, game he played in Ann Arbor against Michigan. The road trip, which included more than ten hours of travel, a four-hour football game, and hours more of meetings and team meals, required nearly twenty-four hours with the team, which would seem to exceed NCAA rules that limited sports participation to twenty hours each week. Yet Colter's log showed only a few hours spent on football for the weekend. How could this be? The NCAA, it turned out, had a loophole in its arithmetic. Time related to a game event—travel, play, team meetings, and everything else—counted for exactly *three* hours against the cap, no matter what the clock said.

Colter's testimony was instructive in another way: it offered a pointed look at how difficult it was to rock the boat in college sports. When announcing the union, Colter had tried to be clear that his beef was primarily with the NCAA, not Northwestern. But only by taking on Northwestern could he take on the NCAA, which created a more ambiguous situation. Northwestern lawyer Anna Wermuth noted that Fitzgerald had created the team's Leadership Council to give players some voice in team rules. Colter countered by saying that Fitzgerald retained 51 percent of the power. "We get an input, but at the end of the day he's the bossman," he said, the last word exploding like a detonated bomb in the courtroom.

Wermuth also brought up Colter's ankle to illustrate how Northwestern took care of players after graduation. Colter, still frustrated with how the injury was handled—he also took painkillers, including a controversial drug called Toradol—was visibly upset on the stand. "So they did say they would reimburse you for the MRI?" Wermuth asked. "After they denied me," Colter interjected. "But I mean there shouldn't be any gray area. I gave—I sacrificed my body for four years. They sold my jersey in the stores, and they should protect me as far as medical coverage." He added, "They're going back and trying to make things right. But you can't just make it right. You denied me."

"Getting on the stand, that was the most nervous I'd been," Colter says. "There were definitely things I wish I could have rephrased, but I felt like their lawyers were attacking me."

A columnist for the *Chicago Sun-Times* described Colter as "slinging mud" and "belligerently grandstanding." Alumni and former teammates wanted to know why he was killing the program. Colter tried to reach out to some former teammates to explain himself. Several told him not to speak to them. An assistant coach later told him he couldn't believe he had referred to Fitzgerald as "bossman." The criticism, Colter said, was fierce— you don't deserve to get paid, you signed up for this, you piece of crap. Soon after, his grandmother—one of his greatest influences—passed away from a neurological disease. She was buried in some of Colter's Northwestern gear. "It was one of the lowest points in my life," he says. "I felt like I had burned all these bridges with Northwestern after I dedicated so much of my life there."

Colter's testimony changed the way some current players viewed the union push too. They debated among themselves in groups in the locker room, some questioning why Colter had so publicly thrown Fitzgerald under the bus. Some felt that Colter, focused on the NFL and away from campus, had less invested in Northwestern than they did. They were left to fight his battle, and they didn't like seeing their coach and their school under fire.

Underlying some of the criticism of Colter was the belief by the school and many of its alumni that Northwestern was the wrong place to highlight the pitfalls of college sports. And in many ways that was true. Northwestern was not a football factory. It had a graduation success rate of 97 percent, the highest in college football's top division, and had a history of providing some medical coverage even after an athlete's playing days had ended. As soon as the NCAA allowed schools to guarantee four-year scholarships, Northwestern was one of the few schools to do so immediately. In truth, the university treated its players about as well as any school—and as well as NCAA rules allowed. This too was part of Northwestern's defense. Colter's concerns were NCAA issues, their lawyers argued.

Northwestern couldn't distribute cost-of-attendance stipends, for example, without the association's approval.

Northwestern called several other players to testify—a long snapper and two offensive linemen—and each presented compelling evidence that Northwestern valued schoolwork. But none refuted Colter's accounting of the hours or the coaches' control. Then came Coach Fitzgerald. He wore a purple tie—Northwestern's color—on the witness stand. "We take great pride in developing our young men to be the best they possibly can be in everything that they choose to do—athletically, academically, socially," he said. But Kohlman got him to concede that the players can spend twenty-four hours on football on a Friday and Saturday, when they travel to away games. He acknowledged he set team rules too. In an interview the year before, Fitzgerald had even called being a student-athlete "a full-time job."

"We won the case with Fitzgerald on the stand," Kohlman says.

A month later, Peter Sung Ohr's decision rattled the foundation of college sports, as the NLRB regional director eviscerated the NCAA's bedrock principle that college athletes were first and foremost students. "The players spend 50 to 60 hours per week on their football duties during a one-month training camp prior to the start of the academic year and an additional 40 to 50 hours per week on those duties during the three- or four-month football season," the ruling said. "Not only is this more hours than many undisputed full-time employees work at their jobs, it is also many more hours than the players spend on their studies." Ohr also noted that Northwestern football reported $235 million in revenue from 2003 to 2012.

Huma was on the phone with a reporter when he got the call that the players had won. He carefully composed himself, got off the phone with the reporter, and then called Colter, who was still training in Bradenton. They laughed, they screamed. "Is this real? Did we really win?" Colter shouted.

"Then things really got crazy," Colter says.

Panic swept athletic departments in the wake of Ohr's ruling, with sports officials outdoing each other with suggestions of doomsday scenarios. Mark Emmert called a union "grossly inappropriate." Former Northwestern president Henry Bienen proclaimed that the university might leave Division I. The Northwestern fencing coach told his team a football players' union could mean the end of varsity fencing. Jim Delany predicted anarchy. "What happens if school A or school B becomes a union school? What would happen?" he told *Chicago Sun-Times* columnist Rick Telander. "I don't know. You don't know. I have no idea! Places where there are unions, places with no unions, no NCAA, no NCAA rules? I think you would have chaos."

It reached statehouses across the Midwest, and Washington too, with politicians also fearing contagion. By the end of the year, lawmakers in Ohio and Michigan pushed legislation barring athletes at public schools from forming a union. Northwestern immediately appealed the decision to the full NLRB in Washington, and a group of congressional Republicans submitted a supporting amicus brief. A House committee called a hearing in May that brought Stanford athletic director Bernard Muir and Baylor President Kenneth Starr (yes, the former Bill Clinton antagonist) to D.C. to lament the unionization drive. If Stanford players unionized, Muir said, the school would look for a new way to run its sports programs. The sky was falling!

The Northwestern football team wasn't even unionized yet. An election was scheduled for April—seventy-six players were eligible to vote, and a majority of the ballots cast had to certify the union. Northwestern, like any employer fighting a union drive, set out to beat the vote. University president Morton O. Schapiro circulated a "Dear Colleague" letter to presidents at other universities saying that "the university has the right to campaign against the union in order to encourage our student-athletes to vote 'No.'" And that's exactly what Northwestern did.

Fitzgerald, no longer equivocating, announced that he had told the players to vote down the union. "I just do not believe we need a third party between our players and our coaches, staff and administrators," he declared at a spring practice. This became the theme of the school's carefully orchestrated campaign—one that was perfectly legal, but heaped immense pressure on the shoulders of a group of eighteen- to twenty-two-year-olds.

It began with new iPads and a trip to a bowling alley when the players returned to practice after Ohr's ruling. (Northwestern counters that the iPads were ordered in December 2013, long before the union movement, and that the team organized regular outings, including several to Chicago Blackhawks games.) Fitzgerald addressed the team about voting down the union. Position coaches talked to players. Parents were e-mailed.

In one e-mail to players, Fitzgerald explicitly equated a vote for the union as a vote against him. He wrote, "The Union is making this a stark choice for you: choose to place your trust in me as your coach, Dr. Phillips, and the men and women who work every day for you at Northwestern, or choose the Union.... Understand that by voting to have a union, you would be transferring your trust from those you know—me, your coaches and the administrators here—to what you don't know—a third party who may or may not have the team's best interests in mind."

The team solicited anonymous questions from players, parents, and staff and compiled a twenty-one-page Q&A document. The message was that a union could result in fewer benefits. Players were allowed, for instance, to travel home for emergencies, but that privilege could become contingent on collective bargaining. One question supposedly submitted by a player: "This is not what we wanted—how can we get back to being students and not employees?" Northwestern's answer: the "process has to go forward, but you can still express your desire to 'get back to being students' by voting 'No.'"

"They reacted like an employer," Adam says. "It was confirmation to me."

To be sure, there were pitfalls to the union approach. A national union representing college athletes—given the different labor laws in every state, and the fact that the universe of college teams included both private and public institutions—was somewhat far-fetched. In some states, public employees weren't even allowed to unionize. The impact on Title IX and what an employee model meant for workers' compensation, unemployment benefits, and potential salaries were unclear. Tax law was another unknown, though the IRS issued an informational letter to a U.S. senator saying the Northwestern ruling did not control the tax issue and it has long been the IRS's position that athletic scholarships are exempt from federal income tax.

There were also real and measurable things the school could do, within the constraints of the NCAA. Northwestern could cut the number of full-contact practices it held (the NFL has stricter limits than the NCAA, which has none during the season). There were also no NCAA rules to restrict Northwestern from guaranteeing long-term health care to players whose football injuries plagued them later in life. And if Northwestern's football players could bargain for those things—benefits that didn't violate NCAA rules—then, the theory went, other schools would follow suit to keep up in recruiting.

These questions, though, were mostly pushed aside as the school threw its weight behind defeating the union push. Fitzgerald hosted a barbecue for players and their families that spring, which at least one player and his family found unusual. (Fitzgerald said the team was inundated with questions about the union and the gathering was meant to help answer them.) Pressures reached the locker room, where Dan Persa, who quarterbacked the Wildcats before Colter, warned players that Fitzgerald could leave if they voted for the union. (Persa said he opposed the union because of the unknowns it would bring and only wanted players to be informed.) Players heard other ominous warnings—that alumni donations could dry up, for instance, or a new $225 million athletic center could be scrapped.

Players got calls from alumni telling them that casting their lots with Colter, who was now persona non grata in Evanston, could hurt their job chances after graduation as the Northwestern alumni network would desert them. One player, wearing a Northwestern football shirt on the train in downtown Chicago, was approached by an alum and told he'd better vote down the union. The common refrain was, how could the players, who had been given so much by their school, bite the hand that fed them? "Some players, especially the younger guys, felt threatened," one player says. "They felt scared, honestly."

Colter, meanwhile, held his pro day at Northwestern to work out for NFL scouts in early April, only to find that some of his former coaches wouldn't speak to him (a Northwestern spokesman explained the school arranged the workout specially for Colter, since he had been injured). As Colter was vilified, a group of Northwestern alumni grew concerned that the university was turning its back on its former star quarterback and that the players were being bullied into voting down the union. They were not pro-union, per se, but they opposed Northwestern's aggressive campaign.

Led by Kevin Brown and Alex Moyer, two former Wildcats who played for Northwestern in the 1980s, a small group went to see Coach Fitzgerald. According to Brown, Fitzgerald was also concerned about the pressure on the players. Brown says Fitzgerald, who denies the story, told them that one player broke down in tears in his office because of the stress of the vote. "Players were torn because they didn't want to disappoint their coach," Brown says. "Players look at their coach like he's a father figure, but it's not necessarily reciprocated. A coach represents the university's interests more than the players' interests. We didn't care one way or the other if they formed a union, but they should be allowed the freedom to exert their rights."

Brown and Moyer called a meeting the week before the vote at a community center in Evanston to voice their concerns to the Northwestern football family. Around sixty former Northwestern football players going all the way back to teams from the 1970s were there, as well as a handful of current players. "I'm worried Kain is becoming a pariah," Moyer said to the group. "He chose to be a pariah," jeered an alum in the crowd.

As the vote neared, Colter and Huma returned to Evanston and called a meeting of players at a hotel near campus. Frustrations had emerged over the recent weeks. Some players didn't like the way their new iPads had been portrayed as bribes; they also wanted to know why other schools hadn't followed their lead. Colter and Huma had said they were talking to players at other unnamed universities, but Northwestern was alone in the spotlight.

It wasn't for lack of trying. According to a player at the University of Illinois, Colter held calls with players there around the time of Northwestern's union push. The player says that word leaked to Illinois coach Tim Beckman and he addressed the team about the possibility of a union, telling players their scholarships would become taxable and they'd lose thousands of dollars. This wasn't necessarily true, of course, but helped kill the momentum, and nothing came of the organizing efforts. (Colter and Huma declined to discuss any unionization attempts at any school besides Northwestern. Beckman said he was unaware of any organizing plans at Illinois and the meeting was meant to be informational. He was fired by Illinois in August 2015 after several players accused him of bullying them into playing through injuries and improperly influencing medical decisions.)

In Evanston, Colter suddenly felt as if his former teammates no longer trusted him. Three months after the cards were signed, everything was different. Northwestern's campaign had worked, he knew. He polled the room and it was clear the school would win the election. Even some of his closest confidants from the previous months weren't with him anymore. Players now questioned his motives: Why had he only given them a day to sign the cards? He also noticed a new split in the team, this one along racial lines, with the African-American players supporting the union and the white players opposing it. "There was a huge divide," Colter says. "The majority of the team was split along racial lines. It was just ugly." Added another player, "If the team had been all black, the union would have gone through."

The players voted on a mild April afternoon. They trickled into the football facility in groups of twos and threes with little to say to the media. As Traveon Henry, a safety, climbed into a ride after the vote, he declined to say how he voted and shook his head. "It's a relief to have it off our plate," he said.

A few months after the vote, Emmert gave a speech in Chicago about the NCAA's renewed reform efforts. Cost of attendance was once again on his agenda, and health care too. "Kain Colter's obviously a very bright capable guy and when you stop and look at the list of issues the Northwestern football team was interested in, they're pretty consistent with what I just said," Emmert said.

Indeed, the legacy of the Northwestern union drive—with or without the union—will always be that it was player-driven, which sent its own jolt through campuses across the country. Lawsuits were drummed up by lawyers. But Northwestern represented a true players' rebellion. And change, as Emmert alluded to, was coming quickly, though not in the way he had hoped.

# Turning the Tables on the NCAA

**YEARS BEFORE HE GOT TO COLLEGE, JOEL BAUMAN'S FATHER WARNED** him about the NCAA. Bauman was a star athlete in Kerkhoven, Minnesota, a town with a population of less than a thousand, two hours from Minneapolis, where he wrestled, ran track, and played football. He also had a talent for music. Adopted at a young age, he was one of Kerkhoven's few African Americans. After discovering Dr. Dre as an adolescent, he started battle rapping online and earned a following.

As he began to think about pursuing wrestling in college, his father had some advice. "Making your own music is great," Bauman remembers him saying. "But be careful. If you get a scholarship, the NCAA will own your name."

Unlike virtually every other college athlete in America, however, Bauman didn't view the prospect of battling the NCAA as a negative. As an aspiring rapper, he thought mostly about the publicity he could reap if the NCAA came down on him. "I just remember thinking the NCAA could make me famous," he says.

Bauman's chance to test his theory came in 2013, during his third year at the University of Minnesota. He was out with a concussion and a friend who had recently landed a job in the music industry reached out to see if he had any new music. Within a week, Bauman wrote, shot, and produced a music video for a song he called "Ones in the Sky," an uplifting anthem about chasing your dreams. He also posted the video to YouTube and iTunes. In his promotion for the video, he noted that he was a Minnesota wrestler.

Not long afterward, the wrestling team asked if it could play the song at a meet. Of course, Bauman replied. Just as he had expected, he soon got an e-mail from Minnesota's compliance department. "You will have to remove your name from any songs that you upload and remove any promotion from your status as a student-athlete," it read.

"I just smiled," Bauman says. "I knew what was about to happen."

What followed was exactly the firestorm he had hoped for. When he declined to take the music down, the NCAA ruled that he was ineligible—and he immediately became the beleaguered athlete taking a principled stand against college sports' most notorious bully. His saga not only generated lots of newspaper and Internet coverage, but he was featured in a segment of *The Daily Show* during the spring of 2013. The segment was titled, sarcastically, "The NCAA's Perfectly Fair Rules."

Bauman played the victim perfectly. "It was like a role," he says. "Think about it. I had a 10 percent scholarship—it basically paid for my books—and I was hurt so I wasn't even wrestling. It wasn't a tough call."

Today, Bauman works in marketing for a holistic foods company, which allows him to continue to work on his music. The job, he says, would never have been possible without the publicity the NCAA helped him attract. "I knew what I was doing the whole time," he says. "The NCAA is pretty predictable."

Even over the phone, you can tell he is smiling.

# CHAPTER 15

# AMATEUR HOUR

O n the morning of June 9, 2014, Sonny and Pam Vaccaro arrived at the federal courthouse in downtown Oakland shortly after dawn. By the time the doors opened at 9 a.m., a line snaked through the courtyard outside the entrance for nearly a block. Vaccaro, with Pam at his side, was at the front. He was positively buoyant. He flitted around the crowd, chatting up anyone he could find: lawyers, journalists, his buddy Ed O'Bannon. "I feel like I've waited my whole life for this," Vaccaro said on this, the first day of the *O'Bannon* trial, five years after he had first spoken to Jon King about suing the NCAA. As part of his preparation for the trial, he had read *Ladies and Gentlemen of the Jury: Greatest Closing Arguments in Modern Law*. He wanted to be ready.

The *O'Bannon* lawyers had good reason to feel confident as the trial began. Months—indeed, years—of taking depositions and obtaining internal documents and e-mails from the NCAA had confirmed that they had chosen the right tack in pursuing a lawsuit built around names, images, and likenesses. "It looks like the NCAA makes money from the licenses," wrote then University of Texas president William Powers in one such e-mail. "Why should we be defendants in this, rather than plaintiffs representing our students?" In another e-mail, the University of Nebraska's chancellor, Harvey Perlman, wrote, "[This] whole area of name and likeness and the NCAA is a disaster leading to a catastrophe, as far as I can tell."

"The documents were a revelation in that they showed that the story we thought was there was, in fact, the story," Hausfeld later said. "It wasn't like there were just a few bad documents"—lawyer lingo for damning documents that can be used, often out of context, to inflame a jury—"but it was their entire culture. There was no ambiguity."

Though it wasn't easy, Ramogi Huma had helped them find six current athletes who were willing to be named plaintiffs along with the fifteen former athletes. Although one quickly dropped out, the other five stayed the course, and one of them, Chase Garnham, a Vanderbilt University linebacker who joined the case after researching the NCAA's bylaws, testified during the trial.

Another reason for the plaintiffs' confidence was that two weeks before the trial began, two companies that had been codefendants with the NCAA, EA Sports and CLC—the Collegiate Licensing Company—settled. EA Sports agreed to pay $40 million to a class of players who had been on its rosters in video games going back to 2003, the first time any commercial entity had agreed to pay college athletes. One of the implications of the settlement was that "but for" the NCAA's restrictions, EA Sports would have gladly paid money to college athletes or former athletes, just as it did when it licensed video games based on professional sports. "But for" is a key concept in antitrust law, basically asking the court to imagine a world in which the restrictions didn't exist.

As the case got closer to trial, Hausfeld had come to rely increasingly on one of the outside lawyers who was helping to bring the case: William Isaacson of Boies, Schiller & Flexner.* The firm, whose managing partner is the famed litigator David Boies, is unusual in that it both does defense work for large corporations and files lawsuits against companies in big plaintiff class actions. Boies, in fact, was a friend of Mark Emmert's and, early on, was not a fan of the case. But he didn't stop Isaacson from joining the *O'Bannon* team. In addition to a lifelong interest in sports—a useful trait given Hausfeld's lack of sports knowledge—Isaacson had a history with Hausfeld; they had also joined forces years before in a long-running

---

* During the time the *O'Bannon* case was being litigated, Joe Nocera's wife, Dawn Schneider, was Boies, Schiller & Flexner's director of communications. She played no role in the lawsuit and did not stand to profit from the outcome.

antitrust class action against a multinational vitamin cartel. Six of the companies had agreed to a $1.1 billion settlement; the pair took a seventh to trial, and won. A lawyer who enjoyed the parry and thrust of a trial, Isaacson was given the task of cross-examining many of the NCAA's star witnesses. He relished his role.

After Judge Wilken dismissed the damages class, Hausfeld had made a shrewd tactical decision: he waived all requests for damages, even for the named plaintiffs. That gave him the right to ask Wilken to try the case herself instead of impaneling a jury. He did this for two reasons. First, the NCAA was using its right to a jury trial as a rationale for delaying the trial by as much as a year. By calling for a bench trial, Hausfeld mooted the NCAA's argument. Second, he reasoned that after five years, Wilken was so well versed in the arguments—and, frankly, seemed more sympathetic to the plaintiffs than the NCAA—that the *O'Bannon* plaintiffs would have a better chance with her than with a jury, which might be more easily swayed by the NCAA's insistence on the importance of amateurism. Indeed, what other judge prior to Wilken had ever concluded that the NCAA could not rely on the *Regents* dicta to justify its practices? None.

Without the *Regents* dicta to fall back on, what did the NCAA have? How could it defend as procompetitive a policy that seemed so anticompetitive on its face: forbidding college athletes from getting paid? That is what the *O'Bannon* trial would reveal.

Ed O'Bannon was first on the stand. The UCLA All-American folded his six-foot-eight-inch frame into the witness chair and told his now famous tale of how a friend's son had recognized him in an EA Sports video game. Much of the rest of his testimony echoed Kain Colter's at the labor hearing in Chicago a few months earlier. At UCLA, O'Bannon had put in forty to forty-five hours each week playing basketball, compared to just twelve on his studies. He felt like an athlete "masquerading as a student," he said.

Two other players also testified: Garnham and former University of Alabama receiver Tyrone Prothro. ("We wanted to show who was making money and who wasn't," Isaacson says.) Garnham testified that he had signed a waiver granting the NCAA use of his name, image, and likeness—despite the NCAA's contention that the players had no such rights to sign over in the first place. He too spoke of the time demands he was under—all the hours during the season, spring practice, and training camp. His major, human and organizational development, was recommended for him by an academic adviser. On cross-examination, an NCAA lawyer pulled up Garnham's Twitter feed, where he wrote of binge-watching the TV shows *Entourage* and *The Walking Dead*. "You were able to spend the whole day watching television; isn't that true?" NCAA attorney Carolyn Luedtke asked.

Prothro's story illustrated a different downside of playing college sports: the risk of a career-ending injury. On September 10, 2005, Prothro made a miraculous catch, reaching his arms around a defender to haul in a touchdown on 4th and 12, during a game against Southern Mississippi. The play was nominated for Pontiac's "Game Changing Performance" contest— the same endorsement deal that had once caused Myles Brand and the NCAA to reexamine its commercial rules—and was named the top play of the season. Pontiac donated $100,000 to Alabama's scholarship fund; Prothro received nothing. His career, meanwhile, ended three weeks later with a gruesome leg fracture. There would be no million-dollar contract, no NFL career, and despite his scholarship, Prothro still owed $10,000 in student loans. He had ten surgeries on his leg, and Alabama had told him it would not pay for an eleventh. Several years after he graduated, he decided to write a book. When he asked Alabama for permission to use some photographs of himself, he was told he would have to pay $10 apiece for them.

Outside the courtroom that afternoon, the NCAA's chief legal officer, Donald Remy, offered up this defense: "Tyrone Prothro is an example of an individual who otherwise wouldn't have access to higher education, and badly wanted that education."

Remy's appearances would become an almost daily ritual. After each day's testimony, a smattering of reporters would gather in the courtyard outside the courthouse, usually under the shade of a palm tree, in what became a makeshift spin room. Hausfeld and Isaacson would debrief for the *O'Bannon* side, while Remy would handle the NCAA's spin.

The son of an army officer, Remy grew up mostly in New Orleans. He went to Louisiana State University and then Howard University Law School. By thirty-two, he was head of the tort division at the U.S. Justice Department, the youngest lawyer to head a major division. From 2000 to 2006, he was the chief compliance officer for Fannie Mae, the mortgage lender—and Republican bête noir—that was put into conservatorship by the government during the financial crisis of 2008. But in 2009, when he was nominated by President Obama to serve as general counsel to the army, the résumé he submitted to the Senate made no mention of Fannie Mae. After a Republican outcry led by Senator John McCain, Remy apologized and withdrew.

By 2011, he had landed at the NCAA, pulling down more than $600,000 in his new post. A smooth talker who wore cowboy boots for luck at the trial, Remy mostly repeated the NCAA's stock defenses in his mini–press conferences: "There is a desire to change collegiate athletics—amateur athletics—into semiprofessional or professional athletics," he said one day in a typical remark. It reminded Isaacson of another trial, one that his firm's founder, David Boies, had worked on years earlier. In 1998, the Justice Department tried Microsoft for antitrust violations, and hired Boies to be the lead lawyer at the trial. Most days after court, a Microsoft PR rep would announce to a group of reporters, "It was another good day for Microsoft." It became a running joke among the journalists covering the trial, who could see with their own eyes that Microsoft was being pummeled almost daily by Boies. Sure enough, the trial judge ultimately ruled against Microsoft.

Like most antitrust trials, long stretches of testimony were numbingly dull to anyone who wasn't an antitrust lawyer or an economist. Yet these same stretches were key, as the dueling economists put forth the critical economic theories that supported their side's position. In addition to Dan Rascher, the economic expert for *O'Bannon* was Stanford's Roger Noll. At seventy-four, the lanky Noll still looked fit enough to play AAU industrial league basketball, something he used to do in the 1960s, with Jerry Tarkanian in the same league. Knowing Tarkanian, in fact, was part of the reason "that I thought the way I did about the NCAA," he says.

Like so many others, Noll had a history of fighting the NCAA. Four decades earlier, he began teaching a class that took a critical look at college sports. Although he had been briefly retained by the NCAA during the *Regents* case, he had long since come to the classic economist's view. "You can go from economists on the far right to the far left," he said, "and everybody who has ever studied the NCAA has always come to the same conclusion: it is nothing more than a cartel for redistributing income from poor people to rich people." He had served as an economic expert in the

*White* case—indeed, Jason White had been his student—and in 2005 he had testified for the plaintiffs when the National Invitation Tournament sued the NCAA, alleging a monopoly on postseason basketball. Noll was in the middle of his testimony when the NIT agreed to be bought out by its adversary. "I got a call in my hotel room, and that was it," Noll recalls. "No monopoly, no guilt, nothing!"

In Oakland, Noll spent eleven hours on the stand over the course of three days, detailing why he believed the NCAA was a classic cartel. He said coaching salaries had increased by 500 percent since 1985, and more than $5 billion had been spent on athletics-related construction projects in recent years. "It's much more efficient to pay people for what they're producing than it is to create a competition for the right to exploit them," he testified.

In Noll's view, NCAA penalties were part of the proof that it was a cartel. Schools pursuing self-interest want to violate the rules, he said, but they are punished. "That's the power of the cartel," he likes to say. For his expertise, Noll earned $800 an hour, which he likened to being a pro athlete. "Getting paid for something I love to do," he later said.

Next up was Rascher, who described the big business college sports had become. March Madness generated more advertising revenue than any sporting event in the country, he said; eight athletic departments had more revenue than the median NHL team in 2012–13; competitive balance was a myth. The best teams already landed the best recruits and won just about all the championships.

The tenor of the trial turned midway through its second week, when the NCAA called to the stand Christine Plonsky, director of women's athletics at the University of Texas. A former basketball player at Kent State with three decades of experience in college sports, Plonsky was an institution. In the mid-1980s, she joined Dave Gavitt's Big East, hired to head public relations at a time when few women held such jobs. There, she and Vaccaro worked closely, since many of the conference's teams were sponsored by Nike. Plonsky moved on to Texas, where she quickly climbed the ladder. "People say she's one of the most influential women in college sports," says former Big East commissioner Mike Tranghese. "I say drop the 'woman.' She's one of the most influential, period."

Plonsky's appearance on the stand marked the beginning of the

NCAA's defense. Not surprisingly, she delivered an impassioned defense of amateur college sports. "The essence of our work is to work with other people's children, really," she said. "They come to us as seventeen- and eighteen-year-olds." The mission of the university is to "transform lives for the benefit of society," and athletics is a key part of that, she continued. Texas had some five hundred student-athletes on its campus, and the school spent, on average, more than $30,000 on each of their scholarships, plus thousands more on medical care, academic support, strength training, and nutrition. Texas even hired the country's first academic coach for its football players, Plonsky told Judge Wilken.

But Plonsky had also been part of the NCAA's commercialism task forces, and she had left a paper trail. Not long after the *O'Bannon* suit was filed in the summer of 2009, then-Big 12 commissioner Dan Beebe sent an e-mail to the Big 12 board of directors in which he expressed concern about exploiting names and images of student-athletes. Plonsky fired back an e-mail to Beebe that turned out to be more prophetic than she realized:

> The case I am stunned at is the O'Bannon case. He wanted [to be] paid for a product that was produced when he was playing. This is like the White case—where fb and bb players can now come to schools and ask for up to $7500 in "cost of education expenses" owed them. And they do not even have to have graduated to get this money. Ridiculous. That money should be directed to services to s-a's in the system TODAY. This is how I feel: if a s-a can sue the ncaa for these two things—one of which (the ea sports video game) only uses school marks and names, not s-a names, then what's to prevent all players from suing us to get a piece of every broadcast rights fee—since clearly we use their names and images in those telecasts?
>
> . . . I view these cases as being the result of the entitlement attitude we've created in our revenue sports. We now have threatening s-a's—many of whom, based on grad rates of the 80s and 90s, sucked a whole lot off the college athletics pipe—and now want to buckle the system at the knees at the expense of today's s-a's.

"Can you tell me what you mean by 'sucking a whole lot off the college athletics pipe'?" Isaacson asked as he began his cross-examination.

Isaacson showed her a copy of Texas's athletic budget. With $165 million in revenue in 2012–13, how much was spent on scholarships? Three percent, Plonsky answered. He showed her one more exhibit, the graduation rates at Texas for the 2006-07 cohort. The football team graduated at 43 percent, the men's basketball team at 29 percent.

On the day Mark Emmert testified, about halfway through the trial, Andy Schwarz arrived at the courthouse early in the morning with a box of doughnuts and a carton of Starbucks coffee. He passed them around to the early birds—Dan Rascher; Sonny and Pam Vaccaro; Ellen Staurowsky, the Drexel University professor who was a longtime NCAA critic; and a handful of reporters. They had all arrived early knowing that although the number of spectators had dwindled during the economic testimony, the line to get into the courtroom was likely to be long again with Emmert on the stand. They stood in a circle and made small talk, mostly about the trial, while waiting for the courtroom doors to open.

In his own way, Schwarz could be as frenetic, and as up-and-down emotionally, as Sonny Vaccaro. That quality had not endeared him to Isaacson; though Schwarz viewed Isaacson as "the best trial lawyer I've ever seen." Isaacson, while admiring Schwarz's abilities, found that his nervous energy and excessive desire to help sometimes distracted from the task at hand—so much so that at one point he exiled him from the courtroom. Once, during a pretrial prep session, Isaacson and Rascher were discussing a particular point that Schwarz knew they were wrong about. He broke in to correct them, but as he ran over to them with his laptop, which he'd forgotten was plugged in, the cord sent a cup of coffee flying, spilling everywhere. A day or so later, in the final "let's get 'em" meeting the night before the trial, Isaacson used the incident as an example of how not to behave in the presence of the reporters and Judge Wilken. Be unflappable, he said—not like Schwarz. Isaacson and Hausfeld had also forbidden Schwarz from tweeting or giving interviews, fearful of his "loose cannon" quality. "My yin and his yang didn't mesh," Schwarz said of his relationship with Isaacson.

With notables like Taylor Branch and *Esquire*'s Charlie Pierce sitting among the spectators, Emmert began his testimony by detailing his career. Soon enough, though, he launched into his defense of the status quo.

College sports, he said, was a campus's "social glue." He added, "People come to watch college sports because it's college sports with student-athletes. To convert college sports into professional sports would be tantamount to converting it into a minor-league sport."

The friendly questioning from Greg Curtner, the NCAA's outside counsel, lasted several hours. Then it was Isaacson's turn to cross examine Emmert. He had been looking forward to it for months, and he and Hausfeld had compiled their favorite documents—all the speeches, e-mails, and conversations where NCAA brass debated commercialism and openly questioned whether they were exploiting players.

Isaacson began by showing Emmert a quote from his predecessor, Myles Brand, who spoke of a crisis of commercialism during one of his annual "state of the association" speeches. He then showed Emmert a similar statement from early in his own tenure, when he too said he worried that commercialism was "overwhelming" college sports. Isaacson presented the head of the NCAA with images of Iowa football players wearing Nike uniforms, playing underneath a giant Nike sign; he later showed Emmert athletes at postgame news conferences in front of backdrops emblazoned with logos for Gillette and Dollar General; he showed him the infamous tweets where Jay Bilas had typed the names of Johnny Manziel and Jadeveon Clowney into the NCAA online store and found their jerseys for sale on their schools' sites.

What, Isaacson asked, had Emmert, the erstwhile reformer, done to act on his concerns over commercialism in his more than three and a half years on the job? Emmert mentioned that the EA video games were discontinued and that the NCAA had stopped selling university jerseys. Did the NCAA look at any of the school websites that were continuing to sell jerseys that could be found by typing the athletes' names? No, Emmert said.

Were there any pending NCAA proposals to curb commercialism that hadn't come about because of a lawsuit or public embarrassment? Isaacson asked. Not that Emmert could think of. Was there anything in the hundreds of pages in the NCAA rulebook that limited commercialism? Emmert had an answer for that one. We only use the names and images of athletes to promote events, not for sponsors to profit, he said. What about the broadcast companies using footage to promote a telecast? "Aren't they doing that for their own financial gain?" Isaacson asked. "You'd have to ask someone who's an expert in the broadcast industry," Emmert said.

Isaacson pressed forward. What about the number of advertisements in stadiums and all around players before, during, and after games? Water bottles at postgame press conferences had to be NCAA brand approved, he reminded Emmert. "It's certainly not where I would prefer the rules be drawn," Emmert conceded. Did the NCAA rulebook define amateurism as forbidding pay to players? It's an interpretation, Emmert answered. Isaacson asked why schools could make money surrounding players with corporate logos, but an athlete couldn't tell fans to buy a can of Coke. That would be exploitation of the players, Emmert answered. This answer perked up Judge Wilken. "Do you consider that to be exploitation of them? Or is it just something you don't want to be happening?" she asked. It was both, Emmert said, because then they'd be making a living off their sport and no longer student-athletes.

Isaacson called up Brand's 2007 e-mail venting his frustrations with the presidents, the one that included these lines: "The presidents want it both ways. They want to be able to rail against commercialism, and they want the revenue that comes with corporate ads. . . . The way they handle all this cognitive dissonance is by blaming the national office." Emmert pled ignorance when asked if he felt the same way. There were also the two memos Emmert received right around the time he took over as president: one from Wally Renfro and the other from VP of communications Bob Williams, both highlighting the growing public discord with the perceived hypocrisy in college sports. Did Emmert have discussions with Renfro about his memo? "Not that I remember," he said, dismissing Renfro, Brand's former right-hand man, as little more than a "provocateur." After a few more questions, Emmert added, "I think you're focusing on the word 'hypocrisy'"—"I am," interjected Isaacson—"more than necessary."

By the time he was finished, Emmert had testified for more than five hours, yet he had offered little more than the same tired talking points the NCAA had been using for years, if not decades. It had the feeling of a last stand. When Judge Wilken asked his opinion of trust funds for paying players (he was, predictably, against them), there was a sense that change would be coming, though its form was still unknown. Emmert had labored through his cross-examination, grew terse at points, and struggled to coherently defend the NCAA's rules. If he couldn't save amateurism, could anyone?

Immediately following Emmert came none other than Jim Delany, who gave his own doomsday warnings: there would be no Rose Bowl if players were paid, and the Big Ten might drop down to Division III. But the Big Ten commissioner did not fall into the same trap as Emmert and Plonsky: he didn't sugarcoat the system. He acknowledged the pitfalls; remarkably, he did so not under cross-examination but during questioning from Luis Li, another lawyer representing the NCAA. He wanted to put a padlock on the gym during the off-season to make sure the NCAA's limitations on practice time were upheld. He wanted athletes to have internships and study abroad. He wanted college sports to be the way it had been when he played for North Carolina nearly a half century earlier.

Hausfeld and Isaacson exchanged a shocked look as Hausfeld stood to cross-examine him. "I didn't have much to ask him," Hausfeld says. "He already said everything we wanted." Delany had always been practical—ruthless and calculating too—and he had developed a distaste for the world he had helped create. Perhaps he was reacting to the recent sea change as well. He'd always had an ability to see around corners, and maybe he was sensing that change was coming and he needed to get in front of it. Either way, his testimony turned out to be a preview of the new position he would stake out—a position as a crusader for reform.

The trial's final week became a hodgepodge of NCAA defense theories. One of their economic experts, Dr. Lauren Stiroh, suggested, absurdly, that as long as consumers weren't affected by the NCAA's rules—such as if there were fewer games on TV—there could be no antitrust harm, no matter the injury to college athletes.

Another NCAA economic witness, Daniel Rubinfeld, had published a textbook in which he called the NCAA a cartel, which hardly bolstered his credibility. Nobel Prize winner Dr. James Heckman presented a study to the court that found that athletics improved academic performance and that college was good for teenagers. Asked if his research was specific to Division I football and men's basketball players, he admitted that it was not. (Heckman earned $2,300 per hour for his troubles.)

The NCAA's other arguments included an insistence that there was no value to players' name and image rights in TV because sports was like news and you don't have to pay for news. Citing the First Amendment and the right to publicity, NCAA lawyers also contended that their broadcast contracts had little to do with the players, but were intended to give TV cameras the right to enter their arenas and stadiums.

Two NCAA witnesses, however, also suggested that modest payments to athletes would have no effect on their concept of amateurism. Former head of CBS Sports Neal Pilson said $5,000 a year for a player wouldn't bother him. Stanford athletic director Bernard Muir said he didn't have a set dollar amount, only that six- and seven-figure payments would be concerning. (Muir was also shown a live view of the school's website, where a photograph of the team's quarterback was for sale—a violation of NCAA rules. Muir said he might have to self-report the indiscretion.)

After the penultimate day of the trial, NCAA lawyer Greg Curtner gave Remy the day off and fielded questions from a handful of reporters. Rubinfeld had said on the stand that the NCAA was not a "classic" cartel that fixes prices. Curtner was asked if that meant the NCAA was a cartel after all. "It's a cartel that does good things," Curtner said, "not a cartel that does bad things." An NCAA flack babysitting the interview looked like she'd seen a ghost.

Mostly, the NCAA's defense had consisted of insisting on the importance of amateurism, just as it always had. As the blogger Patrick Hruby put it, the NCAA's legal theory stated that "athletes can't be paid because they're amateurs, and they're amateurs because they can't be paid."

Writing in *Sports Illustrated*, Stewart Mandel concluded that the NCAA "wasted three weeks mostly trumpeting the same tired clichés its leaders routinely espouse. . . . For that it deserves to lose."

One night during the trial's last week, Vaccaro walked along the San Francisco Bay after dinner. The cool summer breeze made for jacket weather, and Vaccaro had lent his to Pam, leaving him in his shirtsleeves. But he was feeling good. He had thought a lot about old friends the past few days: Jerry Tarkanian, Lamar Odom, Jalen Rose, and the other members of the Fab Five. What struck him most, though, about the three weeks, he said, were the lawyers. He marveled at the crates of documents the firms wheeled in and out of court every day. "There must be fifty, sixty boxes all filled with documents," he says. He could barely express how happy it

made him that lawyers—on both sides—treated the case with such seri-
ousness. "The world is paying attention to us in Oakland," he said.

O'Bannon had similar feelings. When asked by a group of reporters
how he felt upon the trial's conclusion, he said, "I don't know if it's satisfac-
tion or relief, just that we finished. Judge Wilken didn't say, 'You're crazy.'
She didn't say, 'Get out of my courtroom.' She heard the case."

Hausfeld was at the Manhattan Theatre Club with his wife on a Friday
evening in August when Judge Wilken released her decision. Because of a
family rule against cell phones, he didn't learn about the outcome until late
that night, after the production of *When We Were Young and Unafraid*. But
when he did, he was euphoric. In a ninety-nine-page ruling, Wilken delivered a repudiation of amateurism and a resounding win for the plaintiffs.
The NCAA had violated antitrust law; schools couldn't block players from
sharing broadcast and video game money; there was a clear market for
their names and images. "The high coaches' salaries and rapidly increasing spending on training facilities at many schools suggest that these
schools would, in fact, be able to afford to offer their student-athletes a
limited share of the licensing revenue generated from their use of the
student-athletes' own names, images, and likenesses," the judge wrote.

Wilken was especially unkind to the NCAA's hundred-year history of
amateurism. She wrote that the association had changed its definition of
the word whenever it suited it. The association's original bylaws prohibited
scholarships; the NCAA took away the laundry money in the 1970s; tennis
players were allowed to earn $10,000 per year before entering college;
football players could receive $5,500 in Pell Grants, but if they got the same
amount from TV broadcast money they'd be ineligible to play. It didn't
compute. "This record reveals that the NCAA has revised its rules governing student-athlete compensation numerous times over the years, sometimes in significant and contradictory ways," Wilken wrote. "Rather than
evincing the association's adherence to a set of core principles, this history
documents how malleable the NCAA's definition of amateurism has been
since its founding."

She dismissed the NCAA's assertion that college sports was popular
because the athletes weren't paid. There was a loyalty by the fans to their
college team that went well beyond that, Wilken wrote, citing Plonsky's
testimony. "I would venture to say that if we offered a tiddlywinks team,

that would somehow be popular with some segment of whoever loves our university," the Texas administrator had said on the stand.

Competitive balance was a losing argument too, given the millions already spent by the richest schools on their coaches and facilities, and the minimal revenue sharing with smaller schools. Wilken didn't buy integration with the rest of the student body as a defense either, wondering why paying athletes was any more problematic than paying members of student government or writers for the school newspaper. And she found the idea that big-time sports schools would leave Division I "implausible," suggesting they competed in Division I precisely because of the visibility and the revenue it offered.

But perhaps the greatest blow to the NCAA was how Wilken struck at the heart of its *Regents* defense. "Although the NCAA has cited the Supreme Court's decision in Board of Regents as support for its amateurism justification, its reliance on the case remains unavailing," she wrote. The famous dicta, she decreed, "was not based on any factual findings in the trial record and did not serve to resolve any disputed issues of law." It was, essentially, meaningless.

The ruling was hailed as monumental. Vaccaro admitted he was speechless, maybe for the first time in his life. Ramogi Huma called it a great step forward for players. Isaacson said, "The decision goes behind the curtain of amateurism and says there was nothing there." With the NCAA's rules illegal, college sports would never look the same, right? Well, not so fast. As much as Wilken discredited amateurism as college sports' version of the emperor with no clothes, her ruling was more compromise than death knell.

For starters, she explicitly ruled that players should not endorse products, because it "would undermine the efforts of both the NCAA and its member schools to protect against the 'commercial exploitation' of student-athletes." This was a far cry from the free market Schwarz and Rascher had long dreamed of. During the trial, Wilken repeatedly asked lawyers on both sides for alternatives to the NCAA's rigid rules; it became clear she was in search of a remedy that wouldn't overhaul the system, but amend it. During trial, Hausfeld and Isaacson suggested setting aside money for players that they could collect after they left school; to that end they had even set up an organization that could collect payments and then distribute them to former college athletes, the same way ASCAP and BMI distributed music royalties to composers and musicians. Wilken took them up on their offer. Her prescription was a trust fund that college athletes could tap after their playing days were over; she would even allow the NCAA to cap the deferred payments at no less than $5,000 per player per year. It was an olive branch to the college sports establishment. "Consumer preferences might justify certain limited restraints on student-athlete compensation," she wrote. Schools were supposed to be allowed to start offering deferred compensation on August 1, 2015.

The trust fund language bothered many of the reformers. "It doesn't just say there is a cap," Ramogi Huma said. "It specifically seems to allow the NCAA to act as a cartel." Wilken had walked right up to the edge of transforming college sports, but, as a practical matter, she had merely tweaked the system. After the NCAA announced its appeal, even Isaacson wondered what their beef was. "They agree with so much of the ruling, you sometimes wonder why they're appealing," he says.

Still, Wilken's absolute repudiation of amateurism remained historic. "We opened the door," Hausfeld says. "Whoever comes next can charge through it."

# EPILOGUE
# THE SKY DIDN'T FALL

**W**ell before the *O'Bannon* trial took place in the summer of 2014, the case had become an omnipresent cloud hanging over the college sports world. Athletic directors and conference commissioners worried about how it might change the amateur model, which had been so good to them for so long. But the drumbeat of criticism of college sports in the media prompted by *O'Bannon* also caused many of them to publicly vow to do better by their athletes—short of paying them, of course—and to complain that it was the NCAA's governance structure that was holding them back. They recalled, for instance, how the smaller schools with fewer resources had voted down Mark Emmert's 2011 proposal to add a $2,000 stipend to help close the gap between an athletic scholarship and the full cost of attendance.

Thus it was that in 2013, with the top five conferences—the SEC, Big Ten, ACC, Pac-12, and Big 12—having finished their latest round of realignment and having consolidated their power, their commissioners began making veiled threats about what might happen if they weren't given more leeway to set their own agendas. They wanted to offer four-year scholarships, they said. They wanted to have protocols in place when players suffered concussions. And they especially wanted to be able to offer money to players to cover the full cost of attendance. There was talk that the Power 5 conferences (as they were now called) would form their own division, which the press was calling Division IV—or possibly even leave the NCAA altogether.

That fall, a meeting took place between NCAA executives and a number of high-ranking college officials, including several conference commissioners. The subject was more autonomy for the schools in the Power 5. Two days after the meeting, Jim Delany told the press that it had gone well. "We've at least preliminarily concluded we don't want to leave the NCAA, and we don't need a Division IV," he said. "We can have a [March Madness] tournament, everyone can be in it. We can do revenue sharing. We can all brand together. We can all be Division I together. We can all have a big tent.

"But," he added, "the conditions for that are that we need the political autonomy and the political authority to address things we must address on behalf of our student-athletes, on behalf of our universities. We have the resources to do it, and we need the authority to do it."

As the trial date got closer, the calls for reform—not by outsiders like Sonny Vaccaro, but by university presidents and other insiders—became deafening. Weeks before the trial, the Pac-12 presidents published a ten-point reform plan that included full cost of attendance, lifetime education trusts, and improved medical insurance. The Big Ten presidents issued a similar open letter just days after its commissioner, Jim Delany, testified during the trial. Emmert, called in front of a Senate committee soon after the trial ended, was grilled about academic fraud, one-year scholarships, and athletic departments' handling of sexual assault investigations. "I think this hearing is a useful cattle prod that we know the world is watching," he said.

The University of South Carolina, Indiana University, and the University of Southern California unilaterally announced that they would begin handing out four-year athletic scholarships. When players returned to campus for the fall semester, they found that the NCAA had abandoned its longtime release form for the use of players' name, image, and likeness (schools and conferences now issued the form). For practically the first time in the history of the NCAA, colleges were tripping over themselves to do better by their athletes.

And policies were not all that were changing. NCAA headquarters got a jolt in December when University of West Virginia athletic director Oliver Luck was hired as the association's new chief operating officer. Luck, the father of star Indianapolis Colts quarterback Andrew Luck, had been a college quarterback himself, and played a few years as a backup in the NFL. He went on to get a law degree and to make a name for himself as a sports executive for NFL Europe and Major League Soccer, among others; in addition to being West Virginia's athletic director, he also sat on the school's board of governors. Luck was on record saying that athletes had a "constitutional right" to control their own name, image, and likeness. "If we are in fact using name, image, and likeness of student-athletes, they should be compensated," he had said at a conference the year before. He didn't disavow the sentiment as he made his way to Indianapolis.

In early August 2014, less than two months after the *O'Bannon* trial, the Division I board of directors voted 16–2 to give the Power 5 what they were demanding: the flexibility to offer additional benefits to athletes. The following January, during the NCAA's annual convention, the power conferences voted to guarantee four-year scholarships, promising they could no longer be revoked for athletic reasons or injuries. They passed a concussion protocol that had been proposed by the SEC. (The Big 12 objected, complaining that the new protocol still gave coaches too much authority to decide whether a player could return to a game following a concussion.) And by a vote of 79–1, they agreed to give schools the ability to pay the full cost of attendance, which meant a few thousand dollars more for athletes.

Less than a decade earlier, during the *White* case, the NCAA had described cost-of-attendance money as an insidious form of "play for pay" and insisted that it would destroy the amateur model it held so dear. Now those objections evaporated. As Dan Rascher later noted in an expert report in a separate NCAA-related lawsuit, "As 2015 plays out, we are seeing that there has been no ... reaction [to the cost-of-attendance stipend]. No school exited from a Power 5 Conference ... no Division I school announced a unilateral reduction in [scholarship] offers, and most importantly, no school reduced its offers to some football/basketball athletes in order to fund the increase to other athletes. Instead, most schools (both in and beyond the Power 5 Conferences) have seen their total 'wage' bills increase by an amount that can exceed $1 million per year." He quoted Oklahoma State athletic director Mike Holder as saying, "Things get more expensive every year.... It's amazing.... [Nevertheless, w]e'll manage to find the money somewhere. We always seem to."

The cost-of-attendance stipend was a reality, and the sky hadn't fallen.

And, of course, the money kept rolling in. The same month that the Division I membership voted to give schools the ability to offer cost-of-attendance money, the first-ever four-team college football playoff took place. (The four teams vying for the championship were Alabama, Oregon, Florida State, and Ohio State. The Buckeyes won.) Needless to say, it was the lure of money that finally caused the conference commissioners to abandon the Bowl Championship Series and move to the kind of playoff system that most college football fans had long been clamoring for. All season long, the top teams in football fought to be included—at one point, both Mississippi and Mississippi State seemed destined to make the playoffs—which helped the weekly ratings. ESPN had bought the rights to the playoffs, which were sponsored by AT&T, for $7.3 billion over twelve years. The three playoff games wound up generating the three biggest audiences in the history of cable television. The NCAA and the College Football Playoff even struck a deal to fly athletes' families to championship games.

The NCAA's annual convention in 2015 was held in Oxon Hill, Maryland, a suburb of Washington, D.C. It was an appropriate venue. The NCAA had spent $600,000 on lobbying fees the previous year, an indication of where it viewed the future battlefield. The Drake Group and other reformers were calling for a presidential commission to look at how college sports was governed.

A number of the rebels, including Ramogi Huma, Sonny Vaccaro, Kain Colter, and Ed O'Bannon, also decided to meet in Washington during the NCAA convention. They assembled for a strategy session at the NFL Players Association headquarters near Dupont Circle. Former Southern California lineman Bob DeMars screened a rough cut of a documentary he'd been working on for years called *The Business of Amateurs*, featuring, among others, Huma, Andy Schwarz, and Vaccaro. It also profiled several players struggling in postcollege life, like Kyle Hardrick, a former Oklahoma basketball player, who lost his scholarship after he injured his knee and still struggled with pain. He was also in the room watching his own cautionary tale unfold on the projection screen.

The film stoked something in Vaccaro. After it finished, he stood to offer his compatriots a bit of history. He told the story again of making an antigambling film with Nike that the NCAA refused to use. "They don't look out for players," he said. "They've always been cheats. John Wooden fucking cheated. Sam Gilbert was paying his players."

"Watch your mouth, Sonny," said Pam, who was seated beside him.

The next afternoon, the motley crew reconvened on Capitol Hill, holding a briefing for Senate staffers. Down the line they went, each telling his story: Hardrick of his own ordeal; Colter of the union movement; O'Bannon of his lawsuit; Huma of his long struggle; Vaccaro of his even longer struggle. Their implicit message was that the NCAA shouldn't be able to get off the hook with incremental reform; instead, players needed to gain real power to shape their own futures. Watching them all, Pam couldn't help but feel like a proud mother. "They all have something very unique to share and it's so inspiring to see them do it together," she said.

As the group split up to lobby individual offices, they took the short walk down 1st Street to the steps of the Supreme Court. They posed together and Pam snapped a picture. "This is where it could all end," Huma said, pointing up at the neoclassical columns.

That same evening, Mark Emmert opened the NCAA's annual convention. The view from the lobby of the Gaylord Convention Center in Oxon Hill looked out through a great glass façade at the Potomac River. Attendees could get their pictures taken and superimposed on the NCAA's in-house magazine, *Champion*. The NCAA may have been under siege, but not here; these were friendly confines. Emmert's keynote focused on preserving the collegiate model—making sure it worked, as he put it, for the 3 percent as well as the 97 percent, the professional hopefuls and everyone else. He commended schools for guaranteeing scholarships and hoped they would redouble their efforts on academic reform and reducing time demands on athletes. "We don't have the luxury of determining the pace of change," Emmert said. "We can't sit still."

For the first time ever, college athlete delegates—fifteen in all—had both a voice and a vote in the proceedings. Betsy Altmaier, the Iowa professor, had made the trip for her last NCAA convention. She was no longer actively involved in governance, but with her retirement looming she wanted to come and say goodbye to old friends. On an elevator one day, she overheard a group talking about the new roles the athletes were playing in governance. She recalled talking to Myles Brand about putting more students on committees, hearing more from them about all the rules that affected their lives so deeply. Now here they were. "They couldn't believe how eloquent the students were, how much common sense they had," Altmaier says. "It was like we couldn't let them into the room because we were so scared of what they were going to say, and it turned out they're vital and relevant to the debates." She felt a sense of progress, small but real. And now she felt she could retire in peace.

In March 2015, the Court of Appeals for the Ninth Circuit, which is based in San Francisco, heard the NCAA's appeal of Judge Claudia Wilken's *O'Bannon* ruling. Wilken's relief—the $5,000 that was supposed to be set aside for athletes to compensate them for the use of their name, image, and likeness—was supposed to go into effect on August 1, 2015. But in July the NCAA raced to the appeals court, asking that her order be stayed until it ruled. The court agreed to do so. Andy Schwarz was disconsolate after the stay was issued, fearing that it suggested the appeals court was leaning in the NCAA's direction. But others on the team, including Bill Isaacson, were less convinced that the stay offered any clue as to the ultimate ruling. What was clear was that whichever side lost would quickly appeal the case to the Supreme Court.

Even with the *O'Bannon* trial over, class action litigation against the NCAA hadn't let up. Hausfeld was suing the NCAA and the University of North Carolina on the grounds that with the sham classes at the African and Afro-American Studies Department that athletes had been steered to, they had been deprived of the education they'd been promised. There were also several ongoing antitrust lawsuits. *Alston v. NCAA*, filed in early March 2014, "challenges the NCAA's financial aid restrictions that limit the value of athletic scholarship for amounts far below the actual cost of attending college," as its lawyers put it in one brief. The *Alston* team also sought huge damages. A second case, *Jenkins v. NCAA*, filed a week later by renowned sports attorney Jeffrey Kessler, sought no damages at all. Instead, it asked the court to rule that the NCAA's long-standing insistence on amateurism was in fact anticompetitive and thus a violation of the antitrust laws. In other words, Kessler, who helped bring about free agency in the NFL, filed the old "nuclear case" that Ernie Nadel, Andy Schwarz, and Dan

Rascher had unsuccessfully sought to gin up some fifteen years earlier. Judge Wilken was presiding over both cases. Rascher had been retained as an expert in both cases, with Schwarz as an economic consultant.

In late April 2015, the magistrate judge Nathanael Cousins heard arguments over how much Hausfeld and the other lawyers should be paid. Speaking from the bench, he said, "This is a case against a supersized institution in the United States, the NCAA. And the Federal Trade Commission has not gone after the NCAA, and the U.S. Department of Justice Antitrust Division has not gone after the NCAA, various state attorney generals have not. It took thirty-plus law firms spending approximately $50 million with the risk of recovering nothing to make a very adventurous and risky lawsuit that took many years and had a high risk of failure. And the reward for that is that they won at trial."

He continued, "My view is that the result is an exemplary and surprising result given the challenges that they faced in the beginning of the case. . . . Given the huge uphill fight faced by the plaintiffs and their counsel in the beginning of the case, I view this case as being one, if not the most, significant antitrust cases in this era or very close to it. So I view it in the antitrust area as being a very significant victory and one that is going to change the face of a significant part of American culture and the American economy."

In June, he awarded the *O'Bannon* lawyers $48 million in fees.

On August 17, 2015, more than a year and a half after Ramogi Huma turned in union cards to the NLRB in Chicago, the full board in Washington finally issued its ruling on Northwestern's appeal. The five members unanimously agreed not to exert the NLRB's jurisdiction over whether Northwestern's football players were university employees. Perhaps fearful of the consequences of upending the governance of college sports, the board punted. And its nondecision dealt a decisive blow to the players: the regional director's decision was void; the players were not employees; the ballots would never be counted. The status quo reigned.

What puzzled some observers was that the board did not dispute the fundamental facts of the case—that the players worked long hours under the direction of their coaches and were paid for it. The board showed further sympathy for the players' argument, writing it would be happy to reexamine the issue of college athletes as employees should it come up again. The board even went so far as to acknowledge the precariousness of the current system. "We acknowledge that whether such individuals meet the Board's test for employee status is a question that does not have an obvious answer," a footnote in the decision read.

But in practical terms the decision derailed the union movement. As Andy Schwarz wrote on his blog, here was another legal body that seemed unable to consider the personhood of college athletes. "What the NLRB ultimately said was that college athletes have NO venue," Schwarz wrote. "Everyone else has a place to seek redress, even if they lose. You don't even get the right to lose. We don't even hold you in high enough regard to ANSWER your petition."

"This is the federal government not treating college athletes fairly under the law," Huma says. What astounded Huma perhaps more than anything was that the board decision cited "competitive balance" in college sports as a reason to dismiss the petition. In effect, the board was echoing one of the NCAA's longest standing, and least persuasive, rationales. "That part was disturbing," Huma says.

As for Kain Colter, he wrote an e-mail to his former teammates after the decision came out, explaining what the ruling meant, applauding them for standing up and pointing out the myriad changes already under way around the NCAA. "We played a role in that," Colter says. "Those guys should be proud."

On the opening weekend of the 2015 college football season, Colter watched his Northwestern Wildcats upset a ranked Stanford team and cheered his heart out. He hopes one day to sit down with his old coach Pat Fitzgerald and talk out their differences. "I don't think he totally disagrees with everything we did," Colter says. "I think if we could talk, we would agree on a lot and disagree on a few things. I'd love for the relationship between me and Northwestern to be fixed, and the good thing is time heals all wounds."

The Court of Appeals for the Ninth Circuit rendered its decision in the *O'Bannon* case on a Wednesday—September 30, 2015. In a 2–1 decision, it affirmed much of Wilken's decision—the NCAA's amateurism rules did indeed violate the nation's antitrust laws, and Justice Stephens's infamous paragraph in the *Regents* decision was indeed dicta that did not compel lower courts to uphold the NCAA's amateurism defense. Wilken was correct to conclude "that the NCAA's compensation rules were an unlawful restraint of trade," the appeals panel wrote.

And yet, for the third time in the space of eighteen months, people with the power to change how the NCAA did business—and who had concluded that the NCAA's amateurism rules violated the law—blinked. After explaining its conclusion that the NCAA rules were an unfair restraint of trade, the appeals panel actually stripped the plaintiffs of Wilken's tepid remedy—the additional $5,000 a year to be put in a trust fund—and said that paying the cost of attendance was remedy enough. Why? This was the most incredible part of the decision: it said that cash compensation not related to education would not "preserve amateurism." In other words, the amateurism rules violated the law—and yet amateurism had to be preserved in order to retain what made college sports college sports. The NCAA couldn't have said it any better.

The dissenter in the case was the court's chief justice, Sidney Thomas, whose sharply worded dissent exposed the majority's flawed reasoning. "The NCAA insists that this multibillion-dollar industry would be lost if the teenagers and young adults who play for these college teams earn one dollar above their cost of school attendance," he wrote. "That is a difficult argument to swallow."

It's not hard to understand why Wilken, the NLRB, and the Ninth Circuit refused to propose the obvious remedy that their written opinions would seem to require: allowing the players to be paid. Decades of propaganda about the centrality of amateurism to college sports had taken their toll. But they also feared that college sports would be thrown into chaos if schools couldn't pay players—and they didn't want to be blamed. The NLRB practically said as much in its cowardly decision not to decide the issue. Of course, that is what baseball owners said about the prospect of free agency, and Olympic officials about allowing professional athletes to compete. Those fears turned out to be unfounded.

Although Hausfeld quickly declared victory in a press release—and indeed, the appeals court ruling affirming Wilken's antitrust conclusion was certainly at least a partial victory—in truth, the O'Bannon lawyer was devastated. The NCAA, meanwhile, wasn't exactly perturbed by the outcome. In a conference call, Emmert pronounced himself "pleased." There were many observers who felt that Hausfeld would conclude that the case was over, in no small part because he and his fellow lawyers could lay claim to their $48 million. But within days Hausfeld vowed to ask the appeals court for an en banc review, meaning that a number of appeals court judges would rehear the case rather than three. Although en banc reviews are not often granted, it seemed as though Hausfeld had a decent shot at it, especially given that the dissenter was the chief justice. As of November 2015 the en banc request was pending, and it seemed ever more likely that the *O'Bannon* case could wind up at the Supreme Court, where, if the Court agreed to hear the case, it might one day take its places alongside *Tarkanian* and *Regents*, the only other NCAA-related cases important enough to be decided by the high court.

In May 2015, nine months after Wilken's *O'Bannon* ruling and four months after the NCAA convention, Jim Delany circulated an e-mail to all corners of the college sports world: supporters, high-profile critics, media members, coaches, administrators, and presidents. Attached was a twelve-page white paper Delany entitled "Education First, Athletics Second: The Time for a National Discussion Is Upon Us." The e-mail included a link to a website and a new e-mail address (educationfirst@bigten.org) to solicit feedback. "You might be an advocate or a critic or somewhere in between," the e-mail read, later adding, "You can help."

Despite everything he had done to turn college sports into a money machine, nobody, it seems, yearned more for that simpler time when coaches didn't get rich, stadiums didn't grant naming rights, and conferences didn't have their own television networks. Delany was positively misty-eyed about the way things used to be. He wanted athletes in the revenue sports to get a real education, even if it meant having less time to practice. He issued a plea to push college sports toward the academic-centered enterprise he desperately wanted it to be. "Despite its goodness, if the model cannot be defended as educational, it cannot be defended," he wrote.

For several years, Delany had been calling for one reform in particular that really would harken back to the days when he was a college athlete. He wanted football and basketball players to sit out their freshman seasons, which had been the practice until 1972. Delany called his proposal "a year of readiness" that would help high school athletes acclimate to the academic environment of a university without the pressure that came with playing college sports.

The letter was greeted with much derision. Coaches certainly didn't want top players sitting on the bench; other conferences, especially the SEC, were dismissive too. Michael Hausfeld read the proposal and wrote his own letter to a handful of U.S. senators calling Delany's missive a "cry for help." "He's admitting the NCAA has failed," Hausfeld says.

The criticism didn't bother Delany much. He was under no illusions that his year of readiness was going to be embraced, but he wanted people who cared about college sports to start talking about how it could be improved—how it could get back to a place where lawyers wouldn't sue and journalists wouldn't mock its hypocrisy. College sports was his life's work, and he intended to fight for it. He remembered his father and his college coach, Dean Smith. There was no greater lesson in his life than education through athletics, he believed.

"If you were going to get jumped, you would want me with you," Delany said. "I believe in survival and I'm out to do what I can do to save the enterprise; I think other people are not doing enough. What we have in college sports is the envy of the world, an accident of history worth pre-serving and reforming and restructuring. I'm not going to be defined by what some critic says. I'm not going to be defined by what some plaintiffs' lawyer says! I'm going to be defined by my own experience and my own sense of what's right and wrong."

He added, "This is a place to start. Lots of people propose paying play-ers. That's not the answer to our problems."

Delany said this a few weeks after the e-mail went out, sitting in a large, windowed conference room at the Big Ten headquarters in suburban Chicago. The new complex, which cost $17 million, opened in 2013. As he talked, Delany sipped out of a water bottle that had the Big Ten's logo stamped on it.

It confounded Delany that football and basketball players did not achieve the same academic success as athletes in all of the other NCAA sports. Was it because of the time demands? he wondered. Or relaxed ad-missions standards? Or the pressure on the players to perform? Or were the players just not that interested in their education? "If I put you up to bat in a Little League all-star game and you've never played baseball before, you're going to embarrass yourself or get hurt because you're not capable," he said. "You have to make sure the people you're putting into these situations are capable of playing sports, but also of doing the academic work. Otherwise there's exploitation."

As for his own role in TV and conference expansion, coaches' salaries, and the billions of dollars flowing through college sports, Delany admitted that commercialism added to the pressure on athletes, but he added, "I don't rank our commercial success high on that list" of pressures athletes faced.

He placed the blame for college sports' problems on just about everyone and every institution except the Big Ten: the athletes who don't want to be in school; the NBA and NFL, which want to use universities as their free minor leagues; the smaller schools that stood in the way of the Big Ten when it sought change over the years. ("We had to threaten to leave the NCAA just to pass the cost of attendance.") And all that money. "The money changed," he acknowledged.

"Isn't that the point," he was asked, "that money made the system more vulnerable?"

"Then blame ESPN," he answered. "I was here when we weren't very successful, when we didn't have the women's opportunities and our facilities were built in the twenties. Do you get by with bubblegum and sticks and stones or do you take the facilities up to the twenty-first century? Do I believe there should be an antitrust exemption to control coaches and commissioners? I don't. Do I see the dichotomy? I do, but I didn't create it. It's American law."

Roy Kramer and Gene Corrigan, the two long-retired commissioners, now question the big business of college sports and, to a degree, their roles in shaping it. "We never did anything like the Big Ten with Rutgers," Kramer says. "It concerns me what's happening." Delany disagreed. "What's good for the Big Ten has been good for college sports," he said. "I don't spend a lot of time looking over my shoulder. I sleep like a baby."

Delany then offered a tour of the Big Ten's new digs. He pointed out a memento in his office sent to him by former ESPN president George Bodenheimer, whom Delany had outmaneuvered to start the Big Ten Network. It was a gold telescope, indicative of Delany's foresight, and inscribed with a quote from Theodore Roosevelt that read "It is not the critic who counts. . . . The credit belongs to the one who is actually in the arena, whose face is marred by dust and sweat and blood."

The Big Ten commissioner walked to a wall with pictures of famous Big Ten graduates, including Stephen Colbert. A state-of-the-art conference room included portraits of each of the Big Ten's commissioners. Another room served as the replay control room for the slate of Big Ten football games each fall Saturday. "None of the other conferences have anything like this," Delany said, beaming.

In his own way, he was looking forward to the looming legal showdowns. They fed equally his love of competition and his love of ideas. "Let's find out who's right," he said. "When the courts and Congress decide how these statutes are applicable—Title IX, labor law, antitrust law—I'll live with that because I live in America. But access to the courts goes both ways, and if I disagree, then let's get out there and compete."

The final stop on the tour was a walk through a new conference museum, christened the Big Ten Experience. Delany walked over to a wall and pressed a button to play a radio highlight from the famous 1979 basketball championship, the one in which Michigan State's Magic Johnson faced off against Indiana State's Larry Bird. Then he pointed out a virtual reality game that allowed fans to compete as Big Ten athletes. Delany took a turn, choosing to play as a Rutgers women's soccer goalie. He missed the first ball shot at him, but saved the next four.

"This place really has everything you could want," he said.

# AFTERWORD

On a Thursday evening in January 2014, at a party hosted by the NFL Players Association ahead of Super Bowl XLVII, Ramogi Huma met a man named Jeffrey Kessler. Kessler was a renowned sports lawyer; he'd had the NFLPA as a client since the 1980s and had argued the federal court case that gave pro football players their free agent rights in 1992. More recently, he had earned a reputation as the counterforce to the NFL and its commissioner, Roger Goodell, repeatedly going to court to get Goodell-imposed punishments on players reversed. At the time, the *O'Bannon* lawsuit was hurtling toward trial and Huma was in the process of organizing the Northwestern union announcement with Kain Colter. But Kessler represented a new opportunity.

Huma had long advocated in favor of incremental change. But now he wanted something more: he wanted not just, say, better medical benefits for players; he wanted to blow the whole thing up—the whole college sports system. He wanted the lawsuit Andy Schwarz had tried, unsuccessfully, to shop fifteen years earlier, the so-called nuclear case that would seek to invalidate all of the NCAA's rules as violations of antitrust law. If successful, such a case would strike a deathblow to amateurism.

After a brief introduction at the Super Bowl party, Huma and Kessler met two days later for lunch at Carmine's, an Italian restaurant in midtown Manhattan. Huma brought Tim Waters with him; Kessler brought Tim

Nevius, a former NCAA enforcement staffer who had soured on the NCAA's mission and switched sides, joining Kessler's firm, Winston & Strawn. Over a plate of pasta, Kessler made an impassioned argument for why his firm should be the one to file the suit. Huma and Waters were sold.

In March 2014—two months after the union announcement in Chicago, and five months before Judge Claudia Wilken handed down her decision in the *O'Bannon* case—the lawsuit was filed with a group of plaintiffs recruited by Huma. "Jeffrey Kessler Files Against the NCAA," a headline on ESPN.com blared. With everything that was happening—not just *O'Bannon*, but the Northwestern suit, the mounting public criticism of the NCAA, and the broader sense that every day more people were coming around to his view that the NCAA was an unjust cartel—Sonny Vaccaro couldn't help but feel that the Kessler case had the potential to be the final assault, the one that would finally overthrow the college sports establishment.

By the fall of 2017, however, with the Northwestern union victory having been nullified on appeal and the *O'Bannon* ruling defanged by the Ninth Circuit, Kessler's case was all that was left. It was the last big legal threat against the college sports establishment. If the NCAA were going to be forced to change via the courts, Kessler would have to be the lawyer to make it happen.

Tim Nevius was only a year out of law school when he was hired by the NCAA in 2007 as an assistant director of enforcement. Nevius had played baseball at the University of Dayton—he was mostly a utility infielder— and then stayed to get a law degree. After a year doing corporate finance work in Chicago, he applied to the NCAA, and landed in Indianapolis. The first big case he worked on involved a University of Connecticut basketball player, and among other things, Nevius was given the task of interrogating coach Jim Calhoun. "I was twenty-seven years old and I was grilling Jim Calhoun," he says today. "It was a cool job."

But in 2010, he was assigned to investigate a group of Ohio State football players who had sold some of their football memorabilia in exchange for free tattoos and gifts. That experience changed everything for him. Nevius remembers well the media circus that engulfed him when he arrived on campus to interview the players. The meetings were moved to the bowels of the football stadium because of the number of fans and reporters who swarmed the football facility. Part of Nevius's job was to ascertain the exact value of the "extra benefits" the players received. That meant determining the size and number of their tattoos. Nevius had to measure the artwork and then compare the discounts players received to the amounts they should have paid. He found it trivial and absurd. "I remember thinking that it was all pretty ridiculous," he says.

Nevius also had to track down a former Ohio State player named Jermil Martin, who was still living in Columbus. Nevius knocked on the door of his apartment and was greeted by the player's girlfriend and their small child. He was invited in and soon Martin returned home from his job at a fast-food restaurant. As Nevius conducted a lengthy interview, Martin's girlfriend made dinner and occasionally sat next to the player, while the child played with a truck on the floor. Nevius heard Martin's story—how he had been full of such hope when he was recruited, but had transferred after not getting much playing time. His disappointing college football career hadn't led anywhere. Martin had been close to someone at the tattoo parlor where the players got the free tattoos, and he had been given a deal on a used Chevy Tahoe. It turned out to be a lemon. As Martin related the story, tears welled in his eyes. "I left the interview with a pit in my stomach," Nevius says.

Nevius never mentioned his new feelings while working inside the NCAA. "The groupthink was too strong," he says. But within a year, he had enrolled in a master's of law program at Columbia University. Kessler was a Columbia law graduate, and an adviser suggested that with Nevius's sports background, he should reach out to the well-known lawyer. Nevius fired off an e-mail to Kessler. His pitch: Kessler should start a college sports practice. At the time, Nevius wasn't thinking about taking down the NCAA; his idea was that the firm could begin representing universities, high-profile coaches and players who found themselves caught in the NCAA's crosshairs. Kessler agreed and hired Nevius. But the sports practice quickly took a different tack. "I think Jeffrey always had bigger ideas," Nevius says.

Kessler, sixty-three years old and a Brooklyn native, fell in love with antitrust law at Columbia. His first job out of school in 1978 was at a well-known antitrust firm, Weil, Gotshal & Manges, which counted as a client Oscar Robertson, the future NBA Hall of Famer who, in 1970, had sued to prevent a merger between the ABA and NBA, arguing it would reduce players' wages. At Weil Gotshal, Kessler worked under Jim Quinn, the attorney who brought Robertson's lawsuit. (The case eventually settled, allowing the merger to go through and gaining restricted free agency for the players.) Kessler never planned to go into sports, but at Weil Gotshal he found himself in the middle of an emerging players' rights movement. The same year Robertson sued, so did Curt Flood, the St. Louis Cardinals center fielder who argued that baseball's reserve clause—a rule that bound players to their teams in perpetuity—was illegal. After the Robertson case settled, Quinn and Kessler brought a series of follow-up cases on behalf of NBA players that resulted in sports' first salary cap system and eventually unrestricted free agency.

The last holdout against free agency among the three biggest leagues in the United States was the NFL—in 1987 the league even went so far as to use replacement players to break a strike. So Quinn and Kessler recommended a radical strategy to the players: threaten to dissolve the union. Without a union in place, many of the labor restrictions on players—the draft, for example—would be illegal. When the owners still wouldn't budge, the players filed an antitrust lawsuit, which went to trial in the summer of 1992. The three-week trial was Kessler's shining moment, cementing his status as a formidable pro-player sports attorney and forever earning the enmity of the NFL. During one cross-examination, he implied that an NFL executive and Vietnam veteran was a draft dodger. Later, he drew a chart for the jury on a large notepad that compared football players to prisoners and little children; they also had their movements restricted, Kessler told the jury. The players won.

In the ensuing years, Kessler became a go-to attorney for athletes, working on a slew of collective bargaining agreements on behalf of NBA and NFL players—and also representing players who were in disputes with the league. (His highest profile client was New England Patriots quarterback Tom Brady, who Kessler represented during the Deflategate litigation.)

Though he had never been involved in college sports litigation, Kessler had long harbored a dim view of the NCAA. In fact, during the NFL free agency trial, he introduced into evidence a book titled *The NCAA: A Study in Cartel Behavior.* "It's the single greatest exploitation left in major sports," he liked to say of the NCAA. For years Kessler had been the tip of the sword for players taking on owners and leagues; now he had the NCAA in his sights. Kessler—loud, abrasive, confident, and sports savvy—would seem to be the ideal lawyer to press the nuclear case. Unlike Michael Hausfeld, who barely knew the difference between a point guard and a quarterback, this was Kessler's wheelhouse. "Scares me because he's so good," an NFL official once said of Kessler. "It's the capstone to his career," says Kessler's mentor, Jim Quinn.

After the meeting at Carmine's, things moved quickly. Huma had little trouble finding plaintiffs for Kessler, including Bill Tyndall, a football player at Cal-Berkeley, Rutgers basketball player J. J. Moore, UTEP football player Kevin Perry, and Martin Jenkins, a defensive back from Clemson, who became the named plaintiff..

By the fall of 2014, Kessler needed another round of plaintiffs. Some of the original filers had exhausted their eligibility, and according to Nevius, one player dropped out after he was pressured by his school about his involvement in the case. Huma turned to Zach Bohannon, a junior at the University of Wisconsin. Bohannon, a basketball player whose father had been a Rose Bowl quarterback at Iowa, had devoted enormous efforts to educating his teammates about what he saw as the ills of the NCAA—the money flowing into the schools and the exhaustive rules for players. Perhaps his most frustrating moment came during the NCAA tournament in 2013, when he was ordered by a security guard to throw away a water bottle at an arena because it wasn't the brand of the NCAA's sponsor. "The rules are crazy, literally crazy," Bohannon says.

But Bohannon was a junior and Huma and Kessler were hoping for younger players who might still be in college when the case went to trial. Bohannon knew just the one. He had been mentoring a teammate, Nigel Hayes, a thoughtful and intelligent sophomore. "Nigel was going to be a star, and at a school like Wisconsin, we could show how much money the schools were making."

Hayes soon became the lawsuit's most powerful spokesman. He was the latest in the line of college athlete activists that ran through Ed O'Bannon and Kain Colter. Coming out of Whitmer High School in Toledo, Hayes was not a heralded basketball prospect and he arrived at Wisconsin with little fanfare. But he exceeded expectations on the court—and off the court, he listened to what Bohannon had to say. He read a copy of Taylor Branch's damning article in the *Atlantic*, "The Shame of College Sports," and the two talked at length about NCAA history. When Bohannon came to him about signing on to the Kessler's case, he quickly said yes.

Hayes liked to point out that Mark Emmert earned nearly $2 million, while he and his teammates had to rely on the athletic department for snacks because they were broke. He couldn't afford to go home to Ohio to visit his mom. "It was, 'Hey, Mom, love you from Madison, would love to come see you, but I don't have any money,'" Hayes told Vice Sports' Patrick Hruby. "Meanwhile, there are no No. 10 jerseys [Hayes's number] at the [campus] bookstore. Not because they don't sell them, but because they're sold out. That is when I was like, wait a second. There's a little disconnect here."

Hayes would be part of back-to-back Final Four teams in 2014 and 2015, and by his junior year he was an academic all-American. (He was the Big Ten's preseason player of the year his senior season, as well.) And he took advantage of the visibility, using his platform to speak out about NCAA issues.

He pointed out, for instance, that schools used different basketball manufacturers, depending on who they were sponsored by. "I'm not a fan of the Under Armour basketball," Hayes once quipped. "We're supposed to be having fun, but all the money is in these basketballs that colleges play with. But it's an amateur sport, we're just here for fun. It's not really that serious. So I guess any ball should be OK." His senior season, when ESPN was doing its *College GameDay* show before a Wisconsin home football game, he stood in front of the crowd with a sign that read "Broke College Athlete Anything Helps" and urged fans to send money to a Venmo account. There was something familiar about it all—courageous plaintiff, righteous attorney, and, of course, a very worthy cause. Still the question remained: Would this time be any different?

It seemed as though nothing could stem the flood of money that continued to flow into college sports. Texas installed flat-screen televisions in each stall in the football team's locker room. The University of Central Florida announced plans to spend $25 million to upgrade its athletic complex, including the addition of a lazy river—essentially an amusement park—to recruit athletes. Clemson's new $55 million football facility included an indoor slide and a miniature golf course. Coaches' salaries? Those, too, were on the rise. Jim Harbaugh at Michigan earned $9 million in 2016 and Nick Saban at Alabama notched a raise, to $11 million. Every time news of the latest excess broke, Jay Bilas and other NCAA critics would take to Twitter to question why schools claimed to have no money to pay players—but had plenty of money to give coaches raises and build yet another indoor practice facility for the football team.

Arguably no one made out better than Jim Delany, who negotiated a new television deal for the Big Ten in the summer of 2016 with FOX and ESPN worth a whopping $2.64 billion. According to the *Sports Business Journal*, the agreement nearly tripled the conference's annual broadcast revenues. In the aftermath of the new deal, *USA Today* reported that he was due $20 million—that's right, $20 million—in future bonuses. Eric Kaler, the president of the University of Minnesota, explained the payment this way: "Commissioner Delany has provided invaluable leadership for Big Ten member institutions while delivering first-in-class performance during a time of great transformation in college athletics. . . . His compensation is market-competitive, based on an independent third-party analysis, and reflects the value and impact of his leadership."

One notable change during the 2016 football season showed that players were finally becoming savvier about looking out for their own welfare. Ahead of the 2016 bowl games, two of the sport's top stars—LSU's Leonard Fournette and Stanford's Christian McCaffrey—announced they would skip their bowl games rather than risk an injury that would diminish their draft prospects—and leave them with a smaller paycheck. "Very tough decision, but I've decided not to play in the Sun Bowl so I can begin my draft prep immediately," McCaffrey tweeted. There was plenty of hand-wringing from the college sports establishment—concern about the future of bowl games and accusations of selfishness. But there was little they could do. The system was built on leverage over players, and college coaches didn't have any once a player decided to leave school.

As Kessler pushed ahead with his case, he was struck by the similarities to professional athletes' struggle for free agency. When football players first pressed for workplace rights, like raises and pensions in the 1950s, the Chicago Bears owner George Halas argued that they were lucky to play football and, therefore, not "like regular people." "It's the same arrogance," Kessler said. "That athletes are somehow not entitled to the same rights as everyone else, and that these leagues—or in this case the NCAA—knows what's best for them."

During the NFL free agency case, the NFL had to be compelled to turn over financial documents; now Kessler had to ask the court for records from college conferences. Only after the Big Ten was compelled by the court did the conference turn over documents related to the creation of its TV network; the same was true with the Big 12's expansion plans. Jon King, Hausfeld's former partner, was briefly involved in Kessler's case and joined him for a deposition of an NCAA executive. King was riveted by the interrogation, as Kessler insisted on understanding how the athletic department budgets related to whole university budgets. "Jeffrey had this relentless refusal to accept at face value financial information," King says. "The NCAA is essentially saying schools are broke, and he was saying, even though they report these numbers, that's not true. It's exactly what he's done with the pro leagues."

There were two points that Kessler believed made his case a stronger one than the *O'Bannon* lawsuit. The first was that after the cost of attendance stipends were distributed to players, college sports continued seamlessly. In the earlier Jason White case, the NCAA claimed that the full cost of attendance money—which today amounts to between $2,000 and $6,000 a year, depending on the school—would destroy amateurism and college sports. But nothing of the kind had taken place. "Money didn't change anything," Kessler says.

The second development stemmed from the University of North Carolina's fake classes scandal. After initially cooperating with the NCAA, the university had changed course and had chosen to fight back against the NCAA. Thus, when the NCAA sent a notice of allegation to the school in May 2017, North Carolina responded by arguing that the NCAA had no jurisdiction over the matter.

"There is nothing inherently wrong with a student enrolling in a reputedly 'easy' course whether the purpose of taking the course is to balance the student's schedule, remain academically eligible to be a full-time student, meet academic scholarship requirements or to simply boost one's GPA," read the UNC response.

Stunningly, in mid-October 2017, the NCAA's Committee on Infractions announced that UNC would suffer no penalty: "The NCAA defers to its members' schools to determine whether academic fraud occurred," said Greg Sankey, the commissioner of the SEC who led the panel.

Why was this important to Kessler? For decades the NCAA has said education was its raison d'être. They had sold it to the public, as well as to the courts. But now schools themselves were challenging it—and the NCAA was agreeing that it had no jurisdiction over the classroom! If the NCAA couldn't punish a university for committing academic fraud, how could it convince a court it was an educational organization?

After the initial flurry of excitement, however, many close observers became skeptical of Kessler's chances of winning—especially after the appeals court made its ruling in *O'Bannon*, essentially upholding the status quo even though the plaintiffs had ostensibly won the case.

"I just can't see a court opening college sports to a free market," says Hausfeld. Another well-known plaintiffs lawyer, Steve Berman, filed a notable case around the same time as Kessler filed his. Berman's lawsuit sought damages for all the players who did not receive the cost of attendance stipends between 2009 and 2015 (those were the years between when the NCAA discontinued the stipends and then reintroduced them). The case was combined with Kessler's and assigned to Judge Wilken in Oakland. In early 2017, Berman settled the damages piece of his case for nearly $210 million. The good news was that some forty thousand athletes stood to receive checks for between $5,000 and $7,000. But while the settlement was notable for the amount of money, it also represented another legal challenge parried by the NCAA without wholesale changes to its structure. Berman, like Hausfeld, didn't think much of Kessler's chances to blow the NCAA wide open. He thought cash bonuses for staying in school or guaranteed money for graduate degrees were more likely than athletes selling their services to the highest bidder.

Kessler remained undeterred. "We're still asking for a market," he says. If he wins his case and the NCAA's rules are invalidated, Kessler believes the NCAA will be forced to write new rules. The conferences could also step in and implement their own player compensation structures. Kessler quoted Yoda, one of his favorite characters. "'Do or do not, there is no try,'" he says. "My view is we will get this done."

———

Andy Schwarz went into a mild funk after the *O'Bannon* dust had settled, and it was clear that the cartel nature of the NCAA had barely been nicked. He had helped make *O'Bannon* possible, and he had produced dozens of blog posts, articles, and rejoinders making the case for a free market for college athletes. This had been his cause for a decade now, and he wasn't ready to give it up.

So it wasn't long before he dove back in, working with his pal Dan Rascher on the Kessler case. But he also did something else: he came up with a truly radical idea—a whole new way to overturn the status quo.

"When I read your book," he said in an e-mail, "I got very sad at the end where you essentially (and correctly) conclude that we won all the battles and lost the war. I had this feeling of `I just don't have another twenty years to wait for all of the people who read *Deadspin* today to get old enough to be judges.' Because I'm impatient and wasn't ready to just give it up and go back to just running my own life, I started brainstorming about the HBCU league."

HBCU, of course, are the initials for Historically Black Colleges and Universities, whose athletic teams, though still in Division 1, have struggled mightily over the years. They have also struggled financially; many HBCU football teams play early season games against major powers— games in which they are humiliatingly overmatched—to earn paydays that help pay their athletic department's costs.

Schwarz's idea was that a group of HBCU basketball programs would drop out of the NCAA and form their own league, which he called the Historical Basketball League. They would recruit athletes using a tool not available to any Power Five school: cold hard cash, $50,000 to $100,000 per athlete. The athletes would still be students, but in addition to being paid, they would also have the same freedoms any student has to make money on the side. They could endorse products, sign with an agent, sell autographs, accept a free car from the local auto dealer, and even declare for the NBA draft without losing their eligibility.

Here is how Schwarz and the league's other "cofounder," Rick Volante, a lawyer, and Bijan Bayne, a writer, put it in the business plan they devised in 2016:

"The HBL plans to profit from the notion that the demand for college basketball is driven by consumers' demand for high-quality basketball played by bona fide college athletes, rather than being driven by the NCAA's notion of 'amateurism.' 'Amateurism' has created an artificially low price for college athletic talent, which represents a market opportunity for a college-based basketball league, while also creating a barrier against the NCAA's immediate competitive response. In addition, by showing that compensating college athletes will not lead to a collapse of the industry, the HBL represents an opportunity to change perceptions of the market value of college athletes and of the supposed necessity for 'amateurism,' thereby improving the well-being of those athletes, within the HBL and beyond."

The idea of creating a college league that paid players would likely appeal to high school seniors who only wanted to spend a year in college before jumping to the pros—the so-called one-and-done freshmen. But it might well also appeal to other athletes, especially disadvantaged athletes who need to make money while going to school. If the new league attracted enough high-profile players, it would undoubtedly get a television contract, attract big crowds, and receive plenty of coverage from the media.

"There's no amateurism," Schwarz told Vice Sports' Patrick Hruby, laying out his idea. "If we're in a high school recruit's living room, our pitch is that we want to give you a contract for $75,000, with workers' comp, health insurance, and a 401(k). There are opportunities for ancillary revenue on top of that. We offer great campuses and alumni networks. We invite NBA teams to come and to draft you while you're still in school. If and when you make that jump, we are thrilled for you.

"We walk through that menu, and then we ask, 'If you're thinking of going to a school outside of our league, ask them if those same possibilities are there.'"

Of course, Schwarz's brainstorm was as long a shot as Kessler's lawsuit—a longer shot, in fact. In the days of segregation, HBCUs had been powerhouses, routinely sending football players to the pros. Although those days are long gone, HBCU presidents have always been loath to drop out of Division I, much less the NCAA, even though their schools no longer belonged.

And the NCAA would no doubt react with fury. The likelihood of litigation was high. Schwarz and his fellow cofounders had spoken to a meeting of HBCU presidents and had found their reaction to be tepid. But the effort had reenergized Schwarz, and he wasn't about to let it go. The thought of using a market solution to disrupt the NCAA was just too enticing.

Sonny Vaccaro was not intimately involved in Kessler's case, but he was still at it: he gave a speech at Wharton in 2017 and another at the University of South Carolina for the annual College Sports Research Institute conference. In the summer of 2016, he flew to Toronto to meet Spike Lee at the NBA All-Star game, hoping to elicit his support for the cause. "Spike said he hated the NCAA," Vaccaro said. "But he said it's a lost cause—basically, no one cares about it."

But if you got him going, Vaccaro was still the same pugnacious bomb thrower he'd always been. He was incredulous about Delany's bonus. "What they gave him was sickening," he says. "They talk about Wall Street and greed—and here's $20 million." And he was giddy over what the North Carolina case could mean to the NCAA's legal defense. "They've been selling that education shit forever," he says. "Now they don't have a leg to stand on."

His early enthusiasm over the *O'Bannon* case has long since disappeared. He didn't have much faith in Kessler, either. In the fall of 2017, he was focused on writing his memoirs. And he had come to believe that the only way real change would come about was if the players themselves took action by, say, boycotting a bowl game or an NCAA March Madness game. But he has no illusions about how hard it is for young men to potentially sacrifice a pro career to fight the system.

Still, he said, "We gotta keep fighting, gotta keep going to court, gotta keep getting the word out. I'm tethered to this cause. Until they write my obituary."

# ACKNOWLEDGMENTS

Most journalism can't be done without people willing to answer a reporter's questions, and most books built on journalism can't be written without people willing to answer . . . and answer . . . and answer more questions than they ever imagined possible—and over a time span that can last years. So our first thanks goes to eight of the people at the center of this book, all of whom spent far more time with us than they ever imagined when they agreed to participate in *Indentured*: Sonny and Pam Vaccaro, Andy Schwarz, Dan Rascher, Ramogi Huma, Jim Delany, Kain Colter, and Michael Hausfeld. (Another important character, Walter Byers, chose not to be interviewed; he died at the age of ninety-three, as this book was being written. And Myles Brand died in 2009, three years before we began work on the book.)

There were many other key players in the modern evolution of college sports—on both sides of the divide—who don't get their full due in *Indentured* because of the inevitable constraints that come with putting such a sprawling story within the pages of a book. Among those we interviewed were Ernie Nadel, Richard Southall, Wally Renfro, William Isaacson, Len DeLuca, Roy Kramer, Cedric Dempsey, Mike Tranghese, Jim Host, Ellen Staurowsky, Roger Noll, Tim Waters, Ed O'Bannon, Jon King, Scott Tompsett, and Jay Bilas.

Ranae Steiner, one of the *O'Bannon* lawyers, is someone we came to rely on, over the course of several years, as we worked to understand the intricacies of antitrust law and the *O'Bannon* case. Additional assistance came from Dale Brown, Chuck Neinas, Tanisha Boatright, Melodi Dewey, Taylor Branch, Richard Gilbert, Allen Sack, Tibor Nagy, Jason White, James Santini, Tom Jernstedt, Murray Sperber, Richard Johnson, Ken Feinberg, Betsy Altmaier, Mary Willingham, Sharon Lee, Devon Ramsay, Robert Orr, John and Marcia Mount Shoop, Sathya Gosselin, John Sandbrook, Kerry Kenny, and Gary Parrish. When Joe visited Jerry Tarkanian at his home in Las Vegas, the former UNLV coach was too ill to say more than a few words. His story was conveyed during that visit by his wife, Lois, and two of his children, Danny Tarkanian and Jodie Diamant. Lois gave Joe access to the treasure trove of documents she had saved from her husband's two-decade fight with the NCAA. Danny allowed Joe to read his unpublished biography of his father. Betsy Altmaier was equally gracious with her meticulous notes about her work with the NCAA when Ben visited her in Iowa. When Ben conducted a lengthy interview with Mark Emmert (along with Steve Eder), Emmert, knowing full well that our book was unlikely to treat either him or the NCAA kindly, graciously agreed the material could be used for both the *Times* story and the book. We would also like to thank Stacey Osburn and Bob Williams of the NCAA for their assistance.

There were a handful of books we relied on for information and insight. They include: *Unsportsmanlike Conduct: Exploiting College Athletes* by Walter Byers; *The Cartel*, an e-book by Taylor Branch; *Onward to Victory*, the second of Murray Sperber's two histories of Notre Dame football; *The Fifty-Year Seduction: How Television Manipulated College Football, from the Birth of the Modern NCAA to the Creation of the BCS* by Keith Dunnavant; *ESPN: Those Guys Have All the Fun* by James Andrew Miller and Tom Shales; *Undue Process: The NCAA's Injustice for All* by Don Yeager; *Bill Walton: On the Road with the Portland Trail Blazers* by Jack Scott; *Meat on the Hoof: The Hidden World of Texas Football* by Gary Shaw; *The Hundred Yard Lie: The Corruption of College Football and What We Can Do to Stop It* by Rick Telander; and *The Supreme Court and the NCAA* by Brian L. Porto.

Until recently there hadn't been much in the way of in-depth reporting about the NCAA in newspapers or magazines, but one exception was a huge, ambitious series that ran in the *Kansas City Star* during October 1997. The authors were Mike McGraw, Steven Rock, and Karen Diller. Other in-depth articles included stories in the *Los Angeles Times* detailing the relationship between Sam Gilbert and the UCLA basketball program, by Mike Littwin and Alan Greenberg. The most important of these articles was published in February 1982. Another *Los Angeles Times* story that deserves mention is "Summer of Tragedy: Rash of Player Deaths Prompts Reexamination of Our Obsession with Football" by Mike Penner. And of course Taylor Branch's "The Shame of College Sports," published in the *Atlantic*'s October 2011 issue, was not only an important mini-history of the NCAA but marked the beginning of the backlash against the NCAA that we recount in chapter 12.

We would also like to acknowledge the following writers for the great work they have done on the NCAA in recent years: Jon Solomon (*Birmingham News* and then CBSSports.com), Brad Wolverton (*Chronicle of Higher Education*), Steve Berkowitz (*USA Today*), Andy Staples (*Sports Illustrated*), Dennis Dodd (CBSSports.com), Steve Eder (*New York Times*), Tom Farrey (ESPN), and the influential blogger Patrick Hruby.

Ben discovered, and Joe rediscovered, the professionalism, the creativity, and, yes, the fun that comes working with the team Adrian Zackheim has put together at Portfolio/Penguin, as our publisher is now known. Thanks to old friends Will Weisser, Jacquelynn Burke, and Emily Angell (who sadly left for another publishing house just as the final draft was being turned in), as well as new friends Leah Trouwborst, Jesse Maeshiro, Linda Cowan, Tara Gilbride, and Kelsey Odorczyk. Books are team efforts and we were blessed with an exceptional team at Portfolio/Penguin. As for Adrian, Joe has a few additional things to say below.

During the three years we worked on *Indentured*, we were lucky to have some terrific researchers and fact-checkers, including Emily de la Bruyere, Jack Weinberger, and Jacob Fischler. Joe's former assistant, Lydia Dallett, fact-checked large portions of the book as our deadline drew near, and showed her usual grace under pressure. Aaron Feuer found some important documents for us at a courthouse in Los Angeles. We thank them all.

--------

Since there are two of us, we each have friends and colleagues to thank for all the help we received during the time we worked on *Indentured*.

Ben first:

A first book is daunting in so many ways, so I want to first thank Joe for being both a coauthor and a wonderful mentor throughout the process. It has been an absolute pleasure to work with him. I'd also like to thank the terrific team of editors on the sports desk at the *New York Times*. Jason Stallman assigned me (and Steve Eder) a profile of Mark Emmert that among many other stories allowed me to report deeply about college sports and the NCAA. Melissa Hoppert was an instrumental editor on innumerable stories I have written about college sports, and Sam Dolnick worked closely with me on a number of pieces about the Northwestern union drive. Jay Schreiber, Naila-Jean Meyers, Andrew Das, and Connor Ennis have been excellent editors, and I am a better journalist for having worked with all of them. On the business desk, Sunday business editor Vera Titunik green-lighted a profile of Jim Delany that was edited beautifully by Loren Feldman.

Steve Eder, a colleague at the *Times*, was always a great teammate on stories, as were Zach Schonbrun and Marc Tracy. And I'd be remiss if I didn't mention an old buddy from Ithaca College, Nick Corasaniti, who several years ago found me a place to write a few blogs on the *Times's* sports page. I wouldn't be in this business if not for the kind words and advice over the years from a number of journalists, many of them in Chicago. They include Rick Telander, Jon Greenberg, Dan McGrath, David Haugh, Jim Litke, Scott Powers, Rick Gano, Jay Cohen, Paul Sullivan, David Bernstein, Bob Becker, Ron Rappaport, Brad Doolittle, Jonathan Eig, and Solomon Lieberman.

On a personal note, there are certainly too many family and friends to thank, but I can begin with my parents, Leslie and Jonathan, and my sister, Rebecca, who I imagine are excited to again have conversations with me that don't revolve around cost of attendance. My girlfriend, Samantha Swietlikowski, has also been a source of unconditional support, and I cannot thank her enough for all the legal insight she provided—free of charge. Finally, one giant thank-you to friends in Chicago and D.C. and from Ithaca College. I'm very lucky to be so supported and challenged by the people I like the most.

Joe's thank-yous:

*Indentured* is really the brainchild of Adrian Zackheim, who has been my book editor since 2002. About a year after I began writing regularly about the NCAA in my *New York Times* op-ed column, he began badgering me to consider writing a book on the subject. I resisted at first, but eventually I succumbed, and I'm glad I did. In the years we have been working together, I've come to trust Adrian's instincts, his sound judgment, and his straight-shooting style. And he certainly has a way with titles: he came up with *Indentured* before he even saw the manuscript, and *All the Devils Are Here*, the last book I wrote (with Bethany McLean) for Portfolio, was his also.

I originally hired Ben Strauss to serve as my researcher, but it didn't take long for both of us to realize that I—and the book—would be better served if he became my coauthor instead. He is a first-rate reporter and a fine writer, and was invariably an upbeat presence during those dark moments that every author endures. It is no exaggeration to say that this book would never have been completed without him. If I'm lucky, I'll get a chance to write another book with him someday.

My agent, Liz Darhansoff—who is now Ben's agent as well—came to my aid more than once in the three years I worked on *Indentured*. My appreciation for what she did is beyond words. I eagerly seek her counsel and I treasure her friendship.

At the *New York Times*, I would like to extend thanks to Andy Rosenthal, the editor of the editorial page, and Trish Hall and Sewell Chan, who were the top editors at the op-ed page. They gave me the license to write regularly about sports, an unusual subject for an op-ed columnist; whenever she felt there was too big a gap between NCAA columns, Gail Collins would prod me to get back at it. Former *Times* magazine editor Hugo Lindgren assigned me the article that first got me interested in exploring the NCAA and college athletics, and Dean Robinson did his usual terrific job editing that story. Jason Stallman maneuvered to get me press credentials for the 2013 Final Four in Atlanta, where I participated in Mark Emmert's disastrous press conference, described in chapter 12. Colleagues Andrew Ross Sorkin, Peter Lattman, Susan Lehman, and Jonathan Mahler were always ready to lend an ear, as was former *Times* man—and my former boss—Larry Ingrassia.

I owe a large debt of gratitude to Bethany McLean and her husband, Sean Berkowitz, to Steve Parrish, to Sam Waksal, and to the late Robert Silver. I would also like to thank Neil Barsky, Steve Klein, Ken Auletta, Jim Impoco, Dan Okrent, David Boies, Gerry Marzorati, and Andrea Rabney.

My grown children, Kate, Amato, and Nick, have been through this before with me—indeed, Kate, my oldest, was all of six years old when my first book was published in 1994. This time, though, I leaned on them more than I have in the past, and they never gave me anything but their unconditional love in return. They have all become wonderful adults, and I am terribly proud of them.

My young son, Macklin, to whom this book is dedicated, offered a different kind of love, the blind, all-consuming kind that small children give to their fathers. Raising him has been one of the great joys of this, the second, half of my life.

My wife, Dawn, has been a constant source of support, inspiration, and love throughout, and in many ways made it possible for me to write this book. I hope to be thanking her for a very long time to come.

# APPENDIX 1

# EXCUSES, NOT REASONS

## 13 Myths About (Not) Paying College Athletes

By Andy Schwarz

The NCAA and its member universities in the six major conferences[1] are generating over a billion dollars in football profits and over $300 million from basketball[2] on revenues of about $2.9 billion across those same schools. These seventy-three[3] schools earn these profits because, inter alia, they have made a collective agreement, along with the other 272 Division I schools, on the maximum

---

1 By this, I mean the BCS AQ ["Automatic Qualifying"] conferences: the SEC, Big Ten, Big 12, Pac-10, ACC, and Big East, including their eight nonfootball schools (which thus includes Notre Dame, a Big East member that competes in football as an independent). Note that this analysis does not include Utah, which joined the new Pac-12 in 2011, or TCU, which will join the Big East in 2012. See RPIRatings.com.

2 "EADA Survey 2009–2010," https://surveys.ope.ed.gov/athletics/. I derived these figures from the EADA figures for 2009–10, summing the difference between revenues and expenses for football and men's basketball for the seventy-three schools discussed in footnote 1. For the purposes of looking at a true profit numbers, the EADA numbers have several deficiencies. They fail to capture a good deal of revenue generated by football and basketball, either by assigning it to the athletic department as a whole (e.g., television profits from a conference network may be considered all-sports revenue despite being driven by football and basketball) or to other parts of the campus (e.g., profits from the sale of football sweatshirts can be credited to the bookstore). They also tend to overstate expenses, the best example being in the treatment of the cost of athletic scholarships, where cost on the books is often in excess of the actual cost. These all tend to make the profit numbers too low. On the other hand, these numbers do not charge the teams for the capital costs of facilities, which may cause the profit numbers to be overstated. Some of these facility costs are driven by the school's inability to use salary as a means of attracting recruits, so those costs may be higher than they would otherwise be. On balance, as a first approximation, the numbers presented here for the seventy-three schools in question probably gets the profit about right. I would eagerly coauthor a study with any scholars interested in working on the definitive answer to the accounting questions raised in this note.

3 Sixty-six with BCS AQ football and seven just for basketball as of the 2010 college football season. Based on conference realignment, these six conferences now have seventy-four because Utah has joined the expanded Pac-12. And in 2012, it will grow to seventy-five when TCU joins the Big East.

compensation[4] they offer to the college athletes who in large part drive consumer demand for the product.

In any other industry, allowing all 345 employers to form a nationwide wage cartel, while generating nearly 45 percent profit margins, would be an instant target for a Department of Justice or Federal Trade Commission investigation and private litigation.[5] Instead, the BCS AQ conference schools are allowed to generate these profits based on the rarely challenged assumption that the collusion[6] among the 345 schools in Division I is somehow procompetitive. However, there is little or no procompetitive justification for this collusion. The question is often phrased as, "Should we pay college athletes?," but that misses the point. The real question is, "Why do we allow nationwide collusion on player compensation?"

If the current collusion wants to be justified under our antitrust laws, that system should have to make the case that it helps create a product that could not exist in the true competitive environment in which each school (or conference)[7] offers each athlete a level of compensation it deems to be appropriate, without a national agreement. Deviations from this competitive baseline are justified only if the product cannot otherwise exist as a popular product with healthy consumer demand.

Through a century of public relations work,[8] the NCAA has stitched into the national sports fabric a series of myths that purport to provide these procompetitive justifications for the collusive agreement on athlete compensation. The mythmaking powers of the NCAA are mighty, on par with the ancient Greeks. Through a century of hearing these tall tales, you already "know" why paying athletes will never work. Perhaps you've admitted to yourself that college athletes have a raw deal, but then shrugged your shoulders because, of course, college football couldn't exist any other way. Or perhaps you blame Title IX. But

---

4  This compensation comes in the form of athletic scholarships, officially known within the NCAA as "grants-in-aid" (hereinafter GIAs).

5  And possibly also an investigation by the NLRB under the nation's labor laws.

6  Throughout this paper I will refer to this agreement as "collusion" or as a "cartel," though others might prefer the terms "collective agreement" and "joint venture." Feel free to use the more neutral terms; I believe in this case neutrality comes at the expense of accuracy.

7  Daniel A. Rascher and Andrew D. Schwarz, "Neither Reasonable nor Necessary: 'Amateurism' in Big-Time College Sports," *Antitrust*, Special Sports Issue, Spring 2000, 6. As Professor Daniel Rascher and I argued in that issue of *Antitrust*, in the context of multiple regional conferences, a collective cap at the individual conference level may be procompetitive and thus survive a rule-of-reason review.

8  One might use the term "propaganda."

whatever your reason is, recognize that what you are telling yourself is almost certainly an unproven myth based in NCAA assertions rather than fact. It feels true because you've heard it so much, but repetition is not the same as truth. What follows are the thirteen most commonly repeated but false arguments why only collusive-compensation college sports can work and why market-compensation college sports cannot. If you believe any of them unquestioningly, you've fallen for a myth.

## MYTH 1: It's Too Hard to Figure Out How to Pay Players Fairly.

This myth rests deeply in the assumption that if we deign to allow college players to be paid, there would have to be a nationwide agreement by all 345 Division I schools (or perhaps just the 122 in FBS, the Football Bowl Subdivision)[9] as to what each student would get, and it would be a nightmare, with committees meeting annually to review compensation to make sure it was fair to schools and athletes, and endless debates over the optimal pay level.

It makes you wonder how the Software Industry Wage Committee ever decides how much to pay computer programmers and how the Law Firm Pay Commissariat decides on associate and partner compensation each year.

The solution, of course, is just to pay them. There is no need for a central committee to make this decision. Since 1776, with the publication of Adam Smith's *The Wealth of Nations*, we've understood that markets generally find their way to efficient outcomes without the need for a committee, NCAA or otherwise, acting as a wage politburo. No centralized commission or study group is needed to decide what we should pay the athletes.

Let schools make offers, and let incoming high school athletes and their parents decide which to accept. Competition is a wonderful thing, on the playing field and in the marketplace. This is how salaries are set across the world. This is probably how your pay was set.

At first it might be a little messy, just as when a firm prices its stock in an IPO. The initial price may end up higher or lower than the right value, but the company picks a price, sells its stock, and then the market adjusts. For example, LinkedIn went public on May 19, 2011, and closed up 107 percent from its initial offering after two days of trading.[10] The following month, Pandora went public

---

9  The NCAA has rebranded Division I-A as the Football Bowl Subdivision, or FBS. The old Division I-AA is now called FCS, the Football Championship Subdivision.

10  Ari Levy and Lee Spears, "LinkedIn Retains Most Gains Second Day After Surging in Initial Offering," Bloomberg News, May 20, 2011, http://www.bloomberg.com/news/2011-05-18/linkedin-raises-352-8-million-in-ipo-as-shares-priced-at-top-end-of-range.html.

but closed down 20 percent two days after its launch.[11] Opening up the market for student-athletes would not be much different. At first, many schools might continue to offer the grant-in-aid (GIA) package without additional cash. A few programs might want to set the gold standard and offer $10,000 stipends. A few up-and-comers might make a play for some talent and offer $25,000 to see if they could jump-start their programs at a higher level. The following year, maybe a few more schools would up the ante, and maybe some of the Old Guard might start matching offers to avoid losing talent. Just as water finds its own level, so too do prices in a liquid market. A decade in, everyone would have a great sense of what a blue chipper is worth to a program and what it takes to land him. Problem solved.

## MYTH 2: A Market System Will Kill Cohesion.

Often, commentators point out that it would not be fair to pay some athletes on a team and not others, and that the result will be lack of team cohesion. In this view of the world, if a team had stars making more than role-players, blockers would stop protecting better-paid quarterbacks, unpaid power forwards would refuse to throw outlet passes to compensated point guards, and it would become impossible to play college sports.

I wonder how many of these commentators have ever watched the college baseball world series, or NCAA hockey, or most any other college sport, including football at the Division I FCS level. Under NCAA scholarship rules, most schools provide very unequal compensation to their athletes in most sports.[12] In most NCAA teams, some of the athletes are on "full rides,"[13] some are on half

---

11 Lee Spears, "Pandora Plunges Below IPO Price, Reversing Yesterday's Gains," Bloomberg News, June 16, 2011, http://www.bloomberg.com/news/2011-06-16/pandora-plunges-below -ipo-price-reversing-yesterday-s-gains-3-.html. See also Jennifer Saba and Charlie Baldwin, "Update 1-IPO VIEW-Profitless Pandora Picks the Tech Bubble," Reuters, June 17, 2011, http:// www.reuters.com/article/2011/06/17/markets-stocks-ipos-idUSN1728751420110617.

12 There are six sports where the NCAA rules treat a partial scholarship as a full one for purposes of the agreed-upon scholarship quota. This has the effect of making it less common to provide partial scholarships. These six sports are women's tennis, women's volleyball, women's gymnastics, women's basketball, men's basketball, and FBS (Division I-A) football, but not FCS (Division I-AA) football.

13 Left for another day is the myth that the full ride is actually full. The maximum NCAA Division I GIA is prohibited by NCAA rules from actually covering the full cost of attendance, and instead falls about $3,000 short. Every few years, talk of fixing this problem arises, and this year the talk seems particularly promising. There is still plenty of time, however, for this proposal to die in committee like the last time the NCAA took on this issue.

or quarter scholarships, and some get no scholarships at all.[14] These teams very rarely dissolve into chaos because some players are earning four or more times what others are getting. Even in football and basketball, scholarship and non-scholarship players work together cohesively to win games and championships.

Across the country, based on talent, baseball GIAs can range from a full scholarship to no scholarship at all. As one example, one of the schools in the West Coast Conference has thirty-four players on its 2011 baseball team. Three of them receive at least a 75 percent scholarship and another thirteen get a half scholarship or more. Another five get some aid, but less than a half scholarship, and thirteen get no scholarship at all. This disparity in compensation is fairly typical for college baseball, and it is not a secret that better players get better compensation. At the University of California, Berkeley (Cal), one baseball player is on a 75 percent–plus scholarship, ten more are over 50 percent, fourteen got some aid but less than half, and eleven walk-ons get no aid at all.[15] Nevertheless, there is little evidence that cohesion disintegrated because athletes with different levels of talent received different levels of compensation. The WCC team made the college postseason this year and Cal reached the 2011 College World Series in Omaha. According to all accounts, everyone is still on speaking terms.

So if team cohesion depends critically on each team member receiving perfectly identical scholarship offers, it's hard to explain the success of college baseball and softball teams, men's gymnastics, men's and women's lacrosse, etc., where stars sometimes earn full scholarships and most players are on partial scholarships or none at all.

This ability of teams to cooperate successfully despite different levels of pay shouldn't be surprising, since professional sports teams have succeeded since the nineteenth century with pay that varies among the players on a team. Dirk Nowitski earned over $17 million this year, J. J. Barea earned a little more than 10 percent of that, and Ian Mahinmi earned less than half of what Barea

---

14 Recently, the NCAA has required an athlete on baseball scholarship to get at least 25 percent funding. See "Minimum Equivalency Value," Division I Legislation Display, Cite 15.5.4.1, available at https://web1.ncaa.org/LSDBi/exec/bylawSearch?bylawSearchSubmit=Get%20Selected%20Items&multiple=19576&division=1&adopted=0. For all other sports, scholarships can be in the single digits, meaning that some scholarship athletes paid 90 percent or more of their own costs of attending school. Walk-ons continue to pay 100 percent.

15 As an official at Cal stated in private correspondence, "The money is usually distributed based on talent (i.e. the best player will get 85% scholarship, mediocre player will get a stipend + books paid)."

earned.[16] Yet somehow the Mavericks were able to gel as a team and win this year's NBA championship despite Nowitski earning almost twenty-three times Mahinmi's salary.[17] Aaron Rodgers threw nine completions to Jordy Nelson in the 2011 Super Bowl, despite the fact that Rodgers was earning $6 million to Nelson's $475,000, and Rogers was able to hand the ball to James Starks, Green Bay's leading rusher, despite the fact that Starks earned only 5.3 percent of Rodgers's salary.[18] Somehow the Packers overcame this income disparity to win the Super Bowl.

When a team loses, no one even thinks to point to pay disparity as the driver, and when a team wins, no one is shocked by the team's success in the face of seemingly insurmountable lack of cohesion driven by disparities in pay. It's just not an issue because our capitalist society embraces the idea that people making different incomes based on merit work together better than if everyone earns the same amount. In virtually every American industry, different workers earn different pay and yet companies are able to pull together as teams. Think of how equal pay for all worked out for Eastern Europe's cohesiveness. There isn't something special about college football players that make them too fragile to handle what the rest of us deal with on a daily basis.

On the other hand, if we really think equal pay is needed for team cohesion, I'd say we pay the players exactly what we pay the head coach. Coaches would probably make less as a result, and players more. I mean, how can a team pull together knowing their coach is making millions and they are not? I'm surprised they even go on the field at all.

### MYTH 3: Paying Players Will Mean That Schools Cannot Afford to Play Football or Basketball Anymore. After All, Almost All Athletic Departments Are Losing Money Now, So They Would All Go Out of Business If They Were Forced to Pay Athletes.

In terms of myths, this one is a two-headed hydra. It combines the idea that there has to be some sort of wage schedule set by a committee (i.e., Myth 1) with the idea that the result will be that the committee would pick a number that

---

16 "Dallas Mavericks Salaries," HoopsHype.com, http://hoopshype.com/salaries/dallas .htm.

17 Ian Mahinmi earned $762,195. Ibid.

18 Starks earned $320,000 for the 2010–11 NFL season. "Green Bay Packers Players Salaries," SportsCity.

some school can't afford. But a market system of pay will not impose a one-size-fits-all solution, mandatory minimum wage on all colleges.

As an example, currently the University of Texas (Texas) has a choice whether to pay its head football coach, Mack Brown, $5 million per year in base salary. Texas negotiated with Brown, and when the dust settled decided it was in their interest to offer him $5 million (plus bonuses), all without asking permission of the other NCAA schools. Grants to college athletes would be set the same way—each school (or conference) should be allowed to offer each student what it sees fit and let the market sort things out. Across American industries, there are high-paying and low-paying firms, and so there would be high-paying and low-paying schools. Schools that earn less money from football and basketball will make smaller offers, but they will still be able to field teams.

The second head of this myth is the very pernicious idea, which has gained currency since Mark Emmert took the helm of the NCAA,[19] that because the athletic departments at most of the thousand-plus schools in the NCAA lose money as a whole, almost no school can afford to pay their football and basketball players. In essence, the money that should go to pay players is being spent elsewhere, so we're very sorry players, but we're broke.

Of course, this is ridiculous on several layers. The simplest myth to dispatch is that we don't need to lump together the thousand-plus NCAA schools when talking about athletes who will end up being paid in a market-based system. Division II and Division III, the FCS level of Division I, and even a good chunk of the FBS would basically not change in the world where schools can choose to pay their college athletes. Most of those schools are hosting sports on their campus in a much more traditional amateur sense, for the benefit of the athletes, with some level of on-campus interest, and with very little outside fanfare or television coverage. In rare cases, a small school might want to add some cash to their current scholarship offer, but that's unlikely. In the real world outside the NCAA myth bubble, the changes we're talking about are going to take place at the approximately seventy-five schools in the six major conferences.

Just to give this some perspective, these are the football and basketball revenues from all 345 Division I schools, broken down into key categories.[20]

---

19 Tom Farrey and Paula Lavigne, "Selling the NCAA," ESPN.Com, March 13, 2011, http://sports.espn.go.com/espn/otl/news/story?id=6209609.

20 I created this chart based on data obtained from the EADA website—http://ope.ed.gov/athletics/.

| Football and Men's Basketball | Number of Schools | Revenue | Profit | Average Profit per School |
|---|---|---|---|---|
| Six BCS AQ Conferences | 73 | $2.9 billion[21] | $1.4 billion[21] | $19 million |
| FBS non AQs | 56 | $515 million | $39 million | $0.7 million |
| All Other Division I | 215 | $638 million | $18 million | $0.1 million |

What we call the NCAA or even what we call Division I, consists of two or three entirely different economic animals. Seventy-five or so schools are housing massive profit centers on their campuses in their football and basketball programs.[22] For the much larger groups of schools that are running their sports teams as much smaller, break-even activities,[23] sports are just not the same thing at all, and whenever the NCAA asks you to think about college sports economics and tries to talk about Division II and Division III, or even the lower two-thirds of Division I, they are playing hide the ball.

---

21 That's billions with a "b." The other cells are in millions.

22 Victor A. Matheson, Debra J. O'Connor, and Joseph H. Herberger, "The Bottom Line: Accounting for Revenues and Expenditures in Intercollegiate Athletics," College of the Holy Cross, Department of Economics Faculty Research Series, Paper No. 11-01, available at http://college.holycross.edu/RePEc/hcx/Matheson-OConnor_CollegeAccounting.pdf. See also Brian L. Goff, "Effects of University Athletics on the University: A Review and Extension of Empirical Assessment," *Journal of Sport Management* 14 (2000): 85–104, who found that over 70 percent of the schools in major Division I conferences earned over $1 million in profit from their combined football and basketball programs.

23 Again, here EADA accounting can mislead whether schools really break even or not, since some schools will force their books to balance by an accounting entry. The impact of this accounting is much more important for the small schools, some of which may actually be losing money, because those schools simply have fewer off-the-books revenues to even things out. Where Matheson et al. found that almost all BCS AQ schools had profitable football and basketball programs, they found that only three to sixteen non-AQs made profits in football and nine to twenty in men's basketball. See Matheson et al., "The Bottom Line." On the other hand, there have been more in-depth studies of individual small schools (in fact, all of the good studies are of small schools), and they generally show that once all of the off-the-books revenues are added in and all of the overstated expenses are taken out, football is profitable for small schools despite these break-even accounting numbers. See Clifford R. Skousen and Frank A. Condie, "Evaluating a Sports Program: Goalposts vs. Test Tubes," *Managerial Accounting* 60 (1988): 43–49; see also Melvin V. Borland, Brian L. Goff, and Robert W. Pulsinelli, "College Athletics: Financial Burden or Boon?," in Gerald W. Scully, ed., *Advances in the Economics of Sport* (Greenwich, CT: JAI Press, 1992), vol. 1, 215–25. See also Jeremy Howell and Daniel Rascher, "An Analysis and Assessment of Intercollegiate Athletics at the University of San Francisco," University of San Francisco," CSRI Conference (2011), which focuses on sports other than football. See also Brian L. Goff,

Even when we keep the focus on the six BCS AQ conferences, the NCAA still wants to obscure the debate. Mark Emmert, NCAA president, has said that only fourteen NCAA schools make money on sports and so most schools can't afford to pay their athletes.[24] That seems hard to believe given that the seventy-three schools in the AQ conferences earned $1.4 billion in aggregate. But the trick is that the NCAA is throwing in all of the nonrevenue sports, and then asking you to believe that when college football players get paid, so too will college wrestlers, even though football players are bringing in over a billion dollars and wrestlers aren't bringing in anything. That's just not how markets work.

More broadly though, the myth is that the athletic department as a whole is the right unit of analysis and that spending on football compensation will only occur when a school's entire program earns a profit. In other words, if the department loses money, no one gets paid.

But campuses abound with money-losing departments that nevertheless pay the talent. Traditional colleges and universities do not exist to make money, and in general, most of the departments on a campus simply cannot make money. Instead, departments like classics, anthropology, history, and psychology spend more than they bring in, and the school covers the cost of professors, of secretaries, of graduate students, and of academic scholarships with money from donors, with tuition money received, and, in the case of public universities, with taxpayers' money.

Schools do this because having a history department (that has no real source of revenue) is part of the university's mission. If having big-time sports on a BCS AQ school's campus is also part of the total mission of the schools (a statement I think the NCAA would support),[25] then the entire college community

---

"Effects of University Athletics on the University: A Review and Extension of Empirical Assessment," in John Fizel and Rodney Fort, eds., *Economics of College Sports* (Westport, CT: Praeger, 2004), 82, who estimates that when small schools lose money on football and basketball, it's "likely less than $1 million." In my own research, I found that the University of Nebraska–Omaha's Division II football team probably was earning a small profit on the order of $100,000, but the school claimed to be losing $1.3 million on football alone. See Paula Lavigne, "Wrestling with the Truth in Nebraska," *Outside the Lines*, ESPN, May 11, 2011, http://sports.espn.go.com/espn/otl/news/story?id=6488960. In the end, these schools are choosing to keep these programs. So in total, when they add up all of the money and nonmoney reasons for having football and basketball, schools are acting as if they are coming out in the black.

24 Tom Farrey and Paula Lavigne, "Selling the NCAA," *Outside the Lines*, ESPN, March 13, 2011, http://sports.espn.go.com/espn/otl/news/story?id=6209609.

25 This question has actually been examined in the sports management literature. Even though most college and university mission statements do not address particular subunits (like sports), one study showed that about 10 percent of schools with big-time athletics do

should support the program, just as it supports history and psychology and the like.[26]

The idea that before we pay student-athletes the athletic department must make money is a false argument. We do not ask history professors to work solely for room and board because the history department doesn't make money, and in particular, we do not allow colleges to collude on the salaries of history professors in order to help history departments break even. Similarly, we don't ask college sports coaches to work for a price-fixed wage just because the athletic departments don't earn money, although in the past the NCAA has tried to do just this and lost in court.[27]

The profitability (or lack thereof) of the athletic department as a whole should not be an excuse to collude on player compensation. Such an argument would never withstand rule-of-reason scrutiny. Indeed, under the antitrust rule of reason, cost cutting is not a valid justification for otherwise anticompetitive conduct.[28]

But if the NCAA is right that almost everyone is losing money, then why are all of these money-losing schools spending millions on athletic programs now? Why are schools clamoring to get into Division I if it's a money-losing venture? There are now 345 Division I schools; in 1985 there were only 282.[29] Demand to move to Division I has been so great that in 2007 the NCAA imposed a four-year moratorium on new schools from moving up to Division I. This moratorium has

---

explicitly list athletics in the mission statement. Charles T. Clotfelter, *Big-Time Sports in American Universities* (New York: Cambridge University Press, 2011), 28–29.

26  My point is not that providing high-quality sports opportunities is as equally central to the mission of the university as providing a high-quality education. Instead, my point is that if it is the case that the university community is unwilling to spend any of its own money on minor sports, then they should cancel those sports. If instead they *do* value the minor sports, they should spend university money to support them, not dock the pay of their revenue producers to cover it. The fact that football and basketball may be generating a profit is a bad reason to divert those profits to pay for something that no one on campus would pay for if that money weren't just sitting there.

27  Law v. NCAA, 134 F.3d 1010 (10th Cir. 1998).

28  "The NCAA next advances the justification that the plan will cut costs. However, cost-cutting by itself is not a valid procompetitive justification. If it were, any group of competing buyers could agree on maximum prices. Lower prices cannot justify a cartel's control of prices charged by suppliers, because the cartel ultimately robs the suppliers of the normal fruits of their enterprises." *Id.* at 1022. See Phillip E. Areeda, *Antitrust Law*, 1504, at 379.

29  "Big 12 Coaches Favor Expanding NCAA Tournament," CBSSports.com.

only just ended, and immediately new schools are seeking to join.[30] Running a Division I program is much more expensive than Division II. When economic actors are clamoring to spend more, it means that that spending is profitable. Either hundreds of universities are irrational, or, after looking at the total benefit of having great sports on campus, these schools are making a rational decision that paying the current cost of scholarships is actually worth the cost.

Schools want to move to Division I because, taken as a whole, the school thinks Division I is more profitable, in money and in nonpecuniary benefits, than Division II. Maybe the accounting that shows schools losing money is riddled with problems that understate revenues and overstate costs, so they are more profitable than they look.[31] Maybe fielding a quality sports program helps attract better scientists and poets. Maybe donations go up after a March Madness win. Maybe it just feels better to have a Saturday football tradition and the university wants to offer its community that experience. Those are all great reasons to be in Division I, but they are bad reasons to collude with other schools just to keep down the cost of the on-field and on-court talent.

A market system would let us test the NCAA's claim that further spending is impossible. End the collusion for a few years and let's see whether schools think they are too poor to pay for that star recruit, or instead if they decide, on the margin, that the benefits of that athlete continue to exceed his (increased) cost.

## MYTH 4: If We Set Up a System Where Rich Schools Make Larger Scholarship Offers Than Poor Schools, There Will Be No Competitive Balance. Only the Big "Have" Programs Will Get Talent and the "Have Nots" Will Be Left Outside Looking In.

There are two problems with this argument. The first is that it assumes that currently the "have not" schools somehow grab an equal share of talent. They do not. "Haves" recruit great players and consistently win. Have-nots get the leftovers and occasionally luck into hidden gems who gel as seniors and win.

---

30 Doug Lederman, "NCAA Freezes Division I Membership," InsideHigherEd.com, August 10, 2007, http://www.insidehighered.com/news/2007/08/10/ncaa. The University of Nebraska–Omaha will enter Division I for 2011–12. Paula Lavigne, "Wrestling with the Truth in Nebraska," *Outside the Lines*, ESPN, May 11, 2011, http://sports.espn.g o.com/espn/otl/news/story?id=6488960. The University of North Alabama has announced it will begin a six-year transition to Division I in 2011–12. "UNA Board Approves Resolution to Pursue NCAA Division I Status," University of North Alabama Lion Athletics.

31 See note 2 above and accompanying text for a discussion of some of the problems with NCAA accounting.

Kentucky started its 2010–11 men's basketball season against Eastern Tennessee State University (ETSU). I would like to see evidence that Eastern Tennessee State has ever successfully recruited an athlete who was also offered a scholarship by Kentucky. Alabama started its 2010 football season against San Jose State and will start the 2011 season against Kent State, but what top recruit would spurn an offer from Alabama to attend San Jose or Kent?

The current collusive cap on wages has not in any way created a level playing field with respect to the distribution of talent. We don't need to speculate; the proof is in the numbers. Over the last ten years, more than 99 percent of the top 100 high school prospects chose BCS AQs.

### CONFERENCE CHOICE OF TOP 100 FOOTBALL RECRUITS
**2002–11 (1,000 in total)[32]**

| Conference | Recruits | Percent of Total |
|------------|----------|------------------|
| SEC | 303 | 30.3% |
| ACC | 173 | 17.3% |
| Big 12 | 171 | 17.1% |
| Pac-10 | 164 | 16.4% |
| Big Ten | 129 | 12.9% |
| Notre Dame | 36 | 3.6% |
| Big East | 17 | 1.7% |
| Mt. West! | 5 | 0.5% |
| Junior College | 1 | 0.1% |
| MAC | 1 | 0.1% |
| Conf. USA | 0 | 0.0% |
| WAC | 0 | 0.0% |
| Sunbelt | 0 | 0.0% |
| *BCS AQs* | *993* | *99.3%* |
| *non-AQs* | *7* | *0.7%* |

32  I created this chart based on data obtained from Rivals.com—http://footballrecruiting
.rivals.com/.

The myth then points to the successes of Cinderellas and asks, "What about Butler and VCU? How could that happen if we let Duke and UConn buy up all the talent?" But again, we already do let Duke and UConn, and their brethren, buy up all the talent. The amazing and wonderful thing about college sports (basketball in particular) is that despite this massive imbalance in who gets the most talented players, sometimes a bunch of athletes who were overlooked or underrated in high school can find a home at a less prestigious athletic program and turn it into a Cinderella, like the great George Mason Final Four team of 2005–06 or the back-to-back Butler Bulldog teams of 2009–10 and 2010–11.[33] But those schools achieved greatness despite having second choice of talent. If a player is looking at a school primarily as a place to play very high-level college sports, Duke doesn't need to offer cash to win a recruiting war with George Mason, it just has to make a scholarship offer. It doesn't take money for a "have" to steal talent from a "have not"—it just takes interest.

On the other hand, if George Mason wants to win a recruiting war with Duke, it's probably doomed under the current system. Letting have nots use cash is actually the best way to overcome the current unlevel playing field. If we allowed schools to choose how much to offer a player, a current have-not college could use money to steal a player or two from the haves and help begin the climb to the ranks of the elite. If the alumni of ETSU want to fund a powerhouse basketball program, currently they have no dimension on which they can outshine Kentucky. But if they could offer Kentucky recruits $50,000 a year to come to ETSU, they might start winning those recruiting battles frequently enough to become more, not less, competitive with Kentucky.

Finally, it's important to note that the comparative parity of men's basketball is achieved despite the current compensation system, not because of it. The reason we see men's Final Fours with VCUs and Butlers is because the United States produces an amazing amount of high school boys with basketball talent, so that even after all of the big schools get all the stars they can handle, there are still plenty of almost-stars to go around. Contrast this with women's basketball,

---

33 Notice that my examples of Cinderellas both come from basketball. Basketball lends itself better to scrawny seventeen-year-olds blooming into excellent twenty-one-year-olds such that diamonds in the rough can shine at lesser schools. Also the sport needs only five active players at a time, so one impact player can change the fortunes of a school in a way that rarely happens in football. As our current system shows, the best teams get the best players and the best players perform the best. There is no way for a football team to become a powerhouse without spending money to get better players, whether that's under the current system, where the money is spent on coaches and fancy facilities, or under a market system, where some of the money would be spent on the talent.

where there is a greater disparity between the talent among the top tier of recruits and the rest, such that once UConn, then Tennessee, and then Stanford are done, and then once their big conference companions like Notre Dame and Texas A&M finish, there are basically no great women's players left for Butler. For the last ten years, no school from outside the BCS AQ conferences has made the Women's Final Four. Since women's basketball also involves the same national collusion on athlete compensation, but does not achieve even the slightest level of nationwide competitive balance, it can't possibly be the agreement itself that is generating men's parity.

And let's remember that even in men's basketball, the parity in outcomes is somewhat illusory. Over the period 1985–2006, 91 percent of the final AP Top 25[34] in football consisted of schools in the six power conferences. Eighty-three percent of the teams in the men's basketball Sweet Sixteen from 1985 to 2006 and 92 percent of the teams in the Final Four were from those same six conferences.[35] It seems we are not getting very much competitive balance from our nationwide collusion and not much bang for the athletes' sacrificed buck.

## MYTH 5: We Can't Pay Them or Else We'll Have to Cancel Other Sports.

This may only be a half myth, in the sense that in a market system, as the costs of putting on football and basketball rise, such that the profits from those programs decline from astronomical to merely sky-high, it may be the case that some schools in their budgeting priority choose to drop some (most likely men's) nonrevenue sports. It is true that currently those football and basketball profits are being spent in part on subsidizing all of the other sports on campus. And so if those programs are of so little value to the campus community as a whole that with the reduction of the subsidy from football and basketball no one values them enough to pay for them if the subsidy is reduced, they will probably go away.

When the cost of one essential input (e.g., football players) increases without a change in the total money available, the college has less money to spend

---

34 Or Top 20 for years prior to 1989 where ranks 21–25 were not officially assigned. See Patrick L. Dunn, "Past Final AP Polls," RSFC, http://homepages.cae.wisc.edu/~dwilson /rfsc/history/APpolls.txt.

35 See Mark Nagel, Matt Brown, and Chad McEvoy, "Exploring the Myth That a Better Seed in the NCAA Men's Basketball Tournament Results in an Ex Ante Higher Payout," Sport Management Association of Australia and New Zealand, November 2007.

on other things. It has less money to spend on coaches' and administrators' salaries[36] and on weight rooms and practice facilities,[37] but it also has less money to spend on the drama club, on professors and graduate students, on parking enforcement, trash collection, painting campus buildings, and all of the other things it takes to run a university. When it's time to cut the budget to adjust to lower football profits, schools will have to prioritize spending from most important to least, and then cut from the bottom up.

If men's lacrosse is the absolutely lowest priority, that's what we should cut. But if it is the case that men's lacrosse is already the least-wanted activity on campus, then giving money to those least-wanted lacrosse athletes is a horrible justification for diverting money from the athletes whom we do want on campus, whom people are eager to see. If lacrosse and other sports are valuable, let's fund them ourselves without using it as a justification to deny the football and basketball players a chance to earn what they are worth. If lacrosse and other sports are not valued enough to be funded without a massive subsidy, let's not ask the football players to give up a market wage to finance these apparently unwanted activities. Better still, if the campus doesn't value the lacrosse team

---

36  Of the fifty-eight head football coaches in the six major conferences for which salary information was available (eight private schools did not provide data), fifty-two head coaches earned more than $1 million per year in 2010. "Football Bowl Subdivision Coaches Salaries for 2010," USAToday.com, December 9, 2010, http://www.usatoday.com/sports/college/football/2010-coaches-contracts-table.htm. Among the six head coaches who didn't reach the threshold, Washington State's Paul Wulff was employed for a full year and did not have the potential to exceed $1 million after considering bonuses, Baylor's Art Briles earned $878,315 (with no bonus information reported), and the rest had the potential to earn over $1 million after bonuses. Ibid. Seven non-AQ schools also paid their coach over $1 million. Ibid. Even assistant coaches have broken beyond six-figure salaries; for example, Will Muschamp was recently offered $1 million a year to be Mack Brown's defensive coordinator at Texas. Seth Wickersham, "Is Gordon Gee Serious?," ESPN.go.com, http://espn.go.com/college-football/story/_/id/6843627/college-football-ohio-state-president-gordon-gee-recent-football-scandal-espn-magazine. Four of the six BCS AQ conference commissioners earned over $1 million in 2009, and a fifth, Larry Scott of the Pac-10, earned over $700,000 in his first six months on the job. "Four BCS Conference Commissioners Earned $1M," ESPN, June 21, 2011, http://sports.espn.go.com/ncaa/news/story?id=6682234. Interestingly, athletic directors, who are neither responsible for attracting talent like head coaches nor negotiating television contracts like conference commissioners, earned much less. A 2009 study of fifty-one BCS AQ schools found that no athletic director earned more than $1 million (Florida's Jeremy Foley was tops at $965,000), and only ten earned $500,000 or more. See Curtis Eichelberger, "Florida Enters BCS Title Game with Top-Paid Athletic Director," Bloomberg.com, January 6, 2009, http://www.bloomberg.com/apps/news?pid=newsarchive&sid=aYYY_mDwYMkY.

37  With Oklahoma State's announcement of construction of a $16 million project, now all teams in the Big 12 have built indoor football practice facilities. See "Oklahoma St. to Start Work on $16M Practice Site," SI.com, June 21, 2011.

enough to pay for it, we could ask the lacrosse players and parents to pay their own tuition costs, rather than forcing the students who play football and basketball to pay it via collusion. And we could ask the lacrosse fans and interested alums to pay the expenses of lacrosse coaches and travel, rather than colluding to force the students who play football and basketball to cover those costs as well.

Of course, I think the campus as a whole does want lacrosse. Schools want it enough that if we didn't have football revenues to subsidize it, we'd still keep it, much like schools that have lacrosse in Division III,[38] where there are no football profits to spread around.[39] If profits were needed to have men's sports, the entirety of Division III would have vanished long ago.

Instead in Division I, what we have now is a subsidy by young African American men (who comprise a disproportionate number of scholarship athletes in FBS football and the majority of scholarship athletes in basketball throughout Division I)[40] going to support the country-club sports of middle-class whites, all the more shameful if it's done to support activities that are at the absolute bottom of our list of priorities. The current system imposes an involuntary subsidy on students coming from the poorest elements of our society to pay for the activities of the broad middle and upper classes. NCAA president Mark Emmert calls this "a terrible argument," as if somehow his derision can erase

---

38 There are more Division III lacrosse schools than Division I and II combined. "Men's Division III Conference Standings," Inside Lacrosse, http://games.insidelacrosse.com/standings/league/3/DIII (last visited August 4, 2011).

39 "According to an annual survey by the N.C.A.A., every program in Division III loses money. And because of their low profiles, teams in the division have limited cachet among some donors and alumni." Jim Naughston, "In Division III, College Sports Thrive with Few Fans and Even Fewer Scandals," Netfiles.UIUC.edu, November 21, 1997. Of course, this analysis likely suffers from many of the problems of Division I NCAA accounting, but compared to Division I, Division III has fewer revenues to misallocate and no athletic scholarship costs to overstate.

40 As of 2009, 46 percent of all FBS football players were African American. In the same year, 60 percent of all Division I men's basketball players were African American. C. Keith Harrison, *Protecting Their Turf: The Head Football Coach Hiring Process, and the Practices of FBS & FCS Colleges and Universities* (2009), 11–12, available at http://grfx.cstv.com/photos/schools/bca/genrel/auto_pdf/09-football-hrc.pdf. The stars of these sports are even more likely to be African American; the NBA is over 80 percent African American ("NBA Gets High Marks for Diversity in New Study," NBA.com, June 10, 2009, http://www.nba.com/2009/news/06/10/NBA.diversity.ap/index.html), and the NFL is approximately two-thirds African American (Travis Reed, "Study: NFL Has Slightly More Latino, Asian Players," USAToday.com, August 27, 2008, http://www.usatoday.com/sports/football/2008-08-27-1555250552_x.htm).

these economic facts.[41] But as Nobel Prize–winning economist Gary Becker put it:

> A large fraction of the Division I players in basketball and football, the two big money sports, are recruited from poor families; many of them are African-Americans from inner cities and rural areas. Every restriction on the size of scholarships that can be given to athletes in these sports usually takes money away from poor athletes and their families, and in effect transfers these resources to richer students in the form of lower tuition and cheaper tickets for games.[42]

So we really might, in a few cases, decide some of the nonrevenue sports we have on campus really are unwanted given all of the other priorities on campus, and as a result some schools might cancel some programs. But again, recognize that if we did allow football and basketball players to earn a market level of compensation, other inputs would probably become less expensive. This is a very important concept that people often ignore. When economic competition is restricted on a given dimension, it flows into other, less efficient avenues. By allowing the NCAA cartel to dictate the maximum amount each school can pay for talent while allowing that talent to generate excessive profits, we create incentives for schools to find other (expensive) ways to attract that talent. For example, the University of Oregon built the Jaqua Academic Center for Student Athletes, which is a glass palace, combining a Duck Hall of Fame with an exclusive tutoring facility for student athletes and a fancy eatery, all aimed at attracting the best players to Oregon. Millions are spent on lavish facilities like this because the efficient method to attract talent, simply offering a higher compensation package, is not allowed.[43] The so-called arms race in college sports to build bigger and better facilities would be dampened by allowing schools to compete by directly paying those whom the race is trying to influence. If the money is going to be spent anyway, let's direct it to the people generating the

41 "Selling the NCAA," *Outside the Lines*, ESPN, March 13, 2011, http://sports.espn.go.com/espn/otl/news/story?id=6209609.

42 Gary Becker, "The NCAA as a Powerful Cartel," *The Becker-Posner Blog*, April 3, 2011, http://www.becker-posner-blog.com/2011/04/the-ncaa-as-a-powerful-cartel-becker.html.

43 Oregon is not alone. Another classic example is the University of Michigan. See "Stephen M. Ross Academic Center," MGoBlue.com, http://www.mgoblue.com/facilities/ross-academic-center.html (last visited August 3, 2011).

revenue, not large construction firms. If schools could sweeten their offers with cash, they might also be able to spend a little less on the female escorts they currently use as enticements.[44]

The ban on paying players also creates a tremendous windfall for coaches and athletic directors. Recruiting is the lifeblood of a college sports program. If money were an available recruiting tool, it would go to the players. Instead, the money flows to those who are most responsible for getting star players to enroll and play at that school. As discussed above, Mack Brown earned over $6 million in 2009 (after bonuses) because Texas knows he can bring in talent better than other coaches.[45] In the market-compensation world, Texas would not need to pay as much for Brown's ability to charm athletes and their parents; they could show interest in athletes by offering a large annual grant in excess of the cost of attendance. Mack Brown would still be worth millions in this new world, just not six of them per year.

And then some of those millions would be there if we decide we still want a lacrosse team. Or we could spend it on more science courses, or however the university wants to allocate its money, but now we would not be imposing an involuntary subsidy on the eighty-five football and thirteen men's basketball players, asking them to support the rest of the athletic department on their backs.

## MYTH 6: We Can't Pay Them or Else We'd Violate Title IX.

In the analysis above, I focused my examples on men's sports because there is an important government program with the laudable goal of ensuring proper funding for women's sports. Title IX has been one of the great success stories of government-driven social change. So it's a great program, and yet a lot of sports people want to blame Title IX for why America can't do right by the men who play college football and basketball. It's not just a myth, it's a frame-up! We need to stop blaming women for what colleges, through collusion, are doing to male athletes.

The popular misconception is that Title IX mandates equal funding for men's and women's sports programs, with some believing that Title IX requires that each man and each woman get an identical scholarship. It does not do these

---

44  See, for example, Brooks, "Auburn Payroll: Tens of Thousands to Hostesses," *Sports by Brooks*, June 20, 2001, http://www.sportsbybrooks.com/auburn-payroll-tens-of-thousands-to-hostesses-29756.

45  It's not just because he is a good recruiter. Great coaches like Brown also need to do a great job with the talent once they have it, in order to earn their millions. However, excellence in recruiting is a sine qua non.

things, though in theory Title IX does require a rough equivalence in spending on scholarships. In practice this requirement is more commonly violated than met.

Title IX actually aims for gender equity in *participation* and the regulations offer three ways to comply, none of which speak directly to equal funding. One is meeting the needs of all of the underrepresented gender, the second is a subjective concept of progress toward equity, and the third and most common is actual equity in participation.[46] The regulations on participation test whether the number of women playing sports, relative to the number of men, is about on par with the gender split of the undergraduate population: "Whether intercollegiate level participation opportunities for male and female students are provided in numbers substantially proportionate to their respective enrollments."[47] The regulations then explain what this participation requirement means for spending:

> This section does not require a proportionate number of scholarships for men and women or individual scholarships of equal dollar value. It does mean that the total amount of scholarship aid made available to men and women must be substantially proportionate to their participation rates.[48]

So, in theory, if there are more women than men on campus (which is the norm),[49] the participation prong of Title IX requires that more women than men participate in intercollegiate sports. It does not require that the women's programs as a whole spend as much or more as men's programs, nor does it require that any individual female athlete get the same level of aid as any individual male athlete. However, it does require, at least in theory, that the proportion of

---

46 See letter from Gerald Reynolds, Assistant Secretary for Civil Rights, United States Department of Education, July 11, 2003, available at http://www2.ed.gov/about/offices/list/ocr/title9guidanceFinal.html.

47 Office for Civil Rights, "A Policy Interpretation: Title IX and Intercollegiate Athletics," *Federal Register* 44, no. 239 (December 11, 1979), available at http://www2.ed.gov/about/offices/list/ocr/docs/t9interp.html.

48 Ibid.

49 As of 2005, the national male/female ratio for undergraduates was forty-three to fifty-seven. Mary Beth Marklein, "College Gender Gap Widens: 57% Are Women," USAToday.com, October 19, 2005, http://www.usatoday.com/news/education/2005-10-19-male-college-cover_x.htm. Forty-three of the seventy-three schools in the BCS AQ conferences have more women than men on campus. "Best College Rankings and Lists," *U.S. News & World Report*, http://colleges.usnews.rankingsandreviews.com/best-colleges (last visited August 4, 2011).

spending on women's scholarships be "substantially proportional" to women's rate of participation, which has been interpreted to mean that the ratio of spending on women athletes' financial aid be within one percentage point of the ratio of women's participation.[50]

So, how does this hold out in practice? In 2009–10, twenty-two of the seventy-three BCS AQ programs had more women participants than men, but all seventy-three of the BCS AQ conference schools spent more in total on men's sports than on women's sports.[51] All but three of those with FBS football spent more on men's scholarships than women's.[52] Using the "1 percent" test, of the fifty-one schools with more male than female athletes, only seven kept the ratio of spending on women's scholarships within 1 percent of their participation ratio.[53] And of the twenty-two schools in which women comprise the majority of participation, seventeen of those schools nevertheless spent more on men's scholarships (all outside the 1 percent threshold). So, sixty-one of the seventy-three major sports programs are in violation of the (theoretical) requirements of Title IX. From this, I conclude that in practice, Title IX does not actually mean that colleges spend the same on men's and women's sports—not at the program level, not at the individual athlete level, not at the aggregate scholarship level, and not even with a 1 percent cushion relative to participation ratios.

---

50  This interpretation is according to the National Women's Law Center: "the percentages of athletic scholarship money awarded to male and female athletes should be within one percent of their respective participation rates, unless the school can show why a bigger gap is not discriminatory." Linda Bunker et al., "Check It Out: Is the Playing Field Level for Women and Girls at Your School?," National Women's Law Center, September 14, 2011, http://www.nwlc.org/resource/check-it-out-playing-field-level-women-and-girls-your -school. I have not seen this specific 1 percent language from the Department of Education, but I assume it to be true in my analysis that follows.

51  "The Equity in Athletics Data Analysis Cutting Tool," Office of Postsecondary Education, http://ope.ed.gov/athletics/GetDownloadFile.aspx.

52  Ibid. Of schools with FBS football, only the books of Syracuse, Georgia, and UCLA show a higher value for women's athletic scholarships than men's. Interestingly, six schools of the seven non-FBS Big East schools provide more funding to women for scholarships than men. For DePaul, Seton Hall, St. John's, Providence, and Marquette, this task is substantially easier because they do not give football scholarships at all (because they either have no varsity football or compete in Division III). Georgetown and Villanova both play FCS football, with Villanova funding men's scholarships more than women's and Georgetown funding women's scholarships more than men's.

53  Among the fifty-one schools with higher male participation, twenty-three had a spending ratio more than one percentage point higher than their participation rate, seven were within one percentage point (plus or minus), and twenty-one had a spending ratio more than one percentage point lower than their participation rate.

Title IX is also not being applied as a strict rule on equal compensation with respect to coaches. The regulations state that the requirement that schools "provide equal athletic opportunities for members of both sexes" extends to "compensation of coaches." Despite this, all seventy-three of the BCS AQ programs spend more on head coaches for their men's teams than for their women's teams.[54] All seventy-three also spend more on assistant coaches for men's teams than for women's teams.[55] For example, in 2009–10, Rick Barnes, the men's basketball head coach at Texas, earned $1.7 million more than Gail Goestenkors, his counterpart with Texas's women's basketball team.[56] Yet rarely is it claimed that Title IX prevents schools from paying their men's teams' coaches—either at all or more than they pay women's coaches. But if you insist on misreading Title IX to say you can't pay players, that same misreading would mean you can't pay men's teams' coaches more than you pay women's coaches. And we know this just isn't what Title IX means in practice.

Thus, if colleges were to implement a market-based compensation system for athletes along the lines of the market-based compensation for coaches, it is not at all clear that they would have to pay women athletes any more equally to men athletes than they currently do with coaches.

Despite all of this empirical evidence, let's assume that with a market-based compensation system for athletes, enforcement of the letter of Title IX would suddenly emerge to force a stricter standard on schools than currently exists, so that every dollar spent paying male athletes would require an equal new dollar to be spent on women's sports. Or instead, assume that some enlightened schools would choose to undertake this burden voluntarily and would simply commit on their own that spending money to pay male athletes a market rate would also result in equal increases in women's funding, dollar for dollar, even though they currently do not have this intense commitment to spending equity.

Wonderful! Indeed, this might be the greatest boon to women's sports since Title IX itself.

If each new dollar of spending went equally to men and women, the system would function like a 100 percent payroll tax on male college athletes' pay. If a

---

54  The average difference across all sports for head coaches was $2.8 million per school (or $438,000 per full-time equivalent coach per school).

55  The average difference across all sports for assistant coaches was also $2.8 million per school. The average difference per full-time equivalent per school for assistant coaches was $87,000 for each assistant coach position.

56  University of Texas at Austin Information for the Reporting Year: 2010 (last visited August 3, 2011). This data was gathered through my own independent research.

star quarterback is worth $50,000 to a school, and they knew that for every dollar they spent on him they would also need to allocate a dollar to women's sports, then the most they could afford to offer him would be $25,000, knowing the other $25,000 had to go to meet their (theoretical) Title IX pay equity burden. As every school would have this same tax burden, competition for those athletes would be fair, but muted.

Economics teaches us that a high payroll tax will keep salaries down, but not eliminate them.[57] In this extreme interpretation of Title IX's mandate, the system would take advantage of the high demand for male athletes to funnel a lot more money into women's sports (which is the point of Title IX, after all). Title IX doesn't stop male athletes from receiving market-based compensation any more than cigarette taxes have eradicated smoking in this country.

And so regardless of whether Title IX mandates that every new dollar of spending must be spent equally on men's and women's sports, nothing about Title IX makes paying male athletes impossible. The idea that we can blame women for the collusive injustice colleges impose on male basketball and football players is a myth that needs to go the way of Bobby Riggs.

### MYTH 7: The NCAA Sells Amateurism and If We Allow Players to Get Paid, the Popularity of the Sport Will Decline.

This is an oft-heard assertion for which I think there is no evidence and where we can see a lot of counter-evidence.

From 1953 until 1973, in addition to all of the in-kind payments players receive today, college athletes also got "laundry money" that when adjusted for inflation would be over $100 a month today. No one boycotted college sports over laundry money.

Major sports like tennis, golf, and the Olympics all used to be scrupulously amateur for fear of losing viewers. The tide has shifted so much that the PGA Tour now uses money earnings to rank golfers, Wimbledon pays out £1 million

---

57 For example, when Social Security or Medicare payroll taxes go up, unemployment doesn't jump to 100 percent. Philip Morris estimates that cigarette taxes in the United States exceed 50 percent of the final purchase price (http://www.philipmorris usa.com/en/cms/ Responsibility/Government_Affairs/Legislative_Issues/Cigt_Excise_Tax/default.aspx ?src=search), which is effectively a tax in excess of 100 percent. Cigarette sales are obviously still occurring in the United States. In Denmark cars are sold with a 180 percent tax (see Finn Skovgaard, *The Danish Page*), and while this does lower demand, nevertheless Danes buy hundreds of thousands of cars every year (Economist Intelligence Unit, *Economist*, January 1, 2011).

to its champions, and the idea of an amateur-only tennis or golf tournament is quaint.[58]

The idea that no one would watch professional Olympians was shattered when the (professional) Dream Team, led by Michael Jordan, Michael Johnson, and Larry Bird, captivated the world; all are now part of the U.S. Olympic Hall of Fame.[59] Other sports around the world have also gained revenue after abandoning amateurism.[60] I have to question the dire predictions that college sports will die if true students at real colleges also get paid for their athletics, all while continuing to go to class and to play great sports. There just isn't a lot of evidence that says sports are more popular when the athletes are unpaid or underpaid.[61]

If it is amateurism that drives the popularity of college sports, why are Division III[62] stadiums so small? If you had two fifty-yard-line tickets for next year's BCS championship game, and you found out the players for both teams

---

58 Generally speaking, the one amateur invited to the U.S. Open each year is treated as a cuddly curiosity. "Prize Money at Wimbledon (1968–2011)," All England Lawn Tennis and Croquet Club.

59 Jeff Kalafa, "Michael Jordan's '92 Olympic Dream Team," *Bleacher Report*, August 11, 2010, http://bleacherreport.com/articles/433371-jordans-92-olympic-dream-team-was-it-best-basketball-team-ever.

60 Twentieth-century examples include rugby in Australia, New Zealand, and the UK. In nineteenth-century British soccer, the Football Association (FA) was originally amateur until it absorbed a rival professional soccer league, which led eventually (in 1992) to the Premier League, the most watched sports league in the world, "Premier League History," Premier League, http://www.premierleague.com/page/History/0,12306,00.html. Baseball's origins began with amateur teams, then with players being given nonsports fictitious jobs to maintain the illusion of amateurism, until 1869 when the Cincinnati Red Stockings formed as the first professional team, and thereafter the modern major leagues emerged. Toru Mihara, "Labor Negotiations in the Major League Baseball History," Athletes Dream Management.

61 Athletes in the major U.S. professional sports like the NFL and MLB used to receive a very small share of the revenues that they generated, but once a truly free market was introduced through free agency, the athletes began receiving much more money. For example, in MLB in 1950 during the era of the reserve clause, player payroll was 17.6 percent of total team revenue. In 1994 it reached a peak of 60.5 percent and has remained over 50 percent since then. Despite the increased pay, demand for the sport, as measured in total league television team revenue, increased tenfold from 1964 to 2001, after adjusting for inflation (without that adjustment, revenues have increased sixty times over). See Michael J. Haupert, "The Economic History of Major League Baseball," University of Wisconsin–La Crosse, Tables 1 and 5, available at https://eh.net/encyclopedia/the-economic-history-of-major-league-baseball/.

62 Division III colleges do not give any athletic scholarships, just academic or need-based grants. Lynn O'Shaughnessy, "Why Athletes Have an Edge at Elite Colleges," *CBS Money Watch*, June 2, 2009, http://moneywatch.bnet.com/saving-money/article/why-athletes-have-an-edge-at-elite-colleges/307433/.

were being paid, would you give away your tickets? Would you sell them for less than face value? Would you swap them even-up for the Division III championship? Or would you go and watch a great football game played by the (paid) college superstars?

What matters isn't the pay scale; it's the quality of the football and the loyalty to the school. If the University of Florida (Florida) pays its players, will Gator fans switch their allegiance to the University of Central Florida (UCF) Knights? Can anyone credibly make this claim? And yet the NCAA's theory argues that collusive amateurism is a reasonable and necessary practice without which the product could not exist. This theory says that Florida fans would choose UCF because the NCAA sells amateurism and that's what fans want.

Of course, I disagree, and in fact I have trouble believing that anyone other than those paid by the NCAA could argue with a straight face that what makes the product popular is the unpaid status of the players. But we don't need to trust my intuition; we can just end the collusion and let each school decide on its own what its fans want. If it's amateurism that drives demand, the few schools that try paying athletes will quickly lose popularity and have to revert to the old scholarship system. The rule against pay will have been proven unnecessary, but the sport will continue on in the current amateur form. If those schools don't lose popularity, or if they gain popularity as they start to attract more talent, then the claim that amateurism was needed to protect fan interest will be proven false. Look deep inside yourself and ask which scenario you think will hold, say, in Tuscaloosa, Alabama; Austin, Texas; or Columbus, Ohio.

Instead, if we let each school choose its own appropriate level of compensation, fans of college sports would have more choice, not less. Most college athletes (at approximately one thousand schools across Divisions I, II, and III) would continue to receive the same level of scholarship support as they do (or do not) receive now, and would continue to play sports with just as little fanfare while generating virtually no revenue. And for the small percentage of athletes who drive the billions of dollars, fan interest would remain high, even as the players started getting a market level of compensation for their popular product: big-time college football.

## MYTH 8: If Student-Athletes Earn Anything More Than They Currently Get, They Stop Being Students.

As part of the NCAA's claim that it sells amateurism, it's often heard that if college athletes were to be paid, they would stop being students. Mark Emmert, the new NCAA president, advanced this argument on an ESPN story in March.[63] But regular students earn money all the time. Ask your bursar's office if having a paying job disqualifies you for being a full-time student. It doesn't.

James Franco was a paid actor while majoring in English at UCLA, other English majors were paid to work at the library, and still others got money from their families and didn't have to work at all. They were all students.

Northeastern is known for its co-op education program, where undergraduates alternate between the classroom and paying jobs while remaining full-time students. Northeastern has not lost its accreditation, and no student has been stripped of a bachelor's degree because news leaked that a "Northeastern student in a co-op position works full-time (five-days a week) for a period of six-months and is usually paid" and yet "Students on co-op are still considered full-time students."[64]

Forgoing pay is not what turns football players into real college students. Attending college is what does that. Being a college student means being enrolled in real courses at a real school. College athletes are students for all of the nonsports things they do: going to class, joining a study group, and falling asleep in the library. Getting paid when they play football would not change their student status at all, just as a computer science major who creates a successful iPhone app and earns $100,000 from downloads doesn't have to leave the university in shame for having "gone pro."

I guarantee you there is no amateurism test for students who are not athletes. So why do we allow one for students who are athletes in the name of making them more like other students?

If done right, a system where college athletes get paid could easily be crafted to enhance, not diminish, their "studentness." It's easy to imagine athlete's pay packages containing sizable bonuses for graduation instead of (or in addition to) for reaching bowl games.[65] For students with real financial need, a paying job as a football or basketball player could mean passing on a summer job and taking classes instead, allowing them to graduate before they run out of

63 See Tom Farrey and Paula Lavigne, "Selling the NCAA," *Outside the Lines*, ESPN, March 13, 2011, http://sports.espn.go.com/espn/otl/news/story?id=6209609. I presented a dissenting view in the same article.

64 All quotes in this paragraph come from "Parents," Northeastern University Cooperative Education.

65 Another option schools might choose to offer is low (or no) annual pay combined with a deferred payment into a trust fund, which only becomes available upon graduation.

eligibility and the school loses interest in them. On the other hand, schools with a real interest in their athlete will be able to offer a compensation package that includes guaranteed tuition until the student graduates, unlike the current system in which the NCAA limits scholarships to renewable one-year deals so schools cannot guarantee they will pay an athlete's way until he graduates. And of course, well-paid college athletes might be in a much better position to pay for an extra year if they need it out of their earnings from their four or five years of college athletics.

**MYTH 9:** If We Pay Them, Inevitably They Will All Just Become Mercenaries. Alternately, If We Pay Them, We Might as Well Give Up the Charade of Academics and Just Make Them into Mercenaries.

The opposite of "college" is not "professional." As discussed above, there is nothing about paying a college student that causes him to lose his status as a full-time student. Convincing us all that "college" and "amateur" are synonyms is one of the NCAA's greatest sleights of hand. Thus paying students doesn't immediately turn them into faithless mercenaries with no connection to their college or university. We could have that system if we wanted, but it's not required, and if we went in that direction, the popularity of the sport likely would suffer. College sports is great for both reasons, college and sports. I can utter those words without mentioning whether the college students playing sports were paid or not.

We are not limited to a choice between the current system (students paid collusive, in-kind wages) and a system based on pure mercenaries playing for any school regardless of their educational status. We can have a debate over whether college sports could also be professional (i.e., paid a market level of compensation) or if, by their very essence, college sports must always maintain the NCAA's approximation of amateur (i.e., a collusively decided maximum level of cash and in-kind compensation)[66] without assuming that a change in pay will also require a change to the other dimension, college versus no college. We have four choices, not two:

---

66 Generally, a student living on campus with an on-campus eating plan will be paid only in kind, but students living off-campus or without a campus eating plan typically get a monthly paycheck. In total, these payments (whether in cash or in kind) are set collusively at about $3,000 less than the expenses the students incur attending college. So we're really not comparing amateur versus pro, we're comparing collusively low pay to market pay. But for the purposes of this paper, I will follow the common parlance that college players are currently amateur even though that too is a myth.

|  | Capped In-Kind Payment ("Amateur") | Market-Rate Payment ("Professional") |
|---|---|---|
| **College** | Current NCAA<br>*Popular* | My proposal<br>*Likely to be popular* |
| **Noncollege** | True amateurs playing in the park, club Ultimate Frisbee, postcollegiate rugby, etc.<br>*Not popular* | NBA D-League and other minor leagues<br>*Not popular* |

There are good, economically procompetitive reasons why college sports should involve college students, and not just college-aged players who work for, but do not study at, the school for which they play. While NCAA argues that it sells amateurism, I think what the NCAA sells is high-quality sports played by college kids.

A special, demand-enhancing connection develops between alumni and college athletes when those athletes walk onto campus and put on the uniform. Sports fans from that school and the region feel a bond—I went there too, I lived in those dorms, I took those classes, or I've been there and seen them in the library, etc. There really is a special quality to college sports because of the link between college and athlete. The rules designed to keep college sports from being filled with noncollegiate ringers are in a completely different realm than the rules designed to help colleges save money by not paying players. Requiring that athletes also be students is pro-competitive because it strengthens demand for the product (as opposed to the cap on payment, which merely saves costs). Similarly, rules against transfers that prevent students from being traded or from becoming weekly free agents also serve to reinforce that these are real college students[67] and thus also serve a procompetitive role.

The reasonableness and necessity of the collective agreement on ensuring that college athletes really go to college is an excellent contrast with the lack of reason for or necessity of the NCAA's collective agreement on athlete compensation. When the NCAA argues that if the college sport became just a normal minor league, it would be less popular, they are entirely correct, but that would happen only if the athletes lose their true connection to the university, not because they would get paid. What makes college sports so popular is the unique combination of high-quality athletics combined with the notion that the athletes attend school and truly represent the school in competitions. This makes

---

67 As would rules allowing them to earn money from their schools just like other real college students can and do.

the NCAA rule that college athletes be college students procompetitive, in the same way that the lack of necessity for the rule on pay leaves that rule unjustified and anticompetitive.[68]

The 1984 Supreme Court *Board of Regents*[69] decision may be the worst thing that ever happened to college athletes, because, despite the NCAA's arguments to the contrary,[70] it enshrined (in *dicta*) the disastrous idea that for the NCAA to sell a product connected with college also required that "athletes must not be paid."[71] But the dicta got the main story correct: "the NCAA seeks to market a particular brand of football—college football. The identification of this 'product' with an academic tradition differentiates college football from and makes it more popular than professional sports to which it might otherwise be comparable, such as, for example, minor league baseball."[72] The NBA's Development League (the D-League) also pits young, talented, not-quite-ready-for-the-NBA athletes against each other in high-quality basketball. Its lack of popularity might stem from the fact that those athletes are paid. But it's hard to imagine that if you stopped paying D-League players, fans would suddenly flock to see those games and networks would clamor to broadcast them throughout the season. It's easier to imagine those same players being more popular than now if they were on a college team, but still paid. With that in mind, can it really be amateurism that drives interest in sports played by college-age kids just below the NBA's or NFL's level of talent? If not, why do we allow schools to collude to enforce it?

---

68  It's not as if college sports is the only business where there are many jobs that have rules of eligibility. Elected officials and some public employees must reside in the city they serve. Many jobs require a specific degree; to be a doctor you must be an MD, and to cut hair you need a cosmetology license. Such requirements, even across an entire industry, are not akin to price fixing. The NCAA already has academic eligibility requirements, and if the compensation rules change, there is no natural reason to end the requirement that student-athletes be students.

69  National Collegiate Athletic Ass'n v. Board of Regents of University of Oklahoma, 468 U.S. 85 (1984).

70  In the oral argument before the Supreme Court in *Board of Regents*, the NCAA argued that paying the athletes would increase demand for the product. "When the NCAA says, we are running programs of amateur football, it is probably reducing its net profits. It might be able to get more viewers and so on if it had semi-professional clubs rather than amateur clubs." See Oral Arguments of National Collegiate Athletic Ass'n v. Board of Regents of University of Oklahoma, March 20, 1984, available at http://www.oyez.org/cases/1980-1989/1983/1983_83_271.

71  "In order to preserve the character and quality of the 'product,' athletes must not be paid, must be required to attend class, and the like." *Id.* at 102.

72  *Id.*

The D-League isn't popular because no one is an alumnus or alumna of the Rio Grande Valley Vipers and because those Vipers aren't college students. Students and alumni who are fans of a team connect with the team because the players represent them directly. When I asked whether Florida fans could switch allegiance to UCF over the issue of pay, it seemed ridiculous, because who could abandon a beloved alma mater for someplace else? Do Stanford students living in Berkeley suddenly bleed blue and gold? How can we imagine them abandoning the farm simply because Stanford's college athletes started getting paid?

We could get rid of the college in college athlete,[73] but it would not help the athletes and it would not help the fans.[74]

## MYTH 10: What They Get Is Very Valuable, It Should Be Enough. How Can You Say What They Get Is Unfair? I Wish My Kid Got That Deal!

A commonly cited NCAA canard is that because the average college graduate earns $1 million more over the course of the average lifetime, a GIA is worth $1 million. Of course that's ridiculous. The right way to value an asset that is sold

---

73  Or if you prefer, the student in student-athlete.

74  On March 25, 2011, Ralph Nader proposed doing away with all athletic scholarships. "Ralph Nader: Replace Scholarships," ESPN, April 4, 2011, http://sports.espn.go.com/ncaa/news/story?id=6254572. I believe this was primarily an attention-grabbing way of highlighting the plight of college athletes, because Nader offered an alternative to ending scholarships, which was to pay the athletes. But as a thought exercise, it's interesting to imagine what would happen if a law were passed that specifically banned a college or university from giving athletic scholarships. I am certain almost nothing would change. Currently boosters donate to athletic departments, which in turn transfer the money to the university to pay for the athletic scholarships. In Nader's world, those boosters would give money to private foundations that would spring up to pay the way of each school's chosen athletes through special scholarships that look a lot like today's Rotary Club scholarships, except they would go just to athletes. The NCAA would find a way to bless this arrangement as amateur and we'd be right where we are now, except boosters would have a tighter control over athletes, with the threat of a lost scholarship coming not from the coach, but the wealthy fans who control the foundations.

Perhaps it is Nader's intent to actually end college sports. His proposal won't do that, but as it stands, each university currently has a right to do that. In 1939 the University of Chicago, worried at the undue influence of intercollegiate sports on its mission, abandoned big-time sports. "University of Chicago in the Big Ten," HistoryKB.com, May 13, 2004. The Ivy League has never given out scholarships based solely on athletic prowess. Bill Pennington, "Ivy Football and Academics Strike an Uneasy Balance," NYTimes.com, November 17, 2006, http://www.nytimes.com/2006/11/17/sports/ncaafootball/17ivy.html?pagewanted=print. This choice is available to any school now, but almost all of them choose to stay in the business of college sports. The Nader plan is the opposite of a free-market solution, because it imposes a single rule on all schools, treating universities like children, rather than letting the campus community makes its own choice whether to have athletics on campus or not.

in a marketplace is to look at the price at which that asset is sold. If a year at Louisiana State University (LSU) is worth $250,000, why is out-of-state tuition set at $13,800? That said, a GIA is in fact very valuable and of course any parent would love to have the school pick up the tab for one of the most expensive investments they will ever make in their child. Plus, to the extent a student gets into a school that their grades and test scores might not otherwise merit, it's hard to place a specific dollar value on that entrée.[75] But that misses the point entirely. The point is not that college athletes get no value in exchange for playing sports for their schools, since they clearly are getting compensated with a valuable scholarship.[76] If the NCAA did not collude to limit how much each school can offer to incoming high school football and basketball players, those athletes destined for the major conferences would get everything that they currently get and far, far more. The idea is not that the GIA isn't valuable (although the million-dollar claim is laughable), but rather that it is far less than the value of what the schools would gladly pay in a free market, if the NCAA didn't cap compensation.

In 1929, legend has it that Babe Ruth was asked why he deserved to earn more than then president Herbert Hoover. His answer? "I had a better year."[77] The reason that athletes get better scholarships than your kid is that they generally are going to have a much better year, financially, for the school they represent. Sure, I'd like my brainy but nonathletic kid (who will bring no revenue to his college despite having won on *Jeopardy!* before he turned thirteen) to get free tuition, room and board, and required books. Who wouldn't? A few schools give their most desired academic recruits a (true) full ride that is even better than their full athletic scholarship,[78] but generally speaking, college athletes get the best deals a college offers because they are the most valuable. And if the schools were operating in a market system where they could give more, they

---

75 Even still, remember, the economic value of that entrée is really just the difference between the value of the school the athlete wouldn't otherwise merit and the school he would have attended.

76 And again, this also makes clear they aren't really amateurs, all the more so since the NCAA requires that schools make their scholarship one-year renewables rather than allowing them to commit to give the scholarship even if the athlete leaves the team.

77 "Babe Ruth Quotes," Baseball-Almanac.com, http://www.baseball-almanac.com/quotes /quoruth.shtml: "What the hell has Hoover got to do with it [Ruth's contract being bigger than the president's]? Besides, I had a better year than he did."

78 One such example is North Carolina's Morehead-Cain Scholarship, which is a higher-value scholarship than the maximum allowable GIA because it truly covers all six costs of attendance as well as providing a laptop computer and "Discovery Funds" above and beyond normal travel and living expenses. "About Morehead-Cain," http://moreheadcain .org/morehead-cain/.

would, because even at the current full-ride price, college athletes are cheap relative to the profits they bring in, and competition would force schools to pay more to get the most prized recruits.

The critical difference between your high schooler and the incoming athlete is that schools do not (and legally cannot) collude on how much they offer to your kid or mine. In the past when some schools tried to do this, the Department of Justice made them stop.[79] So if your kid didn't get a sweet offer, it's not because of collusion; instead, it's probably because he or she just isn't going to generate millions. And that's the difference—your kid gets what he or she earns, college athletes get only what a cartel allows them to get, even though without that collusion they would get everything they get now and much more.

## MYTH 11: We Can't Pay Them or Else We'd Violate NCAA Rules. These People Are Not Employees!

Although the circularity of this argument should be clear, nevertheless this argument is made all the time by otherwise intelligent people, including the NCAA's Mark Emmert.[80] The primary reason that college athletes are not employees is because the NCAA doesn't pay them. So they aren't employees because they don't get paid and they can't get paid because they are not employees. Amazingly, this completely irrational argument appears to be the new centerpiece of the current NCAA defense. Indeed, if it were not so central to the NCAA's new public relations blitz, I would have hesitated to include it as myth because it's really too inane to be worthy of discussion.

However, since it is the current NCAA position, here goes. This argument is the equivalent of banning airplanes from leaving the ground and then saying air travel is physically impossible because, after all, airplanes don't fly. Other than in name, college athletes are like employees. They perform a service for the school and are compensated via a GIA. For many college athletes, a GIA includes a monthly amount in cash. The school reserves the right to "fire" them at the end of every year, because all scholarships (by NCAA mandate) are one year only, and must be renewed each year,[81] and so many athletes have had their

---

79  It also preemptively prohibited price fixing on tuition and faculty salaries. Sharon Lafraniere, "Ivy League Schools Settle Government's Price-Fixing Suit," *Seattle Times*, May 23, 1991, http://community.seattletimes.nwsource.com/archive/?date=19910523&slug=1284840.

80  Tom Farrey and Paula Lavigne, "Selling the NCAA," *Outside the Lines*, ESPN, March 13, 2011, http://sports.espn.go.com/espn/otl/news/story?id=6209609.

81  A survey by the *Sporting News* in 1994 found that 25 percent of juniors and seniors playing college sports had their coach threaten to terminate their scholarship at some point

scholarships terminated when the school found a better "nonemployee" to do their "nonjob" that there is pending litigation over the practice.[82]

Colleges used to argue that graduate students who serve as teaching assistants on campus were "amateur," but many states have recognized that teaching assistants perform a service like any other employee. Many schools treat graduate instructors as employees, and even the ones that refuse to grant them employee status still pay them. The IRS taxes all of them as employees, whether the schools call them that or not.[83] The only reason that the NCAA is able to say that athletes are not employees is because the NCAA forbids schools from paying them—it's not the reason we can't pay them, it's the result of not paying them (and indeed, we could pay them like graduate teaching instructors and still not call them employees). But whether we do or do not call them employees, the reason they are not paid is because of a collusive agreement among the NCAA Division I schools. End the collusive agreement and this argument goes away too.

## MYTH 12: It Would Be Dangerous to Have Students on Campus with That Much Money. They Aren't Old Enough to Know How to Manage It. Athletes Will Just Blow It All on Bling and Drugs.

The previous myth was deeply illogical, and it's embarrassing that the NCAA, a group of highly educated people, puts it forward as fact. But I am more ashamed by this myth, which I believe is deeply rooted in racism. If our concern were really with college kids having too much money on campus, we would pass a law prohibiting the children of the wealthy from coming to college unless their

---

during their playing career. Gene Wojciechowski, "Player Survey Reveals Flaws in the System," *Sporting News*, April 25, 1994.

82  See Hagens Berman, Class-Action Lawsuit filed October 25, 2010, http://www.hbsslaw .com/file.php?id=663&key=99b3ce7829575cf94aacb1a6dae9decc.

83  There are at least twenty legally recognized graduate student unions. "Recognized Graduate Employee Unions in the USA," CGEU Contact List. From 2000 to 2004, it was the position of the federal government that all graduate students were employees under the NLRA and thus able to unionize. Now the federal position is mixed, with the NLRB stating graduate students are not employees with respect to the right to unionize (which very well might apply to paid college athletes as well), but the IRS stating that they are employees with respect to whether their pay is taxable. "Taxable Income for Students," Internal Revenue Service. "Payment for Services" example: "Gary Thomas receives a scholarship of $2,500 for the spring semester. As a condition of receiving the scholarship, he must serve as a part-time teaching assistant. Of the $2,500 scholarship, $1,000 represents payment for his services. Gary is a degree candidate, and his tuition is $1,600. He can exclude $1,500 from income as a qualified scholarship. The remaining $1,000, representing payment for his services, is taxable."

parents agreed not to provide them with any money. We would have stopped Natalie Portman from going to Harvard with her *Star Wars* riches.

Face it. What the proponents of this argument are really saying is that they are uncomfortable with poor African American adult men, suddenly earning more money than they've ever had before, and facing tough decisions about how to spend or save that money. The images of concern people raise are not of someone blowing the money on trips to Paris to see art in the Louvre. It's Cadillac Escalades, jewelry and tattoos, or guns and drugs that are conjured up as the perils of pay for play.[84] And while sometimes the examples given are white,[85] that's not the stereotype most likely put on display when this argument is trotted out.

We need to stop saying that we do not trust young adults of any race with money and that we're colluding on pay for their own good. We especially need to stop almost-saying that we feel that way because we do not like how young African-American males decide to spend their money. If we are really worried about the financial wisdom of the college athletes who would suddenly find themselves much better off than they are now, then by all means, let's offer

---

84 Some examples from the Internet: "Despite Coach Williams's defense of the idea of paying student-athletes salaries, these same students are continuously making poor irresponsible decisions. Society cannot afford to pay athletes who are being looked up to by countless children across the nation who are indirectly led to believe that student-athletes' behaviors are acceptable. Four University of Tennessee men's basketball players' (Tyler Smith, 23, junior point guard Melvin Goins, 22, junior center Brian Williams, 22, and sophomore guard Cameron Tatum, 21) reputations were all left tainted after they were all arrested during a traffic stop for speeding near campus on guns and weapons charges. Police reported that officers found a handgun with an altered serial number, a bag of marijuana and an open container of alcohol while Tatum was the player driving. Some of the most envied students on campus who play basketball on national television each week, and do not have to pay for a thing in their free time, are found playing with drugs and weapons. Their behavior is childish and irresponsible and should not be tolerated let alone rewarded with additional salaries." Kevin Doran, "Should College Athletes Be Paid?," *SLAM*, March 23, 2011, http://www.slamonline.com/online/college-hs/college/2011/03/should-college-athletes-be-paid/. "Now they want street money AND a $200,000 scholarship? One or the other, not both. I have paid more money to universities than I care to remember, including payments for my wife and three kids. So now you want to pay some chicken shit black or white football player so he can buy bling, ink and a car plus a cell phone, IPod, etc. We all know most, not all, but most, will waste that precious scholarship." John Taylor, "Seven SEC Coaches Would Pay Players—Out of Their Own Pockets," NBC Sports, June 1, 2011, http://collegefootballtalk.nbcsports.com/2011/06/01/seven-sec-coaches-would-pay-players-out-of-their-own-pockets/.

85 "The Naismith College Basketball Player of the Year for 2006 Duke guard J.J. Redick was arrested on a DUI charge the summer after graduating from Duke University right before he was about to enter the NBA Draft." Doran, "Should College Athletes Be Paid?"

financial education classes for all scholarship athletes.[86] Let's end the NCAA rules that prohibit college athletes from having paid financial advisers, agents, or lawyers to guide them with their careers and their money. Instead, the NCAA could provide free financial advisory services and could run an agent clearinghouse to prevent scam artists from exploiting college athletes. Rather than deny athletes a fair market wage because they might waste the money, let's help them invest it wisely.

## MYTH 13: Because a Few College Athletes Are Good Enough to Play in the Major Leagues or Europe, or Because College Athletes Could Choose to Take a Nonsports Job Directly Out of High School, Trying to Change the System Is Anticapitalist or Anti-American.

This myth is often phrased as something like "No one is putting a gun to these guys' heads." "It's a free country, so if they don't like what the NCAA is offering, get a job elsewhere." "Go to Europe." "Pump gas." "Just stop whining if you don't like the offered wage."[87]

Antitrust laws exist for a reason, as do labor laws. A capitalist society should recognize that collusion is damaging to a free-market economy. Indeed, the irony of this myth is that it is designed to prop up the current collusion in the name of capitalism, but the current collusion is basically socialist. The cartel's argument for this collusion is that because some schools may not survive in a competitive market (a questionable premise), all schools should agree to spend the same (artificially low) amount. And like the Soviets, the NCAA creates the legend of students who play football and basketball living together as comrades in a workers' paradise of low- or no-pay equality.

The NCAA maximum allowable athletic scholarship is not a free-market offer. It is a take-it-or-leave it offer by a monopsonist.[88] The smattering of high

---

86  I'm torn over whether making such education mandatory would itself be racist. I think not. I think it's fair to say that eighteen-year-olds of every background would benefit from the NCAA insisting that with newfound riches comes a newfound need for financial savvy and that the presumption that they all need some help to avoid making dumb choices cuts across racial lines.

87  See, for example, Bob Frantz, "Scholarships Are More Than Fair Compensation for College Athletes," *San Francisco Examiner*, April 17, 2011, http://archives.sfexaminer.com/san francisco/scholarships-are-more-than-fair-compensation-for-college-athletes/Content ?oid=2173345.

88  A monopsonist is the buying analog of a monopolist—that is, a single purchaser (here, of talent). See monopsony defined: "single-customer market: a situation in which a product

schoolers who can do better outside the NCAA does not mean the NCAA can escape from the fact that it is the sole option for the vast majority of college-aged athletes. The Hobson's choice they offer (my scholarship or no scholarship) is no choice at all.

## CONCLUSION

The NCAA myths laid out here are in essence a laundry list of potential procompetitive defenses for what on the surface is naked price fixing. Several of the myths[89] can be boiled down to a concern that without collusion, costs would rise. This includes, inter alia, the claim that schools are too poor to pay, that some schools cannot afford to keep up with others, that schools might have to use nonfootball money to support other sports, and even, when properly analyzed, that Title IX makes it more expensive to pay male athletes. It also includes the concern about making students into employees, which in some sense is really a concern about the increasing cost of workers' comp insurance or payroll taxes. But cost savings is a poor antitrust justification for the NCAA's collusion, as *Law v. NCAA* makes clear.[90]

A few of the myths[91] speak to a claim that the NCAA does not have market power, such as when the NCAA posits that anyone who doesn't like their GIA can go play in Europe or pump gas. This seems easily dispatched with a simple analysis of the NCAA's market share in a relevant antitrust market.

A few myths essentially question whether the market is an appropriate or efficient tool for setting prices.[92] I would hope the antitrust laws would not find in favor of an argument that markets are bad vehicles for setting prices.

Finally, what remains is the dubious claim that but for the collusion, the product would not exist. Increasingly, this seems ridiculous. Does anyone feel that next year's BCS championship would have lower ratings or lower attendance if the NCAA stops enforcing a maximum cap on athletic compensation? Of course, this is also an empirical question, which could be answered with data. One way is by natural experiment where some conferences could try paying their athletes, and as the quality players gravitated to those schools, we

---

or service is only bought and used by one customer," available at http://www.bing.com /Dictionary/search?q=define+monopsony&FORM=DTPDIA.

89  See myths 3, 4, 5, 6, and 11 above.

90  "[C]ost-cutting by itself is not a valid procompetitive justification." Law v. NCAA, 134 F.3d 1010, 1022 (10th Cir. 1998).

91  See myths 10 and 13 above.

92  See myths 1, 2, and 12 above.

could determine if fans gravitated away toward lower-quality but unpaid teams. Another is with a well-crafted, unbiased survey that gets at what drives fan interest in the game. It's hard to imagine a fan, when asked what is the best thing about college football, who responds, "Because they are unpaid!" But again, this is an empirical question that can be resolved with further research.

As it stands now, we have an NCAA assertion that the unpaid status of the player drives the popularity of the sport, balanced against a wealth of circumstantial evidence that fans love high-quality college sports and that when sports of all sorts in the past have "gone pro," the fans did not shift away to more amateur endeavors.

When the myths are stripped away, what's left? We could have a vibrant college athletics system where the elite programs pay competitive wages to their athletes and continue to dominate the sports as they do now. Other schools would pay less, get lesser talent, and win less often, just like they do now. Fans would still attend and watch on television. The government would not cut off schools for violating Title IX, because they would comply as much or more than they do now. Costs would rise, but not as much as you might think, because other costs would decline. Coaches would earn a little less, weight rooms would be a little less lavish. And some fairer portion of the billions in revenue would flow to the college athletes who generate them. And that's no myth.

# NATIONAL LETTER OF INDENTURE

## How College Athletes Are Similar to, and in Many Ways Worse Off Than, the Indentured Servants of Colonial Times

By Andy Schwarz and Jason Belzer

It is part of the mythos of college sports: young men and women enter our nation's universities as student-athletes, and after their playing careers have ended, they graduate and go on to great, successful lives. For many, the belief in the transformative power of an athletic scholarship is a true faith. Yet for a significant number of student-athletes, particularly in the sports of basketball and football, the compensation they receive in the form of a free education does little to steer them off a path in which they achieve far less than their more accomplished teammates.

Like many of today's college athletes, Daniel Dulany, a Queens native, came from family of modest means. His father had recently run into financial troubles, so Daniel was forced to transfer from an expensive private school. The free ride he received to Maryland was a blessing for his family. Daniel had always aspired to be an attorney, and promised himself that he would work hard and eventually get into law school.[1]

John Noblin, on the other hand, was a Norfolk native and grew up a Cavalier at heart. A young man from a family of little means, he saw the prospect of four years in Virginia with the opportunity to practice his craft, and a free education along with room and board, as a dream come true. Sure, the days would

---

1 "Daniel Dulany: Indentured Servant to Statesman," Teaching American History in Maryland, http://teaching.msa.maryland.gov/000001/000000/000050/html/t50.html.

be long, especially during the summer grind preparing for the fall season, but he would take to the field in search of glory.[2]

Dulany finished in three years and went to work for George Platter II, a successful lawyer.[3] He traveled to London, and upon finishing law school returned to Maryland and was admitted to the bar. He became a prominent attorney in Annapolis, and later a major land developer.

Hard work and a dream do not guarantee success. Noblin was not as fortunate as Dulany, and eventually entered the construction business.[4] Maybe Noblin was not to blame for his lack of success; maybe it was the fault of his agent, David Warren, for getting him a raw deal in the first place. Whatever the reason, Noblin would become just another statistic in a system where unpaid labor was exchanged for the promise of success that often was out of reach.

Among today's college athletes, for every Daniel Dulany there are many John Noblins. Yet for all the similarities, neither John nor Daniel ever played college sports. In fact, when Dulany immigrated from Queens County, Ireland, in 1703 and Noblin from Norfolk, England, in 1655, it would be more than a hundred years before the University of Virginia or Maryland would be established.[5]

Both Dulany and Noblin came to colonial America as indentured servants, part of a system for recruiting labor to America that flourished in the mid-Atlantic colonies of Virginia, Maryland, and Pennsylvania.[6] Indentured servitude was vital to the immigration of Europeans to the English colonies; by the late 1700s, more than half of all immigrants arriving in Philadelphia were indentured in some form.[7] Indenture was a term for a contract—one which bound the worker to a specific master for a fixed term. Indentured servants were promised free passage across the Atlantic, room and board, and often a chance to get an education or learn a trade as long as they fulfilled their contracts and served their

---

2 "Indentured Servants Basic Search Results," VirtualJamestown.org, http://www.virtual jamestown.org/indentures/search_indentures.cgi?start_page=10&search_type=basic& db=bristol_ind&servant_ln=% (last visited July 26, 2012).

3 "Daniel Dulany: Indentured Servant to Statesman."

4 "Indentured Servants Basic Search Results."

5 "Facts at a Glance," University of Virginia, http://www.virginia.edu/Facts/; "University of Maryland Timeline," University of Maryland, http://www.urhome.umd.edu/timeline/.

6 David W. Galenson, "The Rise and Fall of Indentured Servitude in the Americas: An Economic Analysis," *Journal of Economic History* 44, no. 1 (March 1984): 1–26.

7 Farley Grubb, "Redemptioner Immigration to Pennsylvania: Evidence on Contract Choice and Profitability," *Journal of Economic History* 46, no. 2 (June 1986): 407–18; Farley Grubb, "The Incidence of Servitude in Trans-Atlantic Migration, 1771–1804," *Explorations in Economic History* 22, no. 3 (1985): 316–39.

masters without pay for four years or so. Dulany was one of the few fortunate ones who built a notably prosperous career out of the hundreds of thousands of indentured servants who came to this land with the hope of creating a better life for themselves and their families.

Indentured servants typically lacked the resources to pay their way to a better world and thus faced a hard bargain—stay behind in their old lives with little prospect of advancement or else spend several years working only for room and board and training in the hope of bettering themselves. Some purchased passage by signing themselves into indenture in Europe; their shippers would then sell and assign their contract to a master in the colonies. As the market evolved, however, it became more common for the servants to choose their own master once they reached the colonies, negotiating their best terms they could, including the length of service and whether families could stay together.[8] On average, in exchange for passage across the Atlantic, a male indentured servant arriving in Philadelphia in the mid-eighteenth century could expect to give up 4.4 years of his life working without compensation, save for room, board, and a chance to hone his craft,[9] much as the typical college athlete can expect to spend four or five years earning money for his school paid only in room, board, and tuition and coaching.

Just as the prospects of an average college athlete having a successful professional career are quite small, the chances that an indentured servant would rise to a position of true prosperity or fame were also few and far between.

The system of indentured servitude arose to solve an economic problem—workers in Europe could not afford passage to the colonies of North America, and merchants and farmers in the colonies needed labor. Indentures allowed workers to buy their passage on credit, promising multiple years of labor in exchange for passage to America.[10] Indentured servants earned less than equivalent free laborers, forced to choose between languishing at home or selling themselves at a discount into a system in which masters extracted a portion of their value in exchange for their "free" ride.

Modern-day student-athletes, operating in a system eerily similar to that in which Dulany and Noblin served, face similar challenges—low prospects of

---

8 Servants who sold their own contracts in the colonies were known as "redemptioners." Redemptioners comprised the vast majority of servant contracts sold in Philadelphia in the second half of the eighteenth century. Grubb, "Redemptioner Immigration to Pennsylvania," 408, Table 1.

9 Farley Grubb, "The Market for Indentured Immigrants: Evidence on the Efficiency of Forward-Labor Contracting in Philadelphia, 1745–1773," *Journal of Economic History* 45, no. 4 (December 1985): 855–68.

10 Grubb, "The Market for Indentured Immigrants," 855.

turning professional in their sports after their college careers are over and a system in which a good deal of their value is transferred to others.

Before proclaiming that college athletics is a modern-day form of indentured servitude, it is important to note several important differences. In key respects, college athletes face a more daunting economic reality. Would-be indentured servants actually operated in a vigorously competitive market; the more talented the servant, the better the terms he (or she) could demand,[11] including a reduction in the length of servitude.[12] Servants also made cash payments to lower the length of service and negotiated whether they would receive guaranteed training in a trade and whether education would be provided.[13]

In contrast, athletes heading into college face a solid cartel[14]—an agreement among the otherwise independent colleges and universities that make up the NCAA to fix the price offered for athletes' services, agreeing that no school will offer more compensation than room, board, tuition, fees, and required books and supplies, so there is no direct economic competition.[15] Thus, unlike their skilled counterparts in the days of indentured servants, college athletes cannot receive a cash inducement to sign up or the promise of a cash payment upon completion of their term.

When, after settling litigation on the issue in 2006[16] and with the media questioning why so-called full-ride scholarships don't actually cover the full

---

11  Ibid.

12  As one such example, Daniel Dulany was able to shorten his indenture to only three years because he was more skilled than the average servant. It was common among adult apprentices to hold the minimum length of service at four years. Galenson, "The Rise and Fall of Indentured Servitude in the Americas," 103.

13  Ibid.

14  A cartel of every buyer in the market is a monopsony. This is the buyers' analogy of a monopoly, where there is only one seller. In its dismissal of *Agnew v. NCAA* for failing to state a relevant market, the Seventh Circuit recognized that: "This appears to be a clear monopsony case, since the NCAA is the only purchaser of student athletic labor." Agnew v. NCAA, 683 F.3d 328, 337 (7th Cir. 2012).

15  Although in almost any other industry such a cartel operating out in the open would be a per se violation of the antitrust laws, no one has directly challenged the NCAA front and center on whether this aspect of the cartel is illegal. The NCAA argues that the Supreme Court has blessed its cartel via dicta in *NCAA v. Board of Regents of the University of Oklahoma*. Donald Remy, "Why the New York Times' Nocera Is Wrong," NCAA.org, January 6, 2012, http://www.ncaa.org/about/resources/media-center/news/why-new-york-times %E2%80%99-nocera-wrong.

16  The case was *White v. NCAA*. One of the authors (Schwarz) was one of the three economists who conceived the *White* case, which was settled out of court. See Stipulation and

cost of attending college, the NCAA board of directors sought to allow (but not require) schools to offer their most valued recruits an annual cash payment up to $2,000, the overwhelming majority of the cartel's members voted to forbid such a practice.[17] So on this key dimension, the absence of competition for college athletes has put these athletes in a much worse position, financially, than their counterparts in the days of indentured servants.

In many ways the contracts that indentured servants signed before leaving England for the colonies could be seen as a de facto "letter of intent," similar to the ones student-athletes sign when they commit to play sports at a particular school. Yet unlike student-athletes, the colonial system evolved so that once indentured servants arrived in the New World, they usually had up to thirty days for their contracts to be bought out by a family member, friend, or someone willing to give an advance in order to hire them for their services.[18] The professional baseball world is similar; when a high school player is drafted before college, he can choose to go play professional or enter college with the hope of being redrafted at some later point in time.[19] Of course, this luxury exists because there is a free-market alternative in the MLB, which is willing to put a value on players before they enter college. College football and basketball lack a competitive alternative for recruits.

Though differing in degree, the punishment laid on indentured servants for attempting to get out of their contracts shares much in common with NCAA rules that penalize college athletes if they want to transfer to a different institution.[20]

NCAA bylaws require athletes who transfer to a member institution on the same divisional level to complete a full year of residency before becoming

Agreement of Settlement Between Pls. and Def. NCAA at 3. White v. NCAA, No. CV06-0999 VBF (MANx) (C.D. Cal. Jan. 29, 2008), 2008 WL 890625.

17  Andy Schwarz, "The $2,000 Stipend and the Rule of Reason: An Antitrust Analysis," *Sports Litigation Alert* 8, no. 24 (December 21, 2011), available at http://sportsgeekonomics .tumblr.com/post/15083501409/the-2-000-stipend-and-the-rule-of-reason-an-antitrust.

18  Richard Hofstadter, "White Servitude," in *America at 1750: A Social Portrait* (New York: Knopf, 1971).

19  "First-Year Player Draft Rules," MLB.com, http://mlb.mlb.com/mlb/draftday/rules.jsp.

20  "A student who transfers (see Bylaw 14.5.2) to a member institution from any collegiate institution is required to complete one full academic year of residence (see Bylaw 14.02.13) at the certifying institution before being eligible to compete for or to receive travel expenses from the member institution (see Bylaw 16.8.1.2), unless the student satisfies the applicable transfer requirements or qualifies for an exception as set forth in this bylaw." *NCAA Division I Manual*, art. 14, § 5, cl. 1 (2011).

eligible to play at the new school.[21] Penalties for servants who breached their contracts ranged from extending their contracts by double the time the master lost while they were gone to as much as a ten-to-one penalty authorized in Maryland at one time.[22] Both systems saw extending the period of indenture as the best punishment for seeking mobility.

To the extent that college sports has an interest in preventing athletes from changing teams on a (say) weekly basis, nevertheless rules requiring college athletes to sit out for a year when transferring to another institution go far beyond this legitimate concern, and school and league policies totally prohibiting the transfer to a conference foe or school rival make clear these rules are designed for the benefit of a specific school, not to preserve the legitimacy of the sport. For the majority of college athletes, such policies do nothing but force them to spend extra time in school when they would be better served graduating on time or pursuing their professional careers. And the issue affects a substantial portion of college athletes: transfer rates among Division I men's basketball players are as high as 10.9 percent, and up to 40 percent of all such players won't be playing for their initial teams by their junior year because they transferred, dropped out, or moved on from the sport completely.[23]

Although indentured servants had many more freedoms than slaves, they were still considered chattels of their master and the contracts by which they were bound could be bought and sold at will.[24] Much to the chagrin of the servant, the individual he committed to serve upon his arrival to the colonies could send him off on a whim to much less favorable circumstances.[25] In this respect, the unfortunate reality that servants faced was far worse than, but not entirely different from, the rules that governed scholarship length from 1973 to 2011.

Prior to the 2011–12 recruiting season, NCAA institutions could only grant scholarships to college athletes on a one-year basis, renewable or cancellable entirely at the coach's or school's discretion.[26] Under this system coaches could

---

21  Ibid.

22  Hofstadter, "White Servitude."

23  Jim Halley and Steve Weinberg, "Athlete Movement in Division I Basketball Raising 'Alarm,'" USAToday.com, June 24, 2012, http://www.usatoday.com/sports/college/mens basketball/story/2012-06-24/Athlete-movement-in-Division-I-basketball-raising-alarm /55798356/1.

24  Galenson, "The Rise and Fall of Indentured Servitude in the Americas," 10.

25  Ibid.

26  Louis Hakim, "The Student-Athlete vs. the Athlete Student: Has the Time Arrived for an Extended-Term Scholarship Contract?," *Virginia Journal of Sports and the Law* 2, no. 1 (2000): 145–83.

get rid of an athlete who did not fit into their system or who was not developing as quickly as hoped.[27] Unlike their athletes (who still face a transferring penalty for breaching their letter of intent if their coach leaves), coaches have no waiting period when switching schools, and until this change in the length of a scholarship, schools had no waiting period to replace a player dismissed under a nonrenewed scholarship.

Despite operating under bylaws that purport to be focused on the welfare of college athletes,[28] when the NCAA held a vote to allow (but not to require) schools to offer four- or five-year scholarships, 205 of 330 Division I institutions voted against the new rule and the measure passed by the narrowest of margins, as a supermajority of 207 schools was needed to uphold the ban.[29] This does not guarantee that an athlete will receive a multiyear deal, but at least in this small way competition can work to ensure that the most meritorious will be able to bargain for better terms. Here clearly, as difficult as the NCAA cartel makes it for college athletes, their freedom of movement is several steps above that of chattel.

Although college athletes' freedom of movement is less restricted than indentured servants' freedom was, economically college athletes may fare worse than indentured servants. In both systems, the would-be employers provided room and board instead of paying the going rate for free laborers. Because of competition, the master of an apprentice could expect to pay about 70 percent of what a comparable unskilled free laborer could command over the span of a four-plus-year indenture.[30]

---

27 After taking over the program in the spring of 2012, new SMU head men's basketball coach Larry Brown cut several players from the existing team roster, including starting point guard Jeremiah Samarrippas. When asked for the reasoning behind his decision, Brown told Samarrippas that "[he] wasn't good enough to play for him," despite starting all thirty-one games the previous season. See Mercedes Owens, "Brown's Cutting Down," *Daily Campus* (Southern Methodist University), April 28, 2012, http://issuu.com/smudaily campus/docs/dc042712.

28 *NCAA Division I Manual*, art. 2, § 2, cl. 2.2 (2011). "THE PRINCIPLE OF STUDENT-ATHLETE WELL-BEING: Intercollegiate athletics programs shall be conducted in a manner designed to protect and enhance the physical and educational well-being of student-athletes."

29 The rule had been passed by the NCAA board of directors, so a 62.5 percent supermajority was required to override the bylaw. The override vote received 62.1 percent support, leaving it two votes short of the required 62.5 percent. Josh Levin, "The Most Evil Thing About College Sports," Slate.com, May 17, 2012, http://www.slate.com/articles/sports /sports_nut/2012/05/ncaa_scholarship_rules_it_s_morally_indefensible_that_athletic _scholarships_can_be_yanked_after_one_year_for_any_reason_.html.

30 An unskilled free laborer in the mid-eighteenth century could expect to earn 46.8 Pennsylvania pounds a year if he worked six days per week. The average annualized cost

If the indentured servant were skilled, the master might pay only 55 percent of a free artisan's wage. Considering the risks the master took, for an indentured servant to give up 30–45 percent of his earning potential was perhaps not too steep a price to pay given that he had no other means to pay his own way to the colonies,[31] and the bargain a master received was about comparable to the risks he undertook in committing to four or more years of food, housing, and training.

The situation is noticeably different (and worse) for our modern indentureds, the young and talented men who perform their craft on the gridiron or the hardwood, but lack the ability to negotiate a free-market wage. College athletes are much closer in their economic situation to baseball players in the days of the reserve clause prior to free agency. Under the reserve clause system, a player was bound permanently to the team who signed him first.[32] When a contract ran out, all major-league teams colluded, agreeing not to make an offer to another team's player. In a very real sense, this put him in a state of permanent indenture—Curt Flood famously called himself a "well-paid slave"[33]—and as a result teams could drive very hard salary bargains.

In a seminal work in sports economics,[34] Gerald Scully found that before free agency introduced a relatively free market for players, players earned

---

of an indenture, plus room, board, clothing, and other expenses of the servant, cost 33.6 pounds. In other words, a contract for the right to six days a week of labor sold for 71.7 percent of what six days per week of free labor would have cost. In exchange, the owner of the indenture contract took on the risk of sickness (the servant still needed to be fed and housed when sick, while a free laborer would go unpaid) and of escape. Farley Grubb, "The Auction of Redemptioner Servants, Philadelphia, 1771–1804: An Economic Analysis," *Journal of Economic History* 48, no. 3 (September 1988): 583.

31  The economic literature on indentures has generally concluded that when the risks inherent in a multiyear commitment by a master are taken into account, pricing for indentures was consistent with an efficient market; that is, there were no supercompetitive profits from acquiring an indentured servant relative to a free laborer, despite the pricing difference.

32  According to Paragraph 10A of Major League Baseball's Uniform Player Contract, "If . . . the Player and the Club have not agreed upon the terms of [a new contract offered by the team following the expiration of the Player's original contract], then on or before 10 days after . . . March 1 [of the preceding year], the Club shall have the right by written notice to the Player as said address to renew this contract for the period of one year on the same terms." This contract provision, known as the "reserve clause," essentially gave the team unilateral rights to renew his contract, and thus fundamental ownership over the player in perpetuity unless they decided to release or trade him. James B. Dworkin, *Owners Versus Players: Baseball and Collective Bargaining* (Boston: Auburn House, 1981), 63.

33  For a discussion of Curt Flood's efforts to end the reserve clause, see Brad Snyder, *A Well-Paid Slave: Curt Flood's Fight for Free Agency in Professional Sports* (New York: Viking, 2006).

34  Gerald Scully, "Pay and Performance in Major League Baseball," *American Economic Review* 64, no. 6 (December 1974): 915–30.

approximately 20 percent of their net marginal revenue product,[35] i.e., the rate that would prevail in a free market.[36] At the time of the first challenges to the reserve clause, the standard line was that without this form of indentured servitude, "Professional baseball . . . would simply cease to exist."[37] Even George Steinbrenner famously said that "I am dead set against free agency. . . . It can ruin baseball."[38] Despite these dire predictions, thirty-six years after the end of the reserve clause, the demise of the multibillion-dollar baseball industry has yet to materialize.

At the schools in college sports' six major conferences,[39] the reported value of the athletic scholarship awarded to all football and men's basketball athletes averages between 5 and 10 percent of each respective school's football and basketball revenue. For example, in the Atlantic Coast Conference (ACC), which lies in the heart of where the indenture system was most common in colonial America, its schools[40] provide scholarships that the schools themselves valued (in 2009–10) at an average of $31,675 a year, including the value of room and board.[41] While a scholarship covering approximately 90 percent of the full cost of attending an ACC school is certainly valuable (much as was passage across the

---

35 A "player's marginal revenue product in baseball is the ability or performance that he contributes to the team and the effect of that performance on gate receipts." Ibid., 916.

36 "If the labor market in organized baseball were perfectly competitive, player salaries would be equated with player marginal revenue products (MRP)." Ibid. However, Scully ("Pay and Performance in Major League Baseball," 929) found that "average players receive salaries equal to about 11 percent of their gross and about 20 percent of their net marginal revenue products."

37 Snyder, A Well-Paid Slave, 108.

38 Ocala Star-Banner, March 22, 1977.

39 These six conferences, the ACC, the Big East, the Big Ten, the Big 12, the SEC, and the Pac-12, are also sometimes referred to as the BCS AQ (Automatic Qualifying) conferences, because under the current conference bowl rules (set to expire after 2013) these six conferences' champions receive an automatic bid to one of the five BCS (Bowl Championship Series) bowl games.

40 This average is taken from the NCAA Accounting Submissions for 2010 for Clemson, Georgia Tech, Maryland, North Carolina State, Virginia, and Virginia Tech, received via Freedom of Information Act requests. Efforts to receive the equivalent documents from the other schools in the ACC were rebuffed.

41 When working with NCAA accounting numbers, it is important to recognize that the amount a school charges its own athletic department is not an accurate reflection of the actual costs incurred. As one example, schools typically charge their athletic departments twice as much for books than they cost to acquire, with the profit showing up not on the athletic department's book but on the bookstore's ledger. Nevertheless, while these figures likely represent an overestimate, they can serve as an upper bound of the true cost to a school of providing an athletic scholarship.

Atlantic and four years of room and board to an eighteenth-century stonemason in training), total reported scholarship costs represent only 5.6 percent of the football and basketball revenues of those ACC schools.[42]

What might these athletes earn under competition if the current agreement among all NCAA schools not to compete on economic terms were lifted? One analogy is baseball, where collusion held pay to one-fifth the market value of the players. If the same held true for college athletes, that 5.6 percent figure would rise to approximately 28 percent of revenue. In the ACC that would mean a package of benefits worth, on average, $158,000, of which the currently provided scholarship would comprise 20 percent.[43] Put differently, that could mean the market rate for those one hundred athletes is about $125,000 per year higher than the current indentured value.[44]

Pac-12 figures are similar, with an average reported (public school) scholarship value of $32,732 in 2010–11, equal to 7.3 percent of the average Pac-12

---

42 Total football and basketball revenues specifically assigned by the six ACC schools in the study total $202.9 million, which comprises 88 percent of all sport-specific revenue. This analysis adds in 88 percent of nonsport-specific revenue for an allocated football and basketball revenue total of $321.8 million. Scholarship costs provided by these schools comprise 5.6 percent of the allocated total. Without the allocation, the percentage would be 8.9 percent.

43 This figure is comparable to other recent estimates of the value of an ACC player. For example, Ramogi Huma and Ellen Staurowsky estimate that the average ACC football and basketball athlete is worth $158,466. Ramogi Huma and Ellen Staurowsky, "Study: College Athletes Worth 6 Figures, Live Below Federal Poverty Line," National College Players Association, September 13, 2011. Similarly, Jeff Phillips and Tyler Williams estimate the average football player across all 120 teams in FBS to be worth $137,000 more than he currently receives in scholarships, with the ACC at something close to that average. Jeff Phillips and Tyler Williams, "What Should College Football Players Be Paid?" ESPN The Magazine, June 25, 2012, 103.

44 One critical difference between college athletes and reserve era baseball players is Title IX. Though Title IX is often mischaracterized as making it illegal or impossible to pay male players, it is more fair to say that Title IX might dampen the economic benefits that flow to male football and basketball players in a competitive market. How much depends on a host of factors, but under the set of assumptions that maximize the impact of Title IX, the law could potentially cut the competitive male rate in half—$62,500 rather than $125,000 per player per year. A 50 percent impact likely overstates things—no school in the ACC, public or private, gives women an equal amount of financial aid as men, and on average 42 cents of each financial aid dollar goes to women. Also note that the portion funneled off to women would not necessarily be paid out directly to players—the average ACC women's scholarship only covers 63 percent of a full scholarship, so the first $8 million of these Title IX diverted revenues could go to better fund existing women's scholarships, and the next $35 million could fund scholarships for existing walk-ons rather than to cash payments to women. For a more detailed discussion, see Andy Schwarz, "Excuses, Not Reasons: 13 Myths About (Not) Paying College Athletes," paper presented at the Santa Clara Sports Law Symposium, September 8, 2011.

school's football and basketball revenues.[45] Thus, using the analogy to the reserve era in baseball, the estimated gap between the market rate for athletes and their current indentureship would be approximately $130,000 per athlete.[46]

Moreover, as conference realignment has allowed the major conferences to renegotiate lucrative television deals, the disparity between the revenue per athlete and the school's cost for that student-athlete will increase even further. The Pac-12's new $3 billion, twelve-year deal with Fox and ESPN will grow each school's average broadcast revenue by nearly $16 million.[47] All else equal, this will increase the gap between the collusive terms the athletes are currently offered and the estimated market rate by approximately $50,000[48] per scholarship athlete in football and basketball.[49] But as it stands, the athletes can expect more or less zero of that added revenue to reach them.

Although the lack of reliable data makes it difficult to determine the relative economic impact an indentured servant had on his master's business, doing so for modern-day college athletes in revenue-producing sports is less complicated. In the absence of direct economic competition for athletes, schools compete for the best recruiters, i.e., coaches, as an indirect way of attracting talent.[50] In 2009–10, the University of Texas valued the total grants-in-aid to football players at $3.1 million, less than half of the $6.5 million in total compensation earned by Texas's head coach, Mack Brown. An even greater disparity can be seen in the school's men's basketball program, with head coach Rick Barnes

---

45 Note that while these figures come from the 2010–11 season, which was the final year of the older Pac-10, both the scholarship numbers and the revenues include Colorado and Utah, which tend to increase the value of the scholarship relative to revenues, because these schools' revenues are lower than most of the core Pac-10 schools, but scholarship costs are more comparable because of the NCAA agreement to limit compensation.

46 Again, Title IX could result in as much as half of this, or $65,000, being diverted to increased women's financial aid.

47 The annual television revenues are estimated to increase from a reported $59.5 million to $250 million, which equates to a $15.8 million increase for each of the conference's twelve member schools.

48 This calculation assumes that on the margin, Pac-12 athletes would get 5x6.3% of the $15.8 million revenue increase, or $50,345 for each of the 100 scholarship athletes at each of the twelve schools.

49 Of which, again, half might flow to the male athletes and half to women's financial aid.

50 "In significant part, coaches are paid for the value produced by others, most notably the athletes they recruit. That is, the marginal revenue product of the star players accrues largely to the head coach, rather than to the players themselves. The value produced from recruiting—whose success relies on many factors, such as assistant coaches, the school's conference, its reputation and facilities—is attributed to the head coach." Andrew Zimbalist, "CEOs with Headsets," *Harvard Business Review*, September 2010, 22–23.

earning $3.9 million, 762 percent more than the entire value (approximately $460,000) placed on the scholarships of the athletes he coached.[51] Of course, those numbers do not include the millions in salary paid to assistant coaches or the million-dollar salary of Texas athletic director Deloss Dodds.[52] This phenomenon is not limited to Texas; from 1986 to 2007, college head football coaches' pay increased approximately 500 percent while head men's basketball coaches pay grew 400 percent.[53]

How does college coaches' compensation (relative to their teams' "payroll") compare to that of coaches for professional sports franchises? During the same season that Brown and Barnes earned far more than their entire team, New England Patriots head coach Bill Belichick received approximately 7 percent ($7.5 million) of his team's estimated $115 million payroll. Similarly, the Boston Celtics paid head coach Doc Rivers a comparable 7 percent ($5.5 million) of his team's estimated $83 million payroll that year. The ability of NFL and NBA players to bargain via their unions ensures that the players in those leagues earn a fair share of the revenues they help to produce, and as a result NFL and NBA coaches earn their own competitive salary, but not the value that would otherwise flow to their players without a free market for their labor.

John Rose knew that Charleston was perfectly positioned to become a major player. The beautiful South Carolina weather coupled with an exciting city, almost unlimited resources, and easy centralized access in the South would allow him to build a powerhouse. Rose knew that recruiting top talent would be the foundation for success, yet a once fertile talent pool had begun to dry up. His only solution was a major investment to build something so great that it would serve as a recruiting tool the likes of which rivals had never seen.

One could mistake John Rose for any major college athletics director today. Rose was not an AD, but rather a South Carolina businessman hoping to become a successful commodities trader. Using what money he had, he invested into the construction of the 180-ton merchant ship *Heart of Oak*, which would become one of the greatest commercial trading vessels built in North America since its colonization. The *Heart of Oak* was assembled at great cost and eventually

---

51  Schwarz, "Excuses, Not Reasons," 46.

52  "Athletics Director Salary Database for 2011," USAToday.com, October 6, 2011, available at http://usatoday.com/sports/college/story/2011-athletics-director-salaries-database /50669958/1.

53  As a point of comparison, tenured professor pay grew 30 percent in the same period. Michael Sanserino, "College Coaches' Salaries Continue to Soar," *Pittsburgh Post-Gazette*, March 29, 2012, http://www.post-gazette.com/news/nation/2011/01/15/College-coaches -salaries-continue-to-soar/stories/201101150179.

valued at some £16,000,[54] a fortune in the eighteenth century and more than a million dollars in today's money.[55] Knowing that continued profits from ship-building would require skilled labor at cheap costs, he traveled to England with his greatest recruiting tool, the *Heart of Oak* herself, to sell shipwrights on com-ing to work for him in Charleston as indentured servants.

He failed.

By the late eighteenth century, the market for indentured servants had al-most dried up south of the Chesapeake, due in large part to the proliferation of a far more sinister concept, slavery.[56] With cheap unskilled labor available cheaply via slavery and opportunities in Europe for skilled laborers growing more lucrative, most Europeans no longer were willing to offer sufficient years of servitude necessary to compete with slaves and cover the increasing costs of cross-Atlantic travel.[57] Unlike college athletes, for whom choosing to forgo a scholarship to stay at home is often a guarantee of poverty (and for whom going to Europe is a rare exception),[58] eighteenth-century European laborers had the real choice to stay home and continue to earn a living. Not even John Rose and the *Heart of Oak* could convince the shipwrights, carpenters, silk workers, and other skilled workers to come to America when faced with indentured terms set in competition with the price of acquiring, housing, and feeding a slave.

As social commentators have grappled with proper analogies for the cur-rent collusive market for college athletes, they often reach for metaphors of slav-ery. Civil rights historian Taylor Branch famously wrote that the NCAA has "an

---

54 Lynn Harris, "Shipyards and European Shipbuilders in South Carolina (Late 1600s to 1800)," *Occasional Maritime Research Papers*, http://scholarcommons.sc.edu/cgi/view content.cgi?article=1001&context=mrd_pubs.

55 "Historic Inflation Calculator: How the Value of Money Has Changed Since 1900," ThisIs Money.co.uk, http://www.thisismoney.co.uk/money/bills/article-1633409/Historic-inflation -calculator-value-money-changed-1900.html.

56 The first incidence of one person enslaving another in the colonies that became the United States has been attributed to Anthony Johnson, who himself was a freed indentured servant. "From Indentured Servitude to Racial Slavery," PBS, http://www.pbs.org/wgbh /aia/part1/1narr3.html.

57 Farley Grubb, "Redemptioner Immigration to Pennsylvania: Evidence on Contract Choice and Profitability," *Journal of Economic History* 46 (1986): 200.

58 Over the period 2007–2011, out of all 3-, 4-, and 5-star college basketball prospects (as ranked by Rivals.com), only three athletes have elected to forgo the opportunity to play college basketball to play professionally in Europe: Jeremy Tyler, Yvan Nigarabakunzi, and Brandon Jennings. Until such an option becomes available for the bulk of college athletes, Europe will not serve to break the NCAA monopoly on college athletes' opportunities. Rivals.com, http://www.rivals.com.

unmistakable whiff of the plantation."[59] But while it is easy to see inequity in the level of control that a school exerts over its athletes and the unequal division of the value of their labor, the comparison to slavery breaks down because of the obvious and stark difference between athletes who choose to attend college (however onerous the terms) versus slaves brought involuntarily to this continent and coerced through violence and oppression into unwilling labor.

Acknowledging that college athletes are not enslaved by the NCAA is a far cry from concluding they are exercising free choice in an open market. Instead, what they face is Hobson's choice—the offer of a monopolist cartel where the only choice is "whether you will have this or none."[60] Economic competition is the great protector of the disadvantaged, so powerful that it allowed the most vulnerable colonial laborers to preserve as much as 70 percent of their value, even under extreme conditions of economic hardship that led them to sell themselves into four years of bondage without control of their own movement.

Though not enslaved, college athletes have been denied access to a true market because of the NCAA's nationwide agreement on maximum compensation to athletes. As the NCAA puts it, because "[i]n economic terms the supply-of-labor function is essentially limitless or unresponsive to price," college athletes "will always play sports regardless of compensation."[61] In other words, because college athletes face few other lucrative opportunities, as long as colleges collude to ensure their offers to athletes are not competitive, there is little risk of the athlete going elsewhere.[62]

Left unsaid is what would happen if schools did not collude to fix prices, but instead had to compete for talent, much as farmers and merchants had to compete for the contracts of the indentured servants they sought to employ. As shown above, this collusion likely costs college football and basketball athletes

---

59 Taylor Branch, "The Shame of College Sports," *Atlantic*, October 2011, http://www.the atlantic.com/magazine/archive/1969/12/the-shame-of-college-sports/8643/?single _page=true.

60 For a discussion of the origins of the term "Hobson's choice" and its meaning as "no choice at all, you take what you're given and you like it," see Dave Wilton, "Hobson's Choice," July 3, 2006, http://www.wordorigins.org/index.php/site/hobsons choice/ (citing Samuel Fisher, "The Rustick's Alarm to the Rabbies" [1660]).

61 Remy, "Why the New York Times' Nocera Is Wrong."

62 As discussed above, unlike indentured servants who as the eighteenth century drew to a close found the option to practice their craft in Europe to be lucrative, to date less than a handful of U.S. high school seniors have gone directly to Europe to play basketball professionally without first playing college basketball. Milton Kent, "Why Should Basketball Players Have to Go to College?," NBC News, July 2, 2009, http://thegrio.com/2009/07/02/ what-do-moses-malone-kevin/.

tens or hundreds of thousands of dollar per year. And predictions that the sport is too fragile to survive the hurly-burly of competition seem as likely to prove true as those who predicted baseball's demise in the wake of free agency or of those who told us the Olympics would never survive without the pure amateur ideal.[63] Those predictions proved as true as those who claimed that American civilization itself could not survive without slavery.[64]

Who has benefited from an economic situation that makes indentured servants look relatively well off? That money has flowed to all of the people who provide the indirect tools schools use to compete for talent—to coaches, to administrators, to the construction firms that build the practice facilities and weight rooms used in recruiting—anywhere where there is economic competition for assets that help bring in talent. Ironically, all of these individuals have seen their compensation rise significantly over the last two decades because they have access to the system college athletes are denied, free-market capitalism. Because all other markets in college sports are competitive, those with the talent and work ethic are able to earn their worth, as well as some portion of the players' value, while college athletes face sub-market-rate indentures.

As the history of indentured servants has shown, with economic competition there is economic justice, even for those choosing short-term bondage. As the history of sports such as baseball and college athletics has shown, without economic competition, there is not.

---

63 "The amateur ideal of sportsmanship, fair play and the pursuit of excellence for its own sake is both a noble and a sound one. Whether this ideal depends for its existence on the amateur rules quoted above is quite another question. [Then International Olympic Committee president Avery] Brundage and his supporters believe with religious fervor that it does. 'If we water down the rules now,' one of his staunchest backers told me, 'the Games will be destroyed within eight years.'" Charles W. Thayer, "A Question of the Soul," *Sports Illustrated*, August 15, 1960.

64 See, for example, William Harper, "Southern Justification of Slavery," United States History, http://www.u-s-history.com/pages/h244.html. ("[T]he institution of slavery is a principal cause of civilization. Perhaps nothing can be more evident than that it is the sole cause. . . . Without it, there can be no accumulation of property, no providence for the future, no tastes for comfort or elegancies, which are the characteristics and essentials of civilization.")

# INDEX

Byers, Walter (*cont.*)
  28–29; and compensation for players, 28,
  30, 145–46; criticisms of NCAA by, 14,
  28–30; death of, 14; Dennison case and,
  76; deposition of, 145–46; enforcement
  and, 17–22; and eras of college sports, 91;
  and ESPN television, 95; as first executive
  director of NCAA, 13, 15; impact on
  NCAA of, 13–14, 16, 30; influence on
  Huma of, 74; and injuries/health care,
  75–76; and marketing of NCAA, 27–28,
  29; media and, 16; and names and
  images issues, 30; and NCAA-Big Ten
  relationship, 15–16; personal and
  professional background of, 14–15;
  personality/style of, 16, 25, 29; and
  Presidents Commission, 116; publications
  of, 16, 28, 29, 39, 74, 145, 213, 254; and
  reform of NCAA, 14, 28–30; *Regents* case
  and, 25–26, 28, 29; Restitution Rule and,
  43; retirement of, 28; salary of, 15; and
  scholarships, 76, 146; self-image of, 17;
  and "student-athlete" concept, 13, 75, 76,
  254; *Tarkanian* case and, 39, 42; TV and,
  13, 17, 23–27, 29; Vaccaro and, 37; *White*
  case and, 145–46, 147

CAC (Collegiate Athletes Coalition),
  71–77, 80–85, 243. *See also* National
  College Players Association
Calhoun, Jim, 4, 7
Calipari, John, 214–15
CAPA (College Athletes Players
  Association), 240, 251, 254
Capitol Broadcasting Company, 87
Carroll, Andy, 141–42
Catchings, Haney, 249–50
CBS (Central Broadcasting System): bowl
  games and, 106; conference contracts
  with, 98, 100; expansion of, 189;
  fantasy football and, 159–60; Huma
  and, 71–72, 83; Means-Lang story on,
  110; NCAA television contracts with,
  23, 26, 66, 82, 103, 107–8, 113, 190, 211
CBSSports.com, 213, 214
CFA (College Football Association), 24–26,
  28, 29, 91, 96, 97–99, 100–101, 103

Clark, Brent, 19, 20, 22, 52
CLC (Collegiate Licensing Company), 102,
  193, 266
Clearinghouse, NCAA. *See* Eligibility
  Center/Clearinghouse, NCAA
Clinton, Bill, 219, 227, 258
Clowney, Jadeveon, 231–32, 273
CNN, 252
coaches: agents for, 194; amateurism rules
  and, 37; and assistant coaches-NCAA
  lawsuit, 65, 67, 107, 142; as
  beneficiaries of revenue generated by
  college sports, 102; Brand views about,
  120–21; Byers views about, 16–17; CAC
  and, 81; compensation for, 3, 29, 34, 37,
  53–55, 81–82, 101–2, 107, 110–11,
  120–21, 127, 142, 146, 155, 174, 182,
  193–94, 197, 200, 215, 230–31, 270, 277;
  as critics of NCAA, 214–15; and Delany
  proposal for reform, 291; Emmert
  relations with, 180, 219; and
  enforcement by NCAA, 17–18, 20–21; and
  football, 193–94; high school, 109–11;
  and NCAA bylaws, 9; number of team,
  54; and player activism, 73; and player
  injuries, 283; and players as employees
  concept, 254; "power," 16–17; power/
  authority of, 238, 283; recruitment of
  players and, 109–11, 230; restricted-
  earnings of, 54–55, 65, 67, 107, 142;
  scholarships and, 244; Shaw views
  about, 31; sneaker contracts for, 46;
  sports marketing and, 34, 37; and
  "student-athlete" focus, 77; and time
  with players, 77–78; Tompsett as lawyer
  for, 221; and unionization of players,
  252; and Vaccaro high school activities,
  36. *See also specific person*
Coca-Cola, 27, 83, 101
College Football Playoff, 3, 103–6, 284
college sports: as big business, 193,
  196–97, 270; contradictions in, 17;
  corporatization of, 34; economic
  underpinnings of, 9; as entertainment
  industry, 121; eras of, 91; hypocrisy of,
  274; "plantation" analogy to, 30, 213;
  popularity of, 277; professional sports